Lost In Wonder, Love, and Praise

Chuck Leypoldt

Lost In Wonder, Love, and Praise

Library of Congress Control Number 2014919038
ISBN 978-1-4951-3226-1

For information contact the author/publisher:
Charles Wesley Leypoldt
6840 South 44th Street
Lincoln, NE 68516

Website: www.pylodet.com
Email: pylodet@gmail.com

The title page collage features an art glass image of Charles Wesley from The United Methodist Church in Spring Hill, Kansas, surrounded by photos of pipe organs from the following churches:
First United Methodist, Lincoln, Nebraska
First Trinity Lutheran, Bloomfield, Nebraska
Saint Mark's Episcopal, Lincoln, Nebraska
United Methodist, Albion, Nebraska
United Methodist, Crawford, Nebraska
Bethany Lutheran, Lindsborg, Kansas

Dedication

I've had but one serious girlfriend, and was
incredibly blessed when she married me on July 11, 1970.
We produced two talented children, and gained another by marriage.
We also have three beautiful granddaughters who are gifted
and independent, and make us proud just being who they are.

Chris
Anastasia
Seth
Sarah
Emma
Cora
Olivia

You are the wind beneath my wings!

A Writer's Poem from Olden Days
I thought a thought, but the thought I thought
Was not the thought, I thought I thought.
But, if I think, and again I think,
I'll write it down in pen and ink.

2014 Version
I thought a thought, but the thought I thought
Was not the thought, I thought I thought.
But, if I sweat, and do not fret,
I'll post it on the internet.

Contents

Foreword

I consider Charles Wesley's finest hymn to be **Love Divine, All Loves Excelling** (UMH #384). Line after line it contains inspiring words of the Christian experience. My favorites are "changed from glory into glory" and "lost in wonder, love, and praise." The former expresses the notion that each person is a precious gift, who becomes complete when they grasp divine grace and live for others. The latter speaks to me of discovering the world of nature and ideas, and sharing life with friends and heroes and loved ones, all the while giving thanks for the Creator's generosity.

Joseph Campbell wrote his book **A Hero With a Thousand Faces** in 1949. He encouraged people "to follow their bliss." This helped me see I was on a path which was there all the while, waiting for me, affirming me, providing meaning and satisfaction. Campbell also led me to Schopenhauer, who taught when a person examines their lifetime it can appear as though a novelist has composed a plot in which one's life events seem to be accidental, yet become essential factors in a consistent pattern. In the same way, "people you've met apparently by mere chance became leading agents in the structuring of your life," and I, too, may "have served unknowingly as an agent, giving meaning to the lives of others."[1] I'm still exploring this, but I like where it's taking me.

Except for my dad, grandfather, and the Brooklyn/L.A. Dodgers, my childhood heroes were mostly cowboys. I saw them on Saturdays at the Elite Theater in Crawford, Nebraska, and later on television. Throughout, my greatest cowboy hero was Roy Rogers, and I love the song written by Dale Evans Rogers: **Happy Trails.**[2] And, yes, instructions have been given that it will be sung at my funeral.

Randy Travis released **Heroes and Friends** in 1991. He sang about everyday people who set examples for us, and give us courage to rise above difficulties. He also hailed the loyalties of friendship.[3] His songs and others have helped me define my life journey. In 1991 I announced I would write a book in 1998 after my daughter graduated from college. I'm finally ready to make good on that inaccurate prediction, and what follows is my unfinished story of being lost in wonder, love, and praise.

At Fort Robinson with our grandchildren in 2009

Shared with permission of my youngest granddaughter,
who wrote this when she was in the third grade

If I were a dinosaur, A Oliviasaurus I'd be.
I'd have short green stubby ears and a blue spotted tail, and I'd have long sharp teeth.
I would be friendly for all dinosaurs, eat dead animals,
and make friends with flying dinosaurs in trees.
But since I'm not a dinosaur, I'm happy to be me!

Chapter 1
Cheaters Never Win, Or Do They?

I probably shouldn't be here. My parents were living in the parsonage of a country church west of Oakland, Nebraska when the time came for me to be born. My father called the doctor, and discovered he was out-of-town on vacation. His nurse said to come to the hospital, and Dr. Allen from Craig would take care of things. Dad loaded Mom and 3-year-old daughter Janice into the 1931 Chrysler, and drove into town.

Pretty soon my mother was in the Oakland hospital, and I was in the chute, ready to make an appearance. However, the doctor was late, the nurse was nervous, and Mom was knocked out by ether. Her labor stopped. Obviously, the elderly G.P. arrived just in time, but my dad said he was afraid the doctor's efforts would result in my head being detached. I measured 23 inches on my July 16, 1947 birth date.

Three months later, our family drove to Washington state to visit my uncle and aunt Bill and Beth Hennings. On the way back home, our car hit an obstruction on a gravel road in Wyoming, and rolled into a ditch. We all survived with minor bumps and bruises, and my grandfather came from Omaha to return us to Nebraska.

In February of 1948, my dad went upstairs to his parsonage study. When he opened the door, the space heater exploded, and the old house nearly burned to the ground. I was six months old, and had cheated death three times.

When I was ten, I loved watching the Papillion High School baseball team practice, which took place a block from our home. I was in a spot where I shouldn't have been. A fast ball careened into a foul ball, and hit me squarely between the eyes. I was knocked out cold!

In the fall of 1963, only two months after I got my driver's license, I was driving on an unpaved road about ten miles north of Albion, Nebraska. I hit some loose gravel, lost control, and my 1956 Nash Metropolitan ended upside down in the ditch. An old farmer came by and said, "you're lucky to be alive!" Gordon Belgum, the auto body man from Albion, pulled me out, straightened and repainted a fender for $67.

When I was 20 and a junior in college, I drove a car full of guys down to Marysville, Kansas so we could legally drink 3.2 beer in a bar. It was Friday and on the way home, we stopped in Beatrice at a high school dance. As we were tired, and still in varying stages of drunkenness, we quickly departed up Highway 77. Somewhere along the way, I zipped through a railroad crossing, and heard and saw in the rear view mirror, the unmistakable roar and lights of a diesel locomotive.

Four years later when I was a married man and a student pastor in Thayer County, Nebraska, I drove my 1970 Plymouth Duster to Fairbury for repairs. While traversing south on Highway 81 near Belvidere, I found myself on a railway overpass. Coming toward me was a 14-wheeler whose driver was distracted, and the rig began veering into my lane. There was no place to go, so I stopped, and prepared to vacate my car. At the last second he pulled over, and I continued very slowly to my appointment.

Many years later, in 2003, I was driving my Ford Taurus company car on Highway 9 south of Pender, Nebraska. I came upon a tractor pulling a manure spreader. I slowed to his pace, and followed a while before a straight and level stretch allowed me to pass. Around I went, and the farmer decided to turn left at the same moment, without signaling. I flashed past him, and saw his perplexed glare in the rear view mirror.

Chris was with me in February of 2007, when we survived a crash in another Ford Taurus. You can read about this one on page 200.

The best company car I drove was a 2007 Ford Five Hundred. In the spring of 2008, I was in this vehicle leisurely traveling down Highway 22 in Valley County, Nebraska. Suddenly the car began to accelerate! I immediately tapped the brake to turn off the cruise control, but to no avail. Tap, tap, a few more times and nothing helped. The speedometer was approaching 100; fortunately there was no traffic nor curves to negotiate. I was about to shift into neutral and/or turn off the ignition, when the self-propelleration stopped. My pulse races as I write this.

Last but not least…in 1962 I was fifteen and a high school sophomore. My father was still recovering from the surgery that removed his malignant prostate gland. During halftime of an Albion football game, Ronnie Barnes and I were talking to a carload of guys in the parking lot, and they invited us to ride around for a while. We declined. The next day we learned all the occupants of this car were cited for the dreaded crime of Minor In Possession. The booze was in the trunk, unopened, but every one of the boys got busted. Barnes and I would have faced the same penalty. My dad would have been devastated.

Therefore, I've cheated death ten times, and a fate worse than death at least once. What does it mean? I do not believe an angel was on my shoulder or in my pocket. I do not believe that God intervened to spare my life, else I might think the millions killed in traffic accidents were being punished by divine cruelty. Nor do I think God hurried the doctor to the delivery room to erase a nurse's near fatal error, just as God is not the cause of miscarriages, stillbirths, or natal deaths of any kind.

In the 9th chapter of John's Gospel, there is a story about a man who had been blind since birth. This person talks with Jesus, who spits in the dirt, spreads mud over the man's eyes, and tells him to wash it off in a pool. He returns from the water able to see. The Pharisees investigate, looking for logical conclusions about the blindness and the remedy. The story doesn't exactly say Jesus healed him; it says he followed instructions and was cured. Finally, the formerly sightless one says "I don't know what happened. All I know is I was blind and now I see (my paraphrase)."

Life happens when we are in the right places, and the wrong places. Sometimes we get caught, other times rescued. Often we're lucky, occasionally, not so much.

One might try to analyze life's ups and downs, but I prefer to believe I've simply been lost in wonder, love, and praise more than once. Between 1970 and 2012, I had four employers. I was mostly able to avoid "9 to 5" restrictions, and was pretty much my own boss from day to day. Each time I took a new career path, I started over financially and had to learn some new skills, but I landed on my feet and am now enjoying a secure retirement.

I am Chuck Leypoldt, and you're not. Please continue.

Chapter 2
From Whence I Came

I know where each of my great grandparents were born, therefore I think I am 50% German, 25% Swedish, and 25% English/Irish. Until I decide to get a DNA test, this will have to suffice. My high school German teacher, Mr. Eldor E. Splittgerber, suggested Leypoldt was a Dutch name, and maybe those ancestors had been on the move prior to the 1860's when the Leypoldt branch extended to America. My four grandparents were born in Nebraska, Minnesota, Iowa, and Pennsylvania. I know for sure I am 100% American.

My grandparents came from families with 8, 9, 12 and 18 siblings. My dad's father, George William Leypoldt, was born in Omaha in 1870 and Dad's mother, Maria Bigler Reed, was born in Pennsylvania in 1876. They were both raised in Sarpy County, Nebraska and married in 1911. Soon thereafter they joined several members of the Leypoldt family in Hershey, Nebraska, where they had four children. My father, Woodrow William Leypoldt, was born in 1915 and had three sisters.

My grandmother Leypoldt died in 1943 before my parents were married, and my grandfather Leypoldt died in 1947 when I was a baby. However, my maternal grandparents lived to share my early life, and were very important to me. Ida Marie Sanquist was born on the farm near Elliott, Iowa on October 13, 1892. She was confirmed in the Swedish Evangelical Mission Church in Red Oak, Iowa on June 7, 1908. She moved to Omaha a few years later, where she met and married my grandfather Charles George Hennings.

Grandma's father was August Lars Sanquist who was born in Sweden on December 15, 1842. He came to America with a brother about 1868. He had three wives and fourteen children. His first wife's name is unknown. His second wife was Anna Lisa Augusta Hultman, sister of John Hultman, a well-known musician, pastor, and charter member of the Swedish Mission Covenant Church. August and Anna had six children, including one who was born shortly before her death in 1888. He farmed in both Iowa and Kansas before he married our great-grandmother.

Grandma's mother was Emma Josefina Johnson, who was born in Sweden on July 12, 1855. She came to America about 1882. Her parents, John and Johanna Johnson, also immigrated from Sweden in the 1880's, and settled in the Red Oak, Iowa area. Emma had one child in Sweden, and three more before she married August Sanquist on May 13, 1890. In addition to Ida, they had five boys. My grandmother also had seven half brothers and five half sisters.

My mom's father was Charles George Hennings who was born on a farm near Goodhue, Minnesota on March 13, 1886. In his teens he left home to seek his fortune. He worked as a driver for Dr. Flippin in Stromsburg, Nebraska in 1909-10. He was trained by the John Deere Company to set up and repair tractors for farmers in Nebraska and Iowa, and ended up in Omaha. He broke his right wrist in a motorcycle accident, and because he was a mechanic, learned to use the other one equally well. In those days, the future war hero Eddy Rickenbacker was around Lincoln and Omaha racing cars and flying airplanes. My grandpa, or "Pops" as we called him, was his personal mechanic.

Ida Marie Sanquist and Charles George Hennings were married at First Methodist Episcopal Church in downtown Omaha on January 17, 1917. They moved into a brand new house at 2805 South 34th Street, and lived there for the rest of their lives. Most of those years, Pops was the shop foreman at Andrew Murphy & Sons, a Plymouth garage in Omaha. Their first child, my mother Dorothy Catherine Hennings, was born at the Swedish Mission Hospital in Omaha later that year.

My mother had a brother and a sister. She graduated from Omaha Central in 1935, and won a scholarship to attend Baker University in Kansas, but her bank failed and she lost her college savings. She stayed home, and attended Boyles Business College in Omaha.

My parents met at Camp Sheldon, south of Columbus, Nebraska, in 1941. They were counselors at a Methodist senior high youth institute. Dad was 26 and a senior at Nebraska Wesleyan, as well as a student pastor at Valparaiso. Mom was 23 and an active member of Hanscom Park Methodist in Omaha. They dated for a year, and became engaged in 1942 after he finished college. Dad spent a year at Drew Seminary in Madison, New Jersey, and they were married August 29, 1943 in Omaha and returned to New Jersey for the final two years of seminary.

My Swedish grandmother at age 15

My mother and father from their school days
and with their wedding party on
August 29, 1943

**My Grandmother
Ida Hennings
with her children
1921**

**Chris' Grandmother
Bernice Landon
with her son
1930**

Chapter 3
Vilse Jag Undra, Kärlek, och Lovord[4]

My sister, Janice Marie, was born in New Jersey in 1944. In May 1945, Dad finished seminary, and the family returned to Nebraska. Because the conference year started in September, they lived with my grandparents in Omaha until a pastoral appointment became available. A call came for them to move to North Bend where the pastor, a widower, was retiring. As the folks had no furniture, they made arrangements to purchase his entire household inventory. However, Dad later learned he would be sent to the West Side church near Oakland, and their newly acquired things were sent a few miles north in Burt County. West Side was the largest of about 30 former Swedish Methodist congregations in Nebraska. They had a six bedroom parsonage waiting for a young couple with a toddler. The church had 290 confirmed members plus 63 children in 1945. On their 70th anniversary in 1947, **The Nebraska Farmer** magazine published an article declaring a bright future for the church.[5]

When gender equality was moving forward and improving our society, I heard a cliché: "women should stop having children after age 30." My mother got a slow start, and had two of us before she was 30, and five more while in her thirties. I can remember the first time I saw four of my younger siblings.

My first home was the big old parsonage at West Side. Though I had no memories of living there, it was always a special place in my mind. My folks had many Oakland friends who kept in touch over the years, and we visited there every once in a while. I preached at West Side in September 1996, and noticed the shabby appearance outside and only 25 people showed up for worship. In August 1997 the church closed, and I attended the auction of the church's property. Afterward, I consulted a 1948 Nebraska Conference Journal to review their status when I was a baby. They are representative of many rural institutions: in fifty years, they went from an active group of 350 to zero. I have a story about the West Side church windows on page 215.

I also claim a spiritual ancestor. Charles Wesley was born prematurely in England in 1707, and grew to be a great poet and evangelist in early Methodism, composing nearly 9,000 hymns. 239½ years later (in 1947), my parents honored me by giving me Charles Wesley's name. I became aware of Charles Wesley when I was in the first grade. Easily bored with the sermons at the Crawford Methodist Church, I began thumbing through the hymnal and found the name "Charles Wesley." Sunday after Sunday, I went on a quest to count the hymns ascribed to him. Charles Wesley lives through his music. If you don't believe he is still alive, you have never sung *Hark! The Herald Angels Sing* or *Come, Thou Long-expected Jesus* or *O For A Thousand Tongues to Sing* (UMH 240, 196, 57). As long as music survives, Charles Wesley will live.

When Charles Wesley was 44, he rediscovered theological truth. An Anglican priest, he strayed toward Calvinism which taught God's love is both liberal and liberating and divine grace has no limits. It was hard for him to believe God might be so completely generous. In a 14 verse hymn, he asked, "Depth of mercy, can there be mercy still reserved for me?" (UMH 355) Maybe he thought salvation was dependent upon his own beliefs, or memorizing Bible verses, or regurgitating what others say.

His older brother John was more comfortable with the possibility that human beings could make good decisions, and do good works on their own, perhaps even be "made perfect in love in this life." Calvinists believed that human beings were too arrogant, and they needed to be brought down a notch. Pure Methodists, or Arminians, came to believe that humans were wallowing too much in Victorian guilt, and should be raised up a level.

John Newton, another Calvinist Methodist, gave up the slave trade when he learned that God had forgiven him 1700 years previously. He wrote "Amazing Grace! How sweet the sound that saved a wretch like me. I once was lost but now am found, was blind but now I see (UMH 378)." He helped others see that God was amazingly generous, and that good works naturally follow those who accept the gift of grace.

+++

Although the Swedish language was discontinued long before I was born, the culture still permeated the Oakland community. On one occasion my dad was at a meeting of the West Side men's group, when the locals spent several minutes visiting in their native tongue. Dad listened quietly without the slightest understanding of their discussion. At the next monthly meeting, he discovered that his surprise birthday party had been planned with him in the room! In recent years I've reconnected with my Swedish pedigree, and taken many pictures of Swedish churches and cemeteries throughout Nebraska.

When I was 50 years old in 1998 I baptized my first grandchild, Emma Kathryn, and preached at my son's church in Clatonia, Nebraska. It was a good time for me to share some things about my heritage and growing up in Methodist parsonages. Portions of that sermon follow.

One of my childhood memories was that my father gave very effective one-sentence sermons. These homilies were not the kind you hear in church. As a matter of fact, my dad was taught in seminary that sermons in church should be 30 minutes long and have three main points. We loved our father, but he was not a dynamic speaker. We used to entertain ourselves by counting the pipes in the pipe organ at the Albion church. When we were tired of that, we counted ceiling tiles.

The one-sentence sermons I'm talking about were the ones we heard at home. I don't remember the content of all them, but they were very effective. Mom used a different style, and went into long monologues. But Dad usually needed but one sentence to get his point across. My folks had seven children in thirteen years, but the most dangerous thing they did was to have three boys in three years. My sister Janice is the oldest. I was next. Gary is 20 months younger than I. Doug came along 18 months after Gary, then came Cathy, Steve, and Jim.

Mealtimes were hectic. The youngest would say the blessing, then we dug in. To keep order, Dad would occasionally say, "sit down and be quiet!" or "eat your vegetables" or "no one leaves the table until we're all done eating." My folks must have dreaded bedtime. Mom would announce bedtime was approaching about an hour ahead. Then we would get updates every ten minutes or so. Finally, about 15 minutes after the original deadline, Dad gave us a one-sentence sermon, "get upstairs and get to bed!" and off we'd go. Next we'd engage in pillow fights and wrestling matches, and Gary and I would pick on Doug. Mom would tell us twice more to go to sleep. Then Dad would appear from out of nowhere. By this time, he had no more one-sentence sermons, he was preaching with his huge, open, right hand. And he would always leave us with a final, brief lecture, "If I hear one more peep out of you, I'll be back." And 99% of the time we quietly rubbed our behinds and drifted off to sleep.

One-sentence sermons can be very effective.

Luke's Gospel tells about the time when Jesus went to his hometown synagogue. At the proper time, someone handed him the scroll containing words of the prophet Isaiah, and Jesus began to read: "The Spirit of the Lord is upon me, because God has anointed me to bring good news to the poor. God has sent me to proclaim release to the captives and recovery of sight to the blind, to let the oppressed go free, to proclaim the year of the Lord's favor." The local folks were impressed as Jesus rolled up the scroll, gave it back to the attendant, and sat down. Then he laid a one-sentence zinger on them, "**Today** this scripture is fulfilled in your hearing (Luke 4:16-21)."

Some preachers feel they have received a special call to their vocation. The prophet Isaiah, for instance, was called in a dream - a powerful, motivating dream that he understood to be his call to ministry (Isaiah 6:1-8 NRSV). Isaiah was in the temple at Jerusalem, and tells us he saw God sitting on a high and lofty throne, and that God had a robe, which filled the temple. Giant winged creatures called seraphs floated above God. Isaiah says they had six wings, and he heard them say: "Holy, holy, holy is the Lord of hosts; the whole earth is full of God's glory." Then the foundations of the building shook, and it was filled with smoky vapors of incense used in temple worship. Now Isaiah tells us about his response to what was happening. "Woe is me! I am lost, for I am a man of unclean lips, and I live among a people of unclean lips; yet my eyes have seen the King, the Lord of hosts!" At this time, it was forbidden for humans to see God and live. Isaiah's vision was just a glimpse, but he was scared to death at the sight before him. Next one of the seraphs flew toward him, holding a live, burning coal that had been taken from the altar. The seraph touched the mouth of Isaiah with this coal, and said the heat had removed all guilt and sin from him. Then Isaiah hears the voice of God asking, "Whom shall I send, and who will go for us?" Isaiah had been called, restored, and forgiven. He was ready to respond in service to God. "Here am I; send me!" he said.

Some Christians can tell you about a time, when like John Wesley, they felt their hearts "strangely warmed" and they became a new person. I was never converted or convicted or swept off my feet by a divine seraph, nor did I receive a clear call to preach. One of my seminary teachers, Tex Sample, described a lot of pastors when he said, "… the call to go into ministry is a lot like throwing up. You can put it off for a while…but there comes a time when you have got to do it."[6]

My call was clarified when I first understood prevenient grace: that I was loved, accepted, and nurtured long before I knew it or deserved it. This began at birth, and continued when a servant of God anointed me for service. This is how the great King of Israel and biblical hero, David, got his start. First, many years before, God appointed Samuel to be both a spiritual and secular leader for Israel. He was widely respected, but the people wanted someone else to be their king. They had their eye on Saul, a handsome and wealthy young man from the tribe of Benjamin. After a time, Saul was anointed by Samuel and began his reign (1 Samuel, Chapters 9 & 10).

Several years went by. God was not pleased with Saul, and sent Samuel to anoint a new king. Samuel went to the little town called Bethlehem to find a farmer named Jesse, who had eight sons. One of them was to be the new king, but Samuel does not know which one. When the oldest, Eliab, appears, Samuel thinks his job is easy. But God says, no, "Do not look on his appearance or on the height of his stature, because I have rejected him; for the Lord does not look on the outward appearance, but the Lord looks on the heart."

Each son of Jesse passes before Samuel. Abinadab, Shammah, and the rest are rejected. Samuel is getting worried. "Are all your sons here?" he asks. There was one more, David, the youngest. Just a freckled-faced kid, he was out tending the sheep, and was not even invited to the ritual. But God saw something that God and Israel needed and David was anointed, chosen, to be a servant of God Almighty and a leader for God's people (1 Samuel Chapter 16).

I've come to believe that Christian Baptism is the sign that one has been anointed, called, chosen, and elected into the very special work of serving others through the Church of Jesus Christ. I'm convinced that God calls us all, and we respond according to our various and unique gifts. Some might choose to attend seminary and write sermons for a living - that's one way; but in baptism, the Church ordains all Christians into the ministry. I also believe there is an unseen force that walks with me and gives me little clues about reality along the way.

I was baptized in that little church west of Oakland on February 1, 1948. The District Superintendent from Omaha came out to perform the sacrament. No doubt, the Nelsons and Petersons and Larsons and Sanders and Enstroms and Andersons and Jacobsons were there. And with a few words, and a drop of water drawn from a tap in Burt County, Nebraska, I received the call to ministry. When I realized for myself what grace means, I knew God loved me as though I was the only person in the universe.

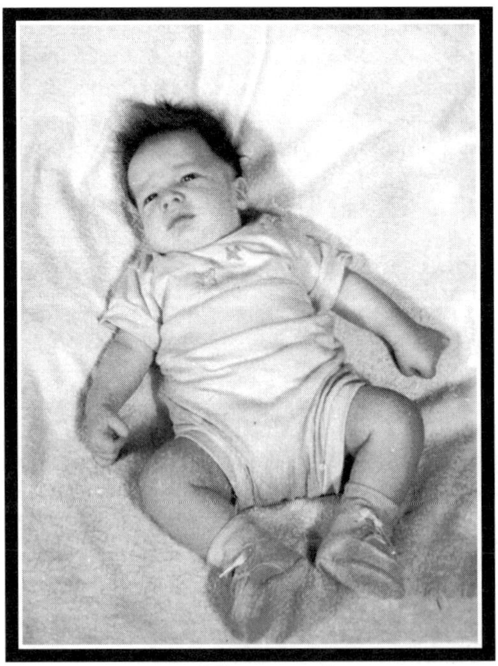

me at three months

Chapter 4
From Diapers To Kindergarten

My dad once told me that Methodist preachers had to move every three years or so if they expected a raise in income. In 1948 he was 33 years old with a wife and two children and moved from a station (one church) to a four-point charge in Howard County, Nebraska. The largest congregation and location of the parsonage was in St. Paul, the Howard County seat. Dad also served Fairdale, a former Swedish church ten miles north of town and two churches (Boelus and Ebenezer) about 20 miles southwest of St. Paul.

St. Paul is the home of the Nebraska Baseball Museum. The Hall of Fame pitcher Grover Cleveland Alexander grew up in the county and is buried in St. Paul. Dorothy Lynch invented the salad dressing that bears her name in St. Paul, and it is produced today about 60 miles away in the little town of Duncan. I wish I could say the city was named for Christianity's most important early leader, but it was tagged in honor of the Paul brothers, who were surveyors that laid out the town site in 1871.

I was less than a year old when we moved to St. Paul, and I have five early memories from living there. My mother said she didn't recall much about the churches and town, either, because she had two little ones when we arrived and two more before we left in 1950.

After six months, Boelus and Ebenezer were added to the Cairo charge, and Dad only preached twice on Sundays. But he decided to jump-start the church at tiny Cushing, about eight miles northeast of St. Paul. They had a building, but had been inactive for a few years. Dad found a nucleus of support, and led services for a year until they were added to the Wolbach charge.

When my friend John Craig became the pastor at St. Paul in 1968, they still had the same parsonage, and I stopped to visit a few times. It was very small, with two bedrooms, and the Craigs had six kids: four in college and two at home, and the parents slept in a travel trailer. When we moved in 20 years previously, my folks had two pre-schoolers, and added two more, so they were forced to sleep in the house! In 1969, the church bought a larger, newer home for their pastor, but the little house on Farnum Street is still there.

Me and Pops in 1948

Enjoying my first car in 1950

I remember riding my tricycle on the tree-lined sidewalk, and playing on the lawn with my dad lifting me inside through an open window. I vividly recall receiving the gift of a kiddie car fire engine on my third birthday, and seeing tiny Douglas Woodrow in September 1950. My last memory was living among the tall boxes the day before we moved to another house.

The St. Paul community was very good to me when I was selling insurance. I added three church customers, and a fantastic retirement facility to my list of sales. The United Methodists have a very nice building about 30 years old. Before they were a customer, I was driving through town on a late November afternoon in 2003. I decided to swing past the church to see if anyone was there.

I knew the pastor well, and he was at the church. I got permission to measure it up, take photos, etc., and sent him a proposal in a few days. I managed to book the sale the next January. It always made me feel extra good to do business with a church formerly served by my father.

In April of 2012, I was driving down St. Paul's main street, and saw the Masonic building. I pulled over to take a picture, and noticed the Baseball Museum and Chamber of Commerce office was on the main level, so I went inside. I asked the chamber manager if she had a key to the lodge area, and she said, "no, but I know somebody who does." She very graciously made a call, and said the lodge secretary would arrive shortly. While I was waiting, I recalled that my father took the initial degrees of Freemasonry when we lived in St. Paul. A brother Mason arrived, and we went upstairs.

I took several photographs, and told him about my dad joining the lodge when we lived in St. Paul. I didn't know exactly when this happened, and asked if there might be a record. He found this on an index card: "Woodrow W. Leypoldt. Petition Rec'd October 20, 1949. Initiated December 1, 1949. Passed March 2, 1950. Raised May 25, 1950. Demitted 5/18/61." That was a wonderful discovery, and I captured it with my Sony a65 camera.

My mother had two little boys in the old St. Paul hospital. After a move to Ravenna (which had no hospital), she came back to St. Paul in 1952 to deliver my sister Cathy. I remembered seeing that 2-story house-converted-to-hospital when Cathy was born, but had no idea where it was or if the building was still standing. In August of 2013 my brothers and I were headed to St. Paul to add the courthouse to our tour, and I called an acquaintance to find the whereabouts of the old hospital. She told me what I wanted to hear. Cathy joined us, and I photographed three little Leypoldts (then 64, 62, & 61) in front of the old hospital.

Ravenna is 40 miles from St. Paul in Buffalo County. In 1950 their Methodist Church burned to the ground, and they weren't getting much done about building a new one. Both Ravenna and St. Paul were in the Kearney District, which was supervised by Dr. Walter Jewett, who had a lot of confidence in my father. He also knew that a family of six required more income, and Ravenna was a "promotion" for my father. We moved there shortly before November 1, 1950. One of my early Ravenna memories was watching my dad shovel coal into the parsonage furnace.

My dad preached at least twice every Sunday most of his ministry. When we were young, he came home from church, gathered us around him, and read the Sunday comics. This gave Mom time to finish dinner, and I remember his voice was always hoarse from leading worship. My father diligently called on his flock, and the farmers sometimes gave him a chicken or two. He carried a gunny sack in his Dodge, and he had an ax he kept in the rafters of the garage. That's how we learned the meaning of "running around like a chicken with your head cut off." Sometimes, there was a bonus egg laid in the trunk as well.

I have a couple of memories about Christmas in Ravenna. One year Santa came to our house and delivered gifts, although we had to wait until Christmas Eve to open them. When he left, Dad looked out the door and said, "looks like Santa got himself a new Ford." The next year Santa showed up again, and I thought it so strange that he had a wristwatch just like my father's. I started demythologizing things at an early age.

My little sister, Catherine Joanne, was born while we lived in Ravenna. My grandparents came out to see the new baby, and they took Janice and I back to Omaha. I was not yet five, and got homesick for the first time in my life. I slept in a small bed near the window in Pops' room. My grandfather, like all good grandpas, snored a little, and that kept me awake. I started thinking how easy it would be for someone to snatch me through that open window. Janice and I were introduced to Grandma's new television set that week.

My mother had a sister who lived with my grandparents. Ida Roberta, "Bobbie," was 19 years younger than my mom, and only 11 years older than me. She was born in 1936 when Grandma was 43, and was quite unexpected. She had cerebral palsy, but we didn't understand what that was. When we were young, Bobbie played with Janice and myself as though we were equals. Later on, when five more little Leypoldts joined the crew, we really upset her structured daily lifestyle.

I started school in Ravenna, and began noticing the world beyond our home. There were three powerful philosophies that guided me: Methodism, Cornhuskerism, and Republicanism. None of these were forced upon me. I just naturally acquired them as a citizen of small town Nebraska in the fifties and sixties. I changed some when I went to college, and even more when I went to seminary.

The next winter, my younger siblings came down with whooping-cough. I wasn't sick, but learned how to mimic the illness and got to stay home from school, which was put to good use on several occasions in the future. In this case our house was also quarantined.

The Ravenna parsonage was very close to the new church under construction. Money was tight, but volunteers were generous with their time as the new building went up. There was a semi-retired contractor in the church who spent a lot of time on the project, and Dad enjoyed that kind of work as well. My father was "low church" and didn't own a pulpit robe until the new church was dedicated. He bought a used black choir robe in Grand Island, and wore it throughout his ministry.

When Dad came back to Nebraska in 1945, he bought a roll-top desk that once belonged to Bishop Homer Stuntz, who served the Omaha Area 1916-24. Possibly this was part of the household they acquired at North Bend. Probably because he was moving to a smaller house, he left it behind in the Ravenna parsonage.

Methodist Church, Ravenna, Nebraska in 1952

Dad with his children at Chadron State Park in 1954

Chapter 5
The Garden Beyond The Sandhills

In the 12th Chapter of Genesis we find the story of Abram being called by God to move to an unknown place. In 1953 our family had a similar experience. It had been an eventful year in Ravenna. Dad had supervised the building of a new church next door, and it was an exciting thing for this five-year-old to witness. I had survived my first year of school. My mother had her fifth child the previous year. The folks were ready to enjoy their family and new church, and a fourth year on the Ravenna-Hazard charge.

When Dad went to AC in June of 1953, he had no expectation of being moved. However, he was beckoned to an audience with Bishop H. Bascom Watts, and told to prepare for a relocation. Then the fateful phone call home was made. I was only five, but I knew something was wrong. When Dad told Mom to start packing, an atmosphere of grief prevailed in our house. Unlike Abram, we had not been sent to an unknown place, but it was close. We were heading for Crawford in the far northwest corner of Nebraska. We did not realize we were going on a sacred journey. We did not feel blessed by the Methodist system.

We United Methodists have an itinerant ministry. That means the call to change pulpits could come at any time. Pastors are still reviewed and appointed on an annual basis. I grew up hearing tales of the olden days from retired Methodist preachers. They talked about going to Conference, and listening carefully when the Bishop read the Appointments, because they could move or stay without warning. John Wesley believed it was important to keep preachers moving, and like Abram they were often called to an unfamiliar future. I'm certain many people, especially spouses and children, did not feel blessed by the Methodist itinerant system.

My father pieced together the circumstances that ensnared him. An elderly pastor serving at Columbus was forced to move, and agreed to go up the road to Madison. However, the Madison folks did not want him, and the Bishop felt the pastor at Crawford had been there long enough, so he was slated for Madison. The guy from Columbus did not want to go west, and had lived in Crawford as a child. Thus, another plan evolved which sent the man from Columbus to Ravenna, and my father ended up in Crawford.

From that time forward, my parents harbored a subtle love/dislike/hate relationship with The Methodist Church hierarchy. In 1953 they had five little children, and made the best of it. Within two weeks, a large Mayflower truck appeared on Grand Avenue in front of the Ravenna parsonage. At the end of that summer day, this van held all our earthly possessions and it headed westward up Highway 2.

My folks carefully packed overnight necessities, loaded us into our 1946 Dodge, and away we went toward the uncertain adventures of Nebraska's panhandle. The family now consisted of Woodrow, 38, Dorothy, 35, Janice and Charles, soon to be 9 and 6, Gary, 4, Douglas, almost 3, and baby Catherine, 11 months. We were two adults and five kids, in a gray Dodge coupe, traveling west in Nebraska in the summer. There was no such thing as air conditioning.

The Crawford parsonage had only two upstairs bedrooms, and my resourceful mother found places for all of us to sleep. Gary and I slept in bunk beds in the hallway, with Doug in a single bed next to us. Janice and Cathy shared a room, and the folks were in the "master." The house was on the edge of downtown Crawford, a block from the train station and next to the church.

Despite our rocky start, Crawford was a fun place to live and we loved it there. It is nestled in the scenic Pine Ridge, where tales of the Old West and a real soldier fort were a part of my life. Long before television was available, we followed the cowboy stories through movies which were shown as week-to-week serials. Nearly every Saturday afternoon, the local theater was filled with kids watching our heroes fight off the bad guys. We loved Roy Rogers, the King of the Cowboys, and his girl Dale Evans. Oh, I so wanted to live in a home on the range, where the buffalo roamed and the deer and the antelope played, where seldom was heard a discouraging word, and the skies were not cloudy all day.

As I grew older and moved to bigger towns, I still longed for the places we sang about in western Nebraska. This became my theme song throughout life. And I'm not alone. Many in America crave an agrarian society. That's why acreages are so popular, and we spend our resources tending over sized suburban lawns.

Soon after moving to Crawford we discovered Fort Robinson, just three miles west of town. It had been an important military outpost when the west was opened to white settlers, and was home to the famous Buffalo Soldiers. In World War I it became the world's largest quartermaster remount depot, when horses and mules were still an integral part of the military. In World War II it was home to the K-9 corps, and also housed prisoners of war.

In 1953 it was mostly empty except for the federal (USDA) beef research station. Some of my friends lived at the Fort, as their parents had jobs there. Our family explored the rugged hills and valleys surrounding Crawford, and we learned the names for the buttes in Dawes and Sioux counties. We picked wild choke cherries that Mom made into jelly. I learned to watch out for red ants, and keep an eye on my little brothers and sister, as those insects bite!

A friend told my mother that red ants carried Indian beads in, around, and under the mounds they constructed. We collected quite a few over the years and the last time we tried was in 2002, when we were in Fort Robinson celebrating Mom's 85th birthday. We got chased out of the Red Cloud Agency site by the park officials, but some of us looked in other places in the area.

In December of 1953, my grandfather called to say Grandma and my Aunt Bobbie were in a car accident. Bobbie was OK, but Grandma's condition was critical, so Dad, Mom, and 18-month old Cathy took off for Omaha. The Congregational pastor and his wife, Jim and Grace Williams, moved into our parsonage, looked after us, and made sure we were ready for Christmas. They were younger than my folks, and had no children. Grandma survived the accident and lived another 19 years.

I remember listening to radio programs including *Jack Benny, Fibber McGee and Molly, Gunsmoke*, and even soap operas. My dad was fascinated by television and he bought a set in 1953, surely one of the first to do so in Crawford. The closest station was in Cheyenne, Wyoming, which was 100 air miles away. Dad put an antenna on the church roof, adjacent to the parsonage, and the snowy signal came in at night.

In 1954 the Nebraska Conference bought some land south of Chadron, which eventually became Camp Norwesca. My father was very involved in developing this site, and we spent many hours at the camp. There is a picture in the Norwesca lodge which includes Dad, Gary, and I. In 2005-2012, my son Seth was pastor in Chadron and chaired the Norwesca Board.

In 1954 a book, **The Nebraska Methodist Story,** was published by the Conference Historical Society. My father's name appears as one who gave leadership to youth ministries through the years.[7]

After school started in 1954, we moved up the hill to a different house. The parsonage was bedroom deficient, and Mom was now expecting her sixth child. Dad found a magnificent house on 3rd and Paddock to rent. It had four upstairs bedrooms and two full baths. There was also a large parlor room right off the front door, for Dad to use as an office. A family of four was living in a trailer near the parsonage. Dad asked them about renting the parsonage, and they went for it. It cost the church nothing, as both houses leased for $40 a month. Since it was on a hill, TV reception was a little better at the new place.

My second grade teacher was Mrs. Marguerite Brashear. She was the mother of Kermit Brashear, Junior, also known as "Buzzie," who was speaker of the Nebraska Unicameral in 2005-07. She wrote this on my report card: "Charles is taking it upon himself to be rather a show-off and entertain the group," which aptly described me for many years.

When I was eight years old, the burdens of being a man took on new meaning. I was the only boy in the 3rd grade who could not ride a bike. Making it worse, my 7-year-old brother had learned the year before, and was now advising me. Another problem was that we only had one bike and, of course, it was my sister's girl's bike. It was easier to ride than a boy's bike, but I didn't dare let anyone see me doing it. I tried and tried. I fell off, I jumped off, I crashed into trees. Sometimes I started off real well, even turned the corner, but our block had a downward slope that seemed to become a steep ramp. The house on the opposite corner of our block had a picket fence along the sidewalk. I swear that fence used to jump out and grab one of my legs every time I went past it.

Finally, I mastered the bike. Jake Reiner from across the street sold us a used boys' bike. I felt like a macho man on wheels for eight years. Of course when I turned sixteen, I discovered a more powerful rule of machismo eliminated "real men" from riding bikes.

A book **Real Men Don't Eat Quiche** was published in 1982.[8] I was never quite sure whether this book was serious or satire. I remember watching a silly movie about men who moved furniture for a living. As you know, it takes people with muscles to move furniture. In the movie, a new crew member was hired but the crew chief felt his name was not right for the job. He said, "You need a new name. You need a real man's name." And this is the part I remember best: "From now on your name is **Chuck**."[9]

Rex Mahlman lived just a couple of houses from our new location, and became my best friend. He was the youngest of five brothers and excelled in sports. Rex was a Yankees fan and in the summer of 1955 I was introduced to baseball. My dad let me use his old ball glove, and I learned to bat and throw and run the bases.

But to keep up with Rex, I needed to do some studying, so I devoured the sports section of the **Omaha World-Herald** and found some books at the Crawford library.

Rex loved those Yankees, and I got a little sick of hearing about them. I discovered that Mr. Branch Rickey, who led the Brooklyn Dodgers until 1953, was a Methodist and two of their star players, Duke Snider and Jackie Robinson, were also Methodists. I also learned the Dodgers had never ever won a World Series.

When the Dodgers won their first World Series in 1955 I was smitten, and have followed them through the years. In 1991 Chris, Ana, and I went west to attend my niece Jennifer's wedding, and spent some time in Los Angeles. I had tickets for a game at Dodger Stadium. We made our way there, and arrived before the gates were open so we retreated to the Olvera Plaza and did some shopping. We also wandered into a neighborhood church, which just happened to be United Methodist.

As six o'clock approached, we headed back to Chavez Ravine, and parked the car. It was a long walk, but finally we were inside one of America's shrines: a place that hosted eight world series. Dodger Stadium, July 31, 1991. It was glorious. Except for our seats. They looked great on the little blueprint order form: third level, first row, overlooking right field. The first row of course overlooked the second level, which looked to be at least a mile straight down! I am a little height-phobic, but Chris was turning green when she found an empty seat several rows behind us.

But really, it was glorious! The Dodgers played the Mets. Orel Hershiser started the game, but left after the third when it was 2-2. Daryl Strawberry hit a home run. Brett Butler stole a base or two. Tommy Lasorda had to come out once to poke and spit and yell at the umpire, and we cheered him on with gusto. Kevin Gross pitched perfectly in relief, and the Dodgers won 6-2. Chris and Ana and I ate Dodger Dogs, and I bought an autographed baseball which I will keep forever. They even flashed a trivia question about some great Dodger who hit over 400 home runs, and finished his career with the Mets. I knew who it was, so I said right out loud, "Duke Snider." And everyone around me knew I was a real Dodger fan, and I'm sure all the other 44-year-old guys were thinking the same warm thoughts about the Duke, and Pee Wee, Roy Campanella, Gil Hodges, and Jackie Robinson. We left the stadium. We had to wait a while in the parking lot. I couldn't believe how light the freeway traffic was at 11 pm. Safely inside the Farm DeVille Motel after a long day, I drifted off to sleep. I was lost in wonder, love, and praise once more, and this time the Big Dodger was by my side.

+++

On June 13, 1955 my mother gave birth to her sixth child, Steven Wayne. Dad took us all down the street in his Plymouth, and parked outside the Crawford hospital. Mom came to the window, and held the baby for us to see. In a few days they came home, and Janice was allowed to hold him but I was not. He was in a bassinet, and I snuck in and picked him up, but my mother came out of nowhere and snatched him away.

Frank Eckhoff was married to Dad's younger sister, Alyce Marie. They lived in Hershey and came to see us in Crawford a couple of times. Frank knew how to get instant laughs from us kids: he wore false teeth, and loved to take them out, make faces, and say silly things. He was a fisherman, and enjoyed the terrain around Crawford.

There was never a fishing pole or a tackle box in our garage when I was growing up. Once Frank brought his fishing gear, and we went on a picnic out west of town. After lunch, he wandered up a stream with his pole. When we found him he had hip waders on, was standing in the stream snagging trout, and throwing them on the bank. I remember touching those cold, slimy creatures with their desolate-looking eyes and thinking, "this is no fun at all." I also recall Frank holding my cousin, Kent Eugene, and they both fell in the water. I still think a school of angry trout tripped them up.

Deer hunting was a big deal in Crawford. Then as now, it was heavily regulated, with limited days given to a time when animals could be killed. People in Crawford, including us when we lived in the big house, rented rooms to hunters. There was never a gun in our house, though. My dad said he had a squirrel gun as a kid, but he had absolutely no desire to hunt for deer. He believed they were beautiful, innocent creatures and deserved to live.

As everywhere there are four seasons in Nebraska, but we call them winter, spring, summer, and football. Each September, I hearken back to the days of my childhood in Nebraska's Pine Ridge country. My father was both pastor and janitor of the Crawford Methodist Church. On Saturday afternoons in the fall, he would take me, at least one of my brothers, and his radio to the church. He would dust and sweep and whisk cobwebs, while we helped "clean church." But from 1 to 4 on those afternoons, we always listened to Lyle Bremser and Nebraska football. They almost always lost, but we loved them anyway. Dad told me when he was my age Nebraska was the best. They beat Notre Dame and Illinois, and Oklahoma wasn't even on their schedule! I wanted to believe him, but it was really hard to imagine.

My family used to frequent an area south of Crawford called Cochran Park. It had wonderful picnic grounds, lots of pine trees, and a mountain stream. It also had a rock formation called the "Giant's Thumb," we tried to climb. Cochran Park was also the scene of the Crawford Community Easter Sunrise Services.

On Easter morning, when it was still quite dark, Dad ushered us from our warm beds, telling us to bundle up, and we would hurry to the Plymouth coupe. A few minutes away, other families were gathering at Cochran Park. It seemed like everyone in town was at Sunrise Services. Then we would sit on a hillside in the chilly morning air, and hear again the story of Jesus dying, being laid in a tomb, and rising from death to once again greet his disciples.

We sang the words of Earl Marlatt: "*Are ye able, said the master, to be crucified with me? Yea, the sturdy dreamers answered, to the death we follow thee.*" And I felt in those moments, and many other times of inspiration, that I really could follow Jesus. Nothing could stop me. If Jesus called me to be a missionary in a foreign place, if I had to sacrifice money and family, if I had to stand up for something unpopular, I knew I could do it. I really meant it when I sang, "*Lord, we are able, our spirits are thine, remold them, make us, like thee divine. Thy guiding radiance above us shall be, a beacon to God, to love, and loyalty* (UMH #430)."

Sandhills cranes in flight

Gary, Chuck and Doug in 1954 and 2011

Chapter 6
The Quest For Double U

1956 was a year of radical changes. I was nine years old, about to enter the 4th grade. Our family moved from the peaceful and panoramic village of Crawford in northwestern Nebraska, to the hustling and bustling suburban town of Papillion, just outside of Omaha. I recall the day in June when the moving van pulled up to our Crawford home. It was strange seeing all our things stretched out on the lawn, while a big green truck gradually received them. I remember saying good-bye to my friend Rex. Late in the afternoon, Mom and Dad and six kids piled into our little Plymouth.

We drove 470 miles to Omaha, arriving at my grandparent's house sometime in the wee hours of the morning. After lunch the next day, we went to Papillion to inspect our new home. It was an aging Victorian style parsonage right next to a brand new stone-veneer church. It was actually a move down for Dad, but Mom wanted to be closer to her mother. We couldn't get much closer, unless we actually lived in Omaha (scary thought even now).

There were some things that hadn't changed much. In Crawford we lived in a huge 4 bedroom house with 10 foot ceilings and a wrap-around front porch. It also had a spiral staircase and a hallway upstairs, that was like a balcony overlooking the downstairs. It was drafty and scary at night. At least the Crawford house had a toilet upstairs.

The Papillion parsonage was also a large two-story building with four upstairs bedrooms, and similar porch with two front doors. On our first night in Papillion we kids learned it was more than scary - it was downright spooky! The worst thing was there was no upstairs bathroom. My brothers and I had to make the necessary trips in the middle of the night down the long, narrow, darkened hallway, which had awful wallpaper with huge flowers that looked like monsters in the shadows. The bare wooden stairs creaked with our descent and, when we grabbed the handrails, they groaned under our tightened grips and sometimes assaulted us with a splinter or two. Next it was down another short hallway, through the dining room (risky - depending on where the chairs were), through the kitchen to the bathroom. Then, of course, we had to make the long trip back to the safety of our upstairs bedroom. Most kids today have no idea what real terror is like. When winter rolled around that first year in Papillion, we found out the house was not only creaky and spooky, it was awfully cold as well.

When we arrived in Papillion, telephones were still on the "number please" system, mail had to be picked up at the post office, the Omar man brought bread, and the Alamito man delivered milk to our front porch. Papillion's 1950 population was 1,034. By the time we moved there in 1956, they had grown to perhaps 1,300. They had only one school building in 1956; high school occupied the top floor and grade school was on the main floor. There was an ancient low-ceiling gymnasium in the old building with three or four rows of spectator seats on east and west sides. A new high school building was finished late in 1956, and the upper grades moved upstairs in the old school. However, the only gym was still in the old building.

Almost immediately television became a centerpiece of our lives. No longer did we flip the dial to see obscure figures in the snow. Now we lived in the shadow of Omaha and two stations, WOW (Channel 6) and KMTV (channel 3), brought all kinds of interesting personalities into our home. We even had a little room off the kitchen we dubbed "the TV room." In 1957, KETV (channel 7) went on the air. A typical school day in 1956-1959, went something like this: breakfast included words of encouragement from *Captain Kangaroo*. After school we caught *The World's Greatest Cartoons*, followed by *The Mickey Mouse Club* and *American Bandstand,* perhaps the world's first reality TV show. After supper, we took in such staples as *The Adventures of Ozzie and Harriett, Red Skelton,* and *Leave It To Beaver* every night.

Mom struggled to get us up on school days, but on Saturdays, we were up early to take in Howdy Doody, Buffalo Bob, and Clarabelle. The television set was like a member of our family, and proved to be a great babysitter as well. Between 1956 and 1960 there were over 50 shows on prime time television that could be classified as "westerns." Even without cable, it couldn't get any better than this: *The Lone Ranger, Sergeant Preston, The Cisco Kid,* and *Wild Bill Hickok* every Saturday morning. At night, we'd watch *Tales of Wells Fargo, Have Gun, Will Travel, Maverick, Rawhide,* and many others.

A. B. Dick was part of our lives every Saturday. Until 1959 my father used his own mimeograph machine to publish the Sunday bulletins, and it was a messy old A. B. Dick model. The Papillion church had no office, and the mimeo was in the church basement. Dad hammered out a stencil (he was a rapid two finger typist), and took it downstairs. Then he smeared the smelly and gooey black ink on the mimeo's cylinder, slapped on the stencil, and he was ready to print.

Next came the slip sheet ritual; Dad kept a supply of old bulletins behind the machine. Because ink didn't dry fast enough, he had to insert an old one in between the newly printed papers. In his early years he must have done all this by himself, but when we were old enough we got the slip-sheet task. Janice hit retirement age (12) when we moved to Papillion, so I was the slip-sheeter by then. When all the bulletins were printed, we sat down and removed the inserts.

The process was not complete until after supper. All the kids took a bath and did other kid things until 9 pm. That's when *Gunsmoke* started, and Dad passed around the church bulletins and we folded them. The old mimeograph wasn't needed in Albion. This church not only had an office and typewriter, they also supplied an A. B. Dick mimeo with quick drying ink and a secretary!

One time, I was discussing mimeographs with my friend and Albion pastor Lester Anderson. He said those machines were so horrible they could make a preacher cuss. Les used to say "shoot, shucks, and phooey!" when he got upset. Dad would utter "it stinks like fury!" when his nostrils were attacked. My generation didn't need much stimulus to lapse into profanity.

It was a slow process to crank and print and slip-sheet a couple of hundred church bulletins every Saturday. It was tiring to stand there sliding those grimy old bulletins in between the new ones. I hated getting ink on my hands, and hated scrubbing them clean even more. But when I was a young preacher doing the same chore with an electric mimeograph and fast drying ink, I would have given anything to spend an hour on Saturdays alone with my dad.

I also grew up with a family named Anderson. As I recall, there was a mom and a dad named Jim and Margaret, a boy they called Bud and two girls, Betty and Kathy. Our family shared many trials and tribulations with the Andersons. A lot of folks came to believe that "father knows best" because of Jim Anderson. Then there was the Stone family with Dr. Alex, who practiced out of his home, and his wife Donna and their children Mary, Jeff, and Trisha. In this case, it was clearly "mother knows best."

Another program I enjoyed watching was *The Adventures of Charlie Chan*, a supposed Chinese detective who worked in London. His oldest son, played by the actor Keye Luke, was called "Number One Son," which I almost borrowed as a title for this book. For a short time I was known by that appellation as well. I was, of course, the oldest son in my family. When I learned about the status appertaining to firstborn sons in days of o're, I fantasized upon what could have been for me.

My dad was the only son in his family and my grandfather, William Leypoldt, was the oldest son in a family of 12 children. His father, Johan George Leypoldt, was also the oldest son in his family. The streak of number one sons has now extended to my son Seth Landon Leypoldt, not that it matters in the least.

There are many references to birthrights and male domination in the Bible, and misogyny continues in many countries and religions, including American Christianity. We were quite surprised when our first child was born, and some folks called us lucky to have a son the first time. When I took the Christian faith seriously, male superiority fell by the wayside for me.

When Christmas drew closer, Mom and Dad made another radical change. Our family had always opened presents on Christmas Eve. We went to church, of course, then we came home and Santa and his elves had invaded our home and the gifts were under the tree. We didn't have to wait for morning.

Inexplicably in 1956, Mom and Dad decided we would open our treasures in the morning rather than Christmas Eve. Perhaps Santa needed more time because there were six of us, but we were not given satisfactory explanations. We kids were not happy; waiting was not a popular concept with any of us. Here we were in an eerie house, probably haunted, and now we had to linger an extra day for Christmas.

The stretch before Christmas was always difficult anyway. My mom was a big Christmas person. She and Dad must have saved all year for the things they gave us. We always got lots of presents. The last Christmas she hosted was in 2004 when she was 87. She had gifts for everyone, whether they were able to be at her house or not. She continued to shop 'til she dropped from Thanksgiving to Christmas, and filled her basement with packages that on Christmas day we devoured in about thirty minutes. But she loved Christmas. From the time we were born she enjoyed giving things away, and making certain we were satisfied. That's why waiting for Christmas is so difficult for many. We have the past to inform us. The anticipation of an event heightens our expected joy, but it can also drive us slightly crazy.

One memory from Papillion is locked into my mind in a very negative way. On a summer day, I encountered the most unpleasant odor I'd ever experienced. It was coming from the kitchen. Dad had visited a gardener who gifted him with a large quantity of cabbage. It made him think about his German grandmother, and a treat she made for her family - sauerkraut. My father was fermenting that stuff in our kitchen to share with us. It was a tough sell for him. I wish my dear father had lived to know that most of his progeny today are lovers of both runza and reuben sandwiches.

One day we were at my grandparents' house in Omaha, and two well-dressed young men came to the door. It had to be on Sunday, because Pops was home and answered the door. I only heard his part of the conversation, and it was not a friendly greeting. The two persisted in wanting to come in for a visit. Finally, Pops said, "We're not interested! We're Methodists, don't come back again!" And he slammed the door shut. The whole thing surprised and intrigued me. Grandma and Pops had a few words out in the kitchen. Something about him losing his temper in front of the children.

When she came back, I said, "Grandma, I didn't know Pops was a Methodist. He never goes to church." Then she explained in her quiet way, "he's not a Methodist, he just doesn't want to have anything to do with Jehovah's Witnesses." Grandma then proceeded to tell us what she knew about them. It was my first exposure to those who sell religion door-to-door.

Easter 1957

When I was ten, tether ball was the rage. In this game, a ball is attached to a cord, which is connected to the top of a pole. Two players stand opposite one another and slap the ball at each other. The one who wraps the rope and ball around the pole wins. Like most games, quickness, coordination, and concentration are the keys to winning. Stature helps a lot, too.

My dad bought this game and installed it in our back yard. I remember one summer day when my buddy, Charlie Sturm, and I were playing tether ball. I think he must have beat me every time, and I was getting pretty tired of losing. So I threw a tantrum, called him some names, and took my ball into the house.

Unfortunately for me, Mom met up with me and asked what was going on. I couldn't admit the truth, so I lied about something Charlie said or did. Mom didn't buy my story, and she took the ball and put it back where it belonged. I stood on the back porch watching the other kids having fun. My worst memory was seeing my dad playing a game with Charlie Sturm. All I could do was snivel and feel sorry for myself.

My dad remained interested in the church's youth ministries, and once more he was a leader in the development of a new camp. The Conference had purchased land near the little village of Fontanelle, and Dad became involved in fund-raising and development of the site. I remember seeing what is now Camp Fontanelle when there were no buildings.

When my youngest brother, James Reed Leypoldt, turned 50 in 2007 I wrote a nostalgic essay about his birth. its titled **The Quest For Double U**, and I've revised it for this publication. Read on.

I've been thinking about the power of "W" lately. This curious letter looks like a double V but is pronounced double U. There are only six major European languages that use the W. The Swedes call it "dubbel-ve," and it did not appear in their official dictionary until 2006. Germans don't really need a "w" because they pronounce it "v" anyhow. The Double U is pretty important to Leypoldts though. Our grandfather was "G. W." and our dad was "W. W." Four of W.W.'s boys have a middle name that starts with W.

There appears to be some clout associated with people who have a middle name starting with W. One former president's best friends call him "W" or "Dubya," although some folks facetiously say this W stands for Wrong. But think about it. Nebraska's greatest politician was George W. Norris. Our most successful football coach was Thomas W. Osborne. I was ordained by Bishop Don W. Holter. One of our greatest presidents was Thomas Woodrow Wilson; another revered by some was Ronald W. Reagan. Someone else who comes to mind is the fictional father: Clark W. Griswold, Jr. The list goes on. There seems to be a mysterious, fraternal, magic in the initial "W." My father-in-law was Harold W. Landon. He had four grandsons using the illustrious "W." My brother Douglas W. Leypoldt has a son named Nicholas W., and grandsons, Colin W. and Dawson W. But the one who wins the prize is my grand-nephew in Oregon, Charles Walter Woodrow Dorr.

Well, enough of this misogynist name game. I'm just recording another episode of our family's history. This one focuses on my baby brother, James Reed Leypoldt, who was born September 16, 1957 (yes, that's Reed, not Weed). It starts in the suburbs of Omaha. In 2013 **Bloomberg Business Week** claimed Papillion was the best town in America to raise kids. It wasn't that great when we lived there, but it's changed a lot. There were less than 1,500 people in Papillion in 1957, with well over 20,000 today.

When the summer of 1957 drew to a close the six Leypoldt children were in for some changes. Cathy would soon be off to kindergarten. Steve was two and giving up his baby bed. The new baby was supposed to arrive before school started. It had been a long, hot summer, and Mom was beginning to wonder if she would turn 40 before her seventh child was born. I'm sure Dad did all he could to make her comfortable, even buying an air conditioner which cooled down one room in the old parsonage. Mom had to admit this child was her idea. Steven was two and he needed a little one to grow up with. She really wanted a girl - the name would be Merrilee Elizabeth. I was really looking forward to the new baby, but I wanted a brother and I don't remember much discussion about boy's names. Mom was set on four boys and three girls.

In those days school started the day after Labor Day. Our school was only two blocks from home, so we had time to dilly-dally around in the mornings. We watched TV, ate some corn flakes, and wondered aloud if Mom was ready to go to the hospital. My clue that something was happening, would be seeing Pops' old 1936 Plymouth in front of our house. Every afternoon I waited anxiously for the 3:45 bell, and dashed down the stairs and out the school door, past Mr. Horne, the well man's truck, and Mr. Arp, the county sheriff's patrol car, hoping to see the old Plymouth.

Fortunately, all this pent up eagerness lasted less than two weeks. On Monday afternoon, September 16, taking the same short route as always, I spied my heart's desire, that wonderful black sedan. I sped up as fast as my ten year old legs would take me, and bounced through the side porch door. Inside was Grandma, Bobbie, and Pops, and the smaller kids. "Has Mommy had the baby yet?" My folks were always Mommy and Daddy until I was around 13, and my voice got deep enough to say Mom and Dad.

"No," replied Grandma, "your daddy will call when the time comes." So we waited. And then we had supper. And waited some more. About 8 o'clock the phone rang. I think I answered, but now I can't remember. Maybe it was Grandma; probably it was Janice who beat me to the receiver. Doesn't matter. Dad was calling from St. Catherine's Hospital in Omaha. He said something like, "you have a new baby brother!" Boy was I excited. We needed another boy. Five made a basketball team. I ran next door to tell the Seybold sisters, then across the street to tell Mrs. Grube, and all the other neighbors who were home. **MY MOMMY HAD A BABY BOY!**

Then I went back home and posed the question that some neighbors had asked me, "what's the baby's name?" Somebody said, "James Reed Leypoldt." Wait a minute, I thought. We have a tradition and this moniker doesn't fit. Yeah, it's a lot better than Merrilee Elizabeth, but where's the double-U? Remember the Leypoldt men all have a middle name that starts with double-U: Grandpa was George W.; Dad was Woodrow W., Charles Wesley, Gary William, Douglas Woodrow, and Steven Wayne. And then along came Jim. Our great-grandfather was James Mitchell Reed. I guess it's OK to recognize another branch of the family tree. It's just too bad Jim would have to spend his life searching for the missing double-U.

We had to wait a few more days to actually see the baby. It was a repeat of Monday: hustling home from school, seeing Pops' old car, and rushing into the house. This time, of course, Mom was there, and in a little bassinet was my new baby brother.

Jim had very pretty red hair, and Mom didn't cut it until he was at least 18 months old. She was still dealing with the Merrilee Elizabeth thing. His hair became a strawberry blond and was real curly. I think he developed long eyelashes as well. Once, when Jim was a little over a year old, I carried him into a school event. One of the teachers asked, "Is this your little sister?" I know he heard it and didn't understand the words, but somehow he knew about the curse of the missing double-U.

Mom called him Jamie for the longest time. The rest of us called him Jimmy. He was really a hyper kid. Mom used to say, "if he was my first, he would have been my last." Our church had no nursery and Mom had quite a time keeping seven of us in line on Sunday mornings. There were four boys aged 2 to 10 to supervise when Jim was a baby.

One time Mom let me stay home with Jim, so she could go to church without having to deal with either of us. There was a wonderful lady in the Papillion church named Blanche Eurek. Every Sunday she would bring us a dozen eggs, and quite often they sat on the dining room table for a while. Jim was probably 18 months old the day I was supposed to be watching him. He was in the dining room and I was in the TV room. I heard him giggling and laughing and talking to himself the way toddlers do. Then I noticed cracking and squishy noises as well. Jim had found the eggs and discovered they could be wonderful toys. That was bad enough, but I thought I could solve the problem with a vacuum cleaner. My baby sitting days were over for a long time.

In 1959 we moved to Albion. The house had three bedrooms upstairs and one down. Mom and Dad thought it better to sleep upstairs with the kids, so Jim ended up in the hall for quite a while. When he was four he played a memorable part in the church

Christmas program, but I'll let him explain that one. It's clear the power of double-U would have helped him then.

I went away to college in 1965, and missed out on a lot of my of little brother's antics. He and Steve and Cathy were home when our father lay sick and dying, and they provided Mom with an enormous amount of help and comfort.

There's a lot more I could say about my little brother. He went to college, got married, raised two kids, worked at the Regional Center, went back to college, worked at a computer store, and now works for the Lincoln Public Schools. He's also a proud grandpa of three beautiful children.

Oh yeah, one more thing: in 1973 Mom and Don Walters got married and moved to Watertown, South Dakota. Jim was in his junior year at Albion High School, so he finished school up there. Watertown High was a lot bigger than Albion, but Jim made the football team there and earned a letter.

Hey! I guess he got himself a **double-U** after all!

James Reed Leypoldt in 2007

+++

My fifth grade teacher was a 20-year-old named Miss Wittick. She was a little overweight and a lot of fun. Some of us kids went to her house one day, and she fed us saltine crackers and real butter. What a treat! Miss Wittick actually changed my name to "Chuck." Heretofore I had been known only as Charles, same as my grandfather Hennings. But on the first day in Miss Wittick's class, she passed around a piece of paper, and told us to write our names and also our nicknames. I could have been Chick or Chas or Charlie or Elvis or Romeo I suppose. But I wrote down "Chuck," and she and everyone else started calling me that.

Papillion parsonage with Pops' 1936 Plymouth

Christmas 1957 with all seven children

My interest in baseball was alive and well in Papillion. Like many others, my love for baseball comes from two perspectives: player and spectator. Actually, there wasn't much difference for me. The coaches always put me in either right or center field, because in little league very few balls got into those places, so I had a reduced chance of getting an error. As a batter I also did a lot of watching. As a matter of fact, the only time I got on base was when I was walked. And I walked a lot because I was afraid to look foolish swinging at bad pitches, and there were a lot of bad pitches. So even when I was a player, I was a spectator.

In the fifties, Dizzy Dean was doing the Saturday afternoon TV games. I've always wondered if he was as good a pitcher as he said he was. The TV commentary improved quite a bit when former Dodger Pee Wee Reese joined ol' Diz, and helped him remember what ball park the game was in. Sometimes at night, I went out to the car, and tuned in Harry Carey on KMOX in St. Louis. I couldn't play worth a hoot, but as a follower, a spectator, a devotee, I knew baseball.

There is a woman I have never met who had a tremendous influence on my early life. My father's grandmother died many years before I was born. Our family tales include the one that she conducted religious services in her home, and imposed her strict ways on those around her. She was a member of another denomination (Free Methodist), and reluctantly became a "regular" Methodist when the family moved to Hershey, Nebraska in the early 1900's.

My dad tried to preserve some of those old ways when we were growing up. Even though he had left home to attend Drew Theological Seminary, the bastion of liberalism, he still remembered Grandma's ways. When I was six, I was invited to the birthday party of a friend on a Sunday afternoon. All the other kids went to a movie, which was something we could not do on Sundays. Perhaps it was a small miracle I had any fun at all that day.

In Papillion we lived a block away from the baseball field. On a Sunday afternoon, I asked permission to go to a game. Dad said, "No - it's Sunday." My mom was not so strict. She was a Presbyterian until age 12 and had a father who voted for Democrats. She intervened by reminding Dad that he was watching a baseball game on television. I think we finally buried Grandma Clara that day.

Being a baseball fan, and living next to a church proved to be hazardous at times. A highly traumatic and unforgettable thing occurred one summer afternoon in 1958. What happened was my fault, and it could have been worse. Well, it was partly Duke Snider's fault. In the middle fifties, he was the most exciting outfielder in the Major Leagues (that is, if you don't include Willie Mays, and he had the obvious weakness of wearing a Giant uniform). In the summer of 1957, at least, I wanted to be like Duke Snider. So I started training for my career. Sometimes I played catch with my brother or my dad, but I also found a way to bounce the ball off buildings and play catch with myself. This is how I got into trouble.

Saint Paul Methodist Church was a lovely white stone building with buttresses along the outside walls of the sanctuary. These are columns of stone that outline the art glass windows. On each column are two flat slabs set at 45 degree angles - one about three feet high, the other maybe six feet from the ground. These slabs made perfect targets for the balls I threw. The lower one acted as a catcher when I wanted to be a pitcher, and the upper one simulated pop flies for me to run under.

The big problem was that in between all the buttresses were the church's art glass windows. As I recall the windows were kind of ugly, dark green things, complete with a traditional Gothic arch. More than once, I was advised by Mom or Dad to stop throwing the ball against the buttresses. "You'll break one of those windows," they said. Of course, I was nearly as accurate as Sandy Koufax by then, and not the least bit worried about the windows, which were two or three feet from the target area.

One fateful summer afternoon, I moved from the side of the church to the front, where it was harder for Mom to see me. The front wall of the church had three narrow windows in the center, also framed by stone buttresses. On the inside, these three were located immediately above the altar. As I hurled the ball toward the slabs, I backed up a step each time. This increased the rebound factor; but it also decreased my precision.

Eventually, I was standing in the street and increasing my speed. Then it happened. The ball made a clunk sound and fell to the ground. My pulse began to race, my throwing hand trembled. I looked both ways. There were no witnesses, and I walked over for an inspection. The window was damaged in its extreme right corner. It looked OK, the frame and lead had stopped the ball.

Then I went inside. The sanctuary was dark and cool and quiet. My eyes sought the three windows above the altar. My heart sank, my stomach ached. Light was pouring in through a silver-dollar sized hole in one of those windows.

I don't remember being punished, or even scolded by my Dad. Maybe it's because I "fessed up" immediately. Or maybe because I looked so terrified, he figured I learned a lesson. I'm pretty sure I quit bouncing baseballs against the buttresses.

I do remember Dad picking up all the pieces of broken glass, taking them to the dining room table, and assembling them together as best he could. He then found the stickiest tape available, and carefully put everything back where it belonged. As far as I know, no one in Papillion ever knew the difference.

I've been inside the Papillion church a few times since we moved from there in 1959. I always look for the broken window (they have a new, much larger sanctuary now and the old one is a library). They've also replaced the glass in the three former altar windows many years ago.

My dad had a temper and sometimes he lost it, and our attitudes were adjusted by his big hand on our small behinds. But, more often than not, he corrected us by his gentle and loving example. That broken window no longer invokes feelings of fear and trembling, rather its a simple reminder of a happy childhood and a father's love and guidance that I still miss very much.

+++

In the summer of 1958 my grandfather had retired, and was planning to take a trip to Goodhue, Minnesota, where he was born and raised. His older brother, Bill, lived in Goodhue and a sister, Lena, was in nearby Red Wing. I think my mother and grandmother cooked up a plan, and it involved me. Mom thought dad needed to get away from a contentious faction in his church, and Grandma didn't want to travel in Pops' 1936 Plymouth. Mom would be left alone to parent her seven children, so she required the least obedient one to take a trip with his father.

One August morning Pops, Grandma, and Bobbie came to Papillion and left the old Plymouth so Mom would have a car, and we loaded up the 2-door station wagon and headed north. Pops was especially close to Bill, his senior by sixteen years. My great-grandfather was kicked by a horse and was an invalid most of Pops' childhood, so Bill was a father figure. We would be staying with Uncle Bill and Aunt Clara.

We made the trip in one day. Upon arrival in Goodhue, we discovered that Uncle Bill was in the hospital. Aunt Clara put us up in her three bedroom house in this little town. The next day we went to Zumbrota to visit Bill, but he wasn't doing well. We went out to what had been the Hennings farm, and Pops thoroughly enjoyed it. The house was still there, though it had been remodeled. One of the barns was standing, and in good repair; Pops found his name that had been carved into a plank 60 years previously.

We went to Red Wing where my great-aunt Lena lived in a one room upstairs apartment on a business block. I'd never seen a home quite like it. Of the eight children, she was closest in age to Pops, and never married.

One morning Pops went to see a childhood friend who lived in Goodhue, and I went along. Returning to Aunt Clara's, we walked by St. Luke's English Lutheran Church, where Pops had been baptized and confirmed. He said, "when you go to catechism for three years you never forget it." I knew Pops wasn't a Methodist, but didn't learn until about 15 years ago that he was a member of Kountze Memorial Lutheran in Omaha all through the years, paying "dues," but seldom attending.

On Sunday, Dad and I went to a church where one of his seminary classmates was the pastor. We always went to church when my father was on vacation, but this was special because Dad got to visit a friend he hadn't seen for thirteen years. I think we were gone for less than a week, but it was a memorable experience for this 11-year-old.

My sixth grade teacher in Papillion was Mrs. Johnson. I remember only two things about her. First, she was a terribly nervous person. I think it had something to do with her teaching during the population explosion. The metro monster on the north, Omaha, was creeping closer and the expansion of Offut Air Base in eastern Sarpy County was also making growth of Papillion a strong possibility.

The administration and school board must have been a little short-sighted.

Without a building program, they began consolidating and took in a large territory all around Papillion in Sarpy County. In the meantime developers in Papillion started two new subdivisions, and the population doubled in five years. It seemed every new family had kids, and every classroom was crowded. Thus, Mrs. Johnson was a nervous wreck. The School Board saw the problem, and by December they added a second sixth grade classroom. However I stayed with Mrs. Johnson. She was still nervous. When she got really frazzled, she always sent me and a few others to see Mr. George, the Superintendent.

The second thing I remember about Mrs. Johnson, was she found a cure for my nearsightedness. Mrs. Johnson wrote something on the chalk board that I couldn't see. After that, she found a cure for this myopia. She did it by making me sit in the front row all through sixth grade. However, this turned out to be a big mistake.

You see, Jim Vance faked being near-sighted so he could sit up there with me. And we drove Mrs. Johnson even crazier. Once more, all she could do was send us to see Mr. George. Later on I went to see Dr. Palmer, the optometrist, in Albion and got my first pair of glasses. In 1967, I started wearing contact lenses. I remained nearsighted, and I remembered Mrs. Johnson's attempts to cure both my orneriness and my sight issues.

+++

When I went to Sunday School at Papillion, we had a "Fisherman's Club." We were supposed to invite someone to Sunday School and if they showed up, we were in the club and got to wear a shiny, brass fishhook in our lapel. I don't think I ever made into that club, but I do remember the story of how Jesus appeared at the Sea of Galilee and called Peter and Andrew and James and John out of their boats and told them, "I will make you fish for people."

This biblical account always bothered me because of Zebedee. Zebedee is kind of an unsung hero in the Bible. Two of his sons, James and John, are important followers of Jesus. His wife Mary shows up a couple of times in Matthew's Gospel. First, she tried to get Jesus to endorse her boys as second and third in command. And secondly, she is named as one of the many disciples who followed and provided for Jesus. But Zebedee evidently stayed on the boat and continued his fishing business. We hear nothing more about him after the day he lost his crew.

I preached a sermon once with the title "The Day Zebedee Lost His Crew." I wrote earlier about not being a fisherman, but I also confess to having sympathy for poor old Zebedee. John Greenleaf Whittier wrote a poem including these words (see UMH #358):

In simple trust like theirs who heard,
Beside the Syrian sea,
The gracious calling of the Lord,
Let us, like them, without a word
Rise up and follow thee.

Though Zebedee apparently stayed with the ship, the four fishermen were models for me. The underlying question was "What does it mean to be a Christian?" The answer is you are a Christian if you've heard and accepted a call to follow Jesus. That's why Zebedee lost his crew; his boys joined the Jesus movement. Note that Jesus took the everyday skills of four persons, and gave them new direction. Peter, Andrew, James and John did not so much drop their nets, as they replaced them.

Albert Schweitzer's famous conclusion was: "He comes to us as one unknown, without a name, as of old, by the lakeside, he came to those men who knew him not. And he speaks to us the same word that he spoke to them, 'Follow thou me.'"[10]

On the south shore of Clear Lake in northern Iowa there was a United Methodist camp called Camp Galilee. Our friends, Bob and Betty Ellis, had a cabin there and we went there often through 1999. We sat under the elms and cottonwoods and watched the skiers and swimmers enjoy the lake. There was a sign on the lakeshore which displayed a quote from J. B. Phillips' translation of Matthew 4:19: "Follow me and I will teach you to catch men!" I've often wondered if Methodist girls in northern Iowa are more aggressive than others.

+++

I delivered the evening editions of **Omaha World-Herald** when we lived in Papillion. I picked up the papers around 4 pm, folded them, and deposited them in a bag slung over my left shoulder. I used to eat Cheetos as I walked along my short route. Thinking back, I wonder if any of my customers noticed any orangish smudges. Years later, after watching **Rain Man**, I started eating Cheetos with a toothpick.[11]

I had a dog on the route that barked and nipped at me when I delivered the paper. Pops was at our house when I was ready to start my deliveries one day, and he went along with me. I told him about that dog and he said he would take the paper to that door for me. Sure enough, the angry canine went after him, but Pops took the rolled up paper and whopped him right on the snout. The little monster never bothered me again.

My grandfather Hennings died very unexpectedly on April 7, 1959. He had a serious heart attack while in his 50's, took time from work to recuperate, and made some life-style changes. He was very slender and looked healthy. He had retired just a couple of years previously, and gave up his only remaining vice: pipe smoking.

My siblings and I were shaken. It was a school day, and I was the last one home that day. I opened the door and everybody was crying. Gary stood up and gave me the bad news. I couldn't believe it. I was his number one grandson and shared his name. I thought he'd be around forever. It was the first time we children had lost someone close to us.

I went upstairs to my bedroom, and after a while my dad came in. He told me he was 13 when his grandfather died, and he said he cried and cried all day and did the same when his grandmother died a few years later. He said it was a good thing to cry, and it meant that you loved someone. That made me feel better, because I'd never seen my father cry.

Randy Travis sang a song titled **He Walked on Water**. It was about a boy's relationship with his great-grandfather.[12] I'm sure a lot of little kids idolized their grandparents; I certainly did. I have fond memories of visiting that little house in South Omaha. They had television before we did. Grandma served pancakes with real butter, and all the 7-up you could drink. When Pops came home from work, he always gave us plenty of attention. At that time in my life, I thought that Pops walked on water.

Pops wasn't perfect. He did things every day my dad avoided his whole life. Pops smoked a pipe, drank a little whiskey, and cussed about Eisenhower. When I was small, I stood beside him and blew out the matches after he lit his pipe. I loved the smell of that tobacco, and that's probably why I became a pipe smoker for a while. On Sunday mornings in mild weather, Pops sat on the front porch and read the World-Herald.

In my pastoral career I dealt with hundreds of grieving persons. I'm sure some of them had private moments of hysteria, but I never witnessed a scene like my grandmother's at the cemetery. I'll just say she was overwhelmed by the loss. We were all sad, but Grandma was never the same after the day she said goodbye to "Charley."

Janice took this picture in 1957

Pops and Grandma shortly before his death

More than once I heard my mother say, "you can take a boy from the farm, but you can't take the farm from the boy," in describing my dad. I remember gardens in both Crawford and Papillion. The biggest one was in Papillion where there was an empty lot across the street from the parsonage. Dad had most of it plowed, and he planted sweet corn, tomatoes, potatoes, lettuce, peas, string beans, and other things. His style was organic, so we learned to hoe, pull weeds, and pluck potato bugs.

One of my friends moved to Papillion from Libya, and introduced us to soccer. I got pretty good at that sport and dodge ball, which were staples of recess activities. We also played a lot of marbles and tether ball. I gradually learned that the less contact, the more I enjoyed sports.

The Russians sent sputnik into space when we lived in Papillion. We were 12 miles from Offutt Air Force Base, headquarters of the Strategic Air Command (SAC). We believed the Communists were planning to attack America, and when they did they would hit SAC first and we would die instantly. I was relieved to get away from this possibility when we moved to Albion, but still worried about my Papillion pals.

We learned another piece of the Communist threat was they would arrest all the clergy, and destroy churches. I watched all 117 episodes of **I Led Three Lives**, and actually believed Joe McCarthy's claim there were known Communists in our government. When the attack included our beloved Dwight Eisenhower, I shifted left a bit.

When Ike left the presidency he told us that a "conjunction of an immense military establishment and a large arms industry is new in the American experience. The total influence - economic, political, even spiritual - is felt in every city, every State house, every office of the Federal government. We recognize the imperative need for this development. Yet we must not fail to comprehend it's grave implications. Our toil, resources and livelihood are all involved; so is the very structure of our society."

He also stated "disarmament, with mutual honor and confidence, is a continuing imperative. Together we must learn how to compose differences, not with arms, but with intellect and decent purpose. Because this need is so sharp and apparent I confess that I lay down my official responsibilities in this field with a definite sense of disappointment. As one who has witnessed the horror and the lingering sadness of war - as one who knows that another war could utterly destroy this civilization which has been so slowly and painfully built over thousands of years - I wish I could say tonight that a lasting peace is in sight."[13] Mr. Eisenhower's farewell address did not have a big influence on me in 1961, but I certainly appreciate it today.

Supposedly, FBI Director J. Edgar Hoover approved each episode of **I Led Three Lives.** Hoover believed the civil rights movement was infiltrated by Communists, and his agents eavesdropped on Martin Luther King, Jr. Even the Kennedy brothers were paranoid about King.[14] I had become an admirer of Dr. King by the time he was killed in 1968.

In 1968 I won the J. R. Gettys Scholarship Award at Wesleyan. It was given by the family of Dr. Gettys, who was once a pastor at First Methodist in Lincoln. I had an interesting encounter with the son of J. R. Gettys that summer in David City. The award required an essay, and mine was mostly about M. L. King's contributions to society. Mr. Gettys thought King was a Communist.

The pastor at David City invited me to preach for him on August 4, and I was happy to do so. He also asked me to share the award essay since Lloyd Gettys was part of the congregation. My hero that day was John McVay, a local clothier who was active in the church and father of my fraternity brother Jack McVay. He had softened Lloyd up a great deal, and I had a nice visit with Mr. Gettys after church.

A few years later I was a pastor, and saw Lloyd at a church meeting and he described a DS in this way: "I don't trust him as far as I can spit, and I can't spit very far." We agreed on that one.

Racism, sexism, xenophobia, marxophobia, and homophobia were part of my childhood and they still creep in on me, but at least I recognize them now. "Free at last, free at last, thank God Almighty, I am free at last."

+++

When I was nine, I discovered a book in the library written by Hartzell Spence. It was his account of growing up as a Methodist preacher's kid in the early part of the 20th century. It is a wonderful collection of stories from a parsonage family with which I could readily identify. Hollywood made a movie using the book's title **One Foot in Heaven.** The author said, "Being a Methodist, father in principle was faithful to the rigid tenets of John Wesley and the Methodist Discipline. We lived by the Discipline. Sometimes we well-nigh ate it, too; for no one who ever lived on a Methodist minister's salary will doubt the miracle of manna from heaven. It came from heaven, or we starved. In rules of conduct, he was as stern as any circuit rider. We of his household [became] balanced, precarious Christians, with one foot in heaven and one on earth, not daring to place both feet solidly either way."[15]

I loved that book and the movie, which I sometimes used in confirmation classes. However, I didn't hear about the Discipline until I went to seminary. I don't think we were worse off financially than most folks in town. We were expected to behave, and my folks practiced corporal punishment. When we were teenagers, Mom was not afraid to tell us "don't do anything to embarrass your father."

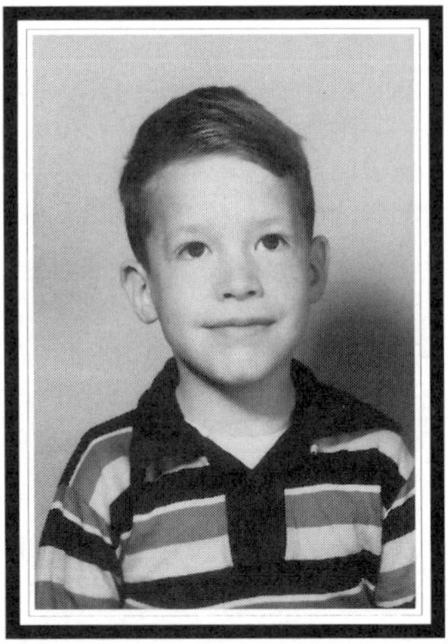

Above: the budding author and photographer at age nine
Below: a picture I took of my parents in 1957

15 years ago I found an envelope with negatives produced by my first camera. This image was one of them.

Chapter 7
Where The Sunbeams Long To Linger

The Papillion church was a difficult one for my dad. It was the largest congregation in the former West German Conference, which merged with the Nebraska Conference in 1926. Thirty years later that constituency still dominated the church leadership. They built a new building in 1955, but in their hearts still prayed to "Vater Unser."[16] During our three years in Papillion, the population more than doubled, as two large housing tracts were developed on the north and south ends of town.

Dad faithfully called on newcomers, and people came to church. Some of the despots were threatened by these suburban usurpers. Another problem was a former Papillion pastor, whose ego was fed by advising his friends in the church. Dad had plenty of support, but had no stomach for a church fight, and asked the Bishop to find another church for him.

Homer Dickerson was the Columbus DS, and had a church he thought would be right for our family. One day in the middle of May 1959, Dad asked me if I wanted to go with him to visit the church at Albion. We left early and met Homer in Columbus. We made a stop at Central City, then drove up to Albion on a gravel highway. We ate lunch at the Sandhills Gateway hotel, and headed to the church.

I thought this was the most beautiful church I'd ever seen, and I fell in love with it. It still reminds me of a castle. Its exterior is brown brick, and on its north and south ends, the bricks form stair steps up to a peak and back down again. On the east the building curves into a semi-circle which outlines the overflow room, and more stair steps form the roof-line. Because the fascia was 4 feet tall in places, this became a perfect area to throw water balloons at the cars passing below on Sixth Street. In the northeast corner is the bell tower, with Gothic windows, and a fort-like appearance on top.

Albion UMC in 2010

The most prominent room inside the church, naturally, is the sanctuary. This space is rectangular and dominated by the pipes of an organ on the west side. It had curved pews with two side aisles, two outside aisles, and a short center aisle about a third of the way. The pulpit was in the center of the chancel, with the altar in front of it. The sanctuary had huge stained glass windows on each side wall. Jesus the Good Shepherd is on the south, and opposite is Mary Magdalene and Jesus in the garden.

In addition to the sanctuary, this building has all kinds of rooms, some very small. The neatest room was the tower room which hosted the Senior High Sunday School Class. Later on, I learned to open an attic door, climb up through the roof and stand atop the bell tower. The basement was mostly a fellowship hall lined by folding doors which contain classrooms. There's a big kitchen down there, too, along with restrooms and storage rooms and miscellaneous rooms.

To my four brothers and I, this huge building that stood next to our house was more than a house of worship. It was a recreational center, where we actually played football in the sanctuary on Sunday afternoons in the winter. Its nooks and crannies were like caves where we groveled looking for treasures. Once Gary and I crawled across the attic above the sanctuary, and found a skylight, long since covered over. The church was a refuge with secret places when the parsonage seemed too small.

The parsonage at Albion was similar to the one in Papillion, a little smaller, but it had an upstairs bathroom and was in better condition. When we moved to Albion about a month later, there was a scheduling mix-up, and the out-going pastor was still in the house. They unloaded our beds, and we slept in the church basement. The next day one truck was loaded, the other unloaded, with many church folks helping out.

This was to be our home for the next ten years. I got acquainted quickly as Sunday school continued through the summer, and there were several in my class. We all loved it there, and Albion always comes to mind when I hear about the "green, green grass of home." And I certainly "love the dear hearts and gentle people who live and love in my home town."[17]

Every Sunday morning we were in church: first, for Sunday School, then at 11 am for Worship. In my high school years, I went back in the evening for Youth Fellowship. Bette Midler was wrong when she sang, "From a distance, God is watching us."[18] God is very, very, close to us. We are not always aware of God's nearness, but when we visit the shrines of our childhood, we quickly remember God's unseen and mysterious presence has always been there for us.

Despite my failures, I still wanted to be an athlete. My brothers and I played baseball and football in backyards and empty lots in Crawford, Papillion, and Albion. Papillion was a baseball town with a town team and a high school team. As mentioned, I was on a little league team, but I was terrible at batting and fielding. In the winter there was a basketball program and I wasn't much better at that sport.

When school started I had some adjustments to make. Because Junior High in Albion started with the sixth grade, I was behind in at least one class: physical education. Our teacher was a gruff, no-nonsense guy named Glen Hilligas. I tried out for all the sports, but neither had talent or the desire to get down and dirty. When I was 13, I had a growth spurt and was the second tallest player on the basketball team, five feet, seven inches, so got a little more time on the court.

One of my heroes in Albion was my 7th and 8th grade English teacher. Mrs. Neva Robinson had a way of making language skills interesting to me, and she encouraged me to read and write. She lived on a ranch in the Sandhills northwest of Albion, but stayed in town during the school year. I remember how surprised I was one summer day, when I saw her in blue jeans, and wearing boots and cowboy hat. She taught me enough that one of the few high school classes I excelled in was Advanced Composition.

Neva lived to age 95 and died in 2001. A few years ago I saw her son, Bilse, who still lives in Albion and told him how much I admired his mother. I said, "she was the best teacher I ever had, and that's saying a lot, because I went to school for twenty years!"

Another Albion resident I fondly remember was Ora Hutchinson, our church organist. The Albion church has a wonderful Estey pipe organ which was installed in 1919, and Ora was sent to Nebraska Wesleyan for special training to play the instrument. She had a few substitutes, but served as head organist for sixty years. Sometimes when I saw her car on the street, I would sneak into the sanctuary and listen to her practice, and it seemed like angels were singing when she glided across the keys and regulated the pedals. She died in 1984 at age 92.

One of my boyhood friends was Ray Dean Sup, but his nickname was Beno. Beno's dad operated Sup's Hatchery. It was no longer a hatchery. They sold a few baby chicks, but their main business was selling and grinding feed for cattle and hog producers.

On Saturdays, Beno would help out at his dad's store, and I used to join up with him for a few hours. It was quite an adventure for me. The tall ceilings were piled high with feed sacks. Beno and I would creep up to the top and find all kinds of pretend places in those deep rows. We could see hills and valleys, boulders to hide behind, even dark caves in which to crawl.

Customers would come and go, and we could spy on them and Beno's dad without being seen. We could be bad guys plotting an ambush, or maybe the sheriff preparing to jump out and arrest somebody. After a while, Beno had to sweep up and I went home. But I've never forgotten the fun and imaginative hours spent in Sup's Hatchery.

In the summer of 1960 we took a vacation trip to the Black Hills and Fort Robinson. My mother was not very excited about the trip for good reason. Imagine seven children between three and sixteen in a 1954 Plymouth station wagon pulling a U-Haul trailer and camping out in a funeral tent. That was the scenario. Mel Levander, the local mortician, graciously loaned us the canvas castle and we were all set.

Dad had reserved a camping spot within view of Mount Rushmore, and we took in all the usual sites in the Black Hills. After a week we packed up, and drove down to Fort Robinson. Four years had passed since we had moved from the area, and we all looked forward to seeing our friends in Whitney and Crawford. We pitched the funeral tent, unpacked necessities, set up the cots, and unrolled the sleeping bags. After supper we took a spin around the Fort and retired early.

In the next few days we picnicked in Sow Belly Canyon, had supper with the Normans in Whitney, searched for Indian beads, hiked around Toadstool Park, shopped the shops in downtown Crawford, and saw many familiar faces. Word got around we were in town, and folks stopped by at the camp ground to visit.

On Friday evening, Pastor and Mrs. Harvey Johnson found us. He invited Dad to preach on Sunday. Dad declined but Harvey persisted, and my father spent some time the next day preparing a sermon. He used one of his classic sermons based on Jesus' instructions, "let the little children come to me," and my younger brother Steve stood beside him as an object lesson.

After church, Pastor and Mrs. Johnson took us all to a local restaurant. After the meal, he encouraged us to get dessert as well. When the check came, 11-year-old Gary asked, "What's all this costing you?" My parents shushed him, but Harvey took it in stride, "not much," he said. But Gary persisted, and proceeded to ask each one of us what we had, and he tried to calculate the cost.

+++

I started High School in 1961. We had over 80 kids in the class, but only a third of us had gone to Albion Junior High. This was because K-8 rural schools were in existence all over Boone County, and the Catholics also had a school. I think it was the last year for freshmen initiation. The boys had to wear baby doll pajamas and shave their legs. We had to be nice to the seniors and eat and drink nasty stuff. Janice was a senior, but I don't remember that she abused me.

One day Gary, Doug, and I were in our bedroom talking about some school experiences, and Dad joined us. Albion had a large vocational agriculture program, and one of my friends told me the best way to castrate sheep was to bite out the testicles. When I said this, they all laughed and laughed. Dad said somebody was pulling my leg, but I found out it was true. When we were teenagers, Dad was a lot more tolerant than Mom. One of his sayings when she went into a tirade was, "simmer down, Dorothy." One time she was upset with all three of us older boys, and made us sit down and be quiet. Then she told Dad, "it's time for you to talk to these boys." After she left the room all he said was, "hello boys."

Janice graduated from Albion High School in 1962 and was salutatorian. She went to Nebraska Wesleyan in the fall. On her first visit home, she told us about a delicacy that we'd never heard about previously - pizza. Later that year, I went to an activity with several kids and our principal. He took us to Valentino's on Holdrege Street in Lincoln, and their signature dishes have been a staple ever since. A small pizza and a pop cost one dollar in my college days.

One of our neighbors in Albion had a large 2-story house, and they rented upstairs rooms to single men. Many of their renters were teachers. One of these was John Rogers who taught English and Sociology during my sophomore year. He was also a graduate of Nebraska Wesleyan and attended our church. One time he asked me if I was planning to attend Wesleyan, and I responded affirmatively. Then he inquired about my career goals, for which I had no ideas. He said, "Chuck, you should be a teacher and I'll give you three good reasons: June, July, and August." He stayed in education throughout his life, and became a Superintendent at one of Nebraska's largest Districts. His youngest daughter, Liz, is engaged to my nephew Kevin.

A young man went to a wise older person and asked about finding meaning in life. The old man told him to go to the Public Library, find the World Book Encyclopedia, and look on page 591 in volume four. The young man did as he was told, and came back saying he found volume 4, and read everything on page 591 but still didn't get his question answered.

The wise old man inquired, "Did you read the article about Ty Cobb?" He certainly did. It said Cobb was the greatest ball player of all time. He played in over 3,000 games, batted 11,429 times, and retired with the highest lifetime batting average ever. "What was his batting average?" asked the older man. ".367" was the answer.

The old man said, “you are correct and the meaning of life is in those numbers.” Still confused, the younger man needed more interpretation. “The greatest ball player in the world failed to get a hit 7,300 times that he went to bat,” continued the old man. “Two-thirds of his times at bat were failures. Meaning in life comes when you realize no one is perfect, and doing your best does not always mean winning first prize.”

I tried basketball, wrestling, and track in high school, with no success. One of my coaches asked me, “are you stupid or just lazy?” I replied, “I don’t know and I don’t care.” I was a score keeper and announcer for the basketball team for three years. My best memories of high school sports were the after school activities. Several of my athletic pals had girlfriends who piled into a car, and drove up and down the streets of Albion until practice was over. While the guys were smashing into one another on the field, or running shin flints on the courts, or lifting weights in the furnace room, I was with the girls! I also acquired a philosophy later echoed in the movie **Teen Wolf:** it’s not whether you win or lose that’s important, it’s how you play the game, and even that doesn’t make much difference.[19]

The summer after my sophomore year, I got a job washing dishes and doing other chores at Camp Fontanelle, near Nickerson, Nebraska, where I had gone for junior high camps. I worked there three summers. The only regret about being away from home that first summer was I turned 16 on July 16, 1963, and had to wait until September to get my driver’s license. There was nothing more important to me than getting that license!

44 years later, in 2007, my granddaughter Cora and I visited the wonderful Dawes County Museum in Chadron. Among their collection of vehicles, is a 1946 Dodge that was similar to one my folks owned when we moved to Crawford in 1953. It made me think about my love affair with the automobile, and I decided to chronicle a few details.

An analyst might ask, “when growing up, what did you like more, cars or girls?” Fortunately I’ve escaped the experience, if not the need, to receive psychoanalysis, but I must admit that’s a good question. In my early years I certainly liked cars a lot more than girls. However, I did kiss the Freimuth girl when I was in first grade, and to this day I have never kissed a car, so maybe the question is irrelevant.

I spent a lot of time with my dad when I was a pre-schooler. No doubt it was because I had three younger siblings before my 5th birthday. Dad took me, and sometimes Janice or Gary, with him on his pastoral rounds just to give Mom a little break. A lot of those excursions, of course, involved the car. And when I was a toddler, it was that 1946 Dodge coupe.

First some ancient history. My dad told me the first car his family owned was a 1920 Model T, aka the Tin Lizzie. They lived in the little town of Hershey. His father won the car in a drawing, and it was brand new. My grandfather didn’t know how to drive and didn’t care to learn, but they kept the car. Hershey was full of Leypoldt relatives, so the car got used and Grandpa Will enjoyed being chauffeured. Dad was only ten when he became the regular driver in the family. He told me this when I was 12, and I must have turned several shades of green with envy. He said there was no such thing as a driver’s license. Those cars didn’t go very fast, and he got pretty well acquainted with the Tin Lizzie.

Dad graduated from Hershey High School in 1933. He and my Aunt Genevieve’s husband, Paul Mason, had taken over the family farm while Dad was still in high school. He farmed until 1937 and had been using the old Model T's engine to power an irrigation pump on the Platte River. He told me it was sold for $1 at his farm sale. He bought a 1929 Chevrolet and went to Barnes Business College in Denver, later to Scottsbluff Junior College and Nebraska Wesleyan. He sold the Chevy to buy Mom's engagement ring in 1942.

My mother was driving a 1931 Chrysler which took the folks to their first home on the Drew campus in New Jersey. That car brought me home from the Oakland hospital in 1947, and was wrecked in Wyoming three months later. Thereupon they acquired the 1946 Dodge Coupe. The Dodge brought Mom home with these babies: Gary in 1949, Doug in 1950, and Cathy in 1952. It took us on a memorable vacation to the Black Hills in 1951. When the whole family was in the car, my favorite place to ride was the shelf above the back seat and under the rear window. When it was just Dad and I, I was in the front seat. No seat belts, no air bags. Heat came by opening a little door under the steering wheel; air conditioning by rolling down a window.

Shortly after moving to Crawford, my father was looking for another car. There were five car dealers when we lived there: Plymouth, Ford, Buick/Willys/Jeep, Pontiac, and Chevrolet. The Chevy garage was west of the parsonage, and all the used cars were in a lot across our fence. It was a great adventure for a kid obsessed with cars! Most of those vehicles were unlocked, and they became playhouses for Gary, Doug, and myself. Some radios came on even without the ignition key. I don't remember getting shooed out of the car lot, but I probably was.

There were two car dealers in the Crawford Methodist Church: Bobby Hays and Frank Anderson. Bobby sold Chevies and Anderson had Plymouths. Even when I was six, I thought it strange that a grown man was named Bobby. I think the folks wanted a station wagon, and Bobby brought one around for us to try out. However, it was a four door and Mom was deathly afraid one of us kids would open a back door and fall out. I recollect being in the car, sitting in the back seat, holding on to the door handle, and hearing Mom say, "see, Woodrow, I told you this would happen. Charles has his hand on the door handle and he's going to fall out and get killed!" So it was my fault that we passed up the superb wagon with the wood grained decals in favor of another 2-door.

Anderson had a 1953 Plymouth coupe that he had driven to California and back. When he heard his pastor was looking for a car, he had a bargain to show him. This little 2-door was as close to a new car as my father ever had. It certainly was no station wagon and it was smaller than the Dodge, but I suppose all five of us kids only weighed about 250 pounds total, so we were able to fit in pretty well. I'm sure the price was right.

This little car took us on a unforgettable trip to the Rockies in 1954, as well as several outings all around Crawford and the Nebraska Panhandle. It brought Steve home from the Crawford Hospital in 1955. It didn't have much of a ledge below the rear window, so I had to sit in the back seat.

In 1956 we moved to Papillion. In Papillion there was a garage on the north end of the church which was available for the pastor. I remember when Dad and Pops overhauled the 1953 Plymouth in this garage. Papillion had a Plymouth dealer named Art Grube, who was a Methodist. In 1958, Art's son Dick married my dad's second cousin, Donna Iske. I was a ring bearer in their wedding. Donna was very pretty, and I still think about her whenever I hear Ritchie Valens' song about another Donna.

Anyhow, Dad was thinking station wagon again and Art came up with a great deal. It was a 1954 wagon with two, not four, doors. Dad was happy. Mom was happier.

Pops checked it over and pronounced it satisfactory. Art was pleased the preacher was happy. The car cost $800, with a trade-in allowance of $400. What a bargain! This car was unique. It had a semi-automatic "Hy-Drive" transmission, that eliminated the clutch except when shifting to reverse. It gave the folks just enough extra room for their growing brood.

A short detour is now in order. Throughout the entire time I shared life with my maternal grandfather, he owned one car. It was a 1936 Plymouth sedan. It didn't seem like an old car when I was young. It was certainly roomier than those coupes my dad was driving, and it had four doors. Pops told me he would give me that old sedan when I turned 16. However, he died long before that date, and Grandma sold the car for $100 in 1961.

Our next move was to Albion in 1959. This also ushered in the closing period of family car history. We had no more babies, but we did have kids that were getting bigger and more difficult to fit into the 2-door, 2-seat station wagon. Because her oldest children were teenagers, Mom was worried about other things now, so the idea of a car with four doors was not so terrifying. Thus in 1960, my dad traded the 1954 Plymouth for a 1957 Custom Suburban wagon.

No picture would do this car justice. It had a 350 V-8 engine with push button automatic transmission. It not only had five doors, but three seats, the rear one facing backwards, with an electric window. It was trimmed in maroon and gray. What a great looking car!

In 1961, we entered the strange new world of a two-car family. Dad found a 1956 Nash Metropolitan at Holmes Motors in Albion. In 1967, I was ready for a car of my own and I found a 1966 Chevy II Nova at Sullivan's in Albion. I traded the old Custom Suburban for this little coupe, and should have kept it a lot longer than I did.

+++

Right before school started in 1962, my father went to the Albion clinic for a physical exam. Dr. Smith detected a tiny growth on his prostate gland, and sent him to a specialist in Omaha. The tissue was examined in two labs. The first report was benign; the second was malignant. Dad underwent a radical procedure that not only removed the gland, but examined all adjoining areas for evidence of cancer. Long before chemotherapy, he was subjected to a variety of treatments aimed at defeating cancer. He was 47, physically and mentally strong, but needed several weeks to recover.

+++

There was a fellow in my hometown named Bob Johnson. When the movie *American Graffiti* and the TV show *Happy Days* were popular, I thought about Bob Johnson. Bob was a "Fonzie" type character: he was tough, he was macho, but he also had time for most of us younger guys. When I was sixteen, Bob was 21. I thought I knew how to drive a car when I got my license in September of 1963; but Bob Johnson taught me how to "really" drive.

My friend Ronnie Barnes told me that Bob Johnson could go from the "Y" south of Albion to the sixteen-mile corner in ten minutes. Math wasn't my best subject, but I knew that at some point, Bob would have to exceed the speed limit to do that. One October evening, Ron and I were cruising in my Nash Metropolitan, when we spied Bob heading south in his 1960 Ford Galaxy 500. Somehow, we managed to intersect him and he invited us for a ride in the fastest machine then operating in Boone County.

Ronnie got shotgun (that means I was in the middle), and we went south on

Highway 14. On the way down, Bob drove moderately, staying under 75. But then he turned around at the sixteen-mile corner. He said, "Clock me, Barnes." And off we went, soaring up and down the hills. We did not need a turbo; Bob Johnson was at the wheel! I snuck a peek at the speedometer only once; we were exceeding 100 miles per hour. Before I had time to be scared, or feel stupid for being involved, the ride was over. Ronnie reported, "ten minutes, fifteen seconds." We went back to town, and drove around like normal teenagers for a while.

Strangely enough, Ronnie and I kept the whole incident to ourselves. We certainly didn't want our folks to know about it. But we weren't very proud of ourselves either. Bob Johnson was one of those persons that some folks would see and say, "That guy will never amount to anything." Karen Freese was a smart, attractive, Lutheran girl. When Bob and Karen got married, some said, "he'll never stay with her." About a year later, Bob and Karen made headlines. They were parents of the first set of triplets - all boys - to be born to Albion parents. Folks said, "Bob Johnson will never be a good father to those boys." After a time, the Johnsons moved to Omaha, and had a fourth son. My brother Doug used to work with him on construction projects.

Suffice it to say, never say never! "Never" is a long time. When we say, "he'll never amount to anything," we presume much more than we know. In fact, when we say these things and believe them, we assume the role of God. We sometimes forget that God's ways are beyond our knowing them. God's mysterious ways are not our ways, and God's thoughts do not always match thoughts.

I haven't seen Bob for over 50 years. His marriage ended and Bob got custody of his four boys. The folks at home were wrong. He turned out to be a successful business man and a pretty good father. Years ago, I read about his triplet sons in the **Omaha World-Herald**. All three were graduating from Kansas University Medical College with highest distinction.

I told this story in an Easter sermon at Plattsmouth in 1993. After church, one of my parishioners told me the same Bob Johnson was now married to her granddaughter.

+++

When I went out for sports in Junior High, I went to Dr. Smith for the required physical. He told me I had a hernia and a hydrocele, and both had been with me since birth. Neither had bothered me, and no doctor had checked my private parts previously. I was doing a few odd jobs that required some heavy lifting, and the rupture was making my life difficult upon occasion. Because of my summer commitments, we decided to get both things fixed in April of 1964.

The women's organization in our conference sponsored a youth mission tour for several years in the Fifties and Sixties. 32 kids (4 from each district) and five adults went on this excursion, and I was fortunate to be one of them in 1964. We went to a few tourist sights, but mostly visited ministries of the Methodist Church including Lydia Patterson Institute in Texas, a couple of schools in New Mexico, and the fledgling Saint Paul School of Theology in Kansas City.

I knew a few of the kids already, but met several more who became lifelong friends. Among my fellow travelers were Dennis Murphy, Randel Anderson, Arlys Boese Eddy and adults John Minert and Ada Draper. One Sunday night we worshiped at Trinity Methodist in El Paso, Texas and it was the first time I beheld an altar call. I was sitting near the back in this huge sanctuary, and people began streaming to the front after the sermon. When I saw Randel and Dennis going up there, I knew I should as well. I wasn't converted that night, but I do remember singing the hymn *Ask Ye What Great Thing I Know*? (UMH #163) for the very first time.

+++

My dad was elected Conference Statistician in 1960 and served for eight years. He was responsible for receiving annual reports from all the Methodist churches in Nebraska, checking them for accuracy, and compiling totals. In those days, the Conference year was June 1 to May 31, and the local church information had to be in a week before the annual gathering during the first week in June. The statistician and his assistants were adding up the numbers when conference was in session.

Dad was paid a small stipend for his work, and he attended several fall workshops at Mount Sequoyah, Arkansas. This gave both my parents an excuse to travel, enjoy the autumn colors, and leave the kids at home. An older lady from our church moved into the our home, provided meals, and attempted to keep order.

In January 1965, Dad had another church-related meeting in a hotel in Oklahoma City. This time he took me, Gary, and Doug along. We were 17, 15, and 14. We drove down in our 1961 Rambler American, and spent the first night in a 2-room suite at Wichita that cost six dollars.

I have a picture of the Hotel Lorainne in Oklahoma City. I'm not sure if we stayed there or not, but we were in the neighborhood. We marveled at the oil wells on the lawn of the state capitol, and all around the city. Dad had an evening meeting, and we boys went to a nearby theater to see **Goldfinger**, starring Sean Connery as 007. After two nights, we headed home by way of Little Rock, where we visited the state capitol building and Philander Smith College.

We drove up the road to Conway and found a motel, then went to Hendrix College. My folks had the habit of stopping at Methodist related institutions, so we ate supper at the college cafeteria. Yum! The next day, we proceeded in a northerly fashion and went through Omaha, Arkansas, population 195. It was a Saturday, and we ended up in Kansas City.

On Sunday, we attended worship at Paseo Methodist in Kansas City, and drove home. We were very fortunate to avoid weather issues. Dad and I took turns driving, and it was the first time I'd driven outside Nebraska. We got to spend several days with our dad and, best of all, he took us out of school for a whole week!

During my high school years, it seemed like we lived in tornado alley. In May of 1965 a twister swept through tiny Primrose, about 20 miles southwest of Albion, and almost destroyed the town. I remember a farmer who lived near Petersburg (north of Albion), whose house was destroyed in a spring storm. He rebuilt, and was wiped out by another tornado exactly one year later.

Our parsonage had a very small cellar. Thus when the sirens sounded, we went to the church basement, and several neighbors joined us there. One summer day, my brother Gary arrived home from work just as the alarms started. My mother was frantically gathering her chicks, and sent me to find Gary. He was in the tub, and I told him to hurry up and get next door. He showed up after the danger had passed.

Much later, in June of 1990, Chris and I were in Albion to attend my 25 year reunion. As we gathered in the gym before the banquet, sirens erupted and an announcement of tornado activity was made. We were directed to go to the locker rooms. Ray Sup and I were sitting together, so we grabbed our wives and went to the girls locker room, which was quite small. I was thinking it, but Ray said, "Gee, I always wanted to see this place!" The storm missed the town, and the dinner and program continued. The next day, we drove by a house five miles south of Albion that was totally destroyed.

I graduated from Albion High School in 1965. I sloughed my way through the first three years, and had a serious case of senioritis the last. Albion's grading system was numerical, "one" being highest. My only "ones" came during my senior year in Bookkeeping, Modern Problems, and Advanced Composition; that's because I was finally doing things that were interesting. I spent my third summer at Camp Fontanelle, and Dad took me to the campus of Nebraska Wesleyan University the last week of August.

Through my first two years of college, my dad's health appeared to be stable. In 1967 he was taking more cancer treatments, but seemed upbeat. The church decided to replace the old parsonage. They looked at a few houses that were for sale, but decided to build on a lot they owned near the church. This gave Dad a project, and he and Mom and a small committee looked at houses in and around Albion, and came up with a design to fit the new location. In the spring of 1968, the new house was under construction, but his health was deteriorating.

Dad was able to preach most Sundays, and the Congregational pastor sometimes helped him with funerals and weddings. The daily administrative tasks and hospital and home visits were difficult. He offered to retire, but the church wanted him to continue as long as possible. Gil Karges was the Lay Leader of the Albion church at this time. He and others made certain the pastoral work continued whenever Dad was unable to do the job. Gil filled the pulpit and invited others to assist. Faithful church members visited hospitals and nursing homes when Dad was unable to do so.

Dad's health began declining rapidly in the summer of 1968. He went to AC only one day in June, and gave his final statistical report. Dad's parishioners in Albion and Loretto loved him dearly. One told him she thought it was unfair that he was suffering, and wondered why God would allow this to happen. He said it was not God's doing, but that he and others were paying the price of misplaced priorities. If more resources were given to curing illness, rather than building weapons of war, perhaps a remedy for cancer could be found.

In 1972 the Albion church celebrated its 100th anniversary and Raymond Maricle wrote this in the history booklet: "Woodrow W. Leypoldt came to serve the Albion church in 1959. Upright, courageous, gentle, honest in all respects, he preached and ministered to his congregation. Under his cautious advice and gentle admonition much was accomplished within and beyond the boundaries of the Albion church. The sanctuary was given a new look. A new tile ceiling was installed and walls redecorated. Pews were re-arranged to provide a central aisle, floors were sanded and new carpets laid and the chancel was re-designed. New folding doors were installed at the rear of the sanctuary and new folding partitions gave the basement larger usefulness for the Sunday school. Repair of the back entrance evolved into an addition with enclosed stairs to both the basement and the first floor.

"The congregation had long dreamed of a new parsonage. Woodrow began with pencil and paper, rule and protractor. The dream was revived. The new parsonage was the structural dream of a pastor and people. One sunny afternoon in the late fall of 1968 he cut the ribbon to a special open house at the new parsonage. He never moved in. In irreversible failing health, he tendered his resignation effective October 15, 1968. Late in his ministry in confidence, he said, 'This is my home, these are my people.'"[20]

From his retirement in October to his death, Dad was in the hospital a few times, but mostly home-bound in the old parsonage. We had our last Christmas together. He wanted so badly to live until his first grandchild arrived, and she was expected in March. However, he took his last breath on February 18, 1969, just four days after his 54th birthday. Jennifer Marie Dorr was born three weeks later.

My father owned no real property when he died in 1969. My mother had three boys in college and three children still at home. She received some benefits from The United Methodist Church and social security, and was able to buy a nice house in Albion. Being a number one son didn't lead to any material gain for me. However, my six brothers and sisters and I did receive a birthright that was imperishable, undefiled, and unfading.

August 1968

Evelyn Johnson, a member of the Loretto church, wrote this poem, gave it to my mother, and it was published in the **Albion News**:

In Memory

Our little town and country-side has heavy hearts, and sad.
We've lost a leader, counselor, and friend, none better could be had.

They say God never takes someone, until his work is done.
And so perhaps in his short years, he lived more than most anyone.

He helped us all when sorrow came, our troubles gladly shared.
He gave so freely of himself, for each of us, he cared.

He loved to share our happiness, to baptize our girl or boy.
To marry our young lovers gave to him much untold joy.

To those of us who knew him well, he taught so many things.
Not all were taught from books or words, but, from what examples bring.

We will not forget his courage, or his faith in God and man.
We'll not forget the quiet way he gave a helping hand.

So even though we miss him, far more than words can tell.
He leaves for us a memory, of how he lived so well.

And as each of us remember him, we'll strive in some small way
To follow his example as we live from day to day.

And because he left us all of this, he lived God's very best.
God knew his work would go right on and he called him home to rest.

This verse from the prophet Micah describes my father's life well, "What does the Lord require of you but to do justice, love kindness, and walk humbly with your God?"

My mother lived 37 years before she joined Dad in that undiscovered country from whose Bourne no traveler returns, and they are buried together in the Rose Hill cemetery, south of Albion. I found this rhyme in another graveyard:

Heaven now retains our treasure,
Earth the lonely caskets keep.
And the sunbeams long to linger
Where our sainted parents sleep.

Albion UMC sanctuary in 2013

pencil sketch drawn by Seth Leypoldt in 1988

Gary, Doug, Chuck, Jim and Cathy in 2013

Good Shepherd Window in Albion UMC

Chapter 8
Before Prairie Wolves Swallowed Plainsmen

I led what might be described as a very sheltered childhood. I was raised in six Methodist parsonages in six small Nebraska towns. My parents did not use alcohol, tobacco, or profanity - ever. We seven children attended worship and church school every Sunday, and participated in all the other church activities. Nearly all the folks we associated with were fine, upstanding citizens and most were Methodists.

Consequently, the idea of evil was never especially bothersome for me. I was taught there were no such things as demons or devils - these were simply images drawn from a pre-scientific age. This was consistent with the theme in Colossians where we are informed that on the cross Jesus disarmed the powers of evil and triumphed over them. And in The Revelation, where Satan is tossed into a lake of fire, never to bother human beings again.

When I got a little older, I discovered that things like alcohol, tobacco, and profanity actually did exist - sometimes they were even found in Methodist homes. I also learned about some far more serious evils – such as war and poverty and racism - and I concluded that the simple answers of childhood were insufficient to explain these issues. Each Sunday, we prayed, "lead us not into temptation, but deliver us from evil." I began thinking that evil was the result of yielding to temptation. If we sinned - did something that we knew we shouldn't - it was our fault, our abuse of free will, that got us into trouble. But it's not always that simple.

Upon my graduation from high school, I received numerous gifts. Many folks gave me five dollar bills or checks for $10, which I promptly deposited in my account at the Albion National Bank, all of which quickly disappeared when I paid my first bill at Nebraska Wesleyan three months later. I also received a fair number of cuff-links and tie tacks, some I still have, but not used in almost 50 years.

At least two of my graduation gifts have survived the years and are still in use. One is my scuffed and worn brief case, and the other is a little book titled **Doing What Is Christian.**[21] This tome has been packed and unpacked at least twenty times in the past 49 years. Its author is Harold Bosley, one of the premier preachers and theologians of the 20th century. He was born in Burchard, Nebraska, a little town in Pawnee County, and graduated from NWU in 1930. After receiving his divinity and doctoral degrees, Bosley became Dean of the Divinity School at Duke University. He ended his career serving as pastor of Christ Church United Methodist in downtown New York City.

His book is about ethics; that is, an interpretation of good and bad behavior, right and wrong approaches to life's problems. In the early days of my life things were pretty clear-cut. Mom and Dad made the rules and when we broke them (or at least when we got caught), we were punished. Some issues that divide society today were not even discussed. Abortion was illegal. Lesbian, bi-sexual, gay, or transgender persons did not exist in my world. We thought it was a good idea to make bombs and build weapon systems because the Communists had missiles aimed at us. We also believed a Communist was anybody who questioned the "American way of life."

We were terribly prejudiced against all kinds of people. We were not violently hateful, but we believed white people were superior to people of color. We were suspicious of Catholics, Jews, Muslims, and Hindus. We thought the poor were poor because they were stupid and lazy. We held that "might makes right," "the majority rules," and white, Anglo-Saxon, Protestants were now God's chosen people.

Big changes were happening in the sixties. Our first Catholic president was murdered. Kids I grew up with were dying in Vietnam. I began rethinking my attitudes regarding race, women, world religions, and issues of war and peace. I learned the majority is not always right and the mightiest among us, such as the captains of industry, were sometimes dead wrong.

I graduated first in the second half of my high school class (37th of 73). I gave no thought to attending any college other than Nebraska Wesleyan in Lincoln. Janice was an incoming senior there, and I had been on campus many times. Several of my friends from Methodist youth activities were schoolmates as well. I scoped out the fraternities on Rush Week, but did not pledge. Wesleyan's enrollment in 1965 was the largest in history for two reasons: baby boomers and the Vietnam war. I was living in Plainsman Hall, the newest of two men's dormitories.

As a freshman, I thought I might be either a Social Studies or English teacher some day. Two semesters of Freshmen English were required, and I enrolled in Dr. John Smith's class. He gave clever lectures, and introduced me to the term "penis envy." He required us to write a theme on an assigned subject every week. The first one I submitted earned me a "F."

I was freaked! However I learned something valuable: keep it short. Dr. Smith wanted every paper to be one page in length, and he was no fan of flowery, descriptive adjectives. He graded on improvement, and by the end of the semester I got a B in English 101.

My second semester English teacher was Miss Bernice Halbert, who had taught at Wesleyan since 1928. She also required a weekly essay, but she liked three pages, eloquent sentiments, and multiple adjectives. I shifted into Halbert mode, but was only getting Bs and Cs until I turned on the charm. Miss Halbert was faculty sponsor for Cardinal Key, the honorary for smart women leaders. One day after class I visited briefly with her, and dropped the name of my sister who was a Cardinal Key officer. I got an A on every paper after that.

Wesleyan had four fraternities and four sororities. Two fraternities were losing members, and the Interfraternity Council approached a handful of non-Greek men to start a new group. I was recruited by them, and signed on to a society we named Phi Sigma Rho. About this time, I learned a song which stuck with me longer than most of my college classes: the one that starts with "Alpha, Beta, Gamma, Delta, Epsilon…"

My mother was the first executive director of the Albion Housing Authority, which was building an apartment complex for "low-income" seniors in Albion. Mom got me a summer job with the firm doing the construction. I remember using a wheelbarrow to haul dirt and rocks and material like that for the first week. On the second week, I helped a guy install fiberglass insulation in the attics of the apartments. In the third week, mercifully, the crew went on strike for some reason and I was able to goof off for a while. However, my father got me a job painting the parsonage.

Toward the end of the summer of 1966, I went to a Methodist Men's retreat at Camp Comeca near Cozad, Nebraska. It is on a bluff about ten miles southwest of Cozad (and ten miles north of Eustis) in Dawson County. It overlooks the beautiful Platte Valley to the north and Midway Lake to the south.

Comeca became a frequent destination when we lived in Eustis, but this was the first time I saw the place. Gil Karges rounded up a couple of carloads of older guys and college students, and we headed toward Cozad. The resource person I met in 1966 was Ernie Logan. He was a lay person working from our national headquarters in Nashville, Tennessee. I remember he encouraged us to do some witnessing to our friends and neighbors. He did not advocate the arm-twisting style that some groups use; he believed the most effective witness was low-key, sincere, Methodist-style sharing.

His message was certainly effective. I still remember much of it after 48 years. He told about the time he walked into a restaurant for breakfast, and encountered a grouchy waitress. It was a nice morning, and he wondered how many people had already had their day ruined by this sourpuss. After listening to her litany of complaints, all he could say in his Tennessee twang was, "This is the day that the Lord has made, let us rejoice and be glad in it."

I don't remember if Ernie claimed to have made an effective witness to the testy waitress, but it certainly worked on me. I've thought about his story on many mornings when things did not necessary look too pleasant. Ernie helped me acquire the philosophy that my attitude is important. If I'm optimistic about an upcoming experience, chances are things will go well. On the other hand, if I'm pessimistic or negative, that certainly makes a difference.

Later in August, it was back to Lincoln and into a fraternity house. We rented a 4-bedroom residence on North 51st Street, a block from campus. Rush did not go well as we were out-manned and lacked experience, but we persevered. The sororities liked us, especially our serenades. I was in the Student Senate and a member of Young Republicans.

Although I was a preacher's kid and immersed in church activities, I was still an unlikely candidate for the ministry. I loved to party. I cussed, smoked, and drank beer. I took a few religion classes at Wesleyan, but settled in with the social sciences. Initially, I chose a sociology major because I noticed a lot of the P.E. majors were minoring in sociology, and deduced it would be an easy route to take.

In the spring of 1967, my sophomore year in college, Mr. Glenn Bush asked me if I would like to be a "student apprentice" at his church in Alvo. Glenn was an ordained Methodist pastor who taught sociology at Wesleyan, and served the people of Alvo part-time. The Lincoln DS had access to an endowment whereby churches could hire students, and the fund would supplement their stipend. It was a great way to try out the ministry, and I signed on to start in September.

In the summers of 1967, 1968, and 1969 I worked for an Albion painter named Dale Smith. Dale was also a farmer, so many days I was alone on the job until mid morning. Sometimes his brother Dewey and father Harley also worked with us, and high school students including my brothers Gary and Doug, worked for Dale. We toiled on brand new houses, business places, and many older homes. Dale had a thirty foot ladder and we used it often.

When painting two story houses you have to climb up the ladder, paint a while, climb down, move the ladder, climb back up, and on and on. I learned something I now call the Belushi shuffle. I found out how to grab the ladder's side rails, jump on the rung, and scoot along without having to climb so often. Of course, I never did this with the 30 foot ladder, or if there was a window nearby, or if the boss was watching.

I really enjoyed painting on those summer days in Boone County. I still have the paint brush Dale gave me when I started, as well as the paint-splattered transistor radio I listened to everyday. We only got two radio stations: KFAB in Omaha and KMMJ in Grand Island. From KFAB, I learned to appreciate the great singer Eddy Arnold and others like him. Garner Ted Armstrong and the "Wonderful World Tomorrow" was on KMMJ, and introduced me to the nonsense a lot of gullible folks were swallowing. I also remember hearing the tragic news of Bobby Kennedy's death, while painting a house in Albion the morning after he died in June of 1968.

Dale was a fun guy and great story teller. He grew up near a little town south of Albion, served in India during World War II, and worked for Boeing in Wichita before returning to the farm. He told me he was a master sergeant in the army, but was demoted to buck private. I asked him why and he said, "there was a young lieutenant I didn't much care for, and he accidentally on purpose fell out of a truck."

Dale was raised a Lutheran, but had drifted away from church. His wife Leah was a faithful member of the Albion First Methodist Church. The only time I saw Dale in a suit was the day he attended my dad's funeral. He encouraged me to be a pastor and said, "kids need to go to church and you'll appeal to the kids." He also called me a half-hippie.

+++

Our fraternity outgrew the house on North 51st and we found a bigger one on 50th and Baldwin. I decided to live in a single room in the brand new Centennial Hall the first semester in 1967. That also put me back on cafeteria food, **and** allowed me to get better acquainted with the freshmen girls, who all lived in the dorms.

This was my junior year in college, and I decided to buy contact lenses. I asked a friend who wore them where he got his lenses, and how much they cost. He said "Go to Dr. Brown and they cost $300." I looked for him in the phone book, accidentally picked the number of Dr. J. E. Burress, and made an appointment anyway. His office was downtown in the Stuart Building.

He was about 70 years old, and his clinic had the look of yesteryear. He examined my eyes and I ordered some hard plastic lenses costing $165, which was a nice surprise. In a week I went back to the Stuart Building, and the optician helped me insert and remove the lenses. I'll never forget how great my vision was when I looked around. I had some irritation for a while. They were easier to put in then to take out, but I was used to them in less than a month.

The same day I got my contacts, I wore them to the college library and Virginia Gewacke saw me and said, "You've got contacts. They make your eyes look violent." Which made me feel pretty good, but later I learned she actually said "violet." In these 47 years I've worn out dozens of contact lenses and glasses. Late in 2014, I experienced the miracles of cataract removal and laser correction.

At the end of the semester, I moved to the fraternity house and went home for Christmas. Eleven years later I saw a movie called **Animal House**[22] and, honestly, there were a lot of similarities between our place and that one. We were never placed on double secret probation, but our housekeeping was pretty much non-existent. From the beginning, we intended to affiliate with a national organization. I'm proud to say two of those groups turned us down, because we were open to men of all races and nationalities. Eventually we became Alpha Kappa Lambda.

Before Nebraska Wesleyan University was created in 1887, the state of Nebraska had numerous Methodist colleges from Bartley to Osceola to Peru, and several places in between. They consolidated into a new school in a new town called University Place, a few miles from Lincoln. Chris' Grandma Grace McGill went there in the 20's and my dad in the 40's. Three kids from my family received degrees from NWU, and 3 others attended as well. Chris and her sisters also went to Wesleyan. Our two children and five of their cousins are also Wesleyan alumni. In the early days NWU was home to the Coyotes. In 1926 University Place was annexed by Lincoln and seven years later Plainsmen replaced Coyotes as a mascot. Plainsmen succumbed to millennial angst in 2000 and were swallowed up by Prairie Wolves, which I guess is a more romantic term for Coyotes.

The seal of Nebraska Wesleyan. It is above the main entrance of the former Rachel Ann Lucas Library

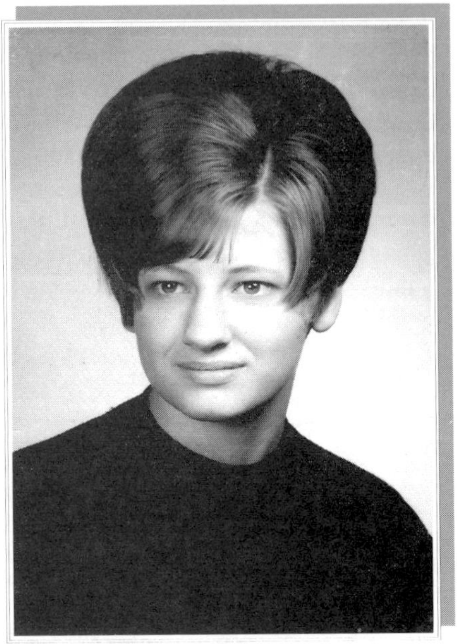

Chuck and Chris in their college days

Keep reading...lightning is about to strike!

Chapter 9
First Date

In 2007 the *Ladies Home Journal* asked their readers to submit stories describing early romantic experiences with their eventual spouses. Chris asked me to write it up, and we sent it to the LHJ. Even though it was probably the best submission, it did not get published. This is a mostly true story, but some names have been altered to protect the innocent.

Fraternity brothers Chuck and Pebbles were unlucky in love. Throughout the first three years of college, they each sought to win the favors of various coeds. Always their standards were high. Chuck and Pebbles, of course, wanted to be seen with the prettiest girls on campus. But there were no secrets in the fraternity house: every date was subject to strict analysis and scrutiny. Chuck and Pebbles were under great pressure to succeed.

Frequently, they received the answer they cherished and squired a lovely lass out on a first date. Sometimes they followed up with a second, maybe a third night on the town. But so very often the magic simply was not there for them. Infrequently, the boys decided on their own not to pursue a relationship. However, usually it was the girl who proclaimed "no more."

Many in the fraternity suffered the same curse. One of the guys went to the local Goodwill Store and brought home an old army helmet. This headdress was appropriately painted brown. Whenever a brother failed at romance, he voluntarily put on the brown helmet for a day or two. Chuck and Pebbles shared the dubious honor of donning of this head covering the most times.

At the beginning of their fourth year in college, they vowed to make some changes. No longer were they interested in finding a "girl just like the girl who married dear old dad." Their quest was to meet and perhaps conquer as many young maidens as possible. They had invested in necessary equipment including contact lenses for Chuck and a 1965 red Mustang for Pebbles. It was a beautiful fall in Nebraska in 1968, and the times were changing for these two young men.

To make the challenge more interesting they made a pact. During October they would each strive to date at least 31 different girls - an average of one per day. There was no prize other than bragging rights, and an end to the dreaded brown helmet syndrome.

And so it began. The phones were busy. Chuck was off to a fine start and had commitments for the first four nights of October. A blonde sophomore named Chris had caught Chuck's attention the previous year, but she was always with other guys and ostensibly unavailable. Now it appeared she was on the accessible list. So he asked and she became date number three. Their first date began at a fraternity party about 20 miles out into the country. Pebbles also had secured a third October commitment, so they all rode together in his Mustang. It was to be a non-alcoholic woodsy for this foursome; Chuck was a church youth group leader, and the second half of the evening was spent at a post-football game church party.

Ironically, Pebbles' date was the object of one of Chuck's previous infatuations. She was a well-built, petite brunette, with bedroom eyes. Her name was Precious. Chris recalled that Precious seemed kind of smitten with Chuck, and the quieter Pebbles and Chris spent a lot of time listening on that night. However, at some point during the evening Chuck realized Chris was awfully special. He was drawn to her pretty smile and deep blue eyes.

He began to wonder…could this be the girl of his dreams? Of course, date number four was already arranged for the following night. Pebbles had failed to line up a fourth tryst, so Chuck was ahead in their silly game. But still Chris was just too good to be true. So the two contestants conferred. "Let's see if these girls will go with us to Omaha tomorrow to see **2001: A Space Odyssey**."[23] They both said yes.

Chuck broke his other date, and on Saturday night the four piled into Chuck's Chevy Nova and headed on down the road. Once again, Chuck and Precious did most of the talking, but Chuck and Chris became a couple that night. The contest was over. A week or so later, one of Pebbles' former girlfriends told him she was pregnant. He then "did the right thing" with Chuck standing up as best man. Shortly thereafter, Chris invited Chuck to meet her parents at their Greenwood farm home, and his bachelor days were soon over. *Author's note: I was truly lost in wonder, love, and praise, going forward.*

+++

When I decided to go to seminary, my first choice was Wesley Seminary in Washington, D.C.; my reason was that I loved politics more than theology. They accepted me, with the provision that I take a couple of college courses in literature. I was impressed with a recruiter from United Seminary in Ohio, and I applied and was accepted there as well. By this time, I had fooled around and fallen in love with Chris Landon. Therefore, consideration of distance from Lincoln crept into my planning.

Dr. Richard Carlyon, a retired pastor and friend of our family, was doing some fund raising and recruiting for Saint Paul School of Theology in Kansas City. He encouraged me to apply there as did Les Lewis, the pastor at Cedar Hill (where the Landons were members), and a recent graduate of Saint Paul. He bought plane tickets for Chris, myself, and another prospective student, and accompanied us to Kansas City.

You might say it was a whirlwind courtship. We met with Dean Bill Case, President Holter, and a few faculty members. We ate in the Great Hall at noon and sat in on a class. Before leaving, I got to meet Dr. Leon Adkins who wrote the great hymn, *Go Make of All, Disciples* (UMH #571), and that pretty much closed the deal.

The flight home was no fun. Long before smoking was banned, the cabin of the small plane was filled with disagreeable effluvia, and I almost upchucked. This was my first flying experience, and last one until going to Israel in 1994. The next week I applied, and shortly thereafter, was accepted as a student at the Kansas City seminary.

I received my degree (Bachelor of Science) on May 18, 1969, and returned to Albion for the summer. I wore my father's plain robe at the graduation ceremony. I also used it when receiving my master's degree, and for both ordinations as well as on Sundays for a few years. It's tucked away a few feet from where I'm typing at this moment. Dad's sketched portrait, which Seth drew while he was in high school, hangs on the wall above my desk.

Mom had purchased a house in Albion from a local dentist (Don Walters), and in May 1969 Gary, Doug, and I moved in to it, with the intention of fixing it up in our spare time. But first, Gary, Phil Meisinger, and I decided to take a trip to the Black Hills and Fort Robinson.

As a pastor, I met dozens of persons who were homeless or close to it. They used to find me at the church or in the phone book. Some needed gas for their car; some a meal or a room for the night. Many wanted to talk and told me how they got where they are. Some knew where they were going; many did not. Fortunately, I was never close to being homeless.

On our outing, Gary, Phil, and I were sort of homeless: sleeping in a tent, eating little, not shaving or showering for three days. One afternoon, I decided to visit the Methodist parsonage in Crawford (where I had once lived). The pastor was not home, but his wife and children were. Without hesitation, they invited me in and fed me. I looked homeless and they took care of me accordingly.

In a week, I was back at Albion and ready to go to work for Dale Smith. But first I needed to return a call to the East Central DS, Max McCamley. He asked if I could preach at the church in Marquette through August. I agreed, and my summer was a busy one. Sunday mornings were spent in Marquette, afternoons and evenings in Greenwood with Chris. Weekdays I painted with Dale Smith, and evenings we worked on Mom's new house.

June 14, 1969 was our first Father's Day since Dad died. It was also my first Sunday preaching at Marquette. A special thing about Marquette was that Dad's cousin, Jollie Rodabaugh, was the church treasurer. Later that summer, Jollie and his wife Ida invited all the family to their place for a reunion. Chris, my mother, my brothers and sister Cathy went to church and several other relatives were at the Rodabaugh place for dinner. Little brother Jim speared a trout in the Big Blue River that day.

At summer's end, the exterior painting of Mom's house was incomplete, and Dale Smith graciously brought over all his big ladders and helped us finish the job. In late August, I loaded up my Nova and drove to Kansas City. It was the first time I'd driven alone in a big city, and I was amazed I found the seminary campus without getting lost. I moved in to Schelkopf Hall late on a Sunday afternoon, and gradually got acquainted with other new students.

On my first trip back to Nebraska in September, Chris and I got engaged. I was for all practical purposes, broke, so she "loaned" me the money to pay for a diamond at Nore's Jewelry in Albion. She claims I never paid her back, but years of good lovin' should be worth something! I made a little money in Kansas City as janitor of the Missouri West conference office, which was across the street from the seminary.

When Christmas vacation rolled around, I spent my days in both Albion and Greenwood. Mom went to Oregon to be with Janice and the new baby. While at the Landon home, Chris' mom Arlene told me something that made me shudder. She said she hadn't been feeling well and she had a lump on her neck. I was back at school a couple of weeks later, and Chris called to give me the bad news. Her mother had what today we call stage four cancer, and she probably would not live six months.

We had decided on a July wedding, and Chris' mother did everything she could to help with the planning. She had a strong faith and always tried to bolster others when they came to see her. If there was any good in this ordeal, it was that she suffered for a relatively brief time and died on April 26, 1970. She was only 43.

Landon Family 1967

Our Wedding Day – July 11, 1970

Chapter 10
Living On Promises

The "death of God" controversy was raging when I started seminary. An Anglican Bishop, John A. T. Robinson, wrote a little book he titled **Honest To God**.[24] He took some ideas from the great continental theologians, and rewrote them into a more down-to-earth, modern way of understanding. Also in the mix were the war in Vietnam, the possibility of nuclear annihilation, Marxism, ecological concerns, and various kinds of human liberation movements.

My seminary education was about learning theology and finding practical ways to improve society. Robinson and others were showing us new ways of defining reality, because frankly, some old definitions were irrelevant. God was not dead, but our understanding of God was misinformed. In other words, it was our belief systems and not the reality of God that was the problem.

It was common for seminarians, especially the married ones, to get a student church for income and practical experience. Several churches in southeast Nebraska had student pastors dating from the establishment of Saint Paul seminary in the early sixties. I asked for an appointment, and the Bishop decided I should serve Cheney and Palmyra beginning in June 1970.

Cheney was and is an unincorporated village on the southeast edge of Lincoln. Palmyra was a little bigger and 14 miles down the road. Each church had about 100 members. The Cheney parsonage was small, but we had few items of furniture. It was to serve as our honeymoon cottage.

As reported earlier, the first car I owned was a used 1966 Chevy Nova that I bought at Christmas in 1967. After a couple of years and many miles, I began to notice and covet a few things my Chevy didn't have, such as an automatic transmission, air conditioning, and power steering. So I convinced myself that the Nova wasn't running well, and I really needed a different car.

One April Saturday in 1970 I spied what must have been the car of my dreams. It was a 1969 Chevrolet Camaro - reddish orange - 307 V-8 with automatic, power steering, and air conditioning. It even had something I'd never heard of, but now I knew I really needed: "posit traction rear end." Unfortunately, I didn't have a wife to slow me down and talk me out of this delusion, so I traded in the car that I thought I couldn't live without two and a half years previously. I got a loan at Nemeco Federal Credit Union, and drove away in my almost new Camaro.

Two months later on a lovely summer eve, disaster struck. I was living in the Cheney parsonage, but spending a lot of time visiting a girl who lived at her dad's house north of Greenwood. It was only about 25 miles. That night, I rolled down the gravel roads of rural Lancaster County, and on to Highway 6. Something strange was happening; my V-8 had no acceleration. I finally figured out I was stuck in low gear. The car of my dreams, with all its special equipment, had a transmission that didn't work. I humbly motored home going 20 miles per hour, hopelessly trapped in low gear.

Our wedding was held at First UMC in Waverly on July 11, 1970. Dr. Ed Mattingly, Wesleyan's Professor of Religion, and my college friend Randel Anderson officiated at the service. The church was full as Chris had a large extended family in the community, and many friends from Alvo and Albion also attended. Our surviving parents had each lost a mate in the recent past, and their absences were keenly felt. Our song was John Denver's **Today**.[25] It was truly the best day of my life; I was definitely lost in wonder, love, and praise that day.

Because of car issues, I borrowed my brother Doug's Ford Falcon, and we honeymooned in the Black Hills and my beloved Fort Robinson. In a week, we were home in our little parsonage. I gave up on used cars, and bought a new Plymouth Duster in August. Chris had a job at the seminary library, and in September we moved into our second home, an apartment in Fisk Hall.

+++

The thing that worried me most about being a pastor was funerals. I asked my dad about it once, and he said he always stuck to a manuscript sermon to avoid an emotional distraction. I asked another pastor, John Craig, about it and he basically said to let go, and let God work things out for me. I followed both pieces of advice throughout my ministry.

My first funeral was a very brief committal service for a relative of one of my parishioners. My second one was a week later in a Lincoln funeral home for Flossie Morton of Cheney. She lived just 2 blocks from the parsonage, so I seen her frequently. I was not yet 23 the first time I knocked on her door. I wanted so badly to say or do something positive and comforting. She was 81 and bed-fast, dying from cancer. After the time of introductions, we began to discuss her illness. She said she knew she would die soon, and asked me what I thought heaven might be like. I can't remember how I answered her. It seems to me she did describe an image or two that worked for her. I think possibly she was strengthened by ministering to me that day. In subsequent visits, we agreed that God would be in Flossie's future and that ending her suffering would be a good thing, which occurred on August 4.

After my first week in seminary in 1970, I returned home to discover a member of the Cheney church had died. I went immediately to his home in Lincoln and no one was there. I later discovered a former pastor had conducted the funeral, and neither he nor anyone else bothered to inform me. Lessons like that stuck with me longer than classroom discussions.

Both believers and unbelievers wonder about life on the other side, and devout people will forever want to know what heaven will be like. Will the streets be paved in gold? Will we recognize our relatives and friends? Will they know who we are? After we're dead, will we be able to watch over our loved ones who are still living? Most everyone wants to know about what we call heaven.

One day a group of Sadducees approached Jesus with a question about life beyond the grave (Luke 20:27-40). They did not believe in the resurrection of the dead, and wanted to embarrass Jesus. So they brought him a riddle. If a man married and died before he had children, it was the custom of the day for his next oldest brother to marry his widow. In their test the Sadducees had the widow marry a man who then died, then his next oldest brother, who died, then the next, until she had married and buried seven brothers. "In the resurrection," they asked Jesus, "whose wife will the woman be?" Obviously, the Sadducees hadn't asked this question for edification. Their purpose was to discredit him.

Jesus told the Sadducees, "God is not God of the dead but of the living," and in another place said, "Follow me, and let the dead bury their own dead." Both these verses helped me understand the existentialist philosophy.

Three years and 20 funerals later my Carleton parishioner, Fannie McCashland, died. She was a committed Democrat who lived in a wonderful Victorian house on the main drag into Carleton. She suffered from diabetes, and had both her legs amputated, hoping it would prolong her life. But in a couple of months she was back in the hospital, and when I walked in, she said, "don't preach me into heaven." I asked what she meant, and she said go home and read First Thessalonians Chapter Four.

I never preached anybody into heaven, always taking the route of St. Paul who taught, "…neither death, nor life, nor angels, nor rulers, nor things present, nor things to come, nor powers, nor height, nor depth, nor anything else in all creation, will be able to separate us from the love of God…" (Romans 8:38). Also, from the prophet Isaiah, "Do not fear, for I have redeemed you; I have called you by name, you are mine. When you pass through the waters, I will be with you; and through the rivers, they shall not overwhelm you; when you walk through fire you shall not be burned, and the flame shall not consume you (Isaiah 431b-2 NRSV)." My aim was to be a comforter, not a philosopher. I've written more on this subject in Chapter 26.

+++

Ed Murphy was a Methodist pastor in Nebraska that I greatly admired. He and my dad were good friends, and attended seminary together. Ed was a popular speaker and had a great sense of humor. When I was in seminary, he was a DS and visited us in Kansas City. He was recruiting students to serve in Nebraska, and told a group that our conference was testing a new plan: when pastors relocated, the spouse and children would stay put, thereby saving a considerable amount of moving expense. Some of my fellow students didn't realize he was kidding.

Several of my friends in seminary served churches without having to travel back and forth every weekend. I talked to some District Superintendents in Kansas and Missouri to see if something like that was available for me. When Ed Murphy discovered I was looking at this option, he suggested Nebraska could do something even better for me, and I was sent to Davenport.

I was the last pastor to live in the Cheney parsonage. A few years after I left, Cheney became part of a parish with three other churches. The senior pastor was a good friend, and I asked him if they still owned the parsonage. He said they did and they were renting it, but their tenant was frequently behind on the rent. This pastor said he visited the renter and told him, "it was time to shit or get off the pot!" He was so shocked to hear the preacher's language, that he'd been current ever since. Even today I am one of the few people in the world who know how to pronounce "Cheney" correctly.

The good folks at Davenport and Carleton agreed to my need to commute and finish seminary, and they also remodeled their beautiful five-bedroom parsonage. The house wasn't quite ready on our first Sunday, so we were invited to stay with Lester and Ruth Urbauer, who lived in a new home next to the parsonage. The Urbauers owned a furniture and appliance store, the biggest one between Hastings, Nebraska and St. Joseph, Missouri. Lester was also the town's funeral director.

On our first Sunday, Lester and Ruth were in church. Someone told me that Lester hadn't been at Sunday worship for almost ten years, because he was offended by a former pastor. I'm proud to say he stuck with me pretty well and, of course, we spent a lot of time together (I had 25 funerals in my 3 years at Davenport). He also sold us a lot of home furnishings at wholesale prices.

Davenport parsonage

You may be surprised to hear that once in a while a "liberal" comment crept into one of my sermons at Davenport. On one occasion, Ruth Urbauer shook my hand when leaving church, and said "I disapprove of what you say, but will defend to the death your right to say it," as ascribed to the French writer Voltaire. Ruth was at the church's 135th anniversary celebration in 2007, and I publicly thanked her for making the comment. She died five years later at age 102.

The first time I experienced a horrible evil, and needed deliverance was when I was a student pastor at Davenport. I had been in the community for six weeks, when a tractor accident claimed the life of Donn Voigt, the 14-year-old son of Mardie and Jim Voigt. Suddenly all my sociological theory and theological wisdom was utterly useless. The entire community was waiting to hear a message of hope from a seminary student who had just celebrated his 24th birthday.

As I considered a funeral sermon, Mardie told me one of her relatives had tried to help her by saying, "Don't worry. This is God's will." She did not agree, but she wasn't quite sure, either. Do some folks believe that God is the source of evil? It's bad enough to think that the Devil is lurking around every corner trying to jab us with a pitchfork, but to think that God would willingly inflict suffering and pain on us, was inconceivable to me.

This was our release: I preached a sermon on God's will. Specifically, "It is not your heavenly father's will that any of these little ones should be lost." There is no comfort or hope in believing that God causes pain and suffering. This is an evil thought from which we must be set free.

I was gratified a year later when one of my parishioners told me she'd overheard a conversation wherein someone from another community had been at the funeral, and felt strengthened by my words. At an equally sad event in Eustis many years later, I heard the Lutheran pastor say "this was not God's will."

After a summer of getting acquainted in Davenport, I returned to my senior year at seminary. Chris had her library job also, so went with me every week. A nice thing about that final year was Gil and Connie Karges were also there. Gil sold his interest in the dairy farm and enrolled at the seminary. They rented a house in the suburbs where their three sons, Todd, Kelly, and Casey, went to school.

Each of their boys are now elders in the Great Plains Conference, as is a daughter-in-law, Cindy Beasley Karges. Gil became a DS and all of them have been outstanding leaders in Nebraska. When Casey was ordained, Gil was interviewed for a newspaper article. He told his story of assisting my father as lay leader, and how this led him to a clergy career. I've often used this illustration to show that a positive outcome can grow out of a tragedy.

My salary in 1971-72 was $5,500. It was the first time I had any real money to give away. I pondered, "how much of this should I share with the church." I decided on $5 per week. It wasn't a tithe, but I was still in seminary, had been married for less than a year, et cetera, et cetera. I had managed to buy a brand new Plymouth Duster. But still, $5 a week would do.

Later that year, I received my first shocking lesson in church stewardship. The Financial Secretary gave me a list of amounts each family gave to the church that year. I discovered my $5 per week made me the biggest giver in the church! From that point on, I was never shy about asking folks to dig down and support the mission of our Lord Jesus Christ.

One of the best bargains in my library is one entitled, **How Karl Barth Changed My Mind.**[26] Karl Barth was a great Christian leader who lived in Europe and worked as a local church pastor, college professor, and finally as a prison chaplain. He died at the age of 82 in 1968. But he left behind books and essays that will forever influence Christian thinking.

I discovered Karl Barth and a great German theologian, Rudolph Bultmann, quite by accident. My teacher Ed Mattingly of Nebraska Wesleyan was no fan of the Continental theologians, and urged us to stick with the more liberal ideas of American theologians. During my senior year in college, he asked me to write a critique of the ideas of Barth and Bultmann. In my research, "I changed my mind."

Karl Barth advocated an evangelical theology, wherein God was about gracious love despite human inadequacy. Rudolph Bultmann made the Bible come alive for me in a new way. He taught me to see mythology as a path to truth. He described Jesus as the Living Word, which interprets all human actions. These two Europeans of another generation caught me by surprise, and helped me to change my mind about some important and basic issues.

In theology, there is a very definite system of ideas that is called "liberalism" or sometimes "modernism." My father and most Methodist pastors who attended seminary between 1920 and 1960 were "liberal" theologians. If you were to ask any of my six brothers and sisters to describe my father, I'm certain none of them would use the term "liberal." He was a gentle and soft-spoken man, but also a very strict disciplinarian. He never smoked cigarettes or drank liquor in his entire life. The crudest thing I ever heard him say was "what the heck," and I still quiver when I think about it. He always voted Republican. He drove Plymouths or Ramblers, and every one was "pre-owned."

When I studied the ideas of Edwin Lewis, Leslie Weatherhead and Harry Emerson Fosdick, I learned how similar they were to my father. You can imagine how surprised I was to hear them called "liberals."

When it came time for me to identify with a particular theological position, I decided that Bultmann and Barth made the most sense to me. Their approach was the rather conservative and traditional notion that God's Word is revealed in Jesus Christ and scripture is the record of this revelation. These ideas are called "neo-orthodox." It was amusing whenever anyone suggested that I had liberal theological ideas. Such a description was not only ignorant, but a good example of trying to label someone in a negative way. If they knew me now!

A short note about the joys of Cornhuskerism is appropriate. A big share of the student body at Saint Paul seminary came from states where the schools of the Big 8 Conference were located. Several of my friends were as supportive of their state universities as I was of mine. During my three years in graduate school, the Nebraska football team not only were Big 8 champs twice, they won national championships as well. Just wanted to say, and said it often in 1969-72, "thank God I'm a Husker fan."

After graduation from seminary in 1972 I was reappointed to Davenport and Carleton, and they had to raise my salary up to the minimum which was $7,300 a year. In June Chris and I joined my mother and 3 siblings, and drove to Oregon to visit sister Janice and her family.

The Davenport community celebrated its Centennial in July 1972, and I was asked to help plan a community worship service. A friend and fellow UMC pastor, Darrel Berg, had taken leave from his Lincoln church to run for Congress, and I suggested him as a speaker. The committee agreed and Darrel preached a wonderful non-political sermon. At dinner and other events, he was able to work the crowd as a politician. Later on he was in our centennial parade. His borrowed convertible wouldn't start, so I let him use my 1972 Mercury Montego, leaving no doubts regarding my political persuasion.

I bought myself a white pulpit robe, and started wearing it that fall. One Sunday I headed up the stairs to the sanctuary, and little Chad Thornton said, "Hi Jesus." I'm sure I gave an extra good sermon that day.

In the fall of 1972, I received an unexpected job offer. There was a time that I considered journalism as a career. I was editor of my high school newspaper for two years, and wrote a column for the **Albion News** during that time as well. NWU did not offer journalism, and when I discarded my English major, my interest in newspaper work also went away. My mother was a close friend of Jack Lough, the publisher of the **Albion News**, and he told her of his desire to ease into retirement.

She was skeptical about my clergy career, and mentioned my name to Jack. He told her to have me stop in to see him next time I was in Albion. When I talked to Jack, he presented a scenario in which I would work for him for a couple of years, he would teach me the trade, and I could buy him out over time. I had just finished seminary, and was learning the role of a small town pastor. I felt I needed to make a serious attempt to follow in my father's footsteps, and thus I told Jack "thanks but no thanks." When I'm back in my hometown, I muse about what my life might have been if I had accepted Jack's offer, and spent my days in Albion, Nebraska.

There were four churches and four pastors in the little town of Davenport when I lived there: two Lutherans, Church of Christ evangelist, and myself. The evangelist was also a student at York College, but the Lutheran pastors and I saw a lot of each other. We drove together to attend the county ministerial meetings at Hebron, and frequented the local café/bar for coffee.

One time I told a slightly off color story, and got a strange look from a member of St. Peter's LCMS. I told his pastor what happened, and he said "don't worry about that guy; he wouldn't say shit if his mouth was full of it." He also told me before council meetings, he felt like bringing in a box of baby toys and passing them around before the session started. The LCA (now ELCA) pastor in Davenport was Andris Grinbergs. He was the uncle of Jeff Grinvalds, who married our daughter in 2009.

The big news around Davenport and Carleton, and in our 1972 Christmas letter, was all about a baby. We were soon to be joyously lost in the wonder of parenthood.

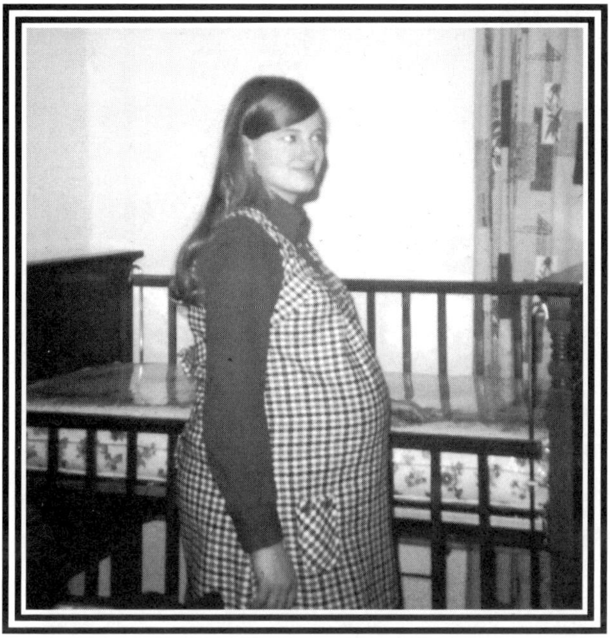

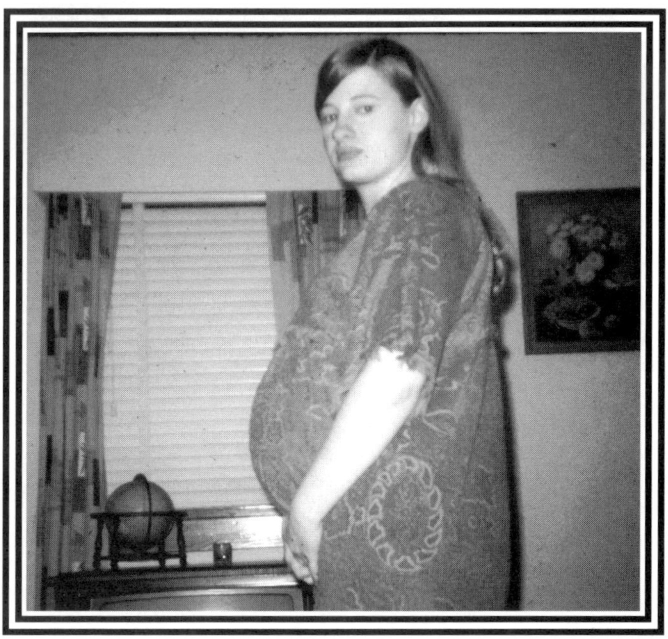

Seth's first day at home

Seth at one month

Chapter 11
Parenthood

A couple of our seminary friends had little ones that we enjoyed in our close-knit campus life. This encouraged us to have a baby as soon as practical, which would be no sooner than the summer of 1972. We started working on the project in the fall of 1971, and were a little anxious when nothing seemed to be happening. On Thanksgiving in 1971 we were at the Landon grandparents, and let slip what we were planning. That prompted Chris' older sister to get to work so she would have the first grandchild, which she accomplished before the next Thanksgiving.

Finally, sometime after my 25th birthday in July, it was confirmed that a baby was due next April Fool's Day. This became our focus. Chris' McGill grandparents came to Davenport, and bought us a baby bed at Urbauer's store. We got a name book and started the arduous search for a handle this little one would have to live with.

In the fall of 1972, Chris and I were in the Greenwood Cemetery looking for some of her ancestors' gravestones. She is deathly afraid of snakes, and was very skittish as we walked around in the tall grass. As we headed back to the car, sure enough, a bull snake slivered its way into our path. Chris screamed and made it to our vehicle quickly. Later on, I came across a superstition that suggested pregnant women who see snakes often deliver children with various physical and/or mental problems.

Our congregations at Davenport and Carleton were excited for us, too. One fellow told me our child would be the first baby in the parsonage for at least 50 years. Since we were pregnant at Advent time, I couldn't avoid sharing a sermon in 1972 with the title "'Tis the Season to be Patient." As everyone knew, Advent had taken on a new meaning in our home. Portions of that message follow.

Perhaps several of you have had experiences similar to mine. My sister is three years older than I, and I remember how excited she was when she went off to the first grade. She would come home and tell me how much fun she was having, and I wanted to go with her, and didn't want to wait another 3 years (it wasn't that great; but that's another sermon entirely).

I was in the first, second, and third grade when we lived in Crawford. The old grade school building had the first four grades downstairs and fourth, fifth, and sixth graders went upstairs. The bigger kids would never let us go up there, and I remember thinking how grown-up and superior it would be to go upstairs. I used to sit in Mrs. Harrison's third grade class, and wish I was a fourth grader just so I could go upstairs (I never did because we moved that summer to Papillion).

I made it to the upstairs in the old Papillion grade school on Washington Street. But while in the sixth grade, I began to daydream about how great it would be to go across the street to the Junior High.

As an eighth grader in Albion I wanted badly to be in high school. On January 16, 1963 I reached 15½ and I commenced the longest 236-day period in the history of a teenager. I was working away from home during the summer, so I had to wait until September to get my driver's license.

Once again my older sister put the pressure on me. She loved college. And as a high school senior, I could not wait to graduate and go to Wesleyan. There I had some of the best days of my life, but when I was 21 and a college senior I was ready and anxiously waiting for the days of graduate school. In between, Chris and I had a ten-month engagement and that was just too long!

As my days in seminary drew to a close, I was looking forward to starting a career and receiving a larger paycheck. Last summer we learned about the wonders of anticipation as we now wait for the arrival of a baby. So here we are at Advent in 1972. A time of waiting. And a time to learn to be patient.

John the Baptizer should be dubbed the patron saint of impatient waiters like myself. He certainly sounded impatient before he realized the Messiah had arrived. John was in prison and looking for a sign - a sign that the long-awaited Messiah had really arrived. That's ironic, don't you think? John the Baptist is the one who first proclaimed his coming. But much has happened to John since we last saw him preaching and baptizing people in the wilderness, and his frustration is showing.

John was expecting a death sentence, and there was one thing he wanted to know before he died. He hoped to hear beyond a shadow of a doubt, that Jesus was really the Messiah. Can you blame him? He had given everything he had, including his very life. He wondered, has it all been in vain? Is it all an illusion or a dream? In the wilderness, John had believed Jesus was the long-awaited Messiah, but in the face of death maybe he had some doubts. Now he wanted to know for "certain sure." He sent some of his followers to find Jesus and ask him, "Are you the one who is to come or are we to wait for another."

Patience is an elusive quality for many. An illustration is the way we deal with Christmas. Decorations go up in the stores when the Halloween candy goes on sale. I've seen several lighted Christmas trees shining through living room windows before Thanksgiving Day. Many folks are confused by Advent symbols. They want Christmas to begin on December 1st. Patience is a key word for Christians at this time.

John was a product of his time. He expected the same kind of Messiah others expected: one who would drive out the despised Romans and establish the realm of God. While languishing in prison, John must have wondered why more wasn't happening. "What's he waiting for?" he might have thought to himself. Why doesn't he drive out the Roman dogs? Perhaps he was disappointed because of faulty expectations.

A principal thing to remember is that God's time and God's ways are not always our own. One reason we are impatient, and one reason we do not appreciate the time of Advent, is because we suppose God works on our schedule. Like John, we want action and things our way, not God's way. But Advent gives us the chance to wait.

We cannot always know God's timetable and God's scheduling, but God is working and appearing. Advent helps us to patiently watch and wait as we learn God's ways. God's arrival at Bethlehem teaches us about expectations, about signs, and about patience. God was doing something unanticipated that first Christmas, including a simple birth in humble surroundings. Sometimes God works slowly, but always surely. Our God is moving, patiently addressing the needs of the world. Let us never lose hope. Joy to the world, the Lord is coming!

April 3, 1973 was a gloomy, overcast day. Chris got up before me and let me know contractions had started. I called the doctor, and he told us to head to Geneva, but there was no hurry. Chris told me to go downtown, and have my coffee because she needed to get packed, and I was making her nervous. I went to Albrecht's Café and drank my coffee, and people asked me if I were a Daddy yet and I replied, "I think this could be the day." But I didn't want to say we were going to the hospital, just in case it was a false alarm.

In 30 minutes I was back home, and we were on our way. It took 40 minutes to get to Geneva, and we were at the hospital about 11 am. Chris and I have different recollections about the rest of the day. I remember attentively caring for her throughout the day, with brief intercessions for personal care. She believes I spent most of the day partying with my college friends who lived in Geneva.

I most certainly was with her about 9:30 pm when Dr. Ashby sent me to the lounge, as fathers were not allowed in his delivery rooms. Seth Landon Leypoldt was born at 9:58 pm on the third day of April in 1973.

When Seth was about a month old, I took him along when I visited an elderly woman in our church. She had not seen the preacher's new boy, so it was quite a treat for her and she asked to hold him. After a while, he began to cry, and she uttered those famous words, "big boys don't cry!" Even when we are 30 days old, society expects us to be macho men!

When we are quite young, we learn there are differences between boys and girls. Once we believed that males were supposed to be dominant, aggressive, and adventurous; females, on the other hand, should be gentle, passive, and sensitive. A challenge for parents is being a good role model, while not allowing these harmful stereotypes to control our children.

The Methodist Episcopal Church retained the dual ordination system of the Anglicans. In 1970, I passed through the process by completing one year of seminary and became a Deacon. From 1784 through 1971 most Methodist Deacons automatically became Elders immediately after receiving a seminary degree. However, in 1972 a year of full-time ministry was added to the ordination requirement.

In the spring of 1973, I submitted a brief statement of beliefs and a sermon manuscript to the Conference Board of Ordained Ministry. I had a short and cordial visit with a couple of board members, and was recommended to the AC for election as an Elder. My ordination took place at First United Methodist Church in Lincoln on June 2, 1973. I was ordained by Bishop Don W. Holter, who was president of Saint Paul School of Theology when I graduated. It was an incredibly moving experience.

The Davenport and Carleton folks celebrated with us following church the next Sunday with a dinner and a short program. Wanda Tegtmeier contacted my mother, who shared several antecdotes from my youth. Wanda used these in a "This Is Your Life" monologue, which everyone enjoyed. My co-pastor in the new parish alignment was present, and told the folks ordination meant I was now in the union. He was referring to elders being guaranteed an appointment forever and ever. Excepting that comment, it was a wonderful day.

My 1973 Christmas letter began with: …the greatest event of 1973 was the arrival of Seth Landon Leypoldt. He brought with him all the joy and happiness for which we hoped. We've spent a lot of time just watching him grow. He is very happy and healthy. Needless to say, we occasionally become boastful and claim unlimited talent for our son. But honestly, we couldn't have ordered a more perfect baby!

Later in June, Seth and Chris spent the week with Grandpa Landon while I toured the Ozarks with a UMYF travel camp.

A good part of our year had been spent adjusting to a new parish structure involving six churches and three pastors. This was an interesting experience. Our parish was certainly not perfect, but I was hopeful the fine lay folks would make something out of it. Our tiny Carleton church voted to close on December 30, so five congregations would remain and the parish continued for 30 years.

In between the bureaucratic maneuvering there was time for pastoral work. I helped with four study groups and taught the confirmation class. There were weddings, baptisms, and funerals; a busy year.

In September we spent about three weeks in Missouri, Nebraska, and South Dakota. This was Seth's first big excursion and he got along fine. Naturally, we enjoyed reminding our Republican friends about their serious error last November. There was a calm serenity in our home, just knowing that we were right about the preacher's son from South Dakota.

1973 ended on two happy notes. I officiated at my mother's marriage to Dr. Don Walters at my home church in Albion and Chris' dad wed Miss Eunice Johnson in Lincoln. Seth doubled his cadre of grandparents in one week!

+++

In 1973 the pastor of the largest church in our Conference retired. It was notable because this man had served the church for 25 years, and during his tenure the Full Membership went from 1,200 to over 6,000. As you can imagine, there was a lot of speculation among the Nebraska clergy as to who might take this appointment. Several of the qualified candidates were heard to say, "I certainly would not want that pulpit." Those of us not in the running said, "me thinks he doth protest too much."

Bishop Moore selected Dr. Ken Hicks, a District Superintendent, to fill this church which was the 10th largest UMC congregation in the United States. I saw Ken a few months later and asked him how the transition was going. He told me that he made a few changes in the Sunday morning order of worship, as most new pastors do. However this church had been singing the same opening hymn - "Holy! Holy! Holy" - for 25 years and the same closing hymn - "Onward Christian Soldiers" - every Sunday as well. Ken said he was finding some traditions were very difficult to change.

There is an old hymn that starts like this (authorship unknown):

"My church, my church, my dear old church, my fathers' and my own. On prophets and apostles built, and Christ the cornerstone. All else beside by storm or tide may yet be overthrown; but not my church, my dear old church, my fathers' and my own."

Jesus had an interesting encounter with the some Pharisees and teachers of the Law. These folks were the keepers of tradition and noticed a few things about Jesus and his friends that were not orthodox. Specifically, they wondered why Jesus' disciples did not wash their hands in ritual fashion. This led to further discussion about kosher foods and what really is pure and impure. This is not the only place in the New Testament that we find Jesus dealing with the problem of tradition (Matthew 9:9-17).

Most of us have feelings about change and preserving tradition. And I think it's fair to say Jesus was not against tradition. His sentiment was, "People were not made to serve tradition, tradition was made to serve people." Many of us have personal rituals or habits that are very important. For some when there is a change in a daily routine, it simply ruins their day. Our church life is the same way. We get used to doing things a certain way, and when changes like new hymnals or new translations of the Bible or new church buildings come along, it can be upsetting.

After Seth arrived, I found myself spending too much time in the house. Having an office at home also meant lugging things back and forth to the church quite a bit. The Davenport church had four small classrooms adjoining the fellowship hall, so I suggested converting one of them to an office. There was a little resistance which surprised me, and even more when I put in a telephone. This molehill/mountain stuff kills churches.

+++

One of our favorite families in Davenport were the Becwars. LeRoy owned a television store and had a large service area. Irene helped at the shop and was a busy mother with four children. LeRoy's passion was magic and he gave shows throughout Nebraska. As the kids grew, the whole family was involved in entertainment. The Becwars were from the Czech community of Milligan, and we got acquainted with many of their extended family.

LeRoy was chair of the Pastor/Parish Relations committee at our church. He handled that job very well. Whenever a parishioner came in to complain about the pastor, he listened patiently, discussed the issue, and always made people say something nice about me before they left. We saw the Becwars many times over the years, and always communicate at Christmas.

Many years later, we lived in Eustis and I was part of the Chamber of Commerce. We contacted LeRoy and Irene to do a magic show at a Chamber event, and they came to our house beforehand. LeRoy asked me if it would be OK to tell a couple off-color stories, and I assured him the folks in Eustis were open-minded. During the show he told the audience that I was once his pastor, and he had taught me the art of hypnotism. He said we were having money problems, and one Sunday I pulled out a gold watch on a chain, and put the folks in a trance. He said I convinced everyone to do exactly what I requested, which was to write some large checks. However, before taking the offering, I dropped the watch and exclaimed "Shit!" Then LeRoy said it took several weeks before they could use the sanctuary again.

Gayle Becwar is the son of LeRoy and Irene, and is an entertainer who has performed internationally. In 1995, Gayle and his fiancé Cindy came to see me at Geneva, and asked if I would lead their wedding ceremony. I was happy to do so, and discovered they were planning to get married at our state capitol building. Gayle had done his first show at the state house when he was small, and wanted to use that site. Because Gayle was a magician and comedian, there were some surprises in the ceremony. When I asked "Gayle, will you have Cindy to be your wife, to live together in holy marriage, etc.," the theme from **Jeopardy** was played on the p.a. system.

Sadly LeRoy had suffered from heart problems for many years, and he died in 1999. We stay in touch with Irene and the rest of the family.

+++

There was a heritage room at the Saint Paul seminary. It was filled with old books including conference journals from Nebraska, Kansas, and Missouri. One day I was thumbing through a Nebraska Conference Journal from 1901. The Hastings DS reported that the "angel of death" had visited the Davenport parsonage, and the young son of the pastor died from a high fever. On a winter night a year later, I was awakened by a roaring sound coming from the room formerly used as an office. I went inside and the window air conditioner was running even though it was not switched on. I unplugged the machine, and later discovered the aforementioned child died in this room.

The Nebraska Conference was convinced the larger parish was going to save the small churches in Nebraska. I was part of this movement, and believed in its merits. However, it turned out to be my undoing at Davenport.

Family portrait – October 1973

The grandparents get hitched – December 1973

Chapter 12
A Home Of Our Own In Ceresco

We wanted to live closer to Lincoln. In October 1973, the pastor serving Ceresco and Ithaca was moved to a new appointment. My college friend Dennis Murphy, who was teaching at Wesleyan, was serving as an interim pastor and told me some nice things about the two churches. I wanted to go there, and asked my DS if it were possible.

He called me in a couple of weeks to say the appointment had been filled, and I was content to wait for something else in the spring. At the end of December I got a surprise call asking me to transfer to Ceresco and Ithaca, effective March 1, 1974, and I agreed to do so. The two churches had been linked together since 1968 with pastors living in the Ithaca parsonage. Ceresco sold their parsonage to reduce indebtedness on the church they built in 1966.

However, the Ceresco folks wanted the pastor in their town and were providing extra compensation to make this happen. We began shopping for a house, and found little available in this town with less than 500 population. But at the right moment a nice dwelling went on the market, we made an offer, and it was accepted.

We bought a 1,100 square foot brick ranch, with full basement, and double garage for $29,000. We had savings enough to reduce the mortgage to $23,200 and our payments were $243 a month including escrow. We were homeowners! The only issue was turquoise trim, which we corrected in the spring. To put this in perspective, my tax and insurance costs alone in 2014 are almost double that 1974 house payment.

Our Ceresco home at 229 West Pine

The Ithaca and Ceresco congregations were very different. Most folks at Ithaca were from the Evangelical branch of the EUB church, while Ceresco was a former Methodist congregation. I was the first non-resident pastor to serve Ithaca, and that was a problem for some folks. Ceresco had a building that could accommodate a 500-member congregation, including a sanctuary that seated 300. Our membership at each church was about 150.

Today we don't think too much about women wearing pants suits to church, but that used to be quite an issue. Alice Eichmeier was a member of the Ithaca church. It was a very conservative country church where the women always wore dresses and the men always wore suits and ties even in the summer. It wasn't air-conditioned, either. Alice broke her leg. It was winter and it was much easier for her to wear flared pants to church, than a dress. And that's what she did; another tradition was shelved in Ithaca.

We had a 9:30 service at Ithaca, and 11 am in Ceresco. Dr. Gerald Hazelrigg, pastor of Dundee Presbyterian in Omaha, was on the radio when I drove to Ithaca. He followed the ecumenical lectionary, as I did. Often, I heard something the Omaha preacher said, and pulled over to revise my sermon. Ithaca had a steady attendance of 100, while Ceresco ranged from 40 in the summer to over 100 when school started.

A few years later, I recalled an evening which was one of the longest and loneliest car rides I ever took. It was in the early spring of 1974. The route was thirteen miles on Highway 77 between Lincoln and my home in Ceresco. It was night time. At that time of year the trees were still bare, and stood out like huge skeletons against my headlights. I don't remember much traffic that night. The wind was blowing in gusts that seemed more powerful with every renewed rush.

As I drove along I remember more than one glance into my back seat to make sure I was really alone in the car. I didn't really want to be alone, but I certainly wanted to be able to choose my driving companions. The reason for my pretend horror that night was that I had attended a movie in Lincoln - and not just any movie. I had gone to see the scariest, most ghoulish, and undeniably unforgettable movie of the year: **The Exorcist**.

I've always been fascinated by stories like that. When I drive through Papillion and see the old Papio Theater, I think about the movies I saw there. I remember going with my sister to see **The Blob,** and how we ran home as fast as we could afterward. A few years later at the Boone Theater in Albion, I saw **The Tingler**. Walking home in Albion was a real adventure because we lived four long blocks from the movie house to our home, and we could not avoid many luminous buildings along the way.

The first one was the worst. The ancient court house was surrounded by dozens of dying Chinese elm trees. Frequently, the clock tower would bang out ten chimes about the time the show was over. We then had a choice. We could go past the Lutheran church, which was even scary in the daytime, or the other way which took us within a half-block of the Funeral Home. We couldn't avoid several old Victorian houses and lots of straggly trees, no matter which way we went.

The Exorcist and those other movies had a lot in common. The theme was that a supernatural power grips a human being or beings and the humans struggle, usually with God's help, trying to destroy the enemy. Among more famous stories with that theme are Frankenstein's monster, Count Dracula, and the Werewolf.

One problem I have is that nobody else in my family likes these stories. So that is why I was alone on that night in 1974. My brother Steve met me at the theater, but I had to drive home alone, hoping all the while there were no demons in my back seat.

The Ceresco church was determined to pay off their mortgage. Our finance chairperson was Art Stewart. His wife, brother, and sister all came to church through the years, but Art kept his gas station open seven days a week until he sold it in 1967. He liked the UM pastor and needed something to do, so starting helping out at the church. He didn't like the guy before me, but he hung in there, and we became buddies.

Shortly after I moved in, he came to see me about the building debt. He said, "I know there are eight families in this church, including mine, that can each give $1,000 to erase the debt." I told him to go for it; and it happened. More gifts of all amounts, an auction, and other fundraisers made up the difference and the church was debt free in September 1974, six months after I arrived. Bishop Holter came on November 17 and we burned the mortgage.

I managed to get my gifted child to write our annual Christmas epistle in 1974. Mommy and Daddy have been talking about a Christmas letter for a couple of weeks, but no results. I decided it was my job. I am still the most important person in the world. I'm almost 21 (months) now, and everyone tells me I am real cute and advanced for my age. Some people say I'm quite athletic, but I'm sure Daddy is only kidding about that Cornhusker football scholarship.

My year has been real eventful. Way back on January 10, I walked alone for the first time. Then we still lived in Davenport. Daddy had six churches to run and he thought he was an old time circuit rider.

On February 3, I said my first word: "hot." That's what Mommy always said about my food. Now I'm much more articulate. My favorite words are "truck," "no," "ow," "don't," "pee-pee," "moo," "daddy," and other assorted babbles.

In March we moved to Ceresco. Daddy takes care of the churches in Ceresco and Ithaca. We live in a nice, brick house, and it has a big garage to play in. Daddy and Mommy really like it here. Daddy told me "I'd rather serve these two churches then any others," so I guess I'll be here a while.

Last month I saw Daddy on television. He was burning the mortgage because our Ceresco church was debt free. That made us all so proud and thankful. Daddy says the Ithaca people are "real good Christians" and they do a lot for needy persons and always over pay their missionary askings.

I like living in Ceresco. I have a big back yard and several playmates on my block. Mommy has a lot of friends her age, and goes to three club meetings each month.

Another nice thing about living here is that I have two grandparents, four great grandparents, and twelve aunts and uncles within 50 miles. It is very gratifying to be the center of attraction so often.

In June we went to AC at Chadron and stayed in a real cabin! Daddy was more thrilled than anyone. In July Daddy and Mommy took the youth group to Colorado and left me home. However, I fooled them and was quite content with my baby sitter. Later in July, Daddy went to Camp Fontanelle so Mommy and I spent a week in Albion with Uncles Jim and Steve. In August we all went to Kansas City for a few days, and then went to see Grandma and Grandpa Walters in Watertown, South Dakota.

Since then, we've pretty much stayed home. Daddy goes to meetings a lot, but he takes me "calling" sometimes. I know where the candy is kept in every business place in Ceresco and Ithaca. Mommy leaves me home with Daddy once in a while and that's a real adventure. I hope you have a nice Christmas and that 1975 will be exciting and eventful for you. I know it will be for me.

+++

In 1975 we invited Dr. John Wichelt, Executive Director of Ministries in our Conference, to preach at an evening service in Ithaca. I discovered that he had been ordained in the Ithaca Ebenezer Evangelical Church in 1935. We put together a surprise program to honor this 40th anniversary. I invited Bishop and Mrs. Holter to attend and they were there as well.

While living in Ceresco I was happy to learn that Art and Mildred Johnson had retired and moved to Wahoo. Art was our Columbus DS for the first five years we lived in Albion (1959-64). Art had served the Fairbury church for 13 years, and his first wife died on Easter before he moved to Columbus. Mildred was the widow of a former Wahoo pastor.

The Johnsons had a special interest in all the families of the Columbus District, and when they heard my father was nearing death they made a special trip to visit him. My mother said it was a very emotional farewell as these two colleagues embraced, and said goodbye to one another.

One of Art's early churches was Carleton. When he saw that I was serving there, he wrote me about his encounter with the Ku Klux Klan in the area. He said they marched into church one Sunday and asked him some questions about his patriotism. He told them what they were doing was not appropriate, and he invited them to disrobe and stay for worship. They were so surprised, they left and didn't bother him again.

I stopped to see the Johnsons one day and he gave me a piece of advice. He said when you visit in someone's home or at the hospital, always take your coat off even when you stay for a short time. People will feel you're not in a hurry, and have time to listen to them. Bishop Monk Bryan also gave some advice that stuck with me. He said when you visit in city hospitals, find the stairs; it's a good way to exercise.

+++

The idea of joining the Masonic Lodge was in the back of my mind for quite a while. One of my fraternity brothers, Clyde Frank, joined his local lodge during the summer between his Junior and Senior years in college. At least two of the second career students in seminary, Bob Ellis and Dick Salmonson, were Masons. Several members of the Davenport church were active Masons and I was invited to some of their social gatherings. I was turned off because a couple of very active Masons were also Methodists, but seldom attended church.

My dad was a Freemason and I remember him going to meetings in Crawford and Papillion, as well as Albion. He had a strange little book with letters and symbols that made no sense. It was intriguing and I tried to decode it. When I was little I asked Dad if I could go with him to a meeting, and he said only members could attend, and there was a guard with a sword to keep away intruders.

When I was a teenager, Ed Maricle asked my dad if my brothers and I would be groundskeepers for the Albion Masonic Lodge, which was a block away from our home. Dad said something like, "they'd be glad to," and then he told us about our new responsibility. In the spring and summer we kept the lawn mowed; in the fall we raked and gathered leaves; and in winter we shoveled sidewalks. The building sat on a large corner lot right across from the school. We always got up early on the days it snowed so we could clear the walks before school. (I grew up in the dark ages when town kids were not allowed to drive to school. If we asked our folks for a ride, they'd lecture us about the even darker ages when they walked 2 miles in 6 foot snow drifts to get to school).

I had no reason to go inside the building, but remained curious about what was happening there. Once when I knew the Albion Lodge was meeting, I made it a point to do some work around the front door. As the members arrived and went into the building, I stretched my neck to get a better look at the inside. Unfortunately the meeting room door was closed; all I could see was the lobby. Somebody went in late after the Lodge had opened. Again I peered in to see what I might see. I couldn't believe it. My dad was telling the truth all those years ago. I saw old Bert Morehead standing outside the assembly room wearing a white apron, and holding a pole with a sword-like point on it.

Shortly after that, my curiosity got the best of me and I figured out a way to get inside the Lodge building, and I wandered around the not-so-mysterious temple room.

There weren't many Masons in my Ceresco church, and those who were attended church faithfully. Jack Lefler, a member of Bethlehem Covenant Church, invited me to an informational meeting at Ceresco's Comet Lodge in early 1975, and I decided to submit a petition for membership. I liked the fact that Comet Lodge had a lot of members who lived in several small towns north of Lincoln, and attended different churches in the area. I was notified of acceptance, and initiation was set for April 24, 1975. Then it got awkward.

I had not discussed lodge membership with my father-in-law, but knew that he was a past master and member of the Unity Lodge in Greenwood. After I invited him to my initiation, he came to see me and told me that lodge membership would be a mistake. He gave me a copy of a book, given to him by a pastor, which maintained Freemasonry was a Satanic conspiracy to destroy Christianity. I was caught off-guard and asked if he was still a Mason. He said he did not attend anymore but his father, who was the lodge secretary, continued to pay his dues.

The book made several false conclusions, and certainly overestimated the ability of this group to destroy God and Christianity. I sent the book back, and thanked my father-in-law for his concerns, but went ahead with ceremonies of the first three degrees of Masonry. Chris' grandfather, Wayne Landon, attended all three rites and offered to pay my way if I chose to become a Shriner, which I did not. When Wayne died in 1988 I was given several of his Masonic artifacts, which I took as a sign there were no hard feelings.

I had researched Freemasonry, and was satisfied it would be a good experience for me. Supposedly it was a "secret society," but I found a book in the Lincoln library that revealed and interpreted almost everything imaginable about its practices. However, I lay awake on my first night as an entered apprentice Mason thinking "how in the world am I going to remember this stuff." The next morning I called my mom to ask about my father's little "code" book, and she looked around but couldn't find it. I had a lot to memorize before I took the next degree.

The thing was it was improper to reveal the esoteric rituals in print. I spent many hours learning the work with my new brother Delbert Lowell, and in a month I took the Fellowcraft degree. About this time one of my parishioners, a nominally active Mason, approached me and loaned me his "code" book. I said, "I thought these were illegal," and he replied, "you can buy one at the Miller & Paine bookstore in Lincoln." I studied this book, and the next time I went to Delbert's house he was surprised at my progress. "You must have found one of those ciphers," he said. I was a bit sheepish, but replied affirmatively. He said it didn't matter to him, but just keep it to myself.

When it came time for my third degree, a friend arranged for a full dress performance. This meant all the characters were wearing costumes of the time period when Solomon was King of Israel, circa 900 BCE, with several Lincoln Masons assisting my lodge in conducting the time-honored ceremony. The event took place in the old lodge hall above Ernie's Store in downtown Ceresco. It was not air-conditioned at that time, but I was possibly the most comfortable one there because I was divested of most of my clothing, including my shoes.

It was an important event in my life, and I wasn't prepared to understand it all. My studying and listening to the experiences of others had brought me to this time, but now it had to become my moment. As they say, "you've got to walk that lonesome valley all by yourself, nobody can walk it for you." The curiosity that began back in my childhood had been partially satisfied, but it was not completely fulfilled until the 10th of July 1975, when I was raised to the sublime degree of a Master Mason at Comet Lodge #229 in Ceresco, Nebraska.

There were only two Masons in the Ithaca church and one of them, Ed Schueneman, was a special friend of mine. He told me why there were so few Masons in Ithaca. Prior to World War I, there were five churches in the Ithaca community: Methodist, Lutheran, and three societies of the Evangelical Association (one in town, two in the country). The three Evangelical groups merged into one, and they joined with the Methodists in 1969. Ed told me the Evangelicals didn't like Masons but several of them, including the pastor, joined the Ku Klux Klan in the early part of the 20th century. Zion Lutheran was still using the German language during the war and one night, the Klan painted the church yellow. But, Ed said, the Masons got the blame. An Ithaca native, Ernest S. Schiefelbein, was Grand Master of Masons in Nebraska 1949-50.

Speaking of the KKK, my dad told me that his father attended a meeting of the Klan near Hershey in the 1920's. Out of curiosity he went to a gathering in an open pasture near town. The Klansmen were adorned in sheets and dunce caps to hide their identity. At one point, Grandpa Will stumbled and a hooded guy said, "watch your step, Will." Dad said he recognized the guy's voice, and had no more interest in the KKK.

Ed also told me a story about one of our church members. He said one Sunday a family in the church had a couple of visiting Japanese college students with them. When this fellow walked into the sanctuary and saw the visitors, he stormed out. Somebody asked him why and he replied, "those people killed my nephew during the war." Ed chuckled and told me, "his nephew died in Europe and was killed by Germans." Ed and his wife Mabel grew up in Ithaca but lived most of their lives on a farm near Memphis. They attended a church which shared a pastor with Cedar Hill, where Chris' family were members. These two churches had many activities together and the Schuenemans knew Chris since she was a baby.

Ed died in July 1975 and Mabel asked a former Cedar Hill-Memphis pastor to participate in the funeral. She said to me, "I want you to give the sermon," and was very definite. Before the service, the guest pastor told me, "I'll do the message, you take care of all the rest." I told him of Mabel's wishes and asked him to offer a prayer, which I think was longer than my sermon. Ed's lodge provided a floral spray with square and compass and the letter G, a first time event in this sanctuary. He did not request a Masonic committal. The former pastor was the one who gave my father-in-law the book on the evils of Freemasonry.

Jack Lefler farmed south of Ceresco, and was a member of Comet Lodge for 63 years and served as Master twice. He was a proficient member for over 50 years, which means he had committed to memory all the rituals and lectures of the three degrees in Blue Lodge Masonry. When I became a Master Mason, Jack gave the second section lecture. 25 years later in 2000, Seth took his third degree at the lodge in Aurora and several members of Comet Lodge went to take part in the ceremony. I acted as Senior

Deacon (the one who guides the candidate), and Jack Lefler again gave the second section lecture.

Jack raised cattle, and a couple of times we bought a quarter of beef from him. Usually you go to a locker, they supply the carcass, cut it up, and put it in the locker. Jack had us come to his home, and we helped him cut and wrap the meat to save a little money. Our lodge was responsible for 2 miles of highway clean-up south of Ceresco. Jack was walking that route while in his eighties. When I was Worshipful Master in 2001, Jack served as Chaplain, which means he sat beside me at meetings and kept me on track.

One time a few of us were talking about a former Master that hadn't been in lodge for quite a while. Jack reminded us that he had family and church responsibilities, and these were far more important. One of my insurance customers was Covenant Cedars Bible Camp at Hordville, Nebraska. I saw pictures displayed from various times in the camp's history. One of these portrayed my friend Jack, who was honored for his many hours of volunteer service to the camp.

It was my great honor to present Jack with a 50 year pin in 2001. On May 17, 2014 Jack Lefler died and has gone to accomplish, in the profound slumber of death, the destiny of all humankind.

I belonged to the Saunders County Ministerium and got to know most of the pastors in the county. The Catholic priest at Valparaiso, John Glaves, became a good friend. One time he noticed my Masonic ring and asked me about it. I wasn't sure where this was going, but it turned out to be quite interesting. He said, "you might be surprised to know I have my grandfather's Masonic ring in my safe deposit box." He went on to tell me three of his grandparents were Methodist, one was a Catholic and therefore his mother was Catholic. He continued, "I happened to be the only male grandson and that's why the ring was given to me." He also told me he would not hesitate to join the Lodge if he weren't a priest.

+++

Shortly before Christmas in 1975, Chris took Seth to Lincoln, and met my mother and sister Cathy at the downtown Miller & Paine store. Seth was 2½ and Chris was six months pregnant with Anastasia. He was one of those children who ignored the normal charts of physical development. He sat up by himself at four months, walked at eight months, refused confinement to cribs and playpens, seldom napped, could not sit still longer than five minutes. He wasn't really "hyper," but came awfully close. At night we used to stand at his bedroom door, watching him in quiet and restful sleep, and marvel that this could be the same little boy who often made Dennis the Menace look like an angel.

That day in the Miller & Paine bargain basement, Chris took her eyes off Seth for sixty seconds and he disappeared. She searched for him among the racks and piles of clothing. Grandma and Aunt Cathy looked all over the basement. Finally, security was called in, and a whole crew of people joined the search. Could he have gone up the stairs and out to O Street? Did someone, not knowing what they were getting into, snatch him away? Chris was asked to stay downstairs and wait, just in case he showed up there.

It was almost time for total panic, when the doors to the freight elevator opened. And there, in a corner, stood a blond-haired, blue-eyed boy, no worse for the wear and terror inflicted on his mother and others. Evidently, he had been standing by the elevator when it opened, empty, and walked right in. Up and down he had gone, unattended, and unbothered. That pretty much ended Chris' day of shopping.

Here's what my 1975 Christmas Epistle had to say:

In the beginning of 1975, God created a new year and presented it to the Leypoldt household. God said "You will have dominion of this year and I will help to make it a good one." But behold the Nebraska winds prevailed and there was much snow. Corporate worship of the Lord was denied on January 12th because of a winter storm. However God blessed the Leypoldt household with a good furnace, color TV, much insulation and snow tires. There was no illness at winter's end.

The days grew longer on the Nebraska plains and the cold wind turned warmer. At spring's commencement on April 3rd, Seth became two and entered the agonizing era of the "terribles." God provided an outdoors so that Seth's terribles would not be confined to the house. And God appointed neighbors and many playmates to fill Seth's days. It was very good. Seth continued to learn new words and sentences and gave commands. Seth occasionally repeated words that society does not condone; but God patiently spared his teacher. In April it came time for the Retzlaffs to begat Teddy. And when he arrived, Seth had another cousin. Behold! It is good and pleasant to dwell in beautiful Nebraska among many friends.

As summer approached, God said unto Bishop Holter, "your man Charles should stay at Ceresco and Ithaca," and it was done. Charles went to Conference in the city of Lincoln and there mingled with many prophets and scribes. And God said to Doug and

Nancy, "you must go now unto the Cathedral at Ceresco. There you will find Doug's brother, the prophet Charles. Tell him you desire to be made one in Christ." It was so ordered and on June 7, God created a new Leypoldt household and sent them to the city of Ralston. And the summer heat fell over the land of Nebraska and the rains did not come. But behold God provided central air conditioning and hoses and sprinklers, and the prophet Charles refused to pray for rain.

On June 28, God said to Charles, "you shall go up to the city of Albion, and there you will find other members of the class of '65, and there you will dine and be merry." And behold **American Graffiti**[27] was discussed and nostalgia prevailed. In July God said "you shall study for one week at Saint Paul School of Theology in Kansas City, and you shall take your family, and live in Fisk Hall ghetto. There you will find other prophets from Dakota and Missouri and Iowa and Kansas." And it was done. The prophet Charles learned little but communed in great measure. In August God sent forth the Leypoldt household westward. To Valentine they journeyed, and onward to Fort Robinson and places of utter wilderness they went. It was good to relax and be in retreat before September's busyness prevailed. And behold the land of Nebraska was parched and the rains did not come, but the Ithaca church paid all its apportionments early.

God appeared to Charles in a dream and said, "it is not good that Seth should be raised alone." The Spirit of God visited the Leypoldt household and alerted nature's way, and behold, Christine conceived in July and now carries a new Leypoldt. The prophet Dr. Moore said, "it shall be a boy or a girl and shall arrive in March." Happiness and expectation now prevail.

The parched Leypoldt lawn turned browner, but autumn's breeze grew cooler. The churches of Ithaca and Ceresco awakened from the summer era of slack, and good attendance returned. God sent a message of goodwill to the prophet's lips, and there was harmony throughout the parish. Forty new dwellings were erected in Ceresco, with sixty anticipated next year. God said unto Charles, "you must visit in those homes, else my people stray to other denominations." Alas, United Methodists numbered few among the transients of Ceresco. God said, "you must improve your church program and make it friendly and inviting to newcomers. This will not be easy." But behold the membership grew steadily and God said, "this is my beloved Charles, in whom I am well pleased, rejoice and raise his salary." And the pastor's bank account grew and waxed strong.

+++

Having a toddler in our home produced scads of sermon illustrations. Chris says my habit of pealing all the skin from a banana, then eating it, is peculiar. One time I was alone with Seth and he wanted a banana; I peeled it and gave it to him. He cried and cried and refused to eat it. When Chris got home she told me why. It needed to be pealed one bite at a time.

Another time I made toast for Seth and spread the margarine in a haphazard manner. He refused to eat it, and I later learned that his mother neatly covered every corner and edge, and never left any unmelted globs on the bread.

Then there was the incident when I asked Seth what he would like for supper. Seth, of course, was always ready for his favorite meal and said, "I'll have a hot dog." I searched the refrigerator's freezer compartment and found a package of what some call "tube steaks."

I said to my little son, "it looks like we're all out of hot dogs. All we have is wieners." Seth was very disappointed and needed to see for himself. The contents of the package certainly looked like the real thing to him, but I insisted they were wieners, not hot dogs.

Finally, he told me, "you can have a wiener, and I'll have a hot dog." Wouldn't it be nice if adults could use that kind of maturity to resolve their differences.

I took Seth with me to visit a parishioner whose husband had recently died. My son was old enough to be comfortable with many folks in the church, and he wandered around the house and asked, "where is your man?" I was a little stunned, but she simply said, "he went away," and that was good enough for Seth.

Don Proett was a Presbyterian pastor in his sixties who was serving the Czech church north of Ceresco. His wife Marjorie had recently died, and I took Seth with me to see him, which Don thoroughly enjoyed. At one point, he looked out the picture window in the manse, and said it was comforting for him to see the church cemetery from the house. Seth was able to understand that Marjorie was there now. When we drove back home and went past the cemetery, Seth said when we get home we need to call an ambulance. "Why?" I asked. "Because we need to get those people out of there," he replied.

Ernie's Store is a large furniture store in Ceresco. One Sunday we saw a Ferris wheel in front of the store, and I took Seth for a ride. I didn't have acrophobia when I was younger, but I must have acquired it, because I was very uncomfortable. It stopped when we were at the pinnacle, and Seth stood up to survey the town. When we got back to ground level, my knees were so weak I almost couldn't walk home.

Seth loved emergency vehicles, and mimicked a siren sound that turned heads. Chris had her wisdom teeth pulled, and we left Seth with relatives for the night. We were watching TV, and the electricity went out a couple of times; then I heard a siren. One of Ernie's warehouses was on fire. I walked down and took a few pictures, but our little boy missed the whole thing.

Our daughter Anastasia Grace Leypoldt was born in Lincoln, Nebraska on February 21, 1976. Her arrival was preceded by an unconventional trip from our house in Ceresco to Lincoln General Hospital, about 30 miles away. She was born on a Saturday, and I gave this sermon the next day.

I had a promising sermon on the drawing board for this morning. It was to have concerned itself with the problems of Yes and No that Saint Paul writes about in 2 Corinthians 1:18-22. That issue is very important for all Christians, as we seek affirmations and ultimate truths. I developed some wonderful illustrations that were to show that God's Yes is always more powerful than our No's or our Yesses. God says Yes to us and all creation through an apparently negative action: the cross of Jesus Christ.

However, a human drama occurred yesterday morning that changed my sermon plans. I don't know what to call my message. Perhaps "Life's Most Unforgettable Experience" or "A Night to Remember" or "February 21st: A Day That Will Live In Infamy!" I suppose it can best be called "Anastasia's Story."

I'm not going to entirely abandon the lessons for this morning; the Gospel makes some points that are relevant to my subject. But, of course, the Gospel touches our lives and our every experience. When I'm through, I hope you will be able to see and feel the power of God's promise in each moment.

Chris and I are believers in "planned parenthood." We scheduled Seth to arrive on a nice spring day in April, and watched him enjoy his first few months in the summertime. Thus when it was time to think about a second child, we planned for March or April again. We all know March weather is far from predictable; but we were playing the odds. We are experiencing one of the mildest winters in Nebraska's history. Not only has the snow been scarce, January and February temperatures have reached 50 and even 60 several times. During Chris' pregnancy we basked continually in the security of this spring like winter of 1976. Friday, February 20th, the weather began to change. First came a gentle rain scattered around by generous amounts of wind. The temperature began to drop, and sleet and snow-covered our Nebraska highways. The weather report sounded strange: blizzard conditions, traveler's advisories.

But on Saturday afternoon the storm would pass, and a moderate climate should prevail. All my life I've gone to bed with the howling sounds of Nebraska wind. It's a beautiful sound when you're inside: safe, warm, contented. Wearing my comedian's mask I actually said to Chris: "This is not a good night to go to Lincoln. If the baby thinks otherwise, you put a stop to it." Very funny, I thought. After all, the due date was still almost three weeks away and Seth's arrival was a little past due. So I settled down to what was supposed to be a long winter's nap.

At 3:15 am, my wife informed me that our baby was planning a coming-out party. My comedic powers at a loss, I got up, and looked outside to see if the weather was as bad as it sounded. It was worse. After a few minutes of discussion and observation we decided the baby had definitely made a decision, and our cooperation was required. We began to pack the suitcase that we had discussed packing for the past couple of weeks. I secured my Kodak KL33 movie camera, while nervously listening to the raging Nebraska wind and wondering about the highway conditions.

I never considered driving us to Lincoln alone. I knew I had friends who could help, so at 4:10 the Joneses were called. Kathy could stay with Seth, and Jerry could decide which vehicle to use for transportation. Within 15 minutes, the Ceresco First Aid Unit was at our door. Three volunteers, including a Registered Nurse would ride with us in the ambulance. Two others would follow in a 4-wheel drive pick-up, armed with another friend - the C.B. radio.

Shortly before 5 am, Saturday, February 21 we were on our way. The weather was terrible! The highway was slick and crusted with snow. The visibility was at times completely nil. We moved slowly southward, noticing several abandoned cars as we went. Several times we swerved on the ice; several times we came to a near halt because of the blinding conditions. However labor was in an early stage, and there was never a glimmer of panic.

At 6 am we pulled into Lincoln General Hospital. Chris went to a labor room; I went to the Admissions Office. As we waited in those pre-dawn hours, the preceding events seemed like a hazy dream. At 9 am I was informed that Chris was going to delivery, and I hastily retired to dress in surgical clothes to witness the continuing drama. I waited with my wife as the doctor encouraged and guided this most beautiful of nature's processes. At 9:18 am a strange little creature came into the world: our sought-after, hoped-for, baby daughter was born.

Before I close I want to preach a little along with this narration. In today's Gospel Lesson we are taught several things. Let me highlight three of them. First: the value of friendship. Quite possibly, Jesus would not have helped the paralyzed man were it not for his friends. The story I have just told you has a similar moral. Chris and I simply could not have brought our baby safely into the world, were it not for the friends who responded. Early yesterday I learned some things about angels. They don't always appear mysteriously; they seldom wear wings; they don't come from a supernatural realm. Angels are friends that God sends to help us in the midst of every problem. The paralyzed man knew his friends, and certainly we know ours. Secondly: persistence pays off. The four characters in our Gospel Lesson weren't stopped by a blocked doorway. They devised a plan to literally tear open the roof. Their plan was to help a friend and they would not be denied! My story contains two kinds of persistence. One had to do with our daughter's desire to be born. That she did not learn or rehearse. She simply cooperated with the ageless plan of life reproducing itself. The second kind of persistence has to do with our friends. One reason I did not panic was because I knew there were alternatives. If all else failed, we would still find a way to bring the baby safely into this world. Our friends were persistent in helping us.

The final comment is this: the power of God is utterly amazing. After Jesus helped the paralyzed man by forgiving his sins, "he got up, picked up his mat and hurried away. They were all completely amazed and praised God saying, 'We have never seen anything like this!'" In our experience God provided persistent friends. We had faith in them. We also had faith in the birthing process, that our doctor was skillful, and that our baby would be healthy. Last night I held that tiny little being, and watched her closely. What else can a father or anyone else say, but, "the power of God is utterly amazing!"

Our baby will be called Anastasia Grace. She is 6 pounds, 4 ounces, 18½ inches long. She has blondish hair. She is short and sweet, like all good sermons. On Saturday afternoon, it did warm up, the sun came out, all was well. Anastasia means "resurrection." Through a stormy experience she came and conquered.

I had some folks at Ithaca who were still fighting the EUB/Methodist union. Methodism stood for pluralism (respecting all opinions), something John Wesley called the "Catholic Spirit." These folks took exception to a few things said from the pulpit. Many of the group were in the choir. They decided to walk out after the anthem and before the sermon, which they had been doing for several weeks before I knew about it.

Most of the choir alcove wasn't visible from the pulpit, and I didn't miss them in the least. One of them called me an apostate for something I said in a sermon. I'd never heard that term before, so had to look it up. It came about because the Nebraska legislature was debating the termination of the death penalty. I said it was a shame that Senator Ernest Chambers, who claimed to be a non-believer, was representing the views of God on this issue.

For a group to claim it was essential to teach biblical literalism, an angry God, eschatological paranoia, and misogyny was sad. They presented an article which attacked the seminary I attended. "Everything's Up To Date In Kansas City," was filled with misleading statements and unqualified lies. I ignored most of their activities, but finally decided with my DS's support, to face it head on. They went away.

At Conference in 1976, I was elected Conference Statistician and Bishop Holter made note of the fact my father had formerly held the position. In August we vacationed at Malta Bend, Missouri, the Nebraska Pine Ridge, and Wagner, S.D. In October we were in Kansas City and Fayetteville, Arkansas.

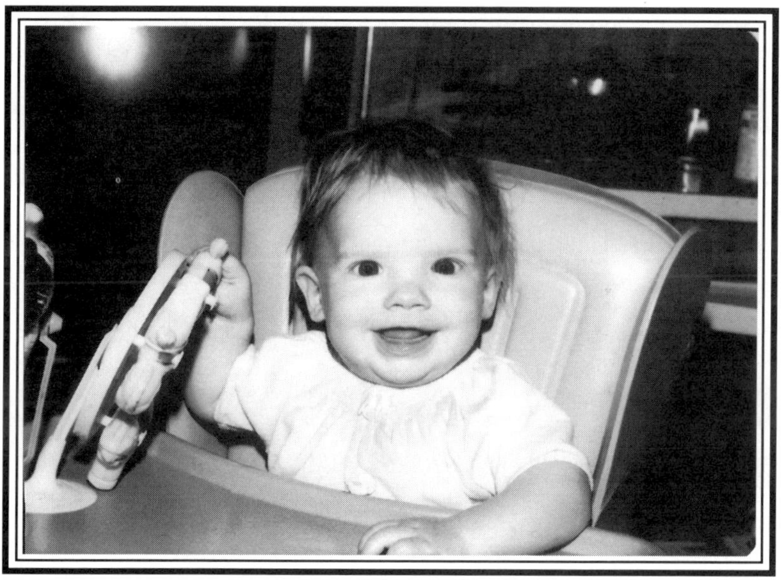

Ana at six months

I wrote about the busy year of 1976 at Christmastime.

Greetings and Happy Holidays! As I was thinking about this annual Epistle, I read an editorial which challenged the validity of Christmas letters. It seems some people fill them with either vanity or heartbreak and the net result is dishonesty. Needless to say, I was threatened by such criticism: my messages are usually quite vain! Recently one of my colleagues sent me a sermon titled "Long Distance Love." This is what we hope to communicate each year.

Our year can be described as both the happiest, and the saddest one we've experienced since our marriage in 1970. The event which outshines the rest was the arrival of Anastasia Grace on February 21. She is the darling of all who meet her. Anastasia is also known as Gracie, Stacy, Sissy and Missy. She is a determined crawler and likes to cuddle.

Seth has passed from terrible two to terrible three. He loves his sister, but gets frustrated when she can't play his games. He started Church School in the fall, and really looks forward to it each week. He has lots of playmates in our neighborhood, and remains very active. His great loves are dozens of little cars, and watching *Sesame Street, Emergency, and Mary Hartman, Mary Hartman*.

We are grateful to be blessed with two happy, healthy children. Chris keeps busy chasing our kids. She also is a part of church groups at both Ithaca and Ceresco. She is treasurer of her extension club, and treasurer of the Lincoln District Minister's Wives. Her biggest job is listening to the woes and disappointments of a certain United Methodist pastor.

My church work keeps me busy. The sadness I mentioned earlier, had to do with several untimely deaths within the parish. I've spent some uneasy moments this year dealing with what some call the "charismatic movement." I continue to have a love/hate affair with the Church, and I'm still trying to roll with the punches of my profession.

We are definitely enjoying our life in the Ceresco community. We appreciate the privilege of owning a house and our proximity to Lincoln. We have some deep friendships within our churches and others in the community.

I followed all the political fun and games this year. My favorite candidate is still George McGovern. This year, however, I started with Birch Bayh, reluctantly switched to Frank Church for the Nebraska primary, and finally jumped on the Carter bandwagon. I am especially pleased with my fellow Midwesterner and Methodist preacher's kid, Fritz Mondale. Nebraska, incidentally, is maturing politically and elected two Democratic congressmen.

+++

In 1976 Nebraska received a new bishop, Monk Bryan, who had been pastor of Missouri United Methodist in Columbia, Mo., for many years. Clarence Forsberg had served Saint Paul UMC in Lincoln since 1962 and replaced Bryan in Columbia. In the spring of 1977, I received a surprise call from Clarence asking me if I would like to be his associate in Columbia. He said the pastor who was running the ministry to college students was leaving, and he would like me to replace him. I had no skills or interests in that type of work, so declined. It was a great honor to be considered, and I might have said yes if invited to be working within the congregation only.

+++

When I started teaching confirmation classes, my decision to avoid the teaching profession was affirmed. I simply wasn't into the preparation and patience that it required. I required the kids to fill out a "sermon review" every Sunday, in which they answered a few questions like "what did you like best" or "what did you like least." One girl wrote she didn't like it when I said, "nothing can separate us from the love of God in Christ Jesus our Lord," because the devil can. I told her later that her argument was with Saint Paul, not I.

About the same time, I had a visit from an independent evangelist who had been advising the separatist Ithaca folks. No mention was made of them, and we had a cordial conversation. When he left, he asked me point-blank, "are you a born again Christian?" To which I said, "of course, I am a United Methodist." A little dumbfounded, he blurted, "that doesn't make any difference." "It does to me," I said and out the door he went.

I was growing weary of the clergy business, and decided the Methodist system was to blame. I visited with the Conference Minister of the UCC, and he sent me to a Lincoln pastor who chaired their ministry committee. I went through the steps, and was granted Privilege of Call in a short time. In the fall I was interviewed and offered a position at a church in South Dakota, but its salary package was insufficient.

My friend Randel Anderson was a year old than I. He and Betty did not have children until 1981, when Grant was born. When Seth was two we visited the Andersons in Valentine, and they showed us an orange tree that had finally sprouted a tiny bud of fruit. Seth quickly harvested it for them. The next year we saw them when Ana was 4 months old. She had been constipated, and we gave her some diluted jello to loosen her up, which she did while Betty was holding her. Thus we blamed ourselves for the Andersons delaying parenthood. Randel later got even by selling me and Seth life insurance policies.

In 1978 my friend and mentor, Vance Rogers, resigned the presidency of Nebraska Wesleyan to run for governor. I did the unthinkable and registered as a Republican in order to vote for him in the primary. See how flexible I am?

Family portrait – August 1976

Crossing the Niobrara by ferry. After a bridge was built, this rig became the Lady of the Lake in Clear Lake, Iowa

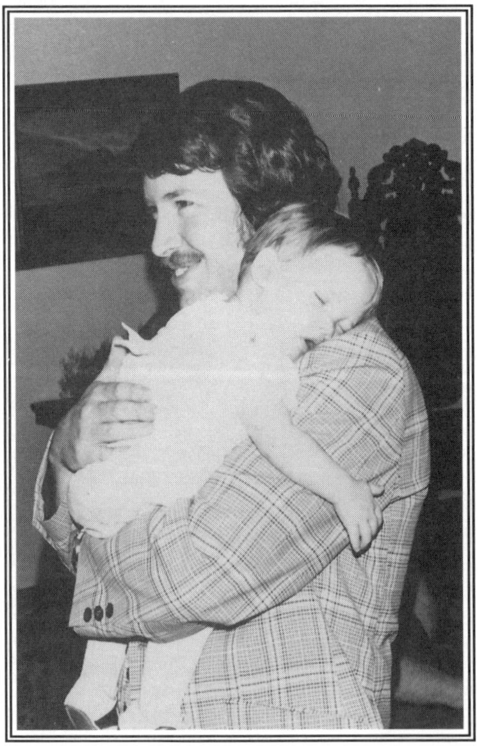

Daddy and his girl

Chapter 13
An Interlude In Hebron

1978 was kind of a mess. I became restless after four+ years at Ceresco, and decided to ask for a change. I was offered a church I thought would be perfect: county seat, only one preaching place, nice parsonage. Unfortunately the DS (the one Lloyd Gettys warned me about), left a few details out of the deal and I pulled back. I decided to stay in Ceresco, but another pastor had been assigned. I went looking for a job in the secular world, but time was short. I turned down an associate position in a 4,000 member church, looked some more, and the call came to go to Hebron.

It was a bit strange to return to Thayer County. The Hebron parsonage was OK. It had a split foyer, so was not practical for a family with little kids. It also had two fireplaces. The previous pastor made a nice office in the lower level, but I found a spot at the church. The church had received an inheritance, and was hoping to build an addition. Bids were opened and the cost was much too high, so these plans were scrapped.

In addition to Hebron UMC, I was also serving the UCC in Belvidere, a little town about six miles north. This made me a part of their denomination, and I still had privilege of call. Two unsolicited offers to serve UCC parishes came my way, but neither warranted further consideration.

At the end of the summer I started pushing a new design for an addition to the Hebron church. Seth was in kindergarten and we were settling in to our new community. Our Ceresco house was sold and we had some money! We bought a microwave and a video cassette recorder. I also sent $100 to the Nebraska State Historical Society, becoming a Life Member, which was probably the best investment I ever made. In addition, we deposited $17,000 into a bank C.D.

Thinking back, I was in a pretty good place. We were in a nice town, the workload was not very demanding, and some new leaders were emerging in the Hebron church. I decided to pursue some accounting classes at Fairbury Junior College, 20 miles away, and take another shot at secular employment in 3 or 4 years.

I went to the H & H Café almost every morning in Hebron, and made friends with several young professionals. An attorney friend bought the old bank building in Belvidere, and he and a young mortician and I jokingly discussed plans to develop a pizza, ice cream, and funeral parlor in the site. I also joined Rotary, and demitted to Hebron Lodge #43, AF & AM.

One of the best kept secrets in Nebraska is the Thayer County Museum in Belvidere. It is the old school house. It has several important displays from the "good old days." The thing I really liked about it was that everything was accessible. Every room was open. You were free to handle and examine the things on display. Many children's museums have signs that read, "Please Touch," which is way of inviting children to really observe and learn from what they are seeing.

I baptized 173 persons in my ministry, but only one by immersion. The Belvidere UCC started out as a merger of Methodists and Disciples of Christ back in the thirties. They compromised by becoming Congregational, then UCC. One family held to the Disciple practice of believer's baptism. A young man of 11 asked me to baptize him, and we did so at the Christian Church in Hebron. It was the first and last time I donned hip waders.

In November the Nebraska football team beat #1 Oklahoma, only to lose to Missouri the next week. Oklahoma got a bowl rematch and beat the Huskers on 1-1-79. What a way to start a new year. I continued at Fairbury JC and was a silent witness to another kind of struggle. There were several Iranian students on the Fairbury campus, and I was in class on February 11, 1979 when Shah Pahlavi was deposed. The teacher announced the event, and the Iranian students spent several minutes discussing things in their native tongue, while we natives uttered not a word.

For Seth's fifth birthday, we bought him a neat little boy's bike with training wheels. He wheeled around on it through the summer and fall, but we left it in the garage all winter. When the nice days of spring grew closer, Chris reminded me of my fatherly duty to teach Seth to ride his bike. Because of my bad childhood experience, I put it off as long as I could, but one Saturday morning we went to the garage. I took off the training wheels, and was prepared to endure the hard task ahead of me. Seth, who was not yet six, hopped on the bike, peddled down the driveway, leaving me behind. He needed no further assistance. He was already a true macho man.

My DS, Don Marsh, was a pretty good fellow and I openly shared what I was thinking, including the possibility of a part-time church, and more time with college classes. I was perfectly content to stay in this low-demand appointment for a few years, was willing to supervise the new addition at the church, and would keep my eyes and ears open for the right change.

What happened next blew my mind. The Douglas church had been a student appointment for at least 30 years. It was close to Lincoln and close enough to Kansas City for seminary students. Both church and parsonage were fairly new. The Bishop was willing to appoint me "to attend school," allowing me to serve part-time at the church and supplement income with other employment. It was better than a dream.

In my single year at Hebron the Catholic world had three Popes. I mentioned the need to pray for our Catholic brothers and sisters on two occasions, and was assailed by a parishioner for doing so. I guess I've always been soft on Catholicism.

Crucifix from Catholic Church in Bellwood

Our children at Easter in 1980

Chapter 14
My Field Of Dreams

Moving after one year, and leaving a church in the middle of a building program raised a few eyebrows. My income was cut in half, but church attendance was higher at my new place. I had new options for college and work, that were impossible in the past. The folks in Burr and Douglas were unbelievably welcoming as well. We also had a chunk of change in First Federal Savings & Loan.

We spent June and July getting acquainted, and took the kids to Silver Dollar City in Missouri. In August I enrolled in Southeast Community College, and starting looking for some part-time work. I had two offers to consider: college bookstore manager and executive director of Girl Scouts in southeast Nebraska. I was just about to accept the bookstore job, when fate intervened.

Harold Boldt was a member of the Douglas church, and owned the local grain elevator and lumber yard. His son-in-law was manager, but because of asthma/allergies he needed to leave. Harold told me he would assume the manager job, and asked me if I could help out as a bookkeeper. He said the hours would be flexible to fit my church and school responsibilities.

In the summer of 1979 one of my college friends, Jim Edington, asked if I would assist a Catholic priest at his wedding ceremony. The wedding was at his fiancé's home church in Duncan, Nebraska on September 1st. We went up for the rehearsal, and stayed overnight at a motel in Columbus. Toward the start of the ceremony, the best man whispered that he didn't have the rings. During the singing of a solo, the priest told me to "take over" and went to his office to find the rings. And I stood before a congregation of Polish Catholics hoping against hope it would be a lengthy mantra.

After the nuptials, we proceeded to the non-air conditioned parish hall for supper. We were met at the door by two young men offering shots of whiskey. We enjoyed the great food and conversation for an hour or so, and then the room began to empty. I asked the priest where everyone was going, and he said the evening mass was about to start. That surprised me, and I wondered aloud if all the folks could walk down for communion. Father agreed, and shook his head.

The next week I started at Douglas Grain, Inc. and evening classes at SCC. In 2005 I was in Albion two weekends in a row. The first was to attend my 40 year class reunion, and the next was to preach at both Albion and Loretto. I used the opportunity to talk some about my Douglas experiences. My sermon title was "Field of Dreams."

Oozing with nostalgia, I said whenever I came home it felt like the future and the past kind of merge together. You think about the ways things were, and the way things are, and the way things might have been. When you're young you dream about the future, and when you're older you try to remember what your dreams were all about.

When I left Albion in 1965 I thought I might like to be a high school English teacher, but my freshman English classes in college were not much fun. I switched to social studies which I kind of liked, but I was really bored by the teacher education courses, so I ended up with a religion minor and went to seminary. Career choices are still tricky things.

I read the average person in American society will change professions five or six times during their working years. I've been pretty lucky. I've only changed career directions four times, and I've learned a lot and been fairly successful. But in many ways, I still didn't know what I wanted to be when I grew up. The comedian Paula Poundstone made this observation: the reason adults ask little kids, "what do you want to be when you grow up," is because they are looking for some good ideas. Theological schools are a good example of this. They are filled with 2nd, 3rd, and 4th career people in their forties, fifties, and even sixties. One of my pastor friends was a woman who was 55 when she received her Master of Divinity degree. She remarked, "I'll still be paying off student loans when I get my first Social Security check."

I told the Albion folks the most interesting and radical change I made was in 1979. I wandered away from the pastorate of a relatively safe and secure county seat church in southeast Nebraska, looking for a possible change in careers. The place where I landed was quite unexpected and educational.

The little town we moved to had a grain elevator and lumberyard/hardware store. The owner asked me to be his bookkeeper. Not exactly my first choice, but a job and something different! And so I began in September of 1979 to learn about milo and soybeans and bushels and hundredweights and moisture content and foreign material and shrink and summary sheets and 40% landlord's share, et cetera, et cetera.

In the following spring, I discovered there was something new and more complicated to this job. Farmers started asking me for prices on things like anhydrous and atrazine. I thought, "maybe I should find out what these things are and do." So I sat down with the local Monsanto representative, and suddenly I had a new career - "Crop Production Specialist."

I knew I was going to be an expert, because I had a brand new **Bladex** hat on my head. My new profession brought a whole new vocabulary with it. For instance, did you know "Sevin" is not a number, but a way of controlling chinch bugs in milo. And "Lasso" and "Round-up" are not just found in cattle-management but are also herbicides. And then there's the word "grass."

As a child I learned to play in the grass, later to cut the grass. In college, I discovered grass was something that made crazy people act sillier. But in crop production, "grass" is something else again. Herein, grass is like weeds, and there are different kinds of poison to destroy the varieties of grass.

Oh yes, I had to learn some new things about the industrial giants - Ciba/Geigy and Dow Chemical. Earlier I considered them "bad guys" - people who manufactured and sold napalm and Agent Orange, whose major product was pollution, and who thrived during the Vietnam war. But I learned they were mostly interested in helping Otoe and Johnson County farmers in the common task of feeding the world, or so they said.

I told my hometown congregation about my later job in the bank, and described my experience in those days as my field of dreams. I was living and working and raising a family in small town America.

+++

In the early part of 1980 I entered the world of computers. Douglas Grain bought an Apple IIe and printer to assist me in billing and inventory. It had two 5.25 inch floppy drives with 64K ram each.

Working at Douglas Grain gave me a chance to get to know people on a different level. I was pastor to many of my customers, but got to know everyone in the area around Douglas. I learned that one fellow had two brand new Ford Galaxy 500 coupes sitting in his garage that were 1964 and 1965 models. They were sold at his estate auction in 2013.

In 1980 the Douglas school superintendent, Don Craig, stopped to see me and said one of the board members was not running for re-election, and suggested I should give it a try. "Why not?" I thought, and took office in June. We were busy, busy, busy, but enjoying every minute as our roots grew deeper in this tiny town.

On a Sunday morning in the Easter season I shared the following with my two congregations: **Some folks do not know how to say good-bye**. For some, when the visit to grandma's house is over, they walk out the door and with a hug and a wave, and they're on their way. For others, the time for parting comes, and they linger at the doorway for five minutes, then ten, maybe even an hour.

Some folks do not know how to say good-bye. I speak from personal experience. I married into a long line of persons who are accustomed to slow good-byes. I have learned that when we go places, I must decide when we should leave. This is an especially big chore whenever we attend one of Chris' family gatherings. It doesn't work just to say, "it's time to go." One needs to make a bit of a commotion before and during the time you are ready to depart.

If it's winter - and that's when most of our gatherings took place - I'd go out and start the car, "revving" the engine several times and checking the dimmer switch several more times. Then, back to the house, stomping my feet loudly even when there's no snow. I'd start carrying things out to the car. I made several trips, each time making a little more noise.

If I was real lucky, someone would actually notice that I'm preparing to leave. Chris always knew, but pretended she doesn't see. When we exchanged glances, it was not always pleasant. After the car was warmed up, I'd get the coats on the kids, load them up and then all three of us sat in the car and waited. After the first fifteen minutes, I'd send one of them back in to tell Mom it was time to go. After another fifteen minutes, I'd dispatch the other one. Of course that almost always defeated me, because the kids stayed and learned the Landon act of saying good-bye, and I was left by myself and my car radio.

Will Willimon said, "Parting, departure, leave-taking is never easy, even when you agree on how to do it. Something, something down deep in us resists the move from presence to absence."[28]

Shakespeare said it well: "Good Night, Good Night! Parting is such sweet sorrow, that I shall say good night till it be morrow."[29]

Schopenhauer was perhaps closest to our thoughts when he quotes a French proverb: "Every parting gives a foretaste of death."[30]

Some folks, and I suspect most of us, do not know how to say good-bye. "The move from presence to absence is a frightening one. When someone is present to us, our space is filled, we are not alone, there is conversation and communion. When someone leaves us, there is crisis. Absence creates a void. What will fill it? Absence means silence. No wonder we fear it, avoid it, cling to the presence, do anything to avoid good-bye."[31]

John's Gospel indicates that our Lord Jesus believed in long good-byes. He starts his thirteenth chapter with these words: "Now before the festival of the Passover, Jesus knew that his hour had come to depart…" Thereupon, John uses four long chapters to record what took place on one night, as Jesus prepared his closest friends for his approaching suffering and death.

The questions of the disciples in these chapters are like inquiries of children. Where are you going? Can we come, too? Who's going to stay here with us? Jesus is about to leave. "What's to become of us?" wondered the Disciples. "I will not leave you orphaned," he had promised. Still, could they be sure? Remember, at this point, theirs was a pre-Easter faith. Unlike us, they did not hear Jesus' promises with the background of the resurrection story.

It's hard to say goodbye, and harder to know how and when to say good-bye. Today when you say goodbye, I don't know where you are going, what tough paths you'll be walking, what burdens you'll be carrying. I do know this: Jesus and the good news of God is always there for us.

Jesus comes to us as a baby, a teacher, a preacher, a crucified criminal, a Risen Lord. He leaves us, but returns as Spirit, and goes again, not to abandon us, but to be close to God who dwells within each one of us.

Some details in this sermon are disputed by my wife.[32]

This is from our 1980 Christmas Letter:

Meow! My name is Tammy. Last winter I took up residence in the Leypoldt home in Douglas, Nebraska. They are a very interesting family - but not very bright. For instance, for the first two months I was here, they called me "Tommy." I finally convinced them I was female, but it was a real downer to be so insulted!

Well anyway, to make matters worse, master Chuck didn't like me very well, and I had to sleep outside for a long time. Then one day, he brought home a broken bag of dog food - ugh! I did eat most of it, but am now enjoying real cat food along with scraps (which I prefer).

Back to this strange family. I'm really indebted to Anastasia (age 4). I followed her home and she began putting milk on the front step for me. She is a real lady who prefers dresses, likes dollies, mother's makeup, perfume by the gallon, and helps in the kitchen which also leads to increased scraps. During summer she also learned to climb trees like her brother, so she could give her mother a surprise. Next year she'll go to kindergarten, and the Leypoldts are taking her to the Palmyra Pre-School three afternoons a week for practice. She gives me a 30 minute recital almost every day, and I get bored listening to her songs and little verses.

Then there's Seth (age 7). He's a second grader, and sometimes I follow him to school. Seth thinks I'm a pillow or a football or something, and carries me all around the house. I growl a lot at him, but so far have restrained my claws. At night I sleep in Seth's big double bed (not by choice, but where else does a pillow belong?). Seth is quite a sports fan, and reads the sports page as soon as the paper comes. And, like all of us, he is dedicated to the Nebraska Cornhuskers. This summer Seth was on the T-Ball team. This kept everyone busy going to games twice a week, plus practice once a week. Seth was catcher for half the game, and I sat behind him and gave him a lot of advice, but the team didn't win any games.

The lady of the house is called Mommy by everyone, but her real name is Chris. She keeps very busy just taking care of the house. On Sundays she teaches a church school class, and she is the president of her extension club. Also, her husband volunteered her to be the superintendent of the Bible school this year. She has been buying baby gifts, too, because there have been five new cousins this year: three Leypoldts and two Landons. Now she is going to a ceramics class, and she can make some of her own gifts.

Master Chuck comes and goes mostly in the dark. He works every day at a lumber yard, and preaches on Sunday. He thinks he's real important now that he's a member of the local school board. He tries to be nice, but I'm cautious around him.

Next year I hear there'll be some changes around here. Chuck gives up his preaching job in June, so we have to vacate the parsonage. I'm sure they will find another nice place to live. Anyway, I hope the Leypoldts will take me with them.

Well, that's life from a feline point of view. On behalf of the Leypoldts, I hope you have a very merry Christmas and a happy new year. Tammy.

+++

In 1981 the local bar/restaurant changed hands. The buyers were a young interracial couple who were well received by the locals. Seth and I went to Lincoln to get our haircuts, and while Seth was in the chair the barber asked me, "how's that colored guy doing at the Douglas bar?" Before I could say anything, my 8-year-old son said "we don't care what color he is!" End of conversation.

As 1981 began, we knew for certain that I would be taking a Leave of Absence from the ministry. Harold Boldt told me I could stay with Douglas Grain as long as I wanted, but I was looking for other possibilities as well. We almost bought a house in Palmyra, but were soon glad the deal didn't go through. My Christian faith had matured to the level that I understood every follower of Jesus was in ministry. Paul makes this very clear in 1 Corinthians 12. I was anointed at Baptism for service, and not necessarily as a full-time pastor.

My transition into banking followed an uncertain path. In Davenport, Ceresco, and Hebron, I knew the bankers pretty well, and mulled over the notion I might enjoy that kind of work. My business experience at Douglas Grain was invaluable, and I picked up some accounting and banking classes at SCC. I talked to Alan Dunlap, Jay Dunlap, and Ross Wilcox, who were bankers and Douglas natives, about a job but got nowhere.

Maynard Dunlap had been with the Farmers State Bank of Douglas for 58 years when I met him in 1979. He celebrated his 80th birthday shortly after we met and, though he lived in Waverly, was at the bank almost every work day. He was alone over the noon hour, and I picked that time to take the Douglas Grain deposits up the street. Maynard invited me to come and sit, and we talked about many things. He knew I was giving up the pulpit and looking toward a new career. But I never came right out and asked him for employment.

In March of 1981 Maynard was on a trip and became ill, so was not at the bank for a month. He and his wife Helen were considering some changes, and consulted a few Douglas friends about me. On Maynard's first day back at the bank, I went up there and told him I heard he might have a job for me. He said, "Yes I do. I want you to start on July 1 and you can work with me for six months, and if you like it, I'll turn things over to you." I prepped for my insurance and real estate licenses, and started spending a little time at the bank almost every day.

We had to move out of the parsonage in June, so needed to find a new home soon. Douglas (population 200) had very little housing available, and we weren't sure what to do. An older couple had a big house that I liked, and I asked the husband if he might consider selling it to me. His reply caught me off-guard, "sure, I would," he said. I was also a licensed Realtor at this time.

I went home, told Chris, and wrote up an offer to purchase for $15,000. He agreed, but I told him his wife would have to go along as well. We waited the rest of the day, and heard nothing. But the next day, she came over to tell us that her husband had not discussed the sale, and was flabbergasted when he brought in the contract. She had no intention of leaving her home.

This same gentlemen died a few years later, and I served as a pall bearer at his funeral. A month later, his wife came to see me at the bank. She handed me 98 one hundred dollar bills that she had found in her late husband's shop. He used to cash his social security check each month, and deposit the money in nicks and crannies of his basement. She eventually found a total of $15,000.

We were lucky to find a farm-house about a mile from town in which to live. We paid $300 per month for this four bedroom house that we occupied for six months. In September, we bought the only house in Douglas that came up for sale in 1981. It had been built by a banker in the 1920's, and sold to another family in the 1940's. It cost us $33,000. Our money was tied up in a certificate of deposit, so we needed to borrow the full amount. I told Maynard about the deal, and he said the house was well worth the money, and I could borrow what I needed from his bank in Waverly. I felt like a real big shot when I drew a draft on the Lancaster County Bank, paid for my house, and signed a note the next day. In November we moved into town.

Our home in Douglas 1981-87

One thing I learned when I was a banker, was that debt should be added to the list of nasty four letter words. Maynard Dunlap also taught me to apply the three "Cs" when making loans: Character, Collateral, and Cash Flow. The most important was the first and most of Maynard's loans, even the big ones, were unsecured when I first started. His way of collateralizing loans was taking a signed Property Statement from each customer every year. The third was obvious: one had to be making money to pay me back. In his 60 years of banking he never foreclosed on or sued a customer in Douglas.

Soon after I started working for Maynard Dunlap, he traded in his 1979 Lincoln Continental for a new 1981 model. He had no idea that Lincoln had down-sized their fleet, and he had trouble getting in and out of the car. After six weeks he bought a new Cadillac, and he tried to sell me the Lincoln at a bargain price, but well beyond my resources. A month or so later, we went to a meeting in Lincoln in our separate vehicles. When the meeting was over, Maynard asked me to bring his Cadillac to the front door as he had parked in the far corner of the lot. I asked for the keys and he said, "they're in the ignition." Sure enough! I found an almost new Cadillac Sedan DeVille with keys to the car, the bank, and his Waverly home, sitting unlocked in a parking lot.

Maynard's sons had utmost respect for their father, even when they questioned his judgment. Alan confessed to me that he would not have put me in charge at Douglas so quickly, but once the decision was made he did everything he could to enable my success. I received on-the-job training from his staff at Milford, and he sent me to a banking school in Kansas City.

I also got to know several other bankers. The Dunlap family owned banks in six Nebraska communities, and partial interest in several others. Their largest was Union Bank in Lincoln. We had monthly meetings and shared concerns and ideas. By the end of September in 1981, I was in the Douglas bank every day as assistant vice president. In November of that year Maynard suffered a stroke, and was unable to walk or drive, so did not set foot in the bank again. I called him often, and went to his house in Waverly several times a month.

One of my tasks was to help Maynard and Helen with their farm accounts, and sometimes their charitable giving. I tried to be a generous and cheerful giver most of my life, but Maynard and Helen had a technique that assured they would always have funds to give away. Every time they received income from any source, they deposited 25% into a special account for tithes.

One time Helen called and asked me to give a special gift of $500 to the Douglas UMC. I took that check to the church on the next Sunday to place it in the offering. I was sitting by a friend in worship, and showed him the check but hid the Dunlap name. I said I'm putting in a little extra today, how about you? He dutifully matched the gift!

When I was in seminary it was announced they had acquired a gift of farmland, which was the largest donation received to that time. When I starting working for the Dunlaps, I was not surprised to learn they were the source of that gift. That family taught me a great deal about Christian stewardship.

When the Douglas church burned down in 1969 they received $60,000 from insurance, and the Dunlap sons joined their parents in giving generously to the building fund. The Milford church was building in 1981, and Alan asked his dad how much he wanted to contribute. "Put me down for $10,000," he said. A few days later, Maynard received a letter from the Milford church thanking him for his pledge of $25,000. He was laughing out loud as he told me what happened and said, "I guess you better send them a check right away before I get hooked for more."

On another occasion, Alan Dunlap told me to contribute $10,000 in bank funds to Saint Paul School of Theology. The school had received a challenge grant, which matched every dollar donated by a graduate of the school. I obediently prepared a cashier's check and sent it on, receiving undeserved accolades in the process.

Another of my interesting chores was making certain we had necessary cash on hand. Because we had so few businesses in town, we had limited cash deposits, and needed to restock currency frequently. Our major correspondent bank was the National Bank of Commerce in downtown Lincoln. Chris and I got in a routine of going to Lincoln every Friday to do some shopping, maybe go to a movie, and pick up currency at NBC. I sometimes had $50,000 in a paper bag that I carried to my car, and kept in the trunk while we did other things. When we got home, we put the money in our freezer as that should be fireproof. The next morning I took the cash to the bank.

During my years in Douglas, I was frequently invited to fill pulpits when pastors were on vacation. On a summer Sunday I went to Pawnee City, DuBois, and St. John's Reformed, a country church between the two towns. St. John's was the only place where I preached when after the benediction, everyone sat down instead of hustling out the door. Much to their credit, all present stayed for Sunday School.

After the 11 am service in Pawnee City, the lay leader told me that a member of their congregation was home bound and in the last stage of cancer. She asked if I would go with her to visit the man, and I did so. A couple of weeks later, Pastor Don Webster sent me a note telling me his dying parishioner appreciated my call, and added, "he died the next day."

I have a plaque on my wall which says I was an Outstanding Young Man in America in 1981. I am not altogether certain who gave it to me, and why I received the honor, but I leave it there anyhow. Chris received similar recognition a few years later.

Our annual Christmas Epistle in 1981 contained the following.

I am writing to you because I've heard you are a generous and sympathetic person. I am an orphan from Japan who came to live with a family in Douglas, Nebraska in October of 1979. Since that time, I've been worked to death every day and they've only given me a bath about three times. Until last month, I slept outside most nights and now I'm in an unheated garage with a half-breed Indian-Italian. Last summer they took him on vacation instead of me!

You will understand my plight best if I give you a few of the grizzlier details; I'll confine myself to the year of 1981. I remember it as being real cold last January. Sometimes they let me inside; sometimes not. My "parents" were living in the Methodist parsonage in Douglas back then. It had a tiny room for me, but sometimes they couldn't get the door shut. Honestly, they treat their Snapper riding mower better than me. Back in January, Chuck (my "dad") was a Methodist preacher, but every weekday he'd take me down and sit me in front of a lumberyard. Sometimes he ran me over to some grain bins, and I'd sit there and breathe in all this milo dust and other yuck you can't imagine!

I did have one up on my roommate. He's bigger than me so he never did get into my room, and had to stay outdoors all winter - night and day. Of course, he's older.

Back to my sad tale. In February, I heard rumblings about some changes. "Mom" (Chris) spends most of her time with my roommate, but Dad mumbles to himself a lot and I can't help but eavesdrop. I discovered we were going to move and maybe Dad was looking for a new job.

In March it became official, my Dad was going to be the new banker in Douglas. I started to worry that he wouldn't want to be seen with me anymore. One day in May

Dad and I went to Lincoln by ourselves. He went into this big building and stayed a long time. When he came out, I discovered he was now a licensed insurance agent. Boy was I glad he'd decided to buy me that new air conditioner to help equalize all the hot air!

In May, my parents took me about a mile out in the country. I figured this was to be my new home. What I didn't know was I expected to do most of the moving. You can't imagine the junk I had to haul. And all those trips. Dad mumbled all the way. I heard him say preachers always get someone else to move them, but bankers are on their own. The new place wasn't too bad. My roommate and I were supposed to have a place of our own, but it seemed like the bicycles and lawnmowers pushed us out most of the time.

In the middle of July, I started the weirdest routine. Every morning (Monday through Friday), Dad would get me up about 6:30 am and make me take him to Milford, 60 miles away. He'd go into a bank there all day, and at 4 pm we'd head back home. On Saturdays he went to the Douglas bank, and stayed until noon. Sundays were really different. I used to take him to Burr every week, but now I go with the whole family to the Douglas church, and Dad doesn't sound hoarse anymore.

Things weren't too bad in August when we stopped going to Milford. Then one Sunday in September I took him to Kansas City. I guess he was trying to make up for not taking me to Clear Lake on the 4th of July. In Kansas City, Dad stayed in a swanky motel and attended a "Banking School." Ha! I know what kind of figures he was studying. Mom showed up later in the week, and then he got a real education.

When we got back home, Dad started mumbling about moving again. This time we made the move in November. My parents bought a nice house in Douglas. I've got my own place (along with my roomie), and I must admit I'm in there almost every night. This house is special because Dad says he and Mom own it, and they'll be in it a long time.

By the way, my parents do have two "real" children. Seth is eight years old and in the third grade. He likes football and baseball and treats me pretty well. But I think he's partial to his bicycle. Anastasia is five and is in kindergarten. She likes dresses and older men. She seems to have a sweet disposition. Both these kids stand on my seats and get me dirty, but also give me a bath once in a while.

My future here is very uncertain. Most bankers won't have anything to do with the likes of me. Dad's boss got a new Cadillac, and Dad said they both had Cadillacs only his was Japanese. That made me feel better. My roomie's name is Pontiac Catalina and he's got a bad cough, and his rubbers are old and worn, his skin is scratched and he's had one eye replaced along with a lot of other operations. I've heard Dad say I was a better bargain than him. But I'm sure Mom likes him best.

Well if you have any sympathy for me, and agree that I'm living in a terribly stressful situation, please send money so I can buy a boat ticket back home. Send your gifts to:

Honda A. C. Cord c/o Leypoldts Douglas, Nebraska

+++

When we went to a Parent/Teacher Conference with Seth's third grade teacher, she told us he was disrupting her class. Whenever someone did something he didn't like, he wrote it down in a special notebook. He was bullied by one of the 4th graders who was a lot bigger than him, and a couple other boys joined in. He was smart enough to know that taking on a mob wouldn't work. So he created a plan that kept all the kids on their toes. We told Mrs. Allen that when the bullying stopped, we'd tell Seth to slow down on the list making.

Because Maynard Dunlap was unable to drive to Douglas, I went to his home in Waverly frequently, and kept him up to date about business and other activities. A long time customer of the bank, who lived close to Palmyra, was having a farm sale. I heard, through the auctioneer, that this farmer had asked the Burr banker to clerk the sale. I really didn't care, as that was one skill I had no interest in developing. But the next time I saw my customer, I said I heard he was having an auction, and I offered to clerk at no charge. He looked perplexed, and said he'd already contracted with someone else.

Another time, I made a little money by assisting a former Douglas resident sell a lot in town. This was somebody that Maynard considered a miser, and she had pulled her money out of the bank, seeking better interest on savings. She used to call me at the elevator almost daily when her renter brought in her share of harvested crops. I guess she liked the way I handled things, but I'd never met her face-to-face.

Her family home had been torn down, but she owned a nice lot, and a couple in town wanted to move their mobile home on to it. I told them I would see what I could do. I called the lot owner and told her about the offer. She was happy to hear from me, and invited me to her home in Lincoln to discuss the transaction. She had a nice, but modest, apartment and was very gracious. She had been a teacher, never married, and retired for 15 years or so. I gave her a check, she signed the deed, and we had a very nice visit. As I left, she dug into her pocket, and gave me a $50 bill. "This is for you, don't give any of it to Dunlap!" she said.

The next time I saw Maynard I told him about both experiences, and he and Helen had a good laugh. They always enjoyed hearing about my banking adventures with people they knew well.

In the summer of 1982, I was given an interesting assignment by the Dunlap family. An investor was considering the purchase of a bank in a small town near Omaha, and it would be managed by Union Bank. Several of us went through the loan files to make certain the buyer was getting a good deal. The bank manager was my dad's second cousin.

The first time I had examiners at the bank, I got along with them pretty well. They asked about our alarm system, and I showed them how it worked (but I didn't tell them it was never turned on). I usually worked for an hour or two after the bank closed, and there was a back door in my office which I opened on nice days, so the screen could let in a breeze. The next morning I got to the bank before anyone else, and noticed I had forgotten to lock the back door the day before. I was sure glad the examiners hadn't followed me in that day.

One criticism they gave me was our practice of leaving keys in the safe deposit boxes. I thought it was strange and I wouldn't do that, but a majority of customers decided it was easier for us to keep the keys. In so doing, it opened us to increased liability. Thus, I changed the policy, and blamed the examiners for making me do it.

About this time I made a loan that went bad. A Douglas resident and bank customer owned a rock truck and decided to retire. He found a young man who was new to our town, and wanted to buy his truck. This fellow needed a loan, and because my customer had vouched for the guy, I wrote him a note and took the truck title. About six months later he was behind on payments.

One evening Chris and I strolled past the home of this errant borrower, and the truck was sitting on the street with the keys in it. The next day I hatched a plan. First I went to the courthouse to seize the title. Rob Focken, our local mechanic, agreed to drive the rig out-of-town for me. We hid the vehicle behind Bob Siefken's barn a couple of miles north of town. Another friend, Darrel Schmidt, put me in touch with an auctioneer who sold this type of equipment. Darrel met me at the auction and bid up the price, and I didn't lose a dime.

I made a loan to another new resident. He was a single fellow who had a daughter in Seth's class. All he needed was $600 for an old pickup, which I later had to repossess. When I told Alan Dunlap about him, he said, "that's OK, we all make missionary loans once in a while."

Our 1982 Christmas Epistle included the following.

Once again we find ourselves in the joyous and busy season of Christmas. The Leypoldt family is occupied with holiday thoughts as they go about their daily chores at home, work, and school. But, alas, one more ritual must be performed before this mid winter rite can be considered truly here. Many have expectantly shuffled through their yuletide mail hoping to find the caustic wit of the Leypoldt epistle. Now, dear reader, the time is at hand and this writer is prepared to share the life and times of a very good year.

In July I began my second year as a country banker, and in November I was promoted to Executive Vice President and Chief Executive Officer of the Farmers State Bank. Many times I'm asked about the "strange" transition from pastor to banker. I believe it has been a casual change from one profession to another. After all, both churches and banks have constituents. In the former we call them parishioners, in the latter, depositors. In both institutions there are good and bad: givers and takers. Bank managers and pastors answer to Board of Directors or Administrative Boards; ultimately they must deal with bank examiners or Bishops. Preachers have their pulpits; bankers have their teller windows. One speaks of prophets, the other of profits. A loan officer will look at your asset/liability ratio; a religious counselor will examine your attitude toward guilt and grace. Evangelists are called upon to seek and save the lost, while a banker must collect bad loans. Clergy hope to nourish their flock, while bankers try to protect your money from straying into Savings & Loans or money funds.

In all things, the ministry prepared me to counsel, exhort, set goals, administer programs, supervise staff, and relate with a variety of personalities. In parish work, I was a generalist. In my present life I continue to wear many hats: banker, Realtor, insurance agent, school board member, church treasurer, village clerk-treasurer. And I still keep in touch with the old life as an occasional guest preacher.

But enough about me. Chris has strengthened her ability in the domestic arts, and serves as cook, dishwasher, laundress, home budget manager, extension club president, PTA volunteer, vacation church school teacher, and member of United Methodist Women.

Son Seth is nine and a fourth-grader at Douglas school. His interests shift from basketball to swimming to T-Ball to football. He has discovered girls, and yet is more interested in the good fortunes of the Big Red. He attended two football games with his father this year.

Daughter Anastasia is six and a first-grader. This spring she graduated from the carefree world of kindergarten and into the horrible shock of a full day of school in the fall. Her interests range from 6-year-old boys to 18-year-old boys; but also has time for kittens and pretty dresses and going shopping with Mom.

We added a new family member last month with the arrival of our 1983 Ford Crown Victoria, so now I don't have to park in the far corner of parking lots when I go to banker's conventions.

In summation, we find our roots deepening in this little community and readily see that our future lies here. Our health has been good and our fortunes are improving, so we look forward to a busy and prosperous new year.

+++

I didn't include the somewhat amusing story about my annual bonus. We held our director's meetings at the home of Maynard and Helen Dunlap in Waverly. The December meeting always included discussion of annual salaries and bonuses, and Alan told me that he and Jay were discussing some changes for me in that regard. We'd had a profitable year and I thought Alan was hinting at a financial boost for me. I got to the Dunlap home before the others, and Maynard said "Let's talk about bonuses. Put yourself down for $500 and give everyone else $200." I went for the stall, and said Alan and Jay were talking about doing something different this year. Fortunately, he agreed to wait for them.

Alan and Jay arrived in about ten minutes, and we went through all the formalities. Thereupon they asked me to go into another room, while they discussed my compensation. Maynard was very hard of hearing, and didn't miss much of the discussion. I heard Maynard exclaim in a loud voice, "TEN THOUSAND DOLLARS!" I heard Alan say I was the lowest paid manager in the most profitable bank the family owned, and Jay said I could leave if they didn't pay me better. Maynard didn't look very happy when I came back into the room, and Alan told me to increase my salary by $3,000 and pay myself a $10,000 bonus.

The Dunlaps owned several farms in Missouri and Iowa and they gave me the responsibility of paying bills, making deposits, and communicating with their tenants. Even after his stroke, Maynard visited his farms a couple times a year. I told Alan I would like to go on one of these trips, and in the summer of 1983 Seth and I joined Alan and Maynard on a trip to Missouri.

+++

I am convinced that one of the most enjoyable games ever invented is the one we call "Hide and Go Seek." Growing up in a large family made this game really special. Before television and video games we enjoyed more physical activities. There were enough of us that no one had to be "it" too often. Depending upon the season, our game would take place in the house, the yard, or if Dad wasn't around, we would go next door to the church. We always found some wonderfully creative hiding places.

One of the neat things about "Hide and Go Seek" is that it is so adaptable. It can be played by as few as two, indoors or outdoors, day or night, all ages can be included. You can have partners or teams. You can set boundaries and time limits. You can combine it with other games like "tag" or "kick the can." We even discovered our cats liked to play "Hide and Go Seek."

You learn a lot about human nature when you play "Hide and Go Seek." Some people always hide in the same place and are real easy to find. Others find incredibly difficult places to hide. Some will brag and tell you where they hid; others are sneaky and keep their best places to themselves. Some will be in a conspicuous spot, but they stay so quiet they go unnoticed. There are the brave ones who quickly and silently move from place to place, eluding the one called "it." Seekers are interesting, too. Some get frustrated quickly and give up before finding all the hiders. Some will look and look with diligence and patience.

I remember playing with my children when they were little. One of them always hid in our bedroom closet. I would look everywhere else and then walk into the bedroom saying, "I just can't find Seth anywhere, I guess I'll quit looking," and a tiny voice would say, "you didn't look in here yet." Some want to be found and some don't. Ana used to giggle with such excitement when you got close, it was impossible to overlook her.

+++

The early 1980's were "boom and bust" years for American agriculture. Inflation was driving interest rates higher and higher, but land prices were rising as well. I remember more than one expert saying, "You'd better buy that farm now, because it will be worth three times as much in ten years." So a lot of farmers and farm banks stuck their necks out to ride the wave of inflation that would take us to the promised land.

Very often, however, our ambition was simply to survive. I read about a farmer who had experienced several bad years in a row. At the end of the harvest season he went to see his banker and said, "I've got some good news and some bad news, which would you like to hear first?"

"Let's get the bad news over with first," the banker replied.

"Okay. With the bad drought and inflation and all, I won't be able to pay anything on my mortgage this year."

"Well, that is pretty bad," the banker agreed.

"Hold on, it gets worse. I also won't be able to pay anything on the loan for all that machinery I bought."

"Wow, things really are bad!" remarked the banker.

"It gets worse. You remember I also borrowed to buy seed and fertilizer and other supplies. Well, I can't pay that back either."

"That's dreadful," said the banker, "now tell me the good news."

"The good news," replied the farmer, "is that I intend to keep on doing business with you."

I remember one of my own farm customers in Douglas telling me that he had gone over to Iowa to purchase a lottery ticket. I asked him what he would do if he won the million dollar prize. He said: "Oh, I suppose I'll just keep farming until it's all gone."

+++

While in Rapid City in 1983 we stayed in a nice motel and there was a theater nearby. Chris and I decided we'd go to the first of National Lampoon's **Vacation** movies. Seth, age ten, was very upset and didn't want to go. He sulked for the first ten minutes but when the family truckster pulled out of the Griswold garage and lost its suitcases, he settled down and laughed heartily throughout the movie.

In September of 1983, a retired gentleman who lived near Palmyra asked if he could borrow money to buy some calves. He was not a customer, but I was acquainted with him and he offered to pledge a $20,000 certificate from a Lincoln savings & loan as collateral. I ran this past Alan Dunlap, and we agreed to the loan of $10,000.

In the middle of October, Alan stopped to see me and asked if I knew of any bank customers who had money in Commonwealth Savings in Lincoln. I mentioned a couple of folks, then reminded him of the fellow who gave us a C.D. as collateral (it was from Commonwealth). His eyes widened, but I said the cattle were worth enough to cover the note. He then proceeded to tell me all he knew about the coming failure of the Commonwealth Savings Company.

Our Christmas Letter in 1983 channeled the great Charles Dickens who helped me create this prose:

The cold December wind lashed angrily at the old man as he shuffled down the street toward the tiny bank. He had walked that same route so long that he could do it blind-folded. "Old C.W." was a legend in this village. Once upright, ambitious, filled with dreams; now a miserable, shrunken reflection of his former self.

As he approached the door, he fumbled with and jangled his keys, unlocking the door. Mechanically, he flipped on the lights, and tore yesterday's date from the wall calendar. "Bah! Humbug!" he muttered as he saw the new date - December 24, 2033. His cold, stiff fingers tore off coat, hat, and gloves. He methodically spun the vault dial; again he could and did do this blindly. He swung open the huge steel door, and the Farmers State Bank was open for business.

He slouched into his large, high-back, leather chair, switching on the computer before him. And he was ready for work. He remained there alone throughout the day. Once he had human help, but now "Cratchit" the computer did it all. Plastic cards and home terminals had replaced the need for employees. So old C.W. sat and dozed as Cratchit blinked and whirred, and occasionally beeped him awake.

At noon, Cratchit sounded off the reminder it was lunchtime, so old C.W. stumbled to the back room to fix a circle meat sandwich, drink some milk, and watch *As The World Turns*. He was then ready to supervise the remainder of Cratchit's work day. At 1 pm he usually had a sound nap, and today was no exception. He began to slumber quite peacefully in his reclining chair, when a rude and scratchy voice called out, "OOOOLD CEE DOUBLE YEW." Again and again it squealed until C.W. responded. "What? Who is it?" queried C.W. "I am the ghost of Christmas past!" proudly returned the voice.

Old C.W. sat straight up and stared at his ghoulish visitor. Cratchit was still spinning and whirling as C.W. inquired, "What is this? Am I on Candid Camera?"

"No, C.W.," the ghost replied. "I'm going to take you back to another year when you were young and active and had all your original parts." Old C.W. was now 86 years old and had nearly every vital element in him transplanted. "O.K. by me," said C.W.

The apparition gently led the old man to another time. He soon discovered it was 1983. The tired and sullen eyes brightened as he witnessed Anastasia's seventh birthday party. He gazed in wonderment at 10-year-old Seth pounding the basketball in the driveway, and kicking the football in the empty lot behind the family home. "1983," pondered old C.W., "that was a very good year!"

Trembling and misty-eyed, he saw Chris busy in the kitchen, taking an accounting course, chairing the annual church dinner, and sending out the meter cards to village residents every month. "I remember that year very well," he mumbled softly. He had human help in the bank back then. He was elected a director and acquired the rather cumbersome title, "Executive Vice President & Cashier." Faintly he heard the theme from **The Godfather**, as he watched the young C. W. at school board meetings, clerking the village board, and attending the Douglas UMC with his family.

He found himself in Lincoln General Hospital, awaiting the surgeon's report after Chris' gall bladder removal. He remembered auditors in the bank that very same week. He sat in the hot August sun at Seth's T-ball tournament, and was poolside when both Seth and Ana passed their swimming tests on their first tries. Suddenly he was in the Black Hills, and the Nebraska Pine Ridge for a lovely and relaxing family vacation.

He climbed the hill to the Douglas school, and saw Seth, a busy 5th grader and Anastasia, and eager 2nd grader. He reminisced over the excitement of an undefeated Nebraska football team watched so carefully by Seth and himself. Then it was Christmas time 1983. Seth and Anastasia and Chris were decorating the tree. There were programs at church and school, and the happiness and warmth of friends and family.

The phantom led him back to his desk, and old C.W. settled again in his high-backed chair. "That was a good year!" he said again. "You were a kind, generous, and happy man in 1983, C.W. said the ghost. "But today you are rich and powerful and yet, miserable. Someday soon the Great Examiner will call for a reconciliation. It would be good if all your accounts were in balance." With these words, the spirit left him and C.W. felt very much alone.

Cratchit was silent. Like human bank employees, he was programmed to drop everything at 3:30 pm. The bank was deathly still, and old C.W. sat in the late afternoon darkness. "Christmas Eve, 2033," he thought. Time had flown so quickly. He wondered, could a withered old cheapskate change? "Yes, I can!" he announced to himself. He could pay higher rates for savings and charge less for loans; he could sell his property and make grants to the needy. Tomorrow was Christmas - a perfect time to start over!

Then Old C.W. thought about his 52 year career. "Can I really change this pattern of my life?" He wondered…rising from his chair and stuffing his rigid body into coat, hat, and gloves. Still muttering to himself about the challenges of change, he walked out the door, locking it behind him. "Can I?"

"NAAAAA!" said old C.W. as he kicked a dog and stumbled up the street.

+++

In 1984 we had new cabinets installed in our kitchen, made electrical and plumbing improvements and installed a new furnace and air conditioner. All this work was completed while we vacationed in Breckenridge, Colorado.

One day we went from Breckenridge to Central City, which on the map looked like a short drive. We didn't realize the route wound through a mountain, was one lane in places, unpaved, and very steep. Chris threatened to get out and walk and I told her "just close your eyes; that's what I do." When we got to our destination, the brakes on our car were literally smoking. We walked around Central City, ate supper, and went back the long way on pavement. At our rented condo, I read a tourist book that told me the local folks call the mountain road we took "The **O My God!** Highway."

After a week in Colorado we went to Yellowstone and saw Old Faithful, grizzly bears, and waterfalls. On the way home, we saw the Little Bighorn battlefield and Fort Robinson. We returned in plenty of time to help my baby brother Jim marry Miss Melissa Doupnik on July 20, 1984 in Lincoln.

A few jokes were floating around the country. Did you hear about the latest medical miracle? They've found a way to transplant a human heart into the body of a banker. What's the difference between finding a dead skunk and a dead banker on the highway? There are skid marks in front of a skunk. Why is a banker's heart preferred by heart transplant patients? It's never been used.

During 1984 I became a director of the Bank of Palmyra. In July of 1984, J.

Woodrow Hearn of Louisiana was elected a Bishop in The UMC, and assigned to Nebraska. Since 1960, Nebraska Bishops had used an allowance to find their own housing, but a new rule required that an episcopal residence be provided. We had some Conference money invested in our bank, so Alan told the conference treasurer we could provide a low-interest loan for the new home. Therefore, I financed a brand new house for the Bishop on Twin Ridge Road in Lincoln. Ironically in 1997, as Conference Treasurer, I purchased a new house for our Bishop and sold the one on Twin Ridge.

At the close of 1983, I was managing a farm bank that on paper looked extremely good. Our total assets were growing steadily, our loan to deposit ratio was at a profitable level, and I had accomplished an important personal goal: zero loan losses. In 1984 we were still very strong, but had to implement stricter security requirements.

High interest rates and low farm prices were taking their toll on small farmers. Washington had a "bigger is better" philosophy, and by the time trickle down economics trickled down to the family farm, there was little, if anything, left. Where I lived in 1984 there was a wet spring that delayed planting, and a September freeze that destroyed most crops.

The FDIC and the State Banking Department started to rate banks on a scale of 1 to 5. "Ones" were the strongest; "fives" would be closed within a year. The bank in a nearby town had the appearance of being rock solid. They had expanded rapidly in the 70's and moved into a beautiful new facility in 1983. We were shocked to learn the FDIC had given this bank a "4." Often, "the bigger they are, the harder they fall."

The bank's owner was directed to find a new manager. This person would be employed by the bank, but supervised by the FDIC. His job was to restore profitability and save the bank from failure. We called him a hatchet man. This scene was repeated in several towns in Nebraska and Iowa. "Hatchet men" were sent to clean up poorly managed banks. Often, foreclosures and liquidations of customers were seen as solutions. Sometimes, there was a necessary change in bank ownership. But the end result was that banking services were retained in most communities.

On November 25, 1984 my wife's younger sister, Kay Abbott, died from cancer. She had fought valiantly for over two years. Chris spent at least one day every week in her Wahoo home, helping in any way that she could. She left her husband, Michael, and two little ones, Rebecca and Matthew.

In 1985 Chris starting keeping a diary, which has helped immensely as I write this memoir. Her first entry on February 6 reads "No school today…took Ana to Dr. Hutchins to see while she is developing so early. Bought her a bra." Our days were filled with routine activities at home, work, school and church. We did a lot of running to Lincoln, Syracuse, Waverly, and Beatrice. The United Methodist Women in Douglas honored both Chris and I with life membership awards in 1985.

In June Chris and I went to my 20th high school reunion in Albion. The next week sister Janice and her family were in town, and we had several get-togethers. At the same time, a big storm went through southern Otoe County, and we lost power for most of the week making it nearly impossible to do business at the bank. In July it was time for a family vacation, and we went to the Eisenhower Library in Kansas, then on to Overland Park, Kansas, and the Missouri Ozarks. We also went to Cedar Falls, Iowa where Ken Grenz and I entertained the local police force. On the way home, we stopped at the Living History Farm near Des Moines.

In September of 1985 Chris was driving home on the Douglas spur, and t-boned a vehicle that made a sudden u-turn in front of her. The driver had seen a piece of junk iron in the other lane, and wanted to get it off the road. The guy she hit was a plain-clothed state patrolman. We were committed seat belt wearers, and Chris' injury was very minor. We decided to trade her 1983 Ford for a much nicer 1985 model.

I was the Village Clerk in Douglas for about four years. One of my duties was managing the business affairs of Rosehill cemetery. At that time, cemetery lots cost $25, and they were big enough to squeeze in eight vaults. I suggested we increase the price to $100, but give people time to get in on the old price. I bought 4 lots for $100 and still own them. Chris thinks we should use the Cedar Hill cemetery. I suppose our remains will end up dependent upon who dies first.

In October of 1985 I had a customer who moved to Wichita, and got behind on a car loan. I had the title to his 1965 Mustang and it was worth more than he owed, but he didn't want to bring it up to Nebraska. It just happened that Alan Dunlap had tickets to the Oklahoma State football game in Stillwater, so Chris and I went with Alan and Phyllis and another couple to the game. We stayed overnight in Wichita, and on Sunday the guy brought his car to our motel. Chris and I then drove home in the Mustang.

Later that month I preached at Endicott and Helvey. The lesson for that Sunday was the story of a farmer who was successful by worldly standards, yet Jesus called him a fool. Jesus did not say the he was a bad person, just foolish. He tells us the meaning of the parable in its introduction (from Luke 12:15, CEV): "Don't be greedy! Owning a lot of things won't make your life safe." The point was that the foolish farmer concentrated so hard on himself and his success, that he left God out of his life. Luke's Gospel tells us often that true happiness comes from sharing wealth, not hoarding it.

The theme for my sermon was "When is Enough Enough?" It was about money and security; about being in control or being controlled. "When is Enough Enough?" That question was beginning to haunt me, at least a little.

My employer and friend, Mr. M. W. Dunlap, died on November 11. His example of generosity and service to others has been very important to me; not to mention, the trust he demonstrated in hiring me, a complete novice, to manage the bank he owned for over 60 years.

On December 19, 1985, the State Banking Department closed the Bank of Panama, which is six miles from Douglas. Alan Dunlap called and asked me if I wanted to buy it. I asked, "What's the lowest amount we can bid?" We were the only bidder at $5,000 for the loans and deposits, and we also bought the property. We doubled our size and acquired a very modern facility. I also gained some new staff persons, and purchased an insurance agency in Panama which increased my volume about 30%.

Coincidentally, the state examiners were at Douglas. We hadn't had a visit for over 2½ years and we were prepared. So it was a bother, but they assured the Banking Department our bank was strong enough to acquire a branch facility.

The Panama deal was the just the end of a very busy year for us. The farm loan situation was not good, and much time was spent developing plans that would save both the farmer and the bank. Reaganomics crippled rural America, and we saw the destruction of Production Credit Associations and Savings and Loans industry. Under Clinton the economy rebounded. Bush II and the hapless Congress stood by as the upper 1% turned us back to Reagan, and nearly destroyed the auto and housing industries as well.

Chris remained active in the UMW and her extension club. She also picked up a very interesting ceramics hobby, and many of her creations were on display in our home. Seth grew to 5'6" and weighed 125 pounds at end of 1985, and had entered Junior High. In November he saw the list of names on the Honor Roll, and asked me what it meant. My son resolved to get better grades, and was on every honor roll/dean's list from that time forward. He also went with me to five Husker football games in 1985, and played basketball in school.

Anastasia was a little lady who likes pierced earrings, make-up, dolls, toys, and sitting on Daddy's lap. She was taking piano lessons every week, and was in a public recital at the church. Both she and Seth were good swimmers, and we took them to Syracuse for this exercise.

Sometimes when I watch Dickens' **A Christmas Carol**, I feel sympathy for old Ebenezer Scrooge. The Christmas of 1985 was like that for me. I was now managing a bank at Douglas with a branch six miles away. We were closing out another disastrous year for farmers and farm banks. Decembers are always busy times for banks, but this was really a tough one.

The Dunlap family made a very wise move in 1985. They hired Daren D. "Bud" Riblett to guide us through the maze of the Farmers Home Administration's guaranteed farm loan program. Bud had served as assistant state director of the FmHA, and really knew his stuff! He was a close buddy of Senator Jim Exon as well. In reality the program was a bank bail-out, but it did enable us to save a lot of farmers.

I spent many hours with Bud. He was a United Methodist, a Freemason, and a native Nebraskan who was a pilot in World War II. The Dunlaps had acquired a bank in Pawnee City and they sent Bud and me down to help write FmHA loan applications. Bud eventually became an officer in the Milford bank.

Family portrait from 1985

One of the saddest things I experienced as a banker involved an 80-year-old farmer, and his 45-year old son. Following harvest in 1985, the younger man told me that he was planning to quit farming, so in January of 1986 we sat down to figure out a way of liquidating his indebtedness. His liabilities far exceeded his current and intermediate assets, thus we needed to refinance the real estate loan. This is where his father entered the picture.

The old man had been a customer of the Farmers State Bank all his life. His parents were among the first depositors in 1919. His son was having trouble obtaining financing from another institution in 1983, and the father wanted to keep the family farm going, so they came to me for help. The only way I could take on the line, was a guarantee secured by the father's 160 acres.

The father had easily agreed to this condition. After three more difficult years, the son was ready to sell out and move to California, leaving his folks to settle with the bankers. Now we sat in the conference room of our country bank. The old man, his son, Alan Dunlap, and myself. After hearing the severity of the situation explained, the father, with his son sitting next to him said to me, "today I wish I never had children." He went on to say things I already knew. One son had already moved away, and this one wanted to follow him, leaving the old man to pay the debt. "I wish I never had children," he said again. How incredibly sad that a piece of rocky, marginal farmland in Johnson County, Nebraska could drive a wedge between a father and a son.

One of my monthly duties in the bank was to make a list of delinquent, and otherwise problem loans. In the first couple of years of my career - the early 1980's - this was a rather pleasant chore. I very seldom had a loan that was more than 30 days past due, and when I did they were relatively easy to work out. One year our only losses were from counting errors that we called "over and short," and accounting errors made by the giant computer at our correspondent bank in Lincoln.

All this started to change in 1984, and by the end of 1985 my monthly chore turned into a nightmare. We weren't concerned about delinquent loans anymore; we wondered if we should make any loans at all. A city-bred examiner from the FDIC was reviewing all customers whose credit line exceeded $40,000. They were all farmers. I think he was down to the C's when he commented, "I haven't seen any positive cash flows in these files." I responded in very dramatic fashion, by pulling open a file drawer, and saying, "This is a farm bank. All my big customers are farmers. You won't find *anything* that looks very positive in here."

At our next monthly meeting, Alan Dunlap told me we needed to change some things in our month-end reports. He said they were no longer concerned with just the delinquent loans; from now on we needed to look closely at all our loans. I started pounding out reports on most of our bank's customers. I visited farms more often. Sometimes I even counted sows and gilts and cows and calves. Occasionally, I checked out the contents of a machine shed.

I grumbled and complained about all this extra work. Alan reminded me why I needed to do these reports. First of all, it looks good to an examiner, and secondly, he said, "we don't want any surprises." In other words, he fully expected we would have some problems, but he wanted to be prepared and have a grasp on every situation. I thus became a predictor and reporter of information. By operating in this careful manner, we were able to avoid being overwhelmed by economic problems that farmers and farm banks experienced during the middle 1980's.

I wrote this fictional story for a sermon in 1992. It was inspired by Jesus' words to one who had received healing (Luke 17:11-19), and built on many news accounts and other stories I heard about the bad times in the eighties.

Many small towns in Nebraska are struggling to survive. Most of them no longer have a school, and only a few businesses remain on Main Street. One tiny community was down to 30 or 40 houses, a combination general store-filling station-post office, a bank, and a church. The bank was managed by a young woman, who had inherited the business from her grandparents. This bank, with its proud past and stately presence on Main Street, gave the people a feeling of security.

One bright, crisp day in November of 1985, the people of this tiny town awoke to a horrible reality. Their Main Street was filled with cars, many with out-of-state license plates. The County Sheriff, who only came around on election years, was assisting 3 or 4 state troopers with traffic control. By noon, news reporters started showing up, including a TV crew from Lincoln.

All the commotion was at the bank. The Banking Department and the FDIC had shut its doors. People were panic stricken. Was their money safe? When would the bank reopen? How could this happen? A few of the braver ones walked up and looked inside the grand old building, and saw dozens of strangers milling around with their calculators and computer read-outs. On the 6 o'clock news and again at 10 pm, Mel Mains on Channel 10 told them the sad news they already knew: their bank was gone forever - a victim of bad management and the weak farm economy.

The next night, a Saturday, the FDIC held a meeting in the church basement. "No one will lose money," the man said, "we'll start paying you off on Monday." He also said those with loans, would have to pay them back within six weeks. This was one reason the bank was in trouble. The owner stuck her neck out to keep the general store-filling station in business. She helped all the young families buy homes, just to keep them in town. When the farmers got dried out, hailed out, and priced out, she rewrote their notes year after year. At the same time, she lived awfully well for a small town girl. She built a new house with an indoor pool, drove a Mercedes, had some very expensive clothes, and spent way too much time in Lincoln or Denver or Los Angeles, visiting her old college friends. She financed all this by taking a huge salary, even though the bank was losing money every year.

Now people's shock turned into resentment against the bank owner. Will she stick around, they wondered? After the FDIC left, the church folks stayed and had an impromptu meeting. The pastor and two council members were asked to visit the former banker. They did so, and found her brash and unrepentant. Of course she would stay in her lovely home, she said. It was all paid for. She had a new insurance job over at the county seat. When the pastor suggested that her extravagance and poor judgment had cost the town dearly, she laughed at all of them saying, "what I did was just business and no big deal."

Things got worse in the little town. The store had to close. Several families lost their homes and farms, because they couldn't find a new lender. Church membership and giving declined dramatically. But the church folks struck back. They had a special meeting and removed the former banker from the membership roll (obviously this was not a United Methodist congregation). When the woman found out about her dismissal, she confronted church members, and showered them with curses. If one of them saw her coming, they crossed the street to avoid her anger. She was shunned; it was like she was forever unclean - an outsider in her own home town.

During the next few years the pastor frequently saw the woman, and spoke to her. She never returned his greeting. Then one day they met quite by accident, in a back aisle of a grocery store in the county seat. "There is seldom a day that passes when I do not pray for you," the pastor said. The woman began to weep.

Two weeks later, on a Monday morning, the woman entered his study. No longer brassy and bold, she admitted she had made mistakes, and deeply regretted the hurt she caused the town and many of its people. In the weeks ahead, the two met frequently for counseling and prayer. Then, one day, she said, "I want to be a part of the church again. I know God has forgiven me, but I won't feel healing until the church takes me back."

He told her he would bring the issue before a meeting of the whole church. When the congregation gathered, the pastor told the people her story. When he finished, a dozen people stood and recounted tales of their encounters with this woman. The pastor reminded them that those clashes took place prior to her confession.

Finally, the vote to restore her as a member took place. It lost by a substantial margin. The pastor sat in stunned silence. The following Sunday, he preached and pleaded for reconsideration. He believed no one could hear the Gospel message, until they exercised this act of healing toward one they had shunned. But they refused to listen.

Jesus' story about ten lepers is the story of separation and forgiveness and rejection and healing. It is a graphic reminder of how we treat outsiders, and how important it is for people to know that they can start over in life. The Bible is full of the Good News of starting over. The Hebrew scriptures tell us of a nation continually being called back to God as they sever the divine connection. Moses, raised as a spoiled aristocrat and hotheaded murderer, and living as a fugitive, starts over as a great liberator and leader of his people. David, anointed to be King when he was an adolescent, slipped into a life crazed with power, and yet grieved over his sin and started over with new direction from God. Hosea, betrayed by his wife who became a prostitute, went himself to the slave market and purchased her, taking her home and loving her, and, with God's help, they started over.

The Bible is filled with characters who were shackled and set free. Peter was a blow-hard, self-styled big shot and occasional coward. He peers into the empty tomb on the first Easter, and starts over as the early church's first Bishop. James and John, jealous, vindictive, hateful, and vengeful, start over as apostles of love. Paul, defender of the status quo, persecutor of the Jesus followers, is overwhelmed by the Risen Christ, and starts his life over to become the greatest missionary who ever lived. So many others: Mary Magdalene, Zacchaeus, Nicodemus, and Thomas, all touched by Jesus, start over and their lives shine on us across the centuries.

The story of Jesus and the ten lepers tells us that God's universal love is extended to all. It also tells us that, perhaps only one in ten of us, begins to truly understand the implications of that love.

The pastor retired and moved away. The little church finally closed its doors. Some of the former members now worship in other towns. Most stay home on Sundays. The former banker found a new church, where she was loved and accepted. Because she told her story of separation and forgiveness and rejection and healing so well, she became a Certified Lay Speaker, and thinks she might enter the pastoral ministry.

The Good News is that God is at work among us today. God still cleanses us of the hurt we cause. God still heals our wounded hearts and minds. God still restores us to wholeness so that we might proclaim God's goodness in service to the world around us.

+++

As recorded earlier, Chris' and my first home was the parsonage of a small church in an unincorporated village just southeast of Lincoln. The town had two churches, a school, a grain elevator, and about 100 people living in thirty houses. Our mail came by rural free delivery, our gas was propane, there was no municipal water or sewer.

Our next-door neighbors were among the most interesting people we've ever known. The parents' names were Earl and Betty. They had three daughters and two sons. The oldest daughter was married, but lived nearby. The boys were about six and eight years old. Earl was a window-washer. He was one of those people who go to the top of high-rise buildings, lower a platform attached to cables down the side, washing the windows as they went. He had service contracts with several firms in downtown Lincoln including Miller and Paine, the National Bank of Commerce, and the old Cornhusker Hotel.

Our houses were only about ten feet apart. Their back door, which was the main traffic route, was ten feet from our bedroom window. With no effort, we kept well-informed regarding all the activities and disagreements in our neighbors' house.

Earl had a deep, gruff voice and laced every sentence with swear words. As a matter of fact, he used cuss words in some of the most creative arrangements imaginable. His loudness motivated others to action. He barked out orders, and his children would scurry around at his direction. Earl had a serious drinking problem, was overweight, and had a recent heart attack. But he kept on working, drinking, and hollering.

Earl and his family were not church goers. The kids occasionally showed up at Sunday School, the oldest girl had a church wedding, and Earl's dad was buried from a church. But that was about the extent of their church-going. We got to know Earl and Betty pretty well. After a while, we began to appreciate them. Eventually, we enjoyed being around them.

It would be kind to call the parsonage we lived in "substandard." It was small, drafty, and rodent-infested. The first peculiar thing we noticed was a strange, tingly, feeling whenever we washed our hands. One time I got a mild shock when I touched the bathtub faucet. The problem was a faulty electric water heater.

We had a lot of thunderstorms that summer. It seemed like the electricity was knocked out at least once a week. The first time it happened, the lights came back on, but there was no water. The well had an electric pump, and the pump had to be restarted and primed manually. I had no idea how to handle this one.

In the fall, we started using our furnace and noticed that it popped and banged before taking off. We found out the flue was full of soot and grime, and needed a good cleaning before the furnace would be safe to use.

With every difficulty, we went to our good church folks and it seemed they were not concerned, or were too busy, and the problem went unsolved. But not so with Earl. All I had to do was ask. He'd crawl down into that well hole, beer belly and all, wheezing and cussing and grunting, and showed me how to prime the pump and how to restart the motor. The furnace went bad on a Friday night, and Earl got somebody to take a look that night and come back and fix it the next day. He chewed on one of the church members until they put in a new water heater.

Earl taught me something about being a neighbor. The last time I saw him was on my front porch in Douglas. Ironically this was Earl's home town, and he owned some property there. At the time I was a banker, village clerk, and a member of the school board. Earl was having financial problems. The village said he owed all kinds of money for past utility bills, and he wanted to transfer his land out of the local school district. I was not the cause, but, I was in the middle of all his problems.

He cussed me out good that day. He told me it was illegal to be the village clerk and on the school board and to hold a real estate license at the same time. I said I thought it was kind of dumb, but not illegal. After a time, Earl left, our problem unresolved.

I couldn't be mad at him. His crisis was enormous. By listening, I felt I had at least bound up his wounds for that day. Sometimes that's the best we can do.

+++

In 1986 we began doing some serious soul-searching about the future. Seth would soon be in High School with Ana closing in on Junior High. We could move to Panama or Palmyra and be in a larger school district. But we loved the Douglas people and how would this be received? How about a fresh start in full-time ministry? Could we afford it?

I started attending a "Barth Study Group" in Omaha with my friend and former DS Merle Zook. I had been out of full-time ministry for seven years. I was successful and relatively happy in my banking career. However, I was starting to ask "when is enough enough?" The fact was that in 1986 as a small-town banker, I made more money than the highest paid pastor in the Nebraska Conference of The UMC. I knew my income would be reduced by more than 50% if I went back to full-time ministry.

Our annual Christmas Epistle contained the following. "On August 30, 1986, I resigned my position as Executive Vice President and Cashier of the Farmers State Bank. I am relieved to report that my resignation was not immediately accepted and that I am still on the job here. I have applied for readmission to Full Connection as a pastor in The UMC, and I hope to receive an appointment at the AC session in June 1987."

We had a few health problems in 1986. In September Chris had a carpal tunnel procedure done on her right hand and quickly recovered, but knew she would do the same with other hand some day. In December, Seth had a bout with pneumonia and was in the hospital for two nights. He had a bad cold and has asthma which compounded the situation.

We took some great trips during the year. In April Chris went to Disney World in Florida with her Grandma Grace McGill. They were gone five days and the kids and I kept house without any problems at all. In July, the whole family loaded up the Crown Victoria and headed east. We stopped first at Clear Lake, Iowa. Then we took a leisurely journey through Illinois, where we stayed in Springfield and took in all the Lincoln memorabilia. We drove across Indiana and Ohio as far east as Canton, where Seth and I went to the Pro Football Hall of Fame. We were in the heart of Amish country, which was very fascinating for me. "A tractor produces debts, but a horse reproduces itself."

In the fall, my brother Steve and I drove to Kentucky, Tennessee, Alabama, Mississippi, and Arkansas. It was great fun as neither Steve or I had been in those states previously. We stayed one night at Nashville and one night at Memphis, among other places. We saw lots of Country Music sights, as well as Graceland Mansion.

In the spring Seth was on the Junior High track team and did pretty well. He ran the 400 and 800 and was also in the long jump, which produced several ribbons. Anastasia was becoming a talented musician. She took piano lessons every week in Syracuse, and was in another recital this year. She also played a solo at the school musical, and sang in the Junior Choir at church. In addition, she was an emerging cat person, and had one of the most beautiful black Siamese cats I have ever seen.

During the spring and summer, the movies came to Douglas. Several scenes for the TV movie **Amerika**[33] were shot in and around town, and one day a Russian tank passed through town. Chris and Ana were in Lincoln, and actually saw Kris Kristofferson at a grocery store.

Both kids were part of a 4-H club in Douglas, and both had several things at the County Fair. Ana got a blue ribbon for a dress she made and modeled. Seth got a purple ribbon for an extensive family tree he made, and it received a blue at the State Fair.

Chris and Seth both taught at the Vacation Church School in the spring. As in other years, church activities remained an important part of our lives. Seth was confirmed in May, and we had all the grandparents at our house for dinner afterwards. I was Church Treasurer; Chris was UMW Treasurer.

Seth was in the 8th grade, stood 5'7", and weighed 150 pounds. Anastasia was a 5th grader, 4'10," weight information unavailable. Seth got all A's first quarter, and was playing basketball for Douglas Junior High. He got out of the hospital just a few days before for the first game and was unable to practice. However, I am proud to report he made 12 of our 25 points.

Chris was on the election board in both May and November. Just to prove I am nominally impartial when it comes to politics, Seth and I went to Omaha to hear President Reagan speak. We did not applaud, but did take pictures.

I was a guest speaker at several churches that year, and in the fall was preaching every Sunday at the Presbyterian Church in North Bend, which was 80 miles north of Douglas. I enjoyed this congregation very much, and gave some thought to applying for the pastoral position. However, there was a restriction on interim pastors doing so.

The Douglas bank had total assets of under $3 million when I started with them in 1981. In 1983, we passed $4 million, and after we acquired the failed Panama bank we were just under $9 million. Not bad for an accidental capitalist.

Our mama cat had a litter in the spring of 1987

Chapter 15
The Wurst Place In Nebraska

There was once a cobbler, who was a happy and contented man. People who passed his shop, laughed and waved when they saw him singing at the top of his voice while fixing shoes. Many people stopped in his shop, just to bask in the warmth of his smile.

One of the people who observed the cobbler was a banker, who sang little and smiled less. He seldom slept well. At first he was irritated by the constant good humor of the cobbler, but as the days passed he was fascinated by him. Finally, he decided to visit the cobbler and discover his secret of happiness. After the two men talked for a while, the banker inquired, "Are you wealthy? Pardon me for asking, but how much money do you make each year?"

"My family is seldom in want," the cobbler answered. "Some days I only fix shoes; no one buys. The shop is closed on holy days, so there is no income at all when we celebrate the witness of a saint. I simply cannot give you an accurate sum."

"How wonderfully simple," the banker said. "I have decided to eliminate your financial problem for the immediate future. Since you have so openly shared your life story with me, I want you to take this gift of 300 gold coins. Please use them whenever you have need."

Overjoyed, the cobbler went home and buried the gold in a corner of his house. The succeeding days brought many changes. He often left the shop to go home when his family was absent, thinking that someone might break in and steal his wealth. He began to lose sleep at night, fearing that people were plotting to steal the gold. Old friends noticed that he did not sing with the same cheer, and he often seemed suspicious when someone stopped in the shop just to chat.

Finally, the cobbler visited the banker with the bag of gold in his hands. "Thank you for your generous gift," he began, "but I cannot afford to be the owner of these gold coins. Please take your money back so that I may again enjoy music, sleep, and my friends. It seems that when I buried the money, I buried happiness at the same time."[34]

+++

I was not seeking martyrdom. During the "farm crisis," I was often on the wrong side of the table, and thus decided to test the pastoral waters once more.

It was a hot and humid day when the movers loaded our belongings in Douglas. We did not leave town until 10:30 pm, and it became a dark and stormy night. As we arrived in Eustis at 4 am on June 9, 1987, a gentle rain greeted us and we slept on the parsonage floor. It was nice enough that we opened the windows in our new home. At eight in the morning, we were awakened by chimes coming from the church. Chris woke from a sound sleep and asked, "do those things go off every morning?" To which I replied, "I don't know, but I'll find out." I hustled over to the church, found the control, and changed the bells to ring at a more appropriate time.

The population of Eustis in 1987 was 470. The UMC had a wonderful parsonage built in 1983, definitely in a superior class as parsonages go. Eustis was recognized in 1986 as one of five small towns in Nebraska that were thriving, rather than declining. It was and is known for its German heritage and has an annual celebration called "Wurst Tag" (Sausage Day in German), which falls on the second weekend in

June. In 1987, it came the same week we moved to town.

On the first Sunday in July I presided at Holy Communion for the first time in six years. Both of my churches were still using little cubes of white bread and grape juice in tiny individual cups. I noticed the juice in Eustis tasted different, and asked the steward what brand it was. "Welch's," she said, and showed me the bottle. It turned out this child of the Depression was watering the drink to save a few pennies.

The Eustis school was very progressive and had updated facilities, including an indoor swimming pool. The town had a grocery store, drug store, clinic, strong bank, several shops supporting farms and ranches, a coffee shop, and two bar/cafes. They were also just 13 miles from Interstate 80 and had cable television, which we greatly appreciated.

The Eustis church was built in 1976. It had a very nice office, with generous shelf and cabinet space. Windows from the old church were moved into the new sanctuary, which gave it a charming atmosphere. I had very talented musicians at both Farnam and Eustis.

One thing about our new community surprised me: even Deutschlanders had difficulty pronouncing "Li - poldt." We quickly came to appreciate the German recipes and Chris learned to make pretzels, which she continues to share. At year end, I discovered reduced income and increased allowable deductions helped us avoid paying income taxes, and we no longer had to feel guilty about supporting the ridiculous Reagan defense build-up.

This story is a part of the folklore of the Eustis and Farnam churches. Throughout most of the 1950's they were served by a pastor named Benjamin Hart. Pastor Hart was diligent and effective in his work and retired from the ministry after he left Eustis in 1960. He was 67 then, and had served as a pastor for 32 years.

During his career, he picked up several methods which became habits that assisted him. He was remembered for visiting all his parishioners in their homes twice a year. He was also very careful to dismiss Sunday services at 12 pm sharp. He controlled his sermon time with a lifesaver candy. He discovered they always took between 12 and 15 minutes to dissolve in his mouth. So when he began to preach, he popped in a lifesaver and when it was gone, he quit.

On one particular Sunday, he finished with the early service at Farnam, and was preparing to leave for the 11 am service at Eustis. As he reached to open his car door, a button fell from the cuff of his suit jacket. He simply picked it up and slipped it into the front pocket of his suit, and drove the twelve miles to Eustis.

Without giving the button another thought, Pastor Hart began his sermon at Eustis in his usual manner. After fifteen minutes, Mrs. Hart knew something was wrong. The preacher continued his exhortation without catching her signal. Another ten minutes went by. All eyes were on the pastor's wife. Finally, the noon whistle blew, and the preacher ran out of things to say. He then noticed the frantic look on his partner's face. He pulled an unused lifesaver from his suit pocket, and in his mouth he found a button. This was one time when a method of time management failed.

Pastor Hart served at Eustis for eight years, and wanted to stay one more and retire. A group asked the Bishop to move him and prevailed. Among his closest friends were Laura and Reinhold Yeutter, parents of former Agriculture Secretary Clayton Yeutter. Because of the mistreatment of their friend, the Yeutters transferred to First Methodist in Cozad. Mrs. Yeutter died in 1989, and gave her home and a generous cash gift to the Cozad church.

My son tried to help me with time management. Shortly after moving to Eustis, he started timing my sermons. I didn't know about it until the end of the year, when he gave me a report which included averages, longest, and shortest. I think he kept it up until he went to college. He wrote the times on a calendar in his room, and I checked it every once in a while.

As a banker, I required every borrower to furnish me with an annual property statement. This helped me to know them intimately. Upon returning to the pastorate, I pondered the idea of having members of my flock complete an annual spiritual inventory, thereby allowing me to better understand their needs. However, I also knew most folks don't want their pastor to know them that well.

Before school started, Seth went out for football. Eustis was playing 8-man, and this was his first year for organized football of any kind. Though there were only 14 on the team, the coach did very little substituting, and the freshmen saw almost no game time. They won 2, lost seven.

In November he went out for basketball, and was one of five boys on the team. In the third game of the season, three guys fouled out, leaving Seth and another freshman on the court. Despite this, they only lost by three points. In January two more boys joined the team and things improved, but they only won 1 game that season.

I wore a clerical collar occasionally when I was young. I did this partly because I wanted to experiment, and partly because I wanted to appear more learned. Often I wore it when I made hospital calls. Once I visited a church member in a Catholic hospital in Concordia, Kansas. Chris and I got some strange looks as we walked hand-in-hand through the lobby. I was adorned in a dark suit and a clerical collar. Chris looked very nice, and was also 8½ months pregnant.

The same year I moved to Eustis, a young friend graduated from seminary and began serving his first church in another small town in southwest Nebraska. This pastor was very "high church." His services were quite liturgical and he wore a clerical collar every day. Two ladies from the church went to McCook to visit with the DS. "Everyone likes Randy," they said, "but you must get him to stop wearing that collar!"

Curtis Trenhaile, the DS, said he would "take care of it." A week later he was in Lincoln and went to a Catholic bookstore, and bought a clerical shirt and collar. The next time he appeared at my friend's church, he wore that collar. No one complained again about the way their preacher dressed, at least not in the presence of our DS.

One of my favorite things in the ministry was a session called the Fellowship of Learning. Held in Grand Island in January, it was a chance to hear some scholarly presentations, lots of gossip, and spend time with clergy friends. Some of us would share intoxicants, and this led to interesting encounters. One year five of us rounded up a sober driver, and went to a local café about 1 am. As the waitress was taking our order, my friend Curtis piped up, "I'll bet you can't guess what we do for a living." She replied, "no, I can't." Then he said we were all Methodist pastors, to the chagrin of everyone else.

The next year we did the same thing, headed to the same eating place, but there was one fellow who hadn't been with us the previous year. In the car I told him what Curtis said the year before. When the waitress showed up, the new guy said, "I'll bet you can't guess what we do for a living." Everybody groaned, and he said, "we're all certified public accountants," and he proceeded to give her tax advice.

William Sloane Coffin, a UCC pastor and chaplain at Yale University, was our featured presenter one year. He was an entertaining speaker and advocate for social justice. While he was talking about another issue, he stopped, and said "you people (UMC) have a got a real problem with your reluctance to accept gay persons into the ordained ministry." Then he went back to his other subject. He was truly someone ahead of the curve.

My family started watching **As The World Turns**[35] in 1956. I got hooked on it because it was on over the noon hour. My grandma was obsessed with it, had a Hughes family picture in her living room, and wrote to Mom with updates as if these folks lived in her neighborhood. In seminary a group of male students were watching ATWT in my apartment. Our wives all had jobs, and one guy remarked, "this is just the reverse of the real world." My classes in pastoral care and counseling involved writing practicums that were later discussed by the group. More than once, I submitted a situation faced by the folks on ATWT.

When Seth was a baby and my office was in the parsonage, I got hooked on a couple more soaps. I discovered several other UM clergy folks were also ATWT devotees. We happened to be eating lunch together at Fellowship of Learning and were discussing the latest adventures of the TV folks. A non-fan asked, "are these people members of your church?" I lost interest and quit watching the show long before it went off the air in 2010.

The movie **Naked Gun** had a scene where the star, Leslie Nielsen, addressed the media wearing a wireless microphone. After his brief speech he went to the men's room with the mike still on, and you can guess the rest.[36] My DS, Curtis, and I were in a pastor's office getting ready to lead a district worship event. The pastor gave us each a wireless mike and we proceeded to joke around and act silly. After a while, the pastor said, "Oh gosh, I forgot those mikes were live!" We stood silent for a few seconds, then he said "just kidding!"

One year I gave the invocation at Farnam High School athletic banquet. The guest speaker was a successful basketball coach from a nearby town. Most of his speech concerned a recent experience wherein he'd fallen from a tree while hunting deer. This left him paralyzed for several months, but he was now gaining strength. Because he was a "born again Christian," he said that as he lay on the ground waiting for help, he asked God why this had happened to him. If he had asked me, I would have said maybe God was punishing him for slaughtering beautiful, innocent creatures.

When I was in high school, I read **No Time On My Hands** by Nellie Snyder Yost, who lived in North Platte. She was widowed in 1968 and later married a Farnam native. They attended Silver Dollar Club dinners at Farnam every month, and I enjoyed visiting with her there.

In June of 1988, Chris and I took our church youth group to Colorado for a week. Janice and her family came to Nebraska that summer, and in July my Mom had arranged for a Beatrice photographer to take a portrait of all eight of us. After that Chris, Seth, Ana and I went to the Centennial Celebration at Douglas, and later went as far south as Dallas. It's a good thing Chris kept a diary, because I forgot that trip.

In 1988 I bought my first personal computer: an Apple "IIc Plus." This was a great little machine with a built-in floppy drive and color monitor. The whole package with a printer cost $1,700. I started writing my sermons on AppleWorks, and using many useful database and spreadsheet programs as well.

In 1988, Seth's sophomore year, the football situation improved. Because of his speed, he became a running back. In his first game at Elwood he had three long rushes and recovered two fumbles, but Eustis lost 52-6. On October 14th, his mother's 39th birthday, Seth scored a touchdown and his team finally got a victory!

The basketball situation was somewhat better for Seth in 1988-89, but being a 5'9" post player was difficult. However, he scored in double figures nearly every game. In their game against Medicine Valley, something very impressive happened. Three Eustis boys fouled out, leaving four on the floor. The MV coach asked for a conference with the referees, and suggested they waive the rule disqualifying players with 5 fouls. His team had a comfortable lead, and he felt there was no reason not to have ten kids playing. The refs agreed, and the game continued. At a special 9th and 10th grade tournament, Eustis beat Elwood with Seth scoring 24 points. His picture was in the **North Platte Telegraph** that week as well.

In November 1988 I was in Baltimore, Maryland. I visited the church called the birthplace of Methodism, and then found Mount Olivet Cemetery. In this cemetery is the grave of pioneer bishop Francis Asbury and in the same lot, E. Stanley Jones is buried. Jones was a great leader of Methodism and missionary to India. I have a dozen of his books including an autographed copy of **Is the Kingdom of God Realism?**[37] I've written more concerning how Dr. Jones helped me develop a theological method in Chapter 26.

During the 1988 presidential campaign, the "L-word" became a hot political issue. The "L-word," of course, was "liberal." George Bush discovered that people were suspicious, even afraid, of liberals. So he proceeded to stick that label on Michael Dukakis at each opportunity. A majority of voters came to believe that liberals like Dukakis would spend us into a depression, release every dangerous African-American prisoner, and destroy all of our traditional institutions. Former Secretary of the Interior James Watt was the champion liberal basher. He said, "I never use the words Republicans and Democrats. It's liberals and Americans." George H. W. Bush won a remarkable come-from-behind, landslide victory.

Most people degrade their opponents by labeling them. In 1964, Lyndon Johnson called Barry Goldwater a "radical" and it stuck. Comedians and columnists have described Dan Quayle as incompetent, and it is nearly impossible for him to shake that brand. We all libel people by labeling them. We do it from our insecurity. We once said, "Sticks and stones may break my bones, but words can never hurt me." But words, labels, do hurt. They are insulting and dehumanizing.

It is never correct to say anyone is completely liberal or conservative; we are always a combination of the two. For instance, when George Bush announced Michael Dukakis was a card-carrying member of American Civil Liberties Union, he implied that the ACLU was a "liberal" organization. In reality, the ACLU has a very conservative purpose: defending the Constitution of the United States, a document written over 200 years ago and based on solid tradition.

In 1989 during a confirmation class discussion at Farnam, a girl asked if there was a literal place called "hell." Before I could give some ideas about the subject, another one asked, "we certainly don't believe in that stuff, do we?" I said no, but still tried to explain the various metaphors the Bible uses for "hell." Some kids told their parents and a few called to ask questions, but a grandmother invited me to discuss the issue. She gave me several reasons why hell was a real place, and asked point blank when our church abandoned the concept of hell. I told her in all honesty, I had been a Methodist/United Methodist my entire life, and knew hundreds of pastors and not one believed the way she did. By implication she, not I, was out of sync with the church.

There continued to be some squabbles at the Farnam church with a very small group. They persisted in scheduling events at the church without consulting me, and I let them know any use of church facilities had to be approved by the Administrative Council. They ignored this, and contacted someone to lead an evangelism event. He called me discuss the situation and I brought this to the Administrative Council. The self-appointed evangelists lost their credibility, and pulled back a little.

One person in this group was upset the new hymnal had included 3 versions of the Lord's Prayer. She especially did not like the ecumenical version which substituted "sins" for trespasses, and left off the doxology at the end. She argued that the version we Methodists used matched exactly what Jesus taught. I asked, "you don't think Jesus spoke in English do you?" "Well, I guess not," she answered.

These molehill/mountain things kill churches. After a while they tried a new tactic, and went directly to Bishop Hearn who diffused the situation, but I must admit I was a wounded healer. When I went back to the pastorate, I naively thought Methodism had been purged of mindless fundamentalism.

Ana, a seventh grader, was slowly realizing her athleticism was much like her parents and concentrated more on musical pursuits. At the spring concert in 1989 she sang a solo, "Put Your Head On My Shoulder."

One of our friends in Eustis was a talented young woman named Wendy Johnson. Wendy's family and ours developed a strong friendship for several reasons. First, they had three teenagers at the same time we had two teenagers. Second, Wendy's uncle Jim Herstein is married to Chris' cousin Wanda, thereby making Amy Herstein a first cousin to the Johnson kids and a second cousin, once removed, to the Leypoldt kids. Third, Wendy's dad was a computer whiz, and contributed generously to my computer habit, even though he remained loyal to Apples and I converted to MS-DOS.

An unusual thing about the Johnson-Leypoldt friendship was the fact that the Johnsons were lapsed Methodists. All five of them were members of the Eustis UMC. The boys faithfully took part in UMYF activities. Their dad was in and out of my office several times a month, and we shared coffee at Das Aulden Haus or the Drawbar on many occasions. But regular worship attendees they were not.

Wendy was the oldest, got straight A's, and won numerous drama awards in High School. I heard her give a presentation at a Mother/Daughter luncheon in our church. Sometime later, we were sitting on the bleachers watching the boys play baseball. I complimented Wendy and told her I would like her to make a talk in church sometime, maybe even speak for me when I went on vacation. To which she replied, "Oh, I could never do that! I'm not very religious." My response was, "Well, neither am I!" Wendy laughed, her mother and dad laughed, some other folks laughed, but at least one regular Methodist was not amused. I heard her say, "Humpf! I'll have to think about that one for a while!"

A basic truth of Christianity is that Jesus came to free us from the yoke of religion. He said: "Come to me all you that are weary and are carrying heavy burdens, and I will give you rest. Take my yoke upon you, and learn from me; for I am gentle and humble in heart, and you will find rest for your souls. For my yoke is easy, and my burden is light (Matthew 11:28-30)." Jesus came to release us from the burdens of the

Law. His Way did not include useless rules and regulations, but simple faith in God and trust in human goodness.

In June of 1989 Seth went to Washington, D.C., New York, and other eastern cities for a 4-H Citizenship Focus. He was with a busload of kids from Frontier and surrounding counties. When he got back, he said, "I didn't know there were any other liberal kids in the state," and he wondered if our church offered anything like this. Of course we did, right up the road at Camp Comeca. He went to Senior High Rainbow Camp that summer, and became involved in District and Conference youth events throughout his high school years, as did his sister.

Wurst Tag was a great fundraiser for many community groups, and very profitable for the three food and drink establishments. For those of us who lived on the edge of downtown, it was challenging. Booze leads to full bladders and empty brains. It was the only night of the year when I locked the church.

Chris was upset with the trash and trespass crowd in 1988, and was prepared for them in 1989. Our town employed extra security, and regular law enforcement was on duty. Several people tried to get in the church, and then urinated in the bushes. Dozens considered our lawn to be a dump. Twice she called security, and they did the best they could. Chris asked people to get off the lawn and finally she loaded the BB gun, and nailed two of the culprits. Late in the evening she heard a group of boys walking back to their cars, and one of them said "watch out for the church lady!" At the next Chamber meeting I brought up these issues, and new policies made for better experiences in the succeeding years.

That summer Ana went to a Junior High camp at Comeca. It was supposed to be United Methodist and the director was a UMC pastor, but he brought some Pentecostal-style counselors with him. She called me to tell me they were pressuring the kids into "salvation decisions." I thought she wanted to come home, but she wanted ammunition! She started counseling the other kids to push back.

One July evening Chris and I went for a walk on the East Canyon Road, south of Eustis. We had a plastic garbage bag with us to pick up the numerous beer and pop cans in the ditch, and on the side of the road. My job was to scour the ditches, scoop the cans up to the road, and Chris would smash them and put them into the bag. More than once, she told me "to watch out for snakes," which are also numerous in Frontier County. But I laughed, and continued inspecting the tall weeds in the trenches. There had been a recent rain, and many of the cans were full of mud and water. Thus, I dutifully shook them empty, before throwing them up to the gravel.

I came upon a treasure. Ten extra-large Coors beer cans were all piled together. I hurried over and began the process of grabbing, up-side-down shaking, and tossing. Chris scrunched them down, and they disappeared into the black bag. The fifth one was different. It was heavy. I figured it was full of something, but when I shook it nothing came out. I gave it a closer look. "Must be caked-up mud," I said to Chris as I threw the can on the road.

Very quickly the mystery was solved. From a peaceful slumber in the silver cylinder, came a slithering serpent. He darted quickly into the ditch, which I more quickly departed. Chris was running so fast that gravel and dust were clouding up behind her. The strange combination of fear and adrenalin, enabled her scream at the top of her lungs all the while she ran. Seth used to run an 11.2 in the 100; his mother would have beaten him that night.

I emerged from the ditch laughing at my wife. I wondered what a passerby would think if they saw or heard what was happening. I thought a minute about going back for the five or six cans still in the ditch. "Naaaah!!" Then I picked up the half-filled garbage sack, and began to jog in Chris' direction. I started thinking about holding that can close to my face, and jogged a little faster. The next walk we took we stayed in town, and left the garbage bag in the garage.

+++

In July 1989, we took a family vacation that included a stop in Albion. Then on to Sioux City on July 19, the same day United Flight 232 crashed. The president of Westmar College was a friend from college, and I introduced him to Seth at the Nebraska UMC conference in June. Seth was starting to think about colleges, and we made an appointment to tour Westmar in Le Mars, Iowa. From there we went to several places in Minnesota, including a baseball game at the Metrodome. We then motored to Clear Lake to spend some time with our Ellis and Grenz friends.

We got back to Eustis on August 2, and learned about a developing soap opera in the communities of Eustis and Farnam. The state required high schools to have an enrollment of 25 to stay open. Farnam had recruited exchange students for several years to guarantee that minimum. They played 6-man football, and were very successful. Enrollment at Eustis had slipped to 38 in 1987, but rebounded. They had some good sized elementary classes, so their future was more secure.

Many schools joined cooperatives to strengthen their programs, especially athletics. A group of Farnam parents asked their school board to work with Eustis to form a football co-op; the board refused. Two families decided to move to Elwood so their boys could participate in sports, and perhaps have a better chance at college athletic scholarships. That left Farnam with five boys.

The Farnam board reconsidered, and asked Eustis to form a cooperative. Two weeks after the football team started practicing, the Eustis school board agreed to the co-op which was good. They also made the Eustis coach an assistant to a fellow from Farnam who had zero experience. Say what? We did some community organizing, and the board flipped flopped. Seth was leading rusher on the football team and scored three touchdowns twice, including one game where he scored all the team's points.

Because of the coop, the 1989-90 basketball team had more boys, thus more potential. Unfortunately they had their third coach in three years, and things went from bad to worse. Seth played through injuries and illness, kept his grades up, and was involved in speech and mock trial. Ana was an 8th grader, was in sports and music, and was doing a lot of babysitting.

We were unable to sell our Douglas house when we moved in 1987. We found renters, but it wasn't an ideal situation. We finally got it sold in 1990 and netted $33,000, which was what we paid for it in 1981. We spent about $17,000 for improvements, so basically paid that amount for renting our own house.

In the spring of 1990 Seth competed in the 100, 200, and 400 yard dashes, and barely missed qualifying for state track meet in the 100. Ana was the discus thrower on her track team. I had five kids in my confirmation class at Eustis, including my daughter. On May 13 she graduated from the 8th grade, and on June 3 she was confirmed at the Eustis UMC.

Congresswoman Virginia Smith had served Nebraska's 3rd District (which included Eustis) for 16 years, and in 1990 decided to retire. Her heir apparent was a state senator from nearby Lexington named Bill Barrett. Though he knew I was a Democrat, our banker Don Brockmeier invited me to a gathering to meet Barrett. It was an informal meeting with a small number in attendance. Don introduced me as a former banker, who was now a pastor in Eustis.

Barrett acted surprised and said, "That's quite a change. Whatever induced you to do it?" I told Mr. Barrett that I was making more money year after year, and I was afraid I would soon be too wealthy to remain a Democrat. I didn't want to risk eternal security by registering as a Republican, so I started preaching again. Don wasn't too amused, but Barrett laughed and laughed. Later on I saw him pointing at me, and repeating my story to a couple of his associates. It's probably a good thing I didn't express my thoughts about nationalizing banks, oil companies, and health care.

May 24, 1990 was a beautiful spring day in southwest Nebraska. That night we were sound asleep with the windows open. I woke up when I heard something hit the deck, which was right outside our bedroom. After a couple more clunks I got up to investigate, and saw baseball-sized hailstones visiting our peaceful village. We were now a three-car family, and Seth's Daytona got clobbered, while the other two were safely inside the garage.

I was having some vision problems in the summer of 1990. For a while I tried the self-cure approach, wearing reading glasses and enlarging everything I read on Sundays. Finally, I went to see Dr. Harvey, the optometrist in Lexington. He put me in a chair and gazed through his slit lamp bio microscope and pronounced, "first problem is you have your contacts in the wrong eyes."

We had another busy summer in 1990. Seth and I both went to AC in June, and he and Ana went to church camp in July. Seth did farm work in Eustis while the rest of us went to Clear Lake. Seth was determined to have a big senior year in sports, so spent many evenings in the school weight room.

In 1989 the UMC in Nebraska began efforts to create several new churches in our state. Known as "Vision Unlimited," its goal was to raise $5 million and start seven new congregations. I was asked to visit seven congregations, and encourage them to get on board with Vision Unlimited.

One stormy night in August of 1990, I went to a small town about fifty miles west of Eustis. They say Montana is big sky country, but if you've been to Frontier or Lincoln County in Nebraska, you can see for miles and miles and when there's a storm coming, it's quite a sight to behold. I arrived safely and found the little white frame church. In the church basement, there were 8 persons representing 55 members. This was a church that did not pay their apportionments, and their fair share for Vision Unlimited would have been about $1,500. They politely listened to my presentation. After a few questions, one of them said, "We are a small, poor church, and we have been saving our money to put a bathroom down here in the basement."

As I drove back home in the darkness, I decided that church would be gone in 20 years. They expressed no desire to help others. Faith dies when toilets take priority over evangelism.

The **North Platte Telegraph** published its 1990 fall sports preview, and Seth was featured as a "player to watch." In the first game at Elwood he had a 70-yard kickoff return for a touchdown and another TD on a 40 yard run from scrimmage. In the second game he was returning a kick and hurt his wrist when tackled, which knocked him out of the game. The next morning we went to Kearney, and found out the wrist was broken.

Obviously disappointed, we headed home and stopped at McDonald's for lunch. In the kitchen, I spied our former Douglas pastor frying hamburgers; he had been forced into retirement for various reasons. On the drive home I tried to be philosophical, and told Seth he would quickly get past his setback, but our former pastor had a lifetime of bad luck. He healed pretty quickly, and was able to play a little at the end of the season.

In December 1990, an unchurched woman living in a village 25 miles from Eustis died. Her mother-in-law was a faithful member of the Eustis UMC, and her family asked me to conduct the funeral in our church. When I met with the family her daughter said, "Mom believed in God, but we don't want any scripture in the service." I politely told her it wasn't possible for me to conduct a funeral without biblical references.

I knew the deceased was a bit unlikable, and was surprised to see one of her brothers-in-law at the service. His wife told me, "he's only here to make sure she's really dead." After the committal a couple told me how much they appreciated my services, and said they had prayed I would say exactly what I said. So I guess they were applauding themselves.

We had a beautiful church facility in Eustis. It was built in 1975 and was fully accessible. It had one design flaw that created huge problems when we lived there. The architect had placed the water pipes in the ceiling above the kitchen. On a Saturday morning in February 1989 I went to my office, and heard the sound of water escaping from busted pipes. I shut off the main source of water, and called my faithful Trustees who called others who helped cleaned up the mess. A plumber repaired the lines. We also discovered the outside shut-off was buried below the sidewalk, and that was corrected in the spring.

In December of 1990 we had a 48 hour period where the temperature remained below zero. Several pipes in the Eustis church froze once again. This time we vented the kitchen ceiling, to allow warmer air to the water lines.

The little town of Eustis had a wonderful newspaper called the **Eustis News.** In February 1991, I read a blurb in that paper that upset me. The editor of the paper, who lived in Curtis, was a United Methodist named "Chas" Greenlee. Chas used his column to take a swipe at our new UMC hymnal. He remarked about how he missed the old songs in church, and how terrible the new hymnals were. You might agree about singing so-called "old hymns," but you'd better get your facts straight before dismissing all the careful scholarship and work that goes into producing a new hymnal. Chas got some time in my next sermon and a rather lengthy letter to the editor.

Having said this, I still don't understand why *Above The Hills Of Time* was left out of the 1989 UMC Hymnal, and why *We Give Thee But Thine Own* has disappeared, but I don't dwell on it too much.

Seth's senior basketball season was a huge disappointment. He had a slow start because his right wrist was still healing. Possibly the best thing to happen was when he accidentally broke the nose of a hotshot wannabe from Brady. He did very well in track and his 400 relay team qualified for state, but a bad hamstring kept him from running.

As written, I was never much of an athlete. I readily admit to living vicariously through the accomplishments of my brothers in high school, my son, and my nephew Ted who played for the Huskers from 1994 to 1997.

Moving On

originally written for our 1991 Christmas Epistle

Seth turned eighteen on April 3 this year and on Saturday afternoon, May 11, he and his eleven classmates received diplomas from Eustis High School. It's hard to describe how I felt that day. I guess I was 40% happy and 60% sad.

I keep thinking about the old days. Times like April 3, 1973 when I was nervously chewing on my pipe, and trying to concentrate on the 10 o'clock news in the waiting room of the Geneva hospital. Dr. Ashby walked in and said, "Well, you've got a bouncing baby boy" (he actually said that). In a few minutes, a nurse pushed Chris and a tiny blue bundle down the hallway in a hospital bed. I walked over and peeled back the blanket, and saw my son for the first time. Five days later I brought them home, and I held Seth for the first time. While Chris rested, I laid him on my chest and he slept there all the rest of the afternoon.

I remember his first day of school in Hebron. We were both acting big and brave, until I stopped the car. He looked up at me with those bright blue eyes, and I decided to walk him to the schoolhouse door. He still wouldn't let go of my hand, so I went with him down the hall to the kindergarten room. And he was scared and I was scared, but we both made it through the morning.

When Seth was six we moved to Douglas, and he was the new kid and got picked on. Later, he was the "rich" banker's son everybody picked on. When he was thirteen, he scored 21 points against Unadilla in THE game of the 1981 Junior High basketball season. From then on he was top dog in Douglas. However, it didn't last long.

He started over when we came to Eustis in June of 1987. He never did bust through the clique that ran things; but he cracked it in several places. In the summer of 1989, he discovered the world was filled with creative ideas and wonderful people. He visited Washington, D.C. and attended a UM youth camp. He started focusing. In 1990 he chose to attend our church's Christmas Conference and family activities instead of staying home to practice basketball. This cost him his starting position, but everyone in town knew Seth was a winner and the coach was a loser. When George Bush and his oil friends started bombing Iraq, Seth wore the green ribbon of protest on his basketball uniform. My little boy was truly an adult.

The pianist starts "Pomp and Circumstance," and we dutifully rise to honor the class of 1991. Seth and the others march across the gym floor and up to the stage, and take their seats. Pastor Gronstal speaks to the kids, and three of them make speeches. The awards and honors are announced. The pianist plays "Wind Beneath My Wings," and the graduates walk out among the crowd to present roses to the mothers. The kids are back on stage. The diplomas are presented. They march out to some rock song chosen by the group.

Afterward our relatives and friends came to our house, and we ate and talked and laughed and saluted the graduate. When they all left, I retreated across the back yard to my church office. I plopped into my chair, raised my feet to the desk, tipped my head back, and closed my eyes. I tried to think about tomorrow's sermon. But instead I felt this tiny, 7-pound boy sleeping peacefully on my chest. And I held him there next to my heart for a few minutes longer.

+++

Since Eustis was a small town and away from major highways, we didn't get many travelers stopping because they needed assistance. The village board had the practice of sending folks to the grocery store for bread, lunch meat, milk or juice; and to one of the gas stations for fuel, and then reimbursing the merchants. One time I was in my church office on a late summer afternoon. A woman came in along with her 14-year-old son. She said they'd been traveling, ran out of money, and needed gas and food. She also said they'd driven around town and thought the Lutheran Church looked a little shabby, so they chose us to help them because we had a newer building.

I called both the grocery store and nearest gas station to make sure they were still open. I explained our town's procedure for traveler's aid. The young man responded in amazement, "don't you have a restaurant in this town?"

+++

After graduation, Seth went to work for Eustis Welding. His major assignment was pounding dents out of irrigation pipe. In between he did a lot of other things. In June, he was the youth representative to AC from the Southwest District. At conference he was recognized with a "Youth In Lay Ministry" award. He was also chosen by his peers to attend the Jurisdictional and General youth convocations. He also attended the AC Youth Ministries Event and Senior High Rainbow Camp.

In July/August of 1991, we went to Oregon for the wedding of my niece, Jennifer, to Bill Hagerup. We drove through Colorado, Utah, and Arizona, and stayed a couple of nights in Las Vegas. It was 113 degrees on this, our first visit, to Sin City. Chris, Ana, and I walked around on the strip, in and out of the casinos. They were building a bigger and better Caesar's Palace. You don't even have to walk into Caesar's; just step on a conveyor belt and it will take you inside. I remember seeing two people outside in the hot sun with a sign that read, "Feed a homeless child tonight." It was hard to believe there would be any poverty in Las Vegas. Very few people, including myself, responded to their plea. We walked past a fountain. Coins, thrown in for luck I suppose, covered the base. Faith dies when we seek the quick buck and ignore hungry children, I thought.

On that same trip we made our way to Victorville, California which is home to Mr. and Mrs. Roy Rogers. Ol' Roy and Dale kept their stuff in a museum in Victorville. A brochure described it this way "...it isn't only about the West. It is about an idealized America, a country of small towns, family farms, fraternal halls, church picnics and Fourth of July parades." In other words, it was about my childhood and yours. They later moved to Branson, and closed completely in 2003.

It was a thrill to learn Roy and Dale brought their children up in a small-town Methodist Church, and that Roy was a Mason and a Shriner. I got to see Trigger the horse, Bullet the dog, and Clarabelle the jeep. I even said, "Hi" to Roy, Jr. or "Dusty" who runs the place.

When we started our tour at 9 in the morning, two ladies a little older than me came in about the same time. At 11:30, when we were leaving, they were still sitting by the front door. You see, Ol' Roy sometimes stopped by his museum and they were prepared to meet up with their old childhood hero. I thought about it, too, but my wife and daughter dissuaded me.

I don't think I joined up when I was little, but I found a certificate in an antique store, framed it, and check it daily to make certain I remain in compliance.

Roy Rogers Rider Club

1. Be neat and clean.

2. Be courteous and polite.

3. Always obey your parents.

4. Protect the weak and help them.

5. Be brave but never take chances.

6. Study hard and learn all you can.

7. Be kind to animals and care for them.

8. Eat all your food and never waste any.

9. Love God and go to Sunday School regularly.

10. Always respect our flag and our country.

+++

Because of his work and other activities Seth was unable to drive out to Oregon with us in July. However, he and his uncle Gary flew from Lincoln to Portland on August 7, and then he came home with us. Less than a week later, we packed him up and sent him off to Nebraska Wesleyan where he moved into Plainsman Hall and reported for football practice the same day. He joined Theta Chi fraternity, Young Democrats, and Nebraskans for Peace. He had found new friends, was cultivating and refining his individuality. He was moving on.

+++

When my kids became active in District and Conference youth activities, I went along as an adult counselor most of the time. We had several youth from Eustis and Farnam, who also became involved during these years. There were summer camps, occasional Sunday afternoon rallies, Youth AC in June and a conference the last week of December.

One day I was driving a carload of kids to a District youth event. We went through Cambridge on highway 34, and I saw the words "Jesus Saves" painted on concrete west of town. One of the kids told me he knew some local boys who crawled up there, and added "Green Stamps" to the message.

At one of the December events we were divided into small groups for discussions. At the first session we introduced ourselves, and said a few things about our lives. At the end of the conference I found out one young man was not who he said he was. He traded identities with a buddy because a girl he liked was in our group. I thought he was clever, and nothing more was made of it. The two boys who made the switcheroo were from Geneva, and six years later were my parishioners.

Kitchen Patrol

Also written for our 1991 Christmas Epistle

Chris now holds down three part-time jobs: Cozad Jack and Jill delicatessen, cook at the Eustis Senior Center, and cook at the Eustis school. She used to work one or two nights per week, so the kids and I had to fix our own supper. Actually Chris left me detailed instructions, and I went from there. Except that I embellished here and there. I always made superb gravy, but the kids wouldn't admit it to me. Ana even told Chris "to keep Dad out of her kitchen." Once my brothers made fun of my French toast which I call "grease bread," but they all ate seconds and thirds.

Lately Chris is working over the noon hour. Now I only have to please myself. I'm thinking of starting a restaurant called "Leftovers." This is some of the best food in the world. All you need is a microwave and barbecue sauces and cheeses. You can add almost anything to a five-day-old casserole, and it will taste great.

The jobs have been good for Chris. It has allowed people to relate to her rather than to a role imposed by a spouse. She also belongs to an extension club, helps with the UMYF, plays for the Cherub Choir, and will be president of a church circle. And she makes great casseroles which get better and better each day.

The Cheerleader

Also written for our 1991 Christmas Epistle

In case you haven't guessed, writing is therapeutic for me. I have a confession to make. I hope I can trust my dearest friends and relatives to keep this confidential.

The problem is that I am in love with a high school cheerleader. I know that sounds dumb, but I can't help myself. I suppose you think I'm going through some kind of second childhood, and maybe I am. But I still can't help it. This girl is so cute and so lively and so perfect. She makes me feel like I'm fifteen again.

I've long preferred cheerleader watching to game watching. Only when Seth played did I pay much attention to the game. Back in Albion I was the cheerleader's advisor. There were no girls' sports in those days, and most girls were confused about things like offense and defense. Also, how many points baskets were worth, and who those guys in the striped shirts were. So I used to sit on the front row, and advise the cheerleaders. The guys on the court were sweating and bleeding and getting whipped most of the time. However, I was across the gym scoring points with the cheerleaders.

I became a pretty darned good judge of cheerleaders. That's some background on why I fell for this girl. She's fifteen and a sophomore at Eustis. She's 5'1" and has strawberry blonde hair. I have to be real careful about my feelings for her because she attends my church. She was in my Confirmation Class a couple of years ago. She sings - sometimes in the choir, occasionally a solo. She plays piano, and gets good grades. I think she ranks first in her class right now.

I really need some help on this one. At ball games, I always sit where I can watch her real good. Once a guy next to me asked me the score and I replied, "I think it's two-bits to four-bits." Another time the coach was yelling at the referee and someone asked, "what'd he say?" and I answered, "Black and White. Fight! Fight!"

At half-time I sit back and watch for her to leave the gym. Then I seek her out and make small talk. She's always nice to me, but I'm sure she has no idea about my infatuation. I suppose I'm not the first 44-year old father of two teenagers who has had this problem, but still it concerns me. My crush on her causes me to do some crazy things. She thinks my 1984 Mercury Cougar is a really fine machine. Sometimes we go for a drive, and I let her take the wheel. Occasionally Chris and I will sponsor teen dances, and I'll get close enough to see who she's dancing with. Once she saw me, and asked me to dance.

I'm sure this thing will pass. If you have any good advice, please write me. I'm uxorious in Eustis.

Ana turned fifteen on February 21, 1991. Soon thereafter she acquired her learner's permit. It's hard to imagine how a tiny slip of paper could cause suicidal thoughts in a grown man. But it did. And I refuse to say anything more about it. Ana was an A student. She was a pianist and a member of the church choir and the Blue Notes, the High School swing choir. She was a delegate to YAC, part of the UMC District and Conference Councils on Youth Ministries all through high school. She attended the CYME and the Senior High Rainbow Camp. In the fall of 1990 she was on the volleyball team, and also began her first year as a cheerleader for the Eustis/Farnam Knights. The problem with her being a cheerleader, is that it causes 44-year-old men to fall in love with her.

Airwaves

Also taken from our 1991 Christmas Epistle

On average I listen to the radio three times during the day: first, when showering and shaving in the morning; second, when going someplace in the car; third, when returning home in the car after going someplace. The first is most important because it helps set the mood for the day.

On my first morning in Eustis I knew I was in trouble. My shower radio only picked up two stations: KRVN-AM and KOOC-FM. The former called itself the "Best Farm Station in the Nation" and the latter cleverly, "KC 104 and-a-half FM." In the car it was better. At least there was an oldies channel in Kearney and a kid station in North Platte. But first thing in the morning I had to live with Paul Harvey, the Kansas auction news, and timely weather reports like, "maybe it'll rain today" and "it will be either partly cloudy or partly sunny in Eastern Montana."

A wonderful thing happened to me on the way to the shower one morning. From the radio I heard Tchaikovsky and Strauss and Debussy and others. I shaved and showered in a symphony. The news was from Washington and London and New York City. The baseball scores were actually from last night's games! More music from Beethoven and Mendelssohn. I didn't even like that stuff before. But after 1,300 mornings filled with live reports from the Cozad City Council and tunes that were mostly about young boys from the country who went to the city and took up with bad girls and got rich and lost it all because the bad girls taught them to drink whiskey, so they went back home in used pickup trucks and met up with nice girls who were married to mean guys who came home from Desert Storm and shot them up, so they left home again and ended up in an alley behind the Grand Ol' Opry and saw Elvis and became Pentecostal preachers, I was ready for something different.

Thank God I'm a country boy who was forced to discover Nebraska Public Radio and KLNE-FM in Lexington!

+++

On May 16, 1992 I found myself in an interesting situation. Both Eustis and Farnam had high schools, and each followed the practice of expecting a local pastor to deliver a sermon at the graduation ceremony. Both towns had two preachers who rotated these duties. I knew a whole year ahead, that in 1992 I would be giving the sermon at both Eustis and Farnam High School graduations. It was my turn; no problem. Eustis always had their ceremony on the second Saturday in May at 2:30, and Farnam the next day at 4:30.

Another element enriches this story. In September of 1991 Lana Kotschwar and Nick Cate came to see me about scheduling a May wedding. I remember our meeting very well. We looked at the calendar. "High School graduations are always the second weekend in May, so let's go with Saturday, May 16," I said. And we were all set.

Some time later, the Eustis Board of Education decided to change their commencement to the third Saturday in May. Fortunately I have learned to use a pencil when recording activities on my calendar. So the adjustment was made for May 16: "Graduation Sermon at 2:30; Wedding at 7 pm." Still later, in the very early days of Spring, I began hearing disturbing rumors about the Farnam High School commencement.

You need to know that this was a particularly unique situation. Chad Hill was the only Senior at Farnam last year. His dad was on the school board. So when the family discovered there were several conflicts on the first and second Sundays in May, it seemed an easy thing to change Chad's graduation date to Saturday, May 16. At a March meeting, when there was still plenty of time to print up this one set of commencement announcements, it was done. My calendar for May 16 now read: "Eustis H.S. graduation sermon at 2:30, Farnam H.S. graduation sermon at 4:30, wedding at 7 pm."

All eleven Eustis graduates and the one at Farnam were forced to endure some prayers and preaching. Nick and Lana got married all right. I slept pretty well that night, but it was definitely a day to remember.

Eustis was the only church I served that also owned a cemetery, which was adjacent to the Lutheran cemetery north of town. Our two churches held joint sunrise services every Easter. One year I suggested we go the cemetery for the service. I gathered the youth at the east side of the graveyard and read some Bible verses, and we sang a couple of hymns. At just the right moment the sun popped over the hill, bright and glorious as it could possibly be.

During our five years in this little town, I was in the Church Cemetery dozens of times. Not just for committals, but on clean-up days, and as a part of an evening walk. The earliest graves in this cemetery are found in the extreme southwest corner. Three children of Gottlieb and Katherine Bartruff were stricken with diphtheria and died within one week. This sad story is repeated in many frontier communities. I can only begin to imagine the grief of parents who lose a child, even an adult one. Twice in my ministry I knew couples who suffered the tragic loss of three children. One was Rich and Donna Lawson of Davenport, whose children were killed while riding home in a school bus. Another was Clarence and Evelyn Stewart of Ceresco, who lost three children to a rare form of cancer.

+++

Dean Weissert told me he and another guy were pouring cement for a new sidewalk at the church. They leveled it, and broke for lunch. When they came back they found bicycle tracks in the fresh cement, and went to a neighbor's house where they saw a bike with wet cement on the tires. The woman asked her son if he had ruined the new sidewalk, and he said, "no." She told Dean, "if he said he didn't do it, I believe him."

Dean was born on the family farm in 1917, and graduated from Eustis High School. He was farming when inducted into the army on 10/16/41, and came back home in September 1945. He married a pastor's daughter in 1947 and had three children. His wife was killed in a car accident in 1959, and in 1963 he married Dorothy and later added another child.

Dean was on the Building Committee when the new Eustis UMC was erected in 1976. He had served in every way possible prior to that. When I came to town in 1987, he volunteered to look after the roses the previous pastor had left behind. We shared many a cup of coffee, and he told me stories about his life and times. His first two years in the army were spent stateside. In 1943 he joined 24,000 soldiers on the Queen Elizabeth, which departed from New York City and he ended up in England.

Dean was a staff sergeant trained in communications. His job was to lay telephone wires, and maintain equipment in the field. On June 6, 1944, he was among the troops who landed on the beaches of Normandy, France. Only 500 of the 2 thousand in his unit survived on Omaha Beach. As they moved inland, the fighting was less intense, but still dangerous. The men sat under the shade of trees to write letters home. Dean went to get paper for a friend, and when he returned, the friend was gone. A shell had killed him, leaving chunks of flesh and bone scattered.

He continued at the front for 318 days. He told me about sleeping in trenches with temperatures below freezing, and going for weeks without a shower or change of clothes. Dean headed back to the U.S. on September 11, 1945. Less than two weeks later, he was back on the family farm in Eustis. In August 1994, he returned to Europe to revisit Omaha Beach and other war sites.

Dorothy died in 2010, and Dean moved to Lincoln the next year to be closer to his children. On April 29, 2014, Dean went with Chris and me to Eustis to help celebrate the church's 130th anniversary. On the way home we ran into a big downpour and pulled to the side of the road. After several minutes of being pelted by marble-sized and larger hail stones, we got back on I-80. Dean, a survivor of D-Day and VE-Day said, "I've never been through something quite like this."

Our friends Conley and Elsie Hinrichs also have Eustis connections. Conley retired from the ministry in 1990, and they have been active in First UMC in Lincoln. He served at Eustis and Farnam from 1966 to 1973. Our denomination promotes "open hearts, open minds, and open doors," but Elsie has lived by this motto her whole life.

A Lutheran farm couple retired, and moved into a house near the Eustis parsonage when the Hinrichses were occupants. Elsie was very welcoming, and helped in small ways to get them settled. The old couple had trouble negotiating steps at the Lutheran church, so began attending the Methodist church, which was more accessible. Elsie and others helped them feel at home in the church. They both died in 1973 and left over $80,000 to the Eustis Methodist Church.

+++

I was getting restless, and convinced myself I should try to move to a church in the eastern part of Nebraska. My DS, Curt Trenhaile, had become a very close friend and tried to get me a "good" move in 1991, but it fell through. In the fall of '91 another DS told me he wanted to send me to Auburn. I was counting on it, and threw my hat into the ring in 1992. Bishop Hearn had changed the process, and once you asked for a change it was very hard to reverse the decision. The Auburn pastor stayed put, and I was out on a limb. Very coincidentally, I met and visited with the Plattsmouth pastor at a meeting in Lincoln. He told me all about the situation there.

A couple of weeks later, Curt called to let me know where I stood in terms of a move. There were very few retirements and fewer moves than usual. They had me in mind for a church near Omaha that was planning to build a new building, and was bursting at the seams. Their current pastor was a recovering alcoholic, and was moving to Pennsylvania. I said, "I hope you're not talking about Plattsmouth." He tried to sugar coat things, but I was stuck.

The worst thing about moving was telling Ana. Since she preferred dramatics and music to athletics, we honestly thought it would be an advantage to be in a much larger school. The next hardest thing was saying good-bye to our friends. We had Bible School programs my last Sunday so I didn't have to preach, but I wept when I stood at the door, balled like a baby in the ride from Farnam to Eustis, and sobbed some more after church in Eustis.

My first funeral in Eustis was for a pioneer woman who had reached the age of 102. Many folks in town were past 90. They had a tremendously active Senior Center. I believed the primary focus of my ministry would be with these Seniors.

I was wrong. In five years, more than sixty babies were born to families in the Eustis/Farnam parish. During several months, a majority of my hospital calls were to see these new babies and their parents. During my time there, baptisms outnumbered funerals by more than 2 to one. Though I had a constituency of over 500, I had a 14-month period with no funerals.

The day we left, the Eustis folks dutifully cleaned, repainted, scrubbed, and readied the parsonage for its new occupants. When we arrived at the Plattsmouth parsonage, it had not been vacuumed. To Ana's credit, she never blamed me for the unwelcome changes in her life. She made new friends, kept up her Conference youth activities, and got a job at Pizza Hut. At the end of the summer she got a kitten we named Cyrus.

Ana and her dad at Confirmation 1990

Seth at Wesleyan 1991

Ana's Senior Picture

Ana at her graduation party 1994

Chapter 16
A Splinter On The Banister Of Life

When the great Hartzell Spence wrote his story about growing up in a preacher's family, he said this about one of his father's appointments: "One town in father's ministry must remain nameless." I almost did the same regarding Plattsmouth. Maybe it was fate. My father's most disappointing experience came from a town south of Omaha that started with "P" as well.

Plattsmouth had its good points. It was the birthplace of the talented artist, John Philip Falter, and his grandparents' home still stood in town and we got to tour the place. John himself escaped at age six and grew up in Falls City. It was also close to Omaha and Lincoln and near both Chris' and my folks, and Seth was only an hour away at Wesleyan.

Shortly after we moved I was at the church when a couple stopped to visit. They were members who had recently moved to Omaha, and wanted to tell me they were transferring their membership. One thing she said stuck with me, "this is the first church we've been part of, when every suggestion made was countered by ten reasons it wouldn't work." Frankly, Plattsmouth UMC's mission statement could have been "we have never done it that way," which of course is the seven last words of any church. I also learned that my four immediate predecessors either left Nebraska or left the ministry, after serving in Plattsmouth.

Previously I had a few skirmishes and disagreements, but had never experienced outright hostility from the git-go. The former pastor was a recovering alcoholic, and he concentrated on other aspects of ministry, and let the entrenched minority have their way. The infamous John M. Chivington was Presiding Elder when the Plattsmouth M.E. Church began in 1857. Perhaps this evil man haunts the church still.

The Eustis/Farnam Charge was the highest salary move in 1992. The DS requested the Plattsmouth folks raise my income to meet their amount, which they did. However, when my first paycheck arrived in Plattsmouth I discovered they were budgeting an incorrect figure for parsonage utilities, and spending far less which meant I was getting a sizable cut in pay. The parsonage system is bad enough, but churches should never pay pastor's utilities.

It was truly the church that time forgot. They had a decaying 90 year old building with virtually no church school space, and a pathetically inadequate office area. On the other hand, we did have potential. They had a Building Committee, and were looking at sites on which to build. There were new folks moving in, and many did show some interest.

One amusing thing happened during church my first summer in Plattsmouth. During my sermon, I noticed the ushers and a few other people observing and commiserating. Not knowing what was happening, I kept on preaching. Afterward I discovered a small but steady stream of water was flowing down the wall behind the pulpit. The A/C units were in the attic, and one of the condenser tubes was plugged.

In July of 1992, the Jurisdictional Conference of the UMC was meeting in Fort Worth, Texas and Chris, Ana, and I decided to travel there. I saw the election of Joel Martinez, the first person elected a Bishop from the Rio Grande Conference, and hung out with Curtis and other friends.

In August our family attended a celebration honoring Bishop Hearn, as he was leaving for Houston. He told about the time he was pastor in Baton Rouge, and went to visit an elderly parishioner who was living with relatives in a small town north of Baton Rouge. This was a special trip for Hearn, because he lived there as a child where his father was a pastor.

When he arrived at his destination, the parishioner was resting and it took a few minutes for her to come to the front room. So her pastor sat and began looking at a book, filled with pictures about the history of this little town. He found a picture of his own second grade class. He said he remembered that day, and how proud he felt because he was wearing brand new overalls. And he found himself in the picture, standing in the middle row clear over to the right.

He read the names of his classmates and flashes of recognition came to him. As he continued looking at their names, he came to his own place on the list - middle row on the right - and it said "unknown." However, that did not spoil the afternoon for him. He remembered it as one of those sacred journeys where God's presence was strong and affirming. I was trying real hard to see my move to Plattsmouth as a sacred journey.

Seth was in his second year at Wesleyan, and moved into the Theta Chi house in August. He was elected to the University's Judicial Council, and began working with the Junior High youth at First UMC in Lincoln. Anastasia turned 16 and got her driver's license. In March she was inducted into the National Honor Society in Eustis, so transferred into that group at Plattsmouth. She attended all the UM youth activities she could find and was a member of District and Conference youth councils and the Conference Board of Church and Society. She had over 100 kids in her class at Plattsmouth, and she managed to stay on the honor roll.

We had a house cat for the first time since 1981. Cyrus was a Siamese-Himalayan who paid a big price for the privilege, as he became a claw-less eunuch on October 5, 1992. We also bought a Mazda 929 complete with power roof, CD player, and leather seats.

I was perhaps being a little too honest in one of my 1992 sermons, part of which follows.

There's a song that advises "Mama said there'd be days like this." Well, Wednesday was one of those days for me: you know the kind when it seems everything is going wrong. Two weeks ago we were visited by some foggy weather here in eastern Nebraska. Chris and I attended a funeral in Waverly that morning, and the fog actually got thicker as we headed that way. We came back home shortly after noon, and things didn't improve much through the day. Ana was at a meeting in North Platte, and was supposed to meet us that night at Seth's fraternity house in Lincoln.

As evening approached we discussed how foolish it was for us to go back to Lincoln in the fog. Perhaps we should call Seth, and tell him to put his sister up in the Theta Chi house overnight. On second thought, we weren't ready for that foolishness either. When it was dark outside, Ana called and we headed out into the fog once more. Traffic was light on Highway 66, and the Church Road and we made it to Lincoln and back home safely.

It reminded me of another time when the fog was much thicker and the trip was longer. This was four or five years ago, and we were on I-80 heading west. The only safe speed was the minimum. Occasionally, a car would pass and it seemed they came from nowhere and disappeared into a vast nothingness. Ahead of us, a car with another nervous driver was traveling less than 40 mph. They appeared like a phantom with their red taillights staring back at us, and then we would follow along too closely, but we were afraid to pass.

It's fair to say that much of life is like driving in a fog. There are times when confusion and disappointment cloud over our hopes and dreams. There are times when our vision is reduced, and there are times when it is just impossible to see more than a day ahead. If we Christians tell the truth, we must admit that matters of faith are more like fog than clear days. We ask "Who is God?" "What is God like?" "How can we believe God cares about human beings?" Because these questions are hard to answer, we often ask the wrong questions and get even more confused.

Another sermon included these words.....Thanksgiving Day 1992 for me, and many of you I'm sure, was a day of relaxation and feasting. I was able to stay in bed a little later than usual, leisurely read through the over-sized edition of the **Omaha World-Herald**, had breakfast and a couple of cups of coffee without feeling I was behind schedule.

At around 11, we headed west to the farm home of Chris' folks. After dodging some unplowed snow drifts, and escaping a slick spot or two we arrived west of Greenwood at noon. There we were met by the wonderful blended aroma of roasted turkey, pumpkin pie, and freshly-baked bread. Eating with this bunch has always been kind of interesting. At our peak we had 22 including great-grandma and grandpa. In our noisiest year we had six children age four and younger. This year there were seventeen of us including five teenage boys in various stages of athletic prowess.

These Landon Thanksgiving dinners have followed a common pattern over the years. We always discuss Nebraska football. Some years we even watch Nebraska football. We always get caught up on the cousins and aunts and uncles and neighborhood gossip. We always schedule the next event - a Christmas feast. We always overeat.

These events have also had many variables. The location has changed from year to year. Our topics of conversation and degrees of affection are always altered during election years. Some years it's nice enough to go outdoors. Great Grandma has watched this event grow and decline as her grandchildren grew up, took spouses, had babies, her son lost a wife and found another, one granddaughter died, one family moved to Texas, her husband died, now she no longer presides over the gravy and dressing detail. It's something that is repeated in many families over the years.

I believe everyone around the table thinks of past celebrations and future ones, too. We passed the food and ate and ate. I took two helpings of mashed potatoes and gravy, and as I did I remembered the horrible year when somebody substituted scalloped potatoes. Throughout the afternoon we engaged in various activities and ate desserts and pretzels and drank coffee and diet Mountain Dew.

At 5:30 I waddled over to a soft chair and started watching the evening news. The lead story was about the starving people of Somalia. It was noisy enough in the house that I couldn't hear much from the reporters, but the pictures spoke loudly. Hundreds of shriveled-up persons stretching out their bony hands for a smidgen of grain. Mothers nursing babies that looked dead already. Fathers pushing wheelbarrows with lifeless bodies covered by dirty blankets. Teenagers laying beside a road without enough strength to whisk away flies from their faces. It was sobering to say the least.

Surely I concluded with some good news, but my attitude was in need of some positive adjustments at the time.

When Advent season approached, hay bales and plastic figures of Joseph, Mary, three wise men, a shepherd, and the baby Jesus were placed in front of the church. Someone told me that the year before a couple of boys (not United Methodists) had taken the baby Jesus, and sent a ransom letter to the church. I laughed and said I thought they were pretty clever, which some in the church didn't appreciate. I also told the choir director that no Christmas music should be used until the Sunday before Christmas and the hymns, chosen by me, were also only Advent hymns. This incensed some folks in the church.

Chris starting working in a school kitchen in February 1993. My DS, Lowen Kruse, asked me to preach at the District Ash Wednesday service and what I said follows.

Ash Wednesday is definitely not on my "Top Ten List of Favorite Holy Days." It almost always hits us in the dreary month of February. It's too soon after Christmas. A lot of folks still have lights and tree decorations to put away. The straw bales that surrounded our nativity scene are still behind the church, too soggy and dirty to be moved.

Epiphany is the season of light and life and growth; of Presentation and Baptism and Transfiguration. I'm not ready for Lent. I don't want to hear about darkness and gloom and fasting and weeping. I want to hear more about the baby at Bethlehem and the Baptizer at the Jordan and the Christ of the Transfiguration Mountain. I'm really not interested in being purged with hyssop, nor am I all that impressed with Paul's afflictions, hardships, and calamities. I'd rather follow the star a little longer; let somebody else hear "You are dust, and to dust you shall return."

Paula Schwed just published a book in which she lists over 100 of her favorite lines from country songs. Most describe the weariness of the human condition and seem appropriate for this time of reproof.[38]

(Here I read several titles)

Ash Wednesday really brings out the cynic in me. I've only attended a service like this one twice in my life; both times it was because I was invited to preach. My sober little church at Ithaca used to have Ash Wednesday services; but those were more of a Lenten kick-off than real reminders of mortality, complete with ashes.

When growing up, I thought Ash Wednesday belonged to the Catholics. As a matter of fact, Lent didn't really begin for us until Palm Sunday when the church was three-quarters full and the babies got baptized. Then we got a real dose of guilt on Holy Thursday - we called it Maundy in those days - and burrowed in with the singing of "The Old Rugged Cross" on Good Friday. Then came Easter, the slate was cleared, and we were ready to think about the good old summertime.

I remember the Catholic kids in high school. We Methodists and Lutherans and Congregationalists thought it was pretty unfair when they were excused in the middle of the morning on Ash Wednesday. Off they went down to St. Michael's, and an hour later they came back with a grimy smudge on their foreheads. Some of them left it there all day, even through basketball practice. We teased them about it, and told them there was nothing scriptural about Ash Wednesday. As a matter of fact, Jesus said it was wrong to show your religion in public. They called us heathens and quoted the Monsignor to us. Finally we pulled out the heavy weapons, and invited them to join us for a fat, juicy hamburger on Friday night.

So, I don't like Ash Wednesday because it's no fun and besides it starts the Lenten season, and, well, I'm just too busy for Lent this year. I have Bible studies and

Confirmation classes and committee meetings to think about. I really don't have time to be contemplative.

But I got serious and pondered a while. Could it be that we need some time to think, to react quietly to what's happening around us? Is it wrong to let a few things slide, and take some extra time just for quietness? Can we believe that God might actually want us to use 40 days or so to listen for some divine direction?

Then there's Tim Vivian, in the most recent issue of **The Other Side** magazine, saying, "...Our families' pasts are our country's past. And, especially during this time of Lent, I find it important to remember - the bad as well as the good, the blood as well as the gold." He continues, "We live in a country of willed and perpetual amnesia, a country whose loss of memory allows us to confuse and jumble together Christianity and capitalism, U.S. and biblical values, so that we no longer distinguish between them...But we can never forget that in the midst of it all we waged war, stole land, wiped out nations, and enslaved other peoples."[39]

A Psalm teaches God wants us to find "truth in the inward being," and wisdom in our secret hearts. Jesus said, "where your treasure is, there will your heart be also." Our faith pleads for a balance between being and doing. As hard as we try we must confess we have left undone many things we ought to have done. Lent helps us focus on where our actions should take us.

We must observe Ash Wednesday and Lent so that God can make Easter happen. Ash Wednesday is a time to draw closer to God, to renew our commitments, and to remember it is God in us, and not us by ourselves, who make good things happen.

+++

I joined the Masonic Lodge in 1975 but had not been very active in the Douglas and Eustis years, because there were no lodges in those towns. I demitted to Plattsmouth Lodge #6 in 1992 and joined the York Rite bodies as well. This means I passed through the Royal Arch, became a Select Master, and was constituted a Knight Templar on March 15, 1993.

A good thing about being in Plattsmouth was connecting with my dad's cousin Marion Reed. Marion was a retired farmer living on the Reed home place north of Plattsmouth in Sarpy County. He was also very active in all the Masonic orders, and was there to conduct me through the above ceremonies.

Our daughter was born with a lazy eye. At sixteen months she had surgery intending to straighten it, but in April of 1993 went back for another procedure. When she came out of surgery Ana said, "my eye hurts" and "it feels like somebody stuck a knife in my eye." Both statements were true. The doctor left in two stitches which were removed later in the day, and I held her hand when this was done. All I can say is she was one tough kid!

Ana was spending a lot of time in UMC activities at the conference level. In addition, she was a delegate to the Jurisdictional youth meeting in Columbia, Missouri. She also went to Senior High camp and the School of Christian Mission during the summer of 1993. In school she was in the Chorus and a member of National Honor Society.

Seth was now a Junior at Wesleyan, and was in a serious relationship with his future wife, Sarah Bernhardt, a student at UNL. Sarah survived gatherings of both the Leypoldts and the Landons in 1993, and Seth met her family in New York during the year as well. He was serving as an intern for Lincoln's First UMC and was a counselor at

Camp Comeca during the summer. He was very busy in college as president of the University Judiciary and was in several other organizations.

The Plattsmouth church had a building committee which had been meeting periodically for several years. I pushed them to do something, and they had an architect draw some plans for an addition to the north side of the church where the old parsonage was still in place. He basically told us we were crazy to do this, and the group got a little more serious about relocating.

I called the pastor of an Omaha church that was getting ready to build, to find out who was assisting them in this process. He gave me the name of a church builder in Kansas, who offered a turn-key approach to constructing churches. He also said this man would be at their church in a couple of weeks. I reported this to the building committee, and they asked me to invite the Kansan to meet with me.

The person I called was Roe Messner, who had suffered financially when Jim and Tammy Faye Bakker's "ministry" fell apart. He later married Tammy Faye. He was very gracious, and said he could meet with me in the afternoon before his Omaha meeting. We walked through our old building, and he affirmed the other architect's opinion. We then climbed into my car, and drove around town looking at possible locations for a new church. Roe was lukewarm about the acreage on the west edge of town, but really liked a space south of the Nebraska Masonic Home.

A couple of us met with the board of the Masonic Home, and they had no interest in selling, so the committee settled on the acreage. The church had been given two farms several years ago, and we needed to convert that property into cash to move ahead. At a church conference April 18, 1993, we voted to buy the real estate by a margin of 52 to 50. My friend Woody Fleming said he looked at me when the result was announced, and my expression made him think of the *Twilight Zone*.

After we purchased the new site, Roe's son Ron Messner presented us with some preliminary drawings. Their fees were reasonable, and I was quite impressed with their philosophy of assisting churches. Of course, the Plattsmouth folks were unable to make any decision, and later sold the acreage. Eventually, they built on to their old church.

On Tax Day (April 15) in 1993, we celebrated by taking Chris to St. Elizabeth's hospital in Lincoln, where she had her second carpal tunnel operation. It all went smoothly and we only spent a couple of hours at the hospital. When healed up, she went back to her part-time job in a school kitchen.

In the summer of 1993 we did something very different: we went on a trip without the kids. We took a leisurely jaunt across Nebraska, staying in Albion, Grand Island, Cozad, Ogallala, Chadron, and North Platte. It was really great to be in church at Eustis on June 27, and see our friends there again. A few weeks later, Ana accompanied us to Minnesota where we visited the huge Mall of America. It was worth seeing - once. I was disappointed to find only one bookstore there. We bought clothes, though (no sales tax on clothes in Minnesota). We spent a few days at Clear Lake in Iowa before returning home.

On the next Sunday, I told my congregation I was thinking about joining a group called the Association of Battered Clergy. I had read about them in the **Omaha World-Herald**. The article described how people might react if they walked out their front door, and were hit on the head with a baseball bat. A healthy person would walk out the back door the next day. A schizophrenic might get hit again but eventually would learn to avoid the attacker. The "co-dependent," a category which includes many clergy, would continue taking a knock on the head each morning until the attacker stopped showing up. Then he or she would probably go looking for the assailant, afraid that the pastor had somehow offended him.

Ana started working at the Pizza Hut in Plattsmouth in September, and also began her senior year in high school. She had her own car and kept up her many activities in the wider church, also finding ways to stem the creeping fundamentalism in Plattsmouth.

I kept my DS, Lowen Kruse, well-informed about the situation in Plattsmouth, and he was very supportive. Bob and Betty Ellis invited us to meet them in Winterset and Des Moines, where we celebrated Chris' birthday on October 14, 1993. About this time I discovered that Nebraska's UMC conference treasurer had resigned, and I applied for the position.

I was interviewed for this job on November 10, but three days later told the position was offered to another candidate, a lay person who was a CPA. I had the support of several persons and was vice-chair of CCFA. I was not a happy camper, but the change would not have been timely for our family either.

Nearly all the fall church meetings were contentious, and I remembered what my friend in Davenport said about passing out baby toys at church meetings. Because the pastor chairs the Committee on Nominations, I skillfully found candidates willing to replace the naysayers. The Committee on Finance attempted to usurp the Administrative Council, so I adjourned their meeting by leaving. The Administrative Council held fast, and recommended a budget which included an increase in pastor's salary. Next came the annual Church Conference in December.

Fortunately these meetings are conducted by the DS, and the pastor only speaks when he/she is requested to do so. This meeting approved the sale of the church's farm property. I was voted a raise, and I'll never forget the support Lowen Kruse gave me that day. At the close of the meeting he said to the assembled crowd, "You and I have been through a lot these past five years and I have gotten to know you pretty well. This guy (pointing to me) may be gone in six months or might be here for ten years. But one thing I know, when he does leave, the problems will still be here."

In October of 1993, I was nominated by the Mount Moriah Commandery in Plattsmouth to be a Holy Land Pilgrim, and in December was notified that I would be taking an all-expense paid trip to the Holy Land in February 1994. My lodge brethren raised a little cash for me to buy souvenirs, and several church members helped as well. I would be flying from Omaha to New York, and then non-stop to Tel Aviv, my first air trip since 1969. I also applied for a passport for the first time in my life.

As the year ended, I wrote in our annual Christmas letter about our children. Seth was a junior in college, maintaining a 3.7 GPA. I said this was better than his parents grades added together, but of course, NWU was more difficult in the sixties. Anastasia was looking forward to her May 22, 1994 graduation. She had done a couple of things in 1993 that the rest of us had never done: 1.) she got all A's and 2.) she went skiing. I confessed to getting only two A's all the way through High School, and had trouble walking, let alone skiing.

During the cold winter of 1992-93 I began understanding why my predecessor opted for a home office. The church office area was carved out of the sanctuary overflow room. The secretary occupied maybe 100 square feet, and the pastor slightly less. One day I measured the master bath at the parsonage, and discovered it was actually bigger than my church office. In November of 1993 I moved several things to the spare bedroom in the parsonage, and did most of my work from there.

+++

The first time I met Alan Dunlap was on October 14, 1970. I remember the date because it was Chris' birthday, and we were in Kansas City. Our seminary had a common meal at noon every weekday, which was a great time of worship and fellowship. Alan was there because the Trustees were meeting, and he was one of them. I introduced myself and Chris, and he invited us to accompany him to a restaurant that evening.

It turned out to be a pretty nice birthday gift for my 21-year-old bride. He drove us to his hotel which had a rotating restaurant on the top floor, and we had a wonderful conversation and meal. After supper, he hailed a cab and sent us back down Truman Road to our Fisk Hall apartment. Little did I know, that I would someday spend six years as part of this man's world of banking.

On the crisp and sunny morning of January 12, 1994, I drove to Milford to attend the funeral of George Alan Dunlap. He was born and raised in the little town of Douglas. He was a country banker in Milford, Nebraska for over 40 years. He was my mentor, friend, and co-worker. When I made a mistake he saw it as a teaching moment, and gave advice along with criticism. When I made a colossal error, he called it for what it was, but then helped me figure out a solution. He died at age 71 of pancreatic cancer.

That afternoon, I met with Bishop Martinez and my Superintendent Lowen Kruse. I knew I had to leave Plattsmouth, and I'd been researching the possibilities. The Bishop asked me to describe my ideal appointment, and I said I would like to be in a rural setting within an hour or so of Lincoln, where both our children would be in college.

On January 16, 1994, I met with the Plattsmouth SPRC. The meeting started with a question: "when do we vote on approving your trip to Israel?" I replied that the Conference policy was that all pastors are entitled to 3 weeks vacation, 1 week continuing education, and an additional month study leave every 4 years. End of discussion. The only agenda item was an advisory vote on my re-appointment to the church. I told them I would be leaving, but they still needed to jump through this hoop. I slept well that night.

It was below zero on February 8, 1994 when Chris took me and my two suitcases to the Omaha airport. At 6 am I boarded Delta Flight 1906 for my trip to Israel. I waited...and waited...and waited. The plane's engines were frozen, and the flight was canceled. My companion on this trip was a young ELCA pastor from Tekamah.

We needed to be in New York by 10 that evening. Now the best we could do was head to Cincinnati at 12:30 pm, and catch a commuter to New York later. So we did what we had to do, and the bags were unloaded and tagged for Cincinnati. In Cincinnati, we learned that a raging blizzard had canceled all flights in and out of New York. We were stymied again. "What about my suitcases," I asked the pretty lady at the Delta desk. "No problem," she said, "everything is taken care of."

Fortunately, I had the modern-day version of a saddlebag slung around my right shoulder. My dear wife had wisely advised me to pack all my necessities, and at least one change of clothing in there. "Just in case," she said. Delta put us up in a motel. End of day one.

We were scheduled to go on to New York at 7 the next morning. But, of course, that flight was canceled. We booked a later flight. "Just where do you suppose our suitcases are?" I asked Brian, my fellow pilgrim. "Oh, these people know exactly what they're doing," he said. And I sat down, tightly grasping my carry-on.

All day we remained in the terminal at Cincinnati. Our flight was delayed over seven hours. But finally our departure was announced. I could see the big burly men loading suitcases on to the plane and I stared at them hoping to see the familiar red of Chris' Samsonite. My carry-on seemed to grow heavier as I dragged myself up the runway and into the plane.

At 8 pm or so we arrived at John F. Kennedy International Airport in New York City. We found the luggage unloading area and waited and watched and waited and watched. Big ones, little ones, square ones, rectangular ones, blue ones, black ones. Down they came and round they went. Then they stopped; and none of them had originated at Omaha, Nebraska. We went to this place and that place and were told this thing and that thing. And the horrible reality sunk in: I would be traveling light on my trip to the Holy Land. My bags were somewhere between Atlanta and Cincinnati and they would put a "tracer" on them and get them to "where ya staying at" as soon as possible.

We flew across the ocean for ten hours, landed in Tel Aviv, and took a bus to a hotel in Jerusalem. When the sun came up, we looked out at a newer part of the ancient city, went to breakfast, and began meeting our fellow pilgrims. Still, no bags, but the guy at the desk said, "we're working on it."

We climbed on a bus and headed for the old city. On this first morning, we went to an overlook to view the ancient city of peace, Jerusalem, and nearby was the Garden of Gethsemane, with its historic olive trees. We saw several other things, but did not enter the holy city. That night we had a gathering in the hotel to introduce ourselves to one another, and discuss the remainder of the trip itinerary. Our group leader asked if those of us who were Masons would like to attend a lodge meeting. He said in the previous year, he attended an Israeli lodge where a Jew and a Muslim were initiated in the same night. What a shame all groups can't live the way we're taught in Isaiah 11:6. Unfortunately, he reported later no lodge meetings were scheduled for this week.

We visited many places in Israel on this journey. Our guide referred us to the New Testament when we visited Bethlehem, Nazareth, Mount Tabor, Tabgha, Chorazin, Capernaum, Via Dolorosa, and the Garden Tomb. We visited Cana, but I failed to buy any wine there. One day we went to the Dead Sea, Jericho, Qumran, and took a cable car to Masada. Another day we were at Megiddo, and later stopped at the border of Lebanon, and walked through a barbed wire chain link tunnel and back. We spent the night on the Sea of Galilee, without realizing where we were. At sunrise I took a gorgeous picture of the lake (it's posted on Google Earth). We crossed the Galilee in a replica of an ancient boat, and ate fish at Tiberias.

Our guide for this pilgrimage was a Jew who grew up in Iraq, but had lived in Israel throughout adulthood. He told us about his mother-in-law, who came to Israel from Poland. She was a blond-haired, blue-eyed Jewish girl, whose parents were captured by the Nazis, and she was sent to a Catholic orphanage. When the German soldiers came to take children to the camps, the nuns pulled her back, telling them she was Aryan.

This guide was a colonel in the Army reserve, and told us battle stories. One was about a Jewish family, living in a Tel Aviv during the 6-day war. They were in apartment, and had a little one they were trying to potty train. They decided to spend their nights in the bathroom. A shell exploded in their building, but they were safe because the toilet was in the middle of the apartment.

While eating lunch one day in Jerusalem, I spotted Dr. Lindsey Pherigo, and immediately went to visit with him. He was a teacher at Saint Paul seminary, now retired, and spending six weeks a year lecturing to tour groups in the Holy Land. It was amazing to be in this place, and happen upon the man who taught me so much about the New Testament.

Our companions loaned us a few articles of clothing, and our bags finally arrived two days before departure. I bought a lot of stuff to take home. One thing I saw and wanted was an olive wood carving of the last supper on a chalice. I tried to barter it down to my price range, but failed. A few years ago, I found and bought one on eBay.

I flew home on February 18, 1994, exactly 25 years after my father's death. I got to our home at 1 pm, unpacked, and slept until Chris woke me for supper. I went to bed early, and awoke at mid morning the next day to the sound of our cat chewing on an olive branch. My roommate throughout the time in Israel, Brian Duane Maas, was elected Bishop of the Nebraska Synod ELCA, on June 6, 2012.

I read about a family member who awoke one Sunday morning and declared, "I'm not going to church this morning and I'll give you three reasons why. First, nobody likes me there and second, whenever I say anything they either ignore me or make fun of me, and finally, it's boring."

To this, the mother in the household replied, as only mothers can do, "Yes, you are going to church this morning and I'll give you three reasons why. First, if you try real hard to like them, they'll start liking you back. Second, once you get to know them better, they'll listen to what you say. And the third reason you're going to church this morning is because you are the pastor."

I kept going to 7th and Main, but I found many diversions in 1994. In March my brother Steve and I drove to El Paso, Texas and we visited Lydia Patterson Institute. This is a High School operated by our church, serving youth who mostly come from Mexico. Teachers at Lydia Patterson receive 70% of the average salaries of other teachers in Texas. They are committed to the ministry in ways few of us can duplicate.

In April 1994, Ana and I flew to Washington, D.C. where we were able to stay at Wesley Seminary at very reasonable rates. Our friend, Josh Davies, was a student at American University and was working for Senator Exon. He took us to many places in the Capitol and other sights in the city. We rented a car and went to Gettysburg and Hershey, Pennsylvania as well.

I attended a pastor's meeting where the subject of clergy recruitment was discussed. One of my colleagues said an important issue for young people considering the ministry is their experience in the local church. A group that practices random acts of kindness and support for others is apt to produce more pastors than one that is known for infighting and clergy abuse. The Albion church has produced nine pastors, and the Eustis church has sent eleven persons into full-time Christian service. Plattsmouth can claim but one, and she made her decision several years after leaving the community.

Some District Superintendents talk freely, some don't. One of them told me he had two pastors retiring, and either place would suit me well. In my January meeting with Bishop Martinez I did not say where I wanted to go, but described the place thoroughly. I was not terribly surprised on March 30, 1994 when the call came offering me a move to Geneva. In my pastoral career, because of various alignments, I had served eight smaller churches within 25 miles of Geneva.

On May 5th Chris, Ana, and I went to Geneva to be formally introduced. After touring the church and parsonage, we had supper, and met with the SPRC for about an hour. We were told there were severe weather warnings for the area, and everyone went home early. On Highway 81 north of McCool Junction, it was raining buckets and then it began to hail. There was an 18-wheeler behind us, and I could see that he was stopping, so I did as well. We sat there for what seemed like an eternity with frozen pellets silencing all conversation. Our car had a sunroof, and I thought surely it would shatter. When it was over, we headed home, and actually had very minor vehicle damage.

Ana received her High School diploma on May 22. We had a big party for her at the Plattsmouth church. She was in the top 10% of her class. We were very proud of her, especially considering her move from a school of 50 students to one of over 500.

The 1994 AC met at Kearney. Seth had turned 21, and I suggested we go to the local strip club. When we got there, I said maybe we should put a newspaper on our heads so nobody would recognize us. It was a warm June afternoon, and the bright sun shone through the door when we walked into the bar. Immediately, I heard a voice, "Hey Chuck! Come and sit over here." There were two tables filled with fellow members of the clergy. In June we moved to Geneva.

Reflecting upon the Plattsmouth experience, I concluded: sometimes you're a windshield, sometimes a bug. One time, I hit a splinter sliding down the banister of life.

In my Arab garb at Las Posadas in Geneva in 1994

Our family on May 20, 1995

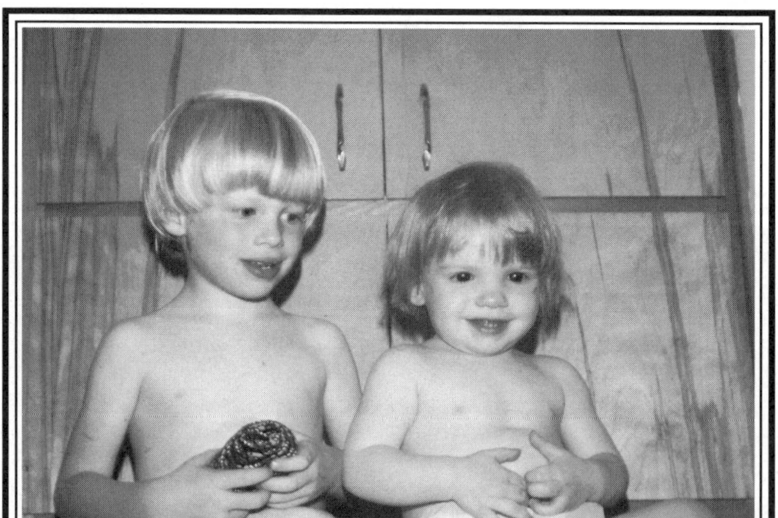

Seth and Ana in 1977

Chapter 17
One Fine Day

When I was a young pastor living in Davenport, Chris and I discovered we would soon be blessed with a baby. As all expectant parents know, there is nervous anticipation associated with a baby's arrival, especially the first one. Our doctor was a kindly, older gentleman in Geneva. He was overweight and smoked a pipe during consultations. But when we asked a question, he answered in ways that we understood. Though his waiting room was crowded, he always treated Chris as if she was his only patient. Within a week after moving to Geneva, I walked downtown and this Dr. Charles Ashby came out of his office, and crossed the street. He came my way as fast as he could, and welcomed me to town.

Then there was the time I needed a little dental work done. There was a dentist in Geneva who had just graduated from Dental School, so I went to him. After the initial exam and x-rays and cleaning and lecture about smoking and coffee drinking, he told me I needed to come back. On my second visit, he lowered the chair, shot me with Novocain, stuffed my mouth with gauze and wire and rubber things. Then with drill in hand, he asked me when I had graduated from seminary. I mumbled, "a year ago." He said, "Well, we're a couple of rookies!" I said, "I wish you hadn't said that." This guy and his wife were part of the Sunday school class Chris and I attended in Geneva.

My second sermon in Geneva included the following. Twenty-five years ago I received my Bachelor's degree from Nebraska Wesleyan. Last night I attended a reunion in Lincoln. A few weeks ago I was asked, along with other members of my class, to write a brief summary of what's happened to me since 1969. This would be put together in a booklet. This is how I began: "My life has been fun, full, and interesting." And so it is.

In many ways, I have been incredibly lucky. Certainly I have been through a few things that were not much fun, but I've always landed on my feet. For as long as I can remember, King David has been one of my heroes. I'm sure that I share this with others who have attended Sunday School. David is a hero to children because of his strength and military success. He is a hero to adults because we see in him a human being, complete with blemishes and horrible failures, whom God continued to love and use in the realm of God.

1 Samuel, chapters 16 and 17, record David's introduction into the court of the reigning King of Israel, Saul. At first, he appears because of his musical ability. This talent enabled him to soothe the troubled soul of King Saul. He accompanied the King everywhere and became his armor-bearer, a sort of "go-fer." Later, David is back at work on the family farm in Bethlehem. His three oldest brothers are soldiers in the service of King Saul, and David's father sends him with food to give to his brothers. While in the army camp, he hears the boasting and challenge of the Philistine giant, Goliath.

One fine day, the young shepherd boy and musician volunteered to go against the mighty warrior of the Philistines. King Saul outfitted David with the king's own armor. However, it didn't fit and David elected to face the giant in the same way he faced the lions and bears, who sometimes stalked his sheep. David picked five smooth stones from the brook, took his sling-shot, and sought out Goliath.

One fine day, a young man named David, without armor or reputation, stepped forward to defend the honor of Israel and Israel's God. He was there because he had been anointed, chosen, to be there. He was there because God gave him the opportunity, and he was successful because God gave the necessary resources. His purpose is found in his own words to Goliath, "You come to me with sword and spear and javelin; but I come to you in the name of the Lord of hosts, the God of the armies of Israel, whom you have defied."

One fine day, David became Israel's hero and their future. This story tells us something about patience. David had to wait for an opportunity. After his anointing, he was still a farm boy for a time, then he sat around and played the harp for crazy old King Saul. After time, he went back and forth, tending sheep for his dad, and toting armor for the king. David was patient. He waited for his time to come.

In 1981, I was a part-time pastor and full-time elevator manager in Douglas, Nebraska. I became friends with the banker in town, who was nearing his 82nd birthday. One fine day, he offered me the chance of a lifetime. He said, "you can work with me for six months, and if you like it, I'll turn things over to you." Let me tell you, I was filled with joy and fear. What a wonderful opportunity - but I had so much to learn.

They did not start me as Executive Vice President. I drove to Milford for five weeks, and worked in the teller window. I did the mail. I counted coins that came from the Tech School's vending machines. I ran the posting machine. I looked and looked for ten cent errors, trying to balance the Daily Statement. But I learned the business. And when the time came, I was ready to do the job.

A week ago Thursday, I was driving to Geneva to spend my first day as your pastor. I quickly grew weary of what I heard on the radio, so I popped in one of my favorite CDs. And I heard the delightful sound of The Chiffons singing *One Fine Day.*[40] Use your imagination and think about David's experience, and your own experience with God, as I read (not sing) this song....

Our human experience is filled with days of challenge. Often, we must learn to wait patiently and expectantly for God to give us opportunities. This is something both King David and the Chiffons can teach us.

One fine day last December, I received a huge envelope from the Grand Commandery of the Knights Templar of Nebraska, informing me that I had been given the gift of a trip to the Holy Land. A few weeks later, I found myself in a boat, possibly a close replica of the fishing boats used in Jesus' time, on the Sea of Galilee. As we put to sea, the weather was calm and beautiful. We left a modern kibbutz guest house, and sailed across to the ancient city of Tiberias. It took about an hour.

One fine day many years ago, at evening, Jesus and his first disciples climbed into a similar boat, perhaps on the same sea, maybe traveling the same route. Jesus was so tired from preaching all day, that he promptly fell asleep. Then a sudden storm came up, and the disciples were literally afraid for their lives. They woke Jesus from his nap, asking, "Don't you care that we're about to drown?"

The Bible tells us Jesus immediately took control of the situation. He rebuked the wind, and calmed the sea. Like King David before him, he used the mighty power of God to challenge and conquer an awesome enemy.

That's what faith is. For the most part we are not in charge of our lives. Sometimes we are lucky, and things go right. Sometimes we are overwhelmed by giants like grief, and hate, and guilt, and depression. But faith teaches us to let go, and allow God's grace to work in our lives.

One fine day, on a battlefield, David surrendered to God's way for him. One fine day, on a boat, the disciples of Jesus discovered the power of the Presence of God. The gift of God is the Cross of Jesus Christ. It tells us each and every day, is One Fine Day to celebrate God's grace and find opportunities to serve and glorify our Risen Lord.

Charlie Hough is about my age. Last year (1993), he was still pitching in the major leagues. He's a knuckleballer. I have no idea how this works. Instead of fast balls, breaking balls, and curve balls, Hough throws knuckleballs. When they work, these pitches are hard to hit and hard to catch. Hough said that if someone hits one knuckleball five hundred feet, he throws the next one the same way, and it will likely do something different. "You're not in charge of what it does," he said, "you're only in charge of letting it go."[41] And that, dear friends, is what faith is.

+++

A week after we moved to Geneva, Chris' brother Bill turned 40. There was and is a school of thought in today's culture which teaches turning 40 is a traumatic event. This has been perpetuated by the greeting card, helium balloon, and novelty t-shirt industries. When Bill met and conquered the big 4-0 with ice cream and cake on June 22, 1994 it was truly a milestone for the whole family. You see, Bill is the baby of the family. He is the youngest of four, and the only boy. Though he had been married for twenty years and had two teen-age sons, his big sisters were still calling him "Billy."

Bill's family announced his birthday in a most clever way. They purchased a display ad in the local paper with a picture of his dad, three sisters, and him when he was 3 years old. It said, "I may be 40, but I'm still a lot younger than my sisters."

Ana technically lived with us during the summer, but she was very busy attending Conference and Jurisdictional Youth Ministries events. In August she went off to Nebraska Wesleyan to live in Burt Hall, and became involved in several campus organizations as well.

In my 18 months at Geneva I had 31 funerals. The first year I had several funerals in Milligan because their pastor was finishing seminary, and gone part of the week. Most of those services were for Czech folks, and I got so frustrated reading names in obituaries that I resorted to first names only. It was common to have services in the morning and a lunch at noon. I got hooked on the sausage-like smoked meats that were always served.

Finally, I asked where I could buy them, and was sent to the locker across the street. I told them what I wanted, and they sent me on with some Wimmers Wieners. I took them home to Chris, and she showed me the same thing in our freezer. The Czech cooks used steam; she boiled them.

York is a little bigger than Geneva, and they had a few more stores and restaurants, so we went up there once in a while. I bought some SAS shoes in a store going out of business, that I wore out a couple of years ago. They also had a Goodwill, several other thrift stores, and a big antique mall. The great theologian, Lotan Harold DeWolf, was an advisor of Martin Luther King, Jr. and graduate of York High School in the twenties. I bought one of his books in the York Goodwill Store for ten cents.

The Geneva church was filled with people willing to give time, talent, and treasure. It was so refreshing to float an idea, and have people respond in positive ways. In the fall of 1992 the UMC published a new Book of Worship, and I attended a workshop to help us make good use of it. One idea I especially liked was Las Posadas, as revised by Raquel Mora Martinez of Lincoln, Nebraska.

I suggested we try a version of it in Geneva, and it took off. We chose one

Sunday afternoon in December, and asked eight families in different parts of town to invite folks to wait for Mary and Joseph to come along. The weather was chilly as we began. One of our families had friends with a very tame donkey and foal, and they were happy to walk the whole route with us. I played Joseph and wore a scarf from Palestine. Every girl under 13, who chose to do so, rode our donkey as we walked through Geneva.

At each house we did a brief responsive reading, and those in the house would join the holy couple on their journey. The final stop was our church. One of our members loved to cook and was an expert in Mexican cuisine, so he managed a festive pot luck in the church hall. Our fellowship hall was filled with people and music, and I am so happy to relive this great memory.

We did things pretty much the same way the next year. The local paper asked children to write a paragraph or two about what Christmas means. One of our girls wrote about Las Posadas, and how she felt a connection with the mother of Jesus when she rode the donkey, and celebrated Las Posadas at the Geneva United Methodist Church.

Here is part of an Advent sermon in Geneva. Advent is the waiting season. It is much like the organ prelude we listen to every Sunday morning. We hear the lovely music. We visit with, and greet one another. We thumb through the hymnal, read the bulletin five or six times. We wait. Some folks don't mind waiting. Some come in only after the opening prayer or hymn. Advent is like the organ prelude. It is a time to wait.

We don't know much about the Hebrew prophet Zephaniah. The only time he shows up in our lectionary is on the third Sunday of Advent. He is unique among the prophets, in that he appears to be a descendant of the great King Hezekiah. He emerged to condemn corruption and perversion in the land of Judah. He also warned of the possible threat of invasions from all directions.

In his third chapter, Zephaniah issued some hopeful words. "Therefore wait for me, says the Lord, for the day that I arise as a witness. For my decision is to gather nations....At that time I will change the speech of peoples to a pure speech, that all of them may call upon the name of the Lord and serve God with one accord....At that time I will bring you home....says the Lord (from the CEV)."

Sometimes it is good for us to wait. In 1994 the city of Lincoln was experimenting with voice controls for pedestrians in the downtown area. I was there in December at 11th and O. As I tried to cross the street, I heard a voice. It said something like, "The east/west crosswalk on 11th Street is clear, you may proceed." Then after a wait, it said, "The north/south crosswalk on O Street is clear, you may proceed." In downtown Lincoln an electronic voice told you when to wait and when to proceed. It's certainly a good time to wait for clearance before walking across a busy street (we're back to lights now).

It's good to wait for a baby to be born. Babies need nine months in their mother's womb before they make their appearance. If you've been close to a premature birth, you know what I mean. Expectant parents are anxious and excited. Sometimes you feel like you just can't wait any longer. But it's a good thing to give the baby all the time he or she needs.

Advent is also the season of starting over. The Good News for today is that God is coming and bringing a new heaven and a new earth. When God becomes a part of your life you know it's time to start over. You've got to start somewhere, right? That's why Advent is so important. That's why the Church won't allow us to rush into Christmas without hearing the messages of Isaiah and John. It's time for a change. But it's important that we start the process correctly.

Part of Las Posadas teaches the importance of waiting. That's why we'll make several stops this afternoon. It will help us remember the time of waiting. The Hebrews waited centuries for their Savior. Mary and Joseph waited nine months for a baby. Advent is the season that answers "Why Wait?" for Christians.

Today we admit before God that it is hard to wait for Christmas. We want to rush into it. We want to celebrate the birthday of Jesus before he arrives. We want to hear the Christmas scriptures and sing Christmas songs before Thanksgiving, because that's when the malls start decorating. But we know this isn't right. We know Jesus deserves better.

+++

We wrote to friends and family at Christmas in 1994 that we had a new home and a new address in a town of 2,300 about 70 miles southwest of Lincoln. We were living in a parsonage surrounded on two sides by a massive brick and stone church. Our congregation numbered about 750.

After some big changes, Chris was resuming more familiar routines. She worked at school kitchens in Plattsmouth on a part-time basis and did the same at the Geneva school. She spent a lot of hours packing and unpacking in 1994. She made pretzels and got rave reviews from those who eat them. She was quilting as we were once again in a house big enough to accommodate quilt frames. She joined both the Bell Choir and Chancel Choir in Geneva.

Seth decided to be the third Leypoldt member of the clergy, and was investigating seminaries. He was leaning toward Boston, and I suggested we go there and take a look in January 1995. I bought the plane tickets, and he called to make arrangements with the school. We learned to navigate via subways and trolleys, and did a lot of walking as well. He was very impressed with the city and the school.

On the way back we made a stop in Evanston, Illinois to visit Garrett Evangelical. They put us up in campus housing, and we attended a class being led by fellow Nebraskan Bob Jewett. So far the weather had been cooperative.

Because it was so much cheaper, we had driven to Kansas City and flown out of KCI. It was overcast when we left Chicago for our flight home. As we approached KCI it was very, very foggy. I lost count of the times the plane circled the runway, and I'll never forget the flight attendant's worried expression. We landed safely, and got to our respective homes in the wee hours.

Here's part of a sermon I preached on January 29, 1995. The morning's Gospel Lesson told us what might happen when a preacher "stops preaching and starts meddling." The previous week we recalled the time when Jesus went to his home town synagogue, read a little scripture, and gave a one-sentence sermon. The folks were impressed. However, the sermon turned into a "question and answer" event and the people became so angry with Jesus that they were ready to throw him off a cliff.

I've heard a few sermons that made me uncomfortable, and quite a few that were downright boring, but none that made me mad enough to want to kill the preacher. This week I heard about a pastor who stood before his congregation at sermon time and said, "My message today has three points: first, there are two billion hungry people in the world; second, you really don't give a damn about them." At this time there was a dramatic pause, as the congregation gasped and squirmed and braced themselves for more. Then the preacher continued, "My third point is most important: you folks are really more concerned that I said 'damn' from the pulpit than you are with the fact there are two billion hungry people in the world."[42]

Jesus got in trouble back in Nazareth because of his call to prophecy. Prophets tell the truth, and sometimes the truth hurts so badly that you want to destroy it. The thing that upset the local folks was the idea that God no longer regarded Israel as a chosen people. Jesus told them that God was looking to outsiders to fulfill prophecy. He told them about the time Elijah bypassed the Hebrews and helped a woman in Sidon; and how Elisha cleansed Naaman, a Syrian leper, and overlooked the many lepers in Israel.

It would be very much like God saying to Christian America, "You are a land of plenty, but you are fat and greedy, from now on I will look to the Muslims and Hindus to accomplish my work." This would not make the folks in my hometown happy. The call to prophecy is that God's word must be heard in all languages and cultures. When we turn inward we fail God, and God will find other messengers.

About 2600 years ago, a priest named Hilkiah and his wife had a son named Jeremiah. When Jeremiah was 16 or 17, the Word of God came to him saying, "Before I formed you in the womb I knew you, and before you were born I consecrated you; I appointed you a prophet to the nations." Jeremiah argued with God, but God insisted and gave him everything he needed to be a prophet.

The work of prophecy is scary. We are called to tell the world it is wrong. Materialism and selfishness are destructive. The word of God to the world is: Repent! Change! Turn around! Give everything away! Stop the killing! War is wrong! Are we listening? Can we understand?

God is calling to us today. There are a variety of gifts in this congregation. There are so many things each of us can do. God gives us the Spirit and the courage to respond, saying, "Do not be afraid .... I will be with you .... I have given you the words you must speak. I have appointed you over nations and earthly rulers, to uproot and to pull down, to destroy and to overthrow, to build and to plant."

+++

One of my parishioners at Geneva was Ron Elznic, who was Geneva's Chamber of Commerce Director. In the spring of 1995, he was facing some heart difficulties and was in a Lincoln hospital. I went to see him on a Saturday afternoon, which happened to be the day before Daylight Savings Time started. We talked about his upcoming surgery, and understood there was a possibility that he might not survive the operation. After a prayer, we chatted some more, and Ron said, "you know, if I don't make it, at least I won't have to go back home and change all the clocks."

Geneva was a great place to preach and I felt a real connection with my listeners there. The following words came from a sermon I gave in May 1995. Not long ago I stumbled across an idea that I found to be especially meaningful, and would like to share with you this morning. I guess you might say it sort of sums up my current philosophy of life. It is, "next year is really important!" Of course, we all know that's true, but think about it, what we believe about next year shapes a lot of what is happening today.

Kathleen Norris writes about this idea in her book, **Dakota: A Spiritual Geography:** "No one waits better than monks, or farmers. The farmers and ranchers of Western North Dakota can wait years for rain. I remember that at the height of a four-year drought, rain came only once all summer, on July 11 .... There was no precipitation again until a sparse snowfall came in November. By early August the grass had turned brown, as if it were late fall, and on windy days the dust was so bad you had to use headlights in the middle of the afternoon .... Farmers and ranchers, whose hopes are so closely bound with the land, speak in terms of next-year country."[43]

"Next year" is really what keeps us going. In farm country, when there's too much rain or not enough, we remain hopeful next year will be a better one. Through illness, economic problems, and personality conflicts, we need to know that "next year" gives us time and gives us hope.

Next year is really special for kids. Changes and challenges of growing up mean tremendous opportunities. For adults, next year includes the fact we are aging. To make matters worse, there is nothing we can do about it except, perhaps, to laugh.

Next year is really important. How we deal with it makes such a difference. Today we are thinking about the ascension of Jesus. I especially like the account we read in the book called Acts. Here Jesus gives the first disciples some parting instructions and then, all of a sudden, he is lifted up by a cloud and disappears from their sight. Then, we're told, the disciples stood by gazing into heaven. It's easy to believe they were bewitched, bothered, or bewildered by what they saw!

But here comes the important part. Two men, presumably angels or messengers of God, said, "Galileans, why are you standing there looking up at the sky? This Jesus, who was taken from you into heaven, will come back in the same way that you saw him go to heaven." These disciples were witnessing the way God determines the future. They were learning that "next year" was already here; that Jesus Christ was truly alive and present today. We sometimes think Jesus is far removed from our lives, too. The lesson of the Ascension is that we need not wait for God; God is truly with us now.

In his Galatian letter, Paul helps us see that God identifies with each of us. He said, "There is no longer Jew or Greek, there is no longer slave or free, there is no longer male and female; for all of you are one in Christ Jesus." Paul was concerned with the distortion of the Gospel. He reminded the Galatians that Jesus died and rose from death, and ascended to God so that he could be forever with us. In these actions, God brings the future into reality right now. Next year is already here.

There is something happening in our little garden spot that helps me to know that next year is important and is happening now. I have been your pastor for almost a year now. I have an obsession that many of you do not know about. I haven't meant to deceive you, and I'm certainly not ashamed of this particular lusty desire of mine. Weeks of soul-searching have empowered me to confess: **I Love Asparagus!**

Over the years we have enjoyed some splendid asparagus. In Davenport and Ceresco and Douglas and Eustis we watered and nourished and harvested this marvelous and tasty green plant. Each summer we watched it grow into feathery bushes, and then in the fall we gently pruned it so it could rest in winter and flourish again the next year.

Our best asparagus came from the Landon farmstead in western Cass County. This land was purchased by Chris' Great-Great-Grandfather in the 1870's. Her grandparents moved into Greenwood in 1949, and took some asparagus with them. We, in turn, transplanted some of it to Douglas and later moved some of it to Eustis.

The entire process is wonderfully parabolic. Something begins as a tiny seed and becomes a huge, clumpy root that year after year sends up shoots. These, when combined with milk and butter and salt and pepper, always taste great and are less filling. Last year, I even ate an asparagus sandwich in a Washington, D.C. restaurant.

When you think about the root coming from a family farm, it's even more special. When you consider the way this plant grew and reproduced and multiplied in two communities while our children were growing up, and while we were actively involved in churches filled with loving and caring friends, it's representative of even more of the good life.

I'm a next year person. I always believe, "Next year things will get better." (I guess that's why I'm still a Dodger fan.) We had a horrible garden spot in Plattsmouth, and our asparagus plant died. But last summer we transplanted some more from the farm in Cass County, and I'm happy to report it's doing well here in Geneva.

The Ascension teaches us the importance of next year. The God of Jesus Christ is the God of every tomorrow. The Good News of Christ's Ascension is that he is alive here and now. He would not be constrained by a physical body. He could not be confined to the narrow limits of ancient Palestine. He must be part of modern Tel Aviv, and Sarajevo, and Mogadishu, and Oklahoma City, and Geneva, Nebraska. "And he departed from our sight," said Augustine, "that we might return to our heart, and there find him."

Seth and Sarah with his college diploma

On May 13, 1995 we went to Lincoln for Wesleyan's commencement. Seth gave the "Prayer for the Journey" at the Baccalaureate, and received his degree "With High Distinction" (GPA above 3.75). He was an Intern at First UMC. He was inducted into Blue Key national honorary in May 1993. He was secretary of Theta Chi and a member of Alpha Theta, Order of Omega, and the Glee Club. Despite the prediction mentioned back in Chapter 11, Seth turned out to be a good athlete and scholar, with only slight OCD tendencies.

A week later, he was married to Sarah Jo Bernhardt at First UMC in Lincoln. It was a wonderful wedding, with all family members present including Seth's great-grandmother Grace McGill. Our friends the Grenzes and Ellises were also there. Sarah had another year at UNL, so Seth took a couple of classes there also and was working at First UMC and Valentino's.

Sarah and Seth on May 20, 1995

+++

That summer I had a bizarre encounter with a fellow from my home town. He was living in a small town in Fillmore County, and was a client at a Mental Health Center in Geneva. He didn't have an appointment, and didn't realize the center was not open every day. He went to the nearby courthouse for information, and because he was notably upset, they sent him to see me.

He was a tough looking guy with long hair, a beard, tattoos, and dressed like a stereotypical biker. He evidently found me easy to talk to, and opened up quickly. At this point, I had no idea that he was from Albion. He told me where he was living and working. He told me he had a 3-year-old daughter, was afraid his marriage was over, and he couldn't live without his little girl. He said he was married the first time when he was young and had five kids, but was a drunk and a bum, and was ashamed to admit he had no relationship with those grown children.

He told me about being drafted after graduation, going to Vietnam, surviving a horrible motorcycle accident, drug and alcohol abuse, and many ruined relationships. When I thought it might be appropriate, I asked him if he went to church. That's when I discovered he was an Albionite. He answered, "I haven't been in church since my mother's funeral at the Methodist Church in Albion, Nebraska."

He'd given me his name when we started talking, but it was a fairly common name. Now I asked him when he graduated, and found out he was a year behind me in school. I told him my name, and because there were so many of us it was easy for him to recall my younger brothers. Albion was just big enough that you couldn't get to know everyone well. I didn't remember his family being part of our church.

I've thought about this incident many times. We were two boys who grew up in the same town at the same time. I went to college, enjoyed a happy marriage and close interaction with two children. I had good health and two successful careers. His life was filled with bad choices, disastrous relationships, poor health, and thoughts of suicide. I invited him to come back and talk, but he never did.

On July 11, Chris and I celebrated 25 years together. We were in Madison, Wisconsin at the time. It was so hot in Nebraska that we went north, and the heat actually followed us up there. However, even that was lucky, because some extra heat is a good thing on the 25th anniversary of your wedding night. A month later, our kids hosted a party for us which most of the family attended. I've always felt lucky Chris is my spouse and friend. I am proud to be her "one-woman man," and will always be.

Anastasia was a sophomore at Wesleyan, and living in Burt Hall for the second year. She was leaning toward a business major. During the summer she stayed in Lincoln, working at a couple of places and spent a week as a counselor at Camp Comeca. Of course she was also a bridesmaid at the wedding.

I was first elected to the Conference Council on Finance and Administration (CCFA) in 1992. This group met 3 or 4 times a year to manage conference finances. There were 11 members (5 clergy & 6 lay persons). In late summer of 1995, we were called to a special meeting because the Conference Treasurer had been dismissed, and she was not going away quietly.

There were some conflicts between her and the program staff regarding fund allocations, but the biggest issue was she had discovered our AC was out of sync with the **Book of Discipline.** Specifically, the BoD states the Treasurer shall be chosen and accountable to the CCFA, not the Personnel Committee, which had been the practice in Nebraska for as long as a Treasurer/Business Manager had been employed. The chair of the CCFA supported the Treasurer, and called this meeting to discuss and take action on the employment of the Treasurer.

We were fortunate to have Bishop Martinez at our meeting, and one of the CCFA members was an attorney who kept us from doing anything to make matters worse. After some testimony-like reports and much discussion, a vote was taken to affirm the Personnel Committee's dismissal. The result was a tie, and the treasurer later resigned.

I was feeling pretty cocky as I prepared my annual Christmas epistle in 1995. It included the following: "I have concluded that I am the luckiest person in the whole wide world. I know that's presumptuous. And probably silly. But that's the way I feel right now. Since I'm doing the writing, you owe me some poetic license. If you keep on reading, you'll understand my conclusion soon enough.

"As 1995 draws to a close, I find I am now the father of a college graduate and a college sophomore, the father-in-law of a college senior, the husband of a pretty woman, and the pastor of perhaps the finest church in Nebraska. I am also ready to embark on a new adventure. I am a lucky man."

Eighteen months previously, I was appointed to serve the wonderful folks in Geneva and was very content to wait for retirement or a conference level position. But it happened sooner than expected. We were packing for possibly our last move until they scatter my ashes on Rose Hill south of Douglas.

Christmas Eve was especially great at Geneva. We had lots of special music including brass accompaniment. The sanctuary, choir sections, and narthex were full. If I had stayed another year, I was prepared to suggest a second Christmas Eve service.

Here's part of my last sermon in Geneva (which came on Christmas Eve): As most of you know, I grew up in Methodist parsonages in six different communities in Nebraska. Because of this, it is a little difficult to call one of these places "home." Only one of these houses is still used as a parsonage, but three of them are still standing. We lived in the Albion house for more than ten years, so that is closest to being home for me. When their new parsonage was built, somebody bought that old house for a couple hundred bucks. They moved it across town, and set it "catawampus," so that the side porch is now the front porch. They also put some new siding on it and attached a garage. It sure looks nice, but it's certainly not "home" anymore.

Having said this, our family will soon leave town and go home for Christmas. Last Thursday, Chris and Ana went "home" for the Landon Christmas and tomorrow we will head "home" for two more gatherings - the McGills and the Leypoldts. Many of you here tonight have already come home to Geneva for Christmas. Some of you, like us, have several more stops called "home" that you must make in the next few days.

In truth, I have not been inside the house I called "home" for over 25 years and Chris' "home" is located ten miles from where her folks now live. I read a survey recently that found Christmas to be the one time of the year when most people want to be home. It led birthdays by 3 to 1 and the 4th of July by almost 5 to 1.

A song tells us, "I'll be home for Christmas, if only in my dreams." Isn't it true that even when we are unable to go home, the feeling of being there remains important, "if only in our dreams." One of the great ironies of this season is that the holiday we want to spend at home, was built around a man and a woman who had a child away from home.

+++

In 1995 one of my Geneva parishioners decided to move to Denver to be close to her daughter. She put most of her belongings up for auction. Chris and I were at the sale. When looking around before the auctioneer began, I found a framed picture which contained what is called "John Wesley's Rule." I decided right away this was something I should buy. After a couple of hours my item was up for sale, and I started the bidding at two and a half. It shot up from there, until just two of us were nodding back to Mr. Underwood. My competitor was Sue Shaw, faithful church worker and friend. When we passed the $20 threshold, doubts set in, and Sue bought my treasure for maybe $25. No harm done.

A few months later I became Conference Treasurer, and we left Geneva with a few parting gifts. One of these was a nicely wrapped package from Sue Shaw. She had enjoyed Mr. Wesley's rules for a time, and passed them on to me - "Do all the good you can...by all the means you can...in all the ways you can...in all the places you can...at all the times you can...to all the people you can...as long as ever you can."

At Geneva, with my Jerusalem stole

Chapter 18
A Move To The Star City

On January 1, 1996 I began my time as Treasurer/Business Manager of the Nebraska AC of The UMC. I was the first member of the clergy to hold this position, and considered myself to be both worthy and well qualified. We started looking for a house when the job was offered in November, closed on it the first week in January, and moved a couple of weeks later. Ana, Seth, and Sarah were all living in Lincoln, so we saw them often.

My day-to-day responsibilities at work involved some unexpected challenges, but I had capable co-workers who assisted me. I discovered a couple of things that were troubling. A pastor had some dogs that trashed a parsonage interior, and some money was found to help the church fix the damage. However, the DS gave the money to the pastor and she disappeared with it. Because of the tension in the past year, there was a lot of paranoia in the office, but, there had been a lot of mismanagement, too.

Our computer system was terrible, and a few folks were into that "we've never done it this way before" philosophy. Later in the year, I bought a new house for the bishop, sold farms to make better use of assets, and bought some land to help plant new churches.

My trip to Dallas on March 18 was a 1-day event. Early in the morning, I boarded a small plane in Lincoln and flew right over Douglas and several farms I recognized. In less than a hour, I was in KCI to board a big plane for Dallas. By noon I was at my meeting, and headed back to the airport at 5 pm. My flight was delayed which would mess up the KCI connector, so I went to Omaha instead and Chris picked me up there. That was the day that was.

That first year I was in every District of our conference at least once, preached in fifteen local churches, and attended meetings in Dallas, Kansas City, Chicago (twice), and Buffalo, New York. In April, I went to the General Conference of our church which met in Denver, and heard Hillary Clinton, a lifelong United Methodist, speak there.

At a meeting in Hemingford, in the northwest corner of Nebraska, I met informally with a group of folks from churches in the area. We talked about mission funding, budgets, pastors' salaries and benefits, and tried to answer concerns. There was a group of five folks who listened attentively, but did not participate in discussions. As the meeting ended, I asked them if they had any questions. A man replied, "we're from Harrison and have never seen a Conference Treasurer before, and just wanted to meet you."

On one occasion, I preached at a little church in the central part of Nebraska. It was in the summer and I had a nice drive there, and arrived quite a while before worship was to start. I drove around town a little, and parked in front of the church. After a few minutes an older woman drove up, got out of her car, and started up the steep front steps. I decided to help her up the stairway. After we got inside the church, she asked if I was visiting the church and when I replied in the affirmative she said, "well, it's too bad you won't to able to hear our pastor speak, there's some bureaucrat from Lincoln taking her place today." The irony is, this was a church once served by my dad.

In July, Chris and I spent a week in Boston. Seth had received a full tuition scholarship to attend seminary there, but when he and Sarah considered the expense of housing and an uncertain job market, they decided to look elsewhere. He applied and was quickly accepted at my alma mater in Kansas City, and she found a job in Lincoln.

We purchased Boston tickets for them to use, so when their plans changed, we went instead. We were there the week of our 26th anniversary. We had a great time walking around town, also taking the trolley, bus, and subways. We went to Trinity Episcopal on Sunday. We also saw the Kennedy Library, old North Church, Harvard and Boston University campuses, Mount Auburn cemetery, and Filene's bargain basement.

Back in the office, the Bishop asked me how Seth felt about his appointment, which surprised me because he hadn't said anything about it. Seth was pretty anxious as he had requested a student church before conference, and they told him to wait until later in the summer. But, he hadn't heard a word. It seemed the DS was upset with me for lobbying her on his behalf, and thought it might be fun to see him sweat. I told the Bishop as much, and Seth received a call shortly thereafter.

Sarah received her degree from UNL in May. Seth was working at Valentino's and First UMC through July. On August 15, they moved to Clatonia and Seth began serving the Clatonia and Swanton churches. They were in a parsonage with their 3 cats and a dog. In September, Seth enrolled at Saint Paul School of Theology, and starting spending Monday-Thursday in Kansas City. Sarah went to work at the Friendship Home in Lincoln.

Shortly after Seth and Sarah moved to Clatonia, we went down to see the house and church. It was a nice sized home with a full basement, but there was water in the basement. I quickly saw one of the problems: an eaves trough was loose and rain was going straight down. I found a 2x4 and propped it up, but it was still full of water. I told Seth to leave it alone and when the trustees come over, maybe one of them would take away the 2x4 and get wet, thereby taking the problem seriously. Believe it or not, that's what happened.

Anastasia turned twenty in 1996, and was in her junior year at Wesleyan. She lived in an apartment about two blocks from campus along with her cats, Gabriel and Alexander. She worked as a host/wait staff at Valentino's for most of the year, and in September started in check processing at Union Bank's main office. She maintained good grades in her business administration major.

I had a disappointing episode concerning Nebraska Wesleyan during 1996. Two members of the CCFA were on the Wesleyan board, and I told them this was a conflict of interest. One agreed, and quickly resigned from CCFA. The other was upset because he was building a resume for future advancement, but he did leave the Wesleyan board. The college was lobbying for increased AC funding, and were telling folks these monies were earmarked for Nebraska UMC students.

As a father of two such students, I was quite surprised. I called the Financial Aid office, identified myself as a pastor and parent of a Wesleyan student, and requested an application for the Nebraska UM scholarship. The director said flatly there was no such scholarship. I then asked where the money sent by the Conference Treasurer went. He said it goes into the general scholarship fund, which was a worthy destination.

At the next session of the CCFA we discussed this matter, and I wrote the university telling them our support would continue, but to make certain there was no further misrepresentations. I was flabbergasted when a longtime friend, who was a Wesleyan Trustee, accused me of being an enemy of the college.

Chris continued her expert cooking with her specialty being the wonderful pretzels she learned to make at Eustis. She led several classes in pretzel-making before we left Geneva. In September Chris became a substitute kitchen helper in various Lincoln Public Schools. It was an ideal situation: she worked fours hours a day (only if she wanted to) and she got to experience a lot of interesting people and places. We had a wonderful attic room in our house on North 74th Street, and Chris had all her sewing things there. She almost always had a quilting project in the works.

In 1997 I began my second year as Conference Treasurer. It was a year of several challenges which affected the financial stability of the conference. UMC conferences depend on funds from local churches called apportionments. A huge problem for me was that over 50% of income came into my office during the last two weeks of the year and, of course, the expenses were paid when due.

We dealt with this by inserting "daily operating reserves" into the annual budget. One day I met with the Bishop and District Superintendents to discuss money. One DS asked about the reserves, and I explained that it was like a savings account: money tucked away for emergencies that exceeded the monthly income. Several of them, who made more money than me, were incredulous.

My home church at Albion celebrated their 125th Anniversary during the year with several events. On one Sunday they recognized those who had gone into full-time ministry, and had each of us speak for a few minutes. I reminisced about the day we moved to Albion in 1959, as described in Chapter 7. I told my home town folks that I was now in charge of scheduling moves for the conference.

I also recalled the Class Prophecy when I graduated high school in 1965, was "Chuck Leypoldt is now a high-ranking official in the Methodist Church." Since I was occupying an office in Lincoln, adjacent to the Bishop, this could be one of the few times such predictions had come true.

A month later in 1997, Mom and six of her children attended the anniversary program in Albion. We all chipped in to help restore the Good Shepherd window in the sanctuary. My mother turned 80 on October 8, 1997.

The annual task of moving pastors around Nebraska was quite challenging. Generally speaking, we had between 50 and 80 moves to schedule within a 3 week period. Only once did I arrange to move a family into a house, before the other was out. A very understanding clergy spouse alerted me to the mistake, and we worked out a satisfactory solution for all concerned.

I had a list of movers who wanted our business, and tried very hard to be accommodating. However, not all pastors were cooperative. The appointment changes were announced 6 to 8 weeks before move times, so I had plenty of time to make lists, send them out, and negotiate changes. The movers contacted pastors, and worked out details as well. Even so, we had issues.

One morning a mover called saying he was at a parsonage, but no one was home. I tracked down the pastor, a single parent. He was in the church office, frantically packing. He said nothing was packed at home yet, but he would call volunteers to help. I told him to go home, and open the house so the movers could get started. It worked out, but criminently!

Another time a pastor had so much chattel, the mover had to send a second large truck. The conference had always paid total cost, regardless of weight. But because of this avarice, we only paid for 16,000 pounds in succeeding years.

One more: an animal lover had such a filthy house with furniture covered in hair and feces, that the movers had to spend the next day power cleaning their van and dry cleaning their wrapping materials. All I could do was refer this to the DS, and offer to reimburse the trucker.

One last horror story came from a pastor who moved from a small town to Omaha. Our guidelines were very clear that pastors were to do their own packing, and he opted to have the moving people do this. I paid the full bill, and asked the pastor to reimburse the conference for his rule violation. This happened right before I left office, but my guess is he got away with it.

One of my responsibilities as Conference Treasurer was to receive and dispose of property acquired when a local church closed. In 1996 the Fairview UMC near Madison voted to close. The DS contacted me, and I hired a local Realtor to put the real estate on the market. In the meantime, Bishop Martinez told me about a church in Mexico that our conference was helping to build. I told him about the Fairview church furnishings. He liked the idea of moving these to Mexico, and I lined up a mover to take them to the border.

All these actions were in an article in the next **Nebraska Messenger**, the conference paper that went to every UMC family in the state. Former members of the Fairview church were infuriated. They claimed they were told by the DS that when the church closed, they could still use the building for local events. This may be true, but it needed to be purchased, and could no longer be called a UM church. I placed all actions on hold.

An attorney in Albion told me he was handling the estate of a woman who left $25,000 to the Fairview church. I said that church no longer exists. In a couple of months, the Conference officers were being sued in District Court at my home county. Fortunately, the president of the Conference Trustees was a very capable lawyer and he picked up the ball and the matter was resolved.

Later that year, the Conference also inherited a property north of Crofton in Knox County. This was a pretty little church, originally known as Salem Evangelical Church, and was built in the 1940's. I'd been to auctions, and knew church furnishings from that era weren't worth much. At the same time, my lodge in Ceresco was discussing new seating in the temple room. If they would provide the labor and truck to move them, I said they could have the furnishings, which we accomplished before the end of the year.

At the end of 1997, I wrote to friends and family to summarize our year. Chris was still working as a substitute in school kitchens. Seth and Sarah were at Clatonia, with same jobs, but now expecting a baby! Ana was a senior at Wesleyan, spent 8 weeks during the summer in Chicago, and now working at the Garden Café in Lincoln.

We didn't get much of a vacation in 1997. The Association of UMC Conference Treasurers met in West Virginia in September, so Chris and I drove there, and took a week off after the meeting. We spent some time in Ohio's Amish Country, and then to northern Iowa to see Bob and Betty Ellis before heading home.

The year of 1998 was an incredible one: the best of times and the worst of times. Our conference was torn apart in 1998, because an Omaha pastor performed a commitment ceremony for two women at his church. A complaint was filed and Bishop Martinez was required by the BoD to take disciplinary action. Because of my respect for the Bishop, and because I was an executive officer in the Conference, I supported his position.

One of our pastors made a profound statement to the press: "Conservative pastors believe what the Omaha pastor did was wrong and he should be defrocked. Liberal pastors believe he was properly performing his pastoral duties." The third group he called institutional liberals: "those who believe the Discipline should be changed, but until then, no pastor should perform the ceremony." The Bishop and I were in the third category.

On January 28, 1998 Chris and I became grandparents with the arrival of Sarah and Seth's daughter, Emma Kathryn. It was certainly a wonder, love, and praise moment to hold your first grandchild! After Sarah's maternity leave ended, we had Emma at our home three or four days each week, which continued until June of 2000.

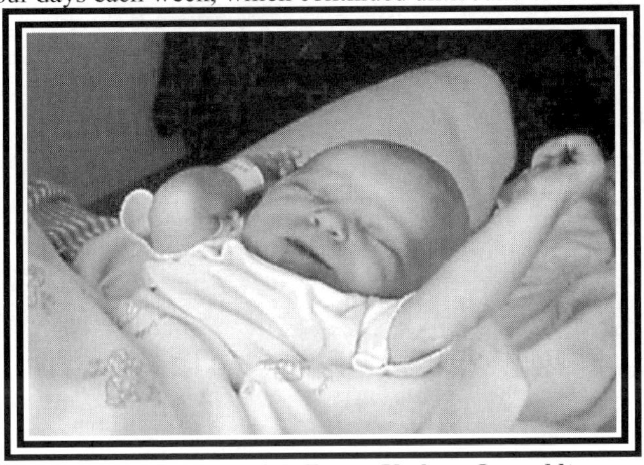

Our first grandchild: Emma Kathryn Leypoldt

In February Chris accompanied me to a meeting in Atlanta. On Sunday we drove to Plains, and saw Jimmy and Rosalynn Carter at their Baptist Church. A picture from that day adorns my study wall.

Ana received her degree from Nebraska Wesleyan on May 16, 1998. We had a big day and most of our family attended a celebration at our house afterward. Her kindergarten teacher, Shelley Irland Lashley, was there as well. Ana went to work at Ameritrade in Bellevue. She was commuting from Lincoln in her 1998 Honda Civic, and preparing to move to Arizona the next March.

Also in May, Seth took Emma to meet Grace McGill at the Waverly Care Center. He placed the baby in Grandma's arms, and told her this was her great-great-granddaughter. She said, "I had two girl babies, Margaret and Arlene." She had three children we knew about: Earnest, Arlene, and Mancel. Who was Margaret?

Soon after we told her younger brother, Art Talcott, what she said. He said that one summer when he was a teenager, he stayed at his sister's house and looked after her oldest son who was a toddler. He said that Grace was sick all summer. He later figured out that she had lost a premature baby, and their father, a country doctor, had disposed of the tiny fetus. Apparently, that was common practice at a time when such births were frequent.

Although Grandma hadn't spoken of it in later years, she never forgot the baby girl she loved and mourned. We were so glad she got to meet and hold Emma, as she died about a month later.

Grace McGill meets her great-great-granddaughter

This was my report to the AC in June of 1998:

In the past year I celebrated my 50th birthday, became a grandfather, and watched my youngest child graduate from college. I also viewed the church in which I was baptized being sold at public auction. All this put me in a reflective mood. I've been both an observer and a participant in the Nebraska Conference for the past 50 years. I've actually been inside a majority of church buildings in our conference - most of which are in rural areas. I believe we need a new organization. We have the MFSA, UMW, UMM, and UMYF; we also have the AUMEN, ARMS, and Order of the Elder. But I think we really need one more group. I am, therefore, announcing the creation of the Redneck Assimilated Theologians - RAT for short.

If you've ever taken the youth group for an overnight retreat at an interstate rest area, you might be a RAT.

If you've ever conducted a wedding where the best man was a huntin' dog, you might be a RAT.

If you've ever referred to the United Methodist Women leadership team as the Spice Girls, you might be a RAT.

If any of the kids in your youth group are named Opie, Skeeter, Bubba, Thelma Lou, or Newgene, you might be a RAT.

If you've ever used a Jerry Clower story in a sermon, you might be a RAT.

If you know who Jerry Clower is, you might be a RAT.

If you have white, green, red, and purple baseball caps, and you wear them around town at the appropriate seasons, you might be a RAT.

If you've ever searched for and downloaded redneck jokes for your sermons, you might be a RAT.

If your dog brings something home and you serve it at the next church potluck, you might be a RAT.

If you install a clapper device to dim the sanctuary lights during your sermon, you might be a RAT.

If the Bishop visits your church and you introduce him as our "supreme dude," you might be a RAT.

It was well received, but I kept my day job for a while longer.

+++

In July we saw a Dodger game in Saint Louis and in August we visited the Grand Canyon. Seth continued his studies in Kansas City and serving the Clatonia and Swanton churches. Sarah was with the Friendship Home in Lincoln. Chris was doing her substitute kitchen work with the Lincoln Public Schools and we were watching Emma 3 or 4 days a week.

Several friends in the Conference warned me there was a coup d'état in progress. Three staffers at the Conference office prepared a document containing unfriendly descriptions of my work performance and complete falsehoods, and presented these to the chair of the CCFA. He gave this document to me, and I met with an attorney which completely diffused them. However, there was no wonder, love, or praise left for me at 49th and Saint Paul in Lincoln, Nebraska.

In the fall of 1998, I began actively looking for new employment. I started with my contacts in banking, and was immediately offered a branch manager position. However, I was committed to staying in Lincoln, and the position required a move. A friend put me in touch with a banker who was looking for someone with my qualifications. I met with him, and received another offer requiring a move. I was invited to interview at the bank in Davenport. Nothing came of that, but I was directed to a similar opening in Doniphan. Even though I was not finding exactly what I wanted, all this was encouraging because I learned there were jobs, and I was being favorably considered. But still, the main thing was I didn't want to ask Chris to move again.

On December 5, 1998, Seth and I officiated at the wedding of my nephew Nick Leypoldt and Suzanne Smith. I told the group that I felt this couple would have a happy marriage because whenever they had a fight, someone always said, "I'm sorry" and Nick always said, "that's OK." This was almost the same joke I told at his parent's wedding 23 years previously.

Lone Tree Road near Scribner, Nebraska

Ana receives college degree in May 1998

A poem I wrote on October 3, 1998

30 years ago was our first kiss
We've had so many years of bliss
You're a grandma and still a lovely miss
So very often I've been remiss
You've always helped me avoid abyss
You are my lovely Chris

Grandpa and Emma in October 1998

Chapter 19
Revisiting The Learning Curve

One of my responsibilities in the Conference Office was caring for property and insurance. I knew the local Church Mutual agents and the division manager, Craig Wessman, who lived in Des Moines. I worked with Craig to set up a group workers' compensation program in 1997. In November 1998, I discovered one of the local CMIC agents had moved to another job, and I immediately called Wessman. He was happy to hear of my interest, and said he would be advertising the position and doing some interviews in December.

Meanwhile, the bank at Bennet was advertising for a loan officer. Their manager was Lee Anderbery, who worked with me in Douglas, and their president was Brad Clark, a college classmate. They asked me to interview, and offered me a job. I met previously with Wessman, and he called January 10 asking me to be a regional representative for Church Mutual Insurance. It's almost worse to choose between two opportunities, than to be looking for work.

The Bennet job had a guaranteed salary and benefits, and a promise for advancement in the company. The main drawback was the daily commute of 20 miles, and the need to buy another car. CMIC had an office near our home, a company car, good benefits, but lower initial pay (it also offered commissions and incentives). I decided to go with Church Mutual.

I informed the Bishop of my decision to leave the treasurer position March 1, and decided to request clergy retirement status on the same date. On February 28, I cleaned out my office, parked the conference car, and starting driving a 1998 Pontiac Grand Am, leased by CMIC.

On March 1, I drove to Des Moines for a week of training at the Division Office there. Craig Wessman took me through a huge training manual which introduced me to the company, and the peculiarities of establishing values for church buildings. One needed to identify building type, ceiling height, HVAC systems, art glass, pipe organ rank, sanctuary furnishings, and other things to get a proper cost estimate. CMIC provided me with 100 foot cloth tape measure. I suggested a steel one would be more practical, and Craig said the company provides this one and that's the one we should use. I politely tuned him out after that.

In June I was renewing a policy at Genoa, and needed to get a new church diagram. As I was struggling with the primitive tape measure, a church member told me to get a measuring wheel which I did. Later, Craig was with me when I was quoting a boarding school with several buildings. He and I divided the structures to get diagrams. He saw me using the wheel, and asked to borrow it.

Most of my time in Des Moines was spent calling Nebraska United Methodist churches to discuss, and hopefully enroll them, in the conference workers' compensation program. The next week, I moved into my new office at 303 North 52nd Street in Lincoln. I shared this office with Dave Allen, who had been with CMIC for 10 years, and gave me more valuable training than anyone else in the company. Dave and I were very different in many ways. He had quit the Republican Party because it was too liberal; I was and am among the greenest of Democrats. He was raised Methodist, but was searching for a more austere faith; I was ashamed of how conservative the UMC had become. We were like siblings who bonded because of a common enemy: the "parental" home office. Dave helped me deal with our inefficient software, and advised me on ways to work the insurance system to my advantage.

Dave also enlightened me on the "three Ps:" Product, Presentation, and Price. Church Mutual's multi-peril coverage for religious organizations was the industry standard. We needed to know all about it and explain it well to prospects and customers. But to get it sold, the premium needed to be competitive.

My training process continued with me accompanying Dave on his customer and prospect visits, and weekly sessions with Wessman either in Lincoln or Des Moines. By May I was pretty much on my own, and picked up two new customers that month. Dave and I shared that cubby hole on North 52nd, and a bigger one near the Gateway Mall for the next 12 years.

One of my early customer visits was with a pastor in Columbus, who had literally inherited the job from his grandfather, who founded the church. This guy was very capable, but his only training for the ministry was being a Sunday school teacher and other volunteer work. After his grandfather died, the family hired an outsider as pastor, but he was soon gone and the mantel fell to this young man. When he discovered I had a seminary degree, he asked all kinds of questions about sermon organization and counseling. I gave him what advice I could, and he was always happy to see me through the years.

I also had an interesting conversation at the Assembly of God in Thedford, whose young pastor was very personable. After discussing insurance business, I asked him about his career. He said he moved to Thedford from Plattsmouth, which had a very small AG congregation. He had come to town about a month after we left. It was uncanny to hear his stories of disappointment there that paralleled my own.

My travels took me to a unique church in North Loup, Nebraska. This was the only Seventh Day Baptist church in Nebraska, and they also owned a camp ground which I insured. The church traces their heritage from England to Rhode Island to Wisconsin. In 1870, members of the congregation heard of homesteads available in North Loup and within a few years, virtually the whole congregation moved and established this beautiful church. On one of my visits, I met the granddaughter of the founding pastor. She and her husband took me to the camp, and shared several fascinating stories with me.

I decided to attend the clergy session at annual conference in June 1999, sitting in the back row of Wesleyan's Weary Center. When leaving, I told a couple of my friends, "gotta go, I've got a real job now!" I did go back to the Memorial Service the next evening, as the choir from the Eustis church was there. The preacher for the evening was Cal Leeds, who gave a remarkable message, even though he was suffering from terminal cancer. A few months earlier, he warned me about the effort to "fire" me, and jokingly predicted he would outlive my employment in the conference office.

I did not attend the retirement service, but Seth brought me a plaque which I found when moving in 2013, and put above the door to my study. When I was a young pastor, I looked forward to hearing the stories told by retiring pastors. A few took the opportunity to chastise the system for its weaknesses, but most told lighthearted, sentimental tales. I'd known Keith Bruning since I was six, and he retired in 1975. He said, "I always told my kids that in the church you'll find the best people in town, and the worst people in town, and often you can't tell the difference." I went to seminary with Olin Belt who was 20 years older than me, and in his retirement message he thanked me and another student for encouraging him to come to Nebraska. He also told a great story about one of his lay persons who I knew well. Olin had been a plumber before he went into the ministry, and the little church at Ohiowa had no indoor lavatory because of sewer line issues. Olin figured out a way to get one installed, and when he moved on this parishioner said, "We always wanted a bathroom in our church, and Olin made that possible. Now every time we use the toilet, we'll think of Olin." Another one, Jerry McInnis, was very practical and spoke to the clergy bibliophiles in the audience: "I've accumulated a lot of books over the years, and now I'll have time to read them."

On July 17, 1999, the day after my 52nd birthday, I traveled to Merrill, Wisconsin for training at the home office of CMIC. I was there until August 5th, which was the longest time Chris and I have been apart. There were a dozen other new regional reps in attendance. The "class" sessions were pretty dull, but after hours we experienced the night life in Merrill and nearby towns. I drove my company car up there, and when the session was over, went to Garner, Iowa where Bob and Betty Ellis lived. Chris had made her way there by bus, and met the Ellises at a little town called Boondocks. We had a great time, but I don't think she'll ever take the bus again.

I spent the rest of the summer getting used to my new job. Chris went with me on a long trip to visit the UMC conference properties in Chadron, Scottsbluff, McCook, and Cozad. In the fall Seth returned to Kansas City to finish his final year at Saint Paul, and Sarah was working in Lincoln. This meant we had Emma at least 3 days each week, which was wonderful!

In September my buddy John Charles stayed with us, and we attended our 30-year class reunion at Wesleyan. In October, I organized a surprise party for Chris' 50th birthday at Douglas.

When my seminary days were over and I was a "full-time" pastor, I mulled over the issue of my appearance. Specifically, should I wear a coat and tie on a daily basis. My father only dressed up when necessary: Sundays, funerals, weddings, meetings. One of my friends advocated the "dress for success" philosophy. There were six pastors in the Davenport-Carleton vicinity and only one wore a tie on a daily basis, so I stuck with the informal majority.

When I went into banking I was expected to "suit up" daily, but only did so when the boss was in town or when I went to a meeting. One time I forgot to tell my Douglas co-workers that Alan Dunlap would be at the bank later in the morning. When I showed up in a suit, they chewed me out. In Eustis and Geneva I went downtown for coffee almost every morning, and when I appeared in suit and tie, someone always asked if I was conducting a funeral that day.

As Conference Treasurer, I was the only male staffer who dressed informally, except for meetings. CMIC had a written dress code wherein men were supposed to wear tie and jacket daily, except Friday. This never happened in the Lincoln office except when the manager was in town, and that was seldom.

CMIC furnished me with a company car, albeit a crummy Pontiac Grand Am, but I really enjoyed traveling the back roads and by-ways of Nebraska. This windshield time produced a lot of introspective thinking. One realization was I had made a subtle, yet profound, shift in vocation. Previously, as pastor and small town banker, I had a calling. I was doing something that effected meaning and enhanced people's lives. Beginning March 1, 1999, my worth as a human being was measured by the number of contacts, invitations to quote, persuasive meetings, and closed contracts I achieved. My new job had elements of service, but the bottom line was sales.

I was going through a metamorphosis. It wasn't traumatic, and I had plenty of time for self-analysis as I wandered around the state. In my life, I had made numerous changes of opinion, conquered a few bad habits, switched political parties, learned to like diet Coke, and cozied up to a few people I didn't like when I first met them. I used to think Apple Computers were superior to IBM-compatibles, and I once believed Ford cars were worse than Chevies, but experience transformed me.

There were and are some things I don't think I'll ever give up: I was born, baptized, bred, billowed, and bolstered in Methodism. I'll probably always be partial to blue-eyed blondes. I doubt I'll ever be a vegetarian, or put on another pair of roller-skates. I didn't think I would accomplish much in my introduction to the church insurance world. I only picked up five new customers my first year.

+++

Among the Protestants in Nebraska, the largest groups are UMC, ELCA, and LCMS. The LCMS provided me with quite a few interesting stories. My dad had an incredible experience in Crawford back in the fifties. The pastors met to plan an interfaith Thanksgiving service to be held at the Bethlehem LCMS building. My father preached from the Lutheran pulpit. This was reported to the District President, and the church was instructed to destroy the pulpit and replace all the flooring surrounding it. I don't know what happened to their pastor.

Many years later I had a similar experience. In 1976 a woman at Ithaca died. I knew her well as she had been attending our church with her daughter, but she was a Lutheran from nearby Ashland. When I stopped to visit the daughter, she told me they wanted me to conduct the funeral. However, they were told I could not use the pulpit so they did not ask. This was an American Lutheran (now ELCA) congregation.

In October of 2001, I had a meeting with the council at one of my LCMS customers. Before the meeting started, the pastor spoke about an interfaith gathering in Yankee Stadium which included a LCMS District President, David Benke. He said he had attended a Nebraska District pastor's conference and a resolution to censure Benke failed, and he was concerned there might be a split in his denomination. A LCMS pastor in Newtown, Connecticut was criticized for doing the same thing in February 2013. My view of ecumenism was very different, but I kept my lip buttoned.

There is a LCMS congregation in north Omaha that is quite unique, as they are nearly 100% African-American. They had a black pastor for many years, but when he retired they had problems finding a successor. They hired an interim pastor who was working at Boys Town, had a doctorate, was a UMC elder, and an African American. The LCMS District President told him he could not continue unless he was working toward a degree at a LCMS seminary. He did not tell the church to destroy their pulpit, though. And I'm pretty certain no one knew their preacher was a Freemason.

I went to a LCMS customer in Omaha, and found they had an interim pastor. This person had been a hospital chaplain for several years, and was the first LCMS pastor I'd seen with hair in a pony tail. We visited a while and I decided to ask, "do you think the LCMS will ever ordain women?" His answer was, "never say never."

I got to know several of my pastor customers pretty well over the years. Three LCMS pastors who were close to my age died in 2012, my last year with CMIC. John Emslie of Blair died of a heart attack in February 2012 at the age of 68. Duane Fahr of Bloomfield was a month younger than me. He had been in the sanctuary with a wedding party for pictures on a Saturday afternoon. He couldn't be found when it was time to start the ceremony, and they found him dead in his office. Bob Reimer was a pastor in Wahoo and also farmed near Belgrade. He died on May 24, 2012 in an accident at his farm. He was also 68.

From time to time I insured the LCMS camp in Nebraska and two of their high schools. The great scholar Martin Marty was born in West Point, and grew up in Battle Creek where his father was the LCMS school principal. As brother Martin later switched to the ELCA and attended Trinity UCC in Chicago, most folks in Battle Creek don't call him a favorite son.

I've been fortunate to see Garrison Keillor in person three times, and we listen to him every Saturday on PBS. In October 2004, we saw him in Omaha where he helped promote the camping ministries of the LCMS, ELCA, and WELS churches in Nebraska and Iowa. At one point he talked about family squabbles, and he said in his family they dealt with arguments and differences of opinion by singing. He then led all the Lutherans, and at least two Methodists, in singing "A Mighty Fortress Is Our God."

Another unsung Nebraska hero is Dr. Walter Brueggemann, who I met in seminary. He is an immanent scholar of the Hebrew scriptures and was born in Tilden, Nebraska, while his pastor father served what is today the Peace UCC. That was the home church of my stepfather, and his cousin Hall of Fame outfielder Richie Ashburn. Peace UCC became my customer in 2001.

In November of 1999 I was invited to preach at the UM churches in David City and Bellwood. The Gospel lesson was Matthew 23:1-12 and my sermon was titled, "Perfection and Total Depravity." Portions of what I said follow.

Near my home town of Albion, up in Boone County, Nebraska, lies the little community of Saint Edward. It is a pretty little town with tree-lined streets and attractive homes. When I was growing up, Saint Edward was famous for two things. First, it had a huge dip on Main Street (which is also Nebraska Highway 39). This dip was so big you literally had to slow down to 5 miles per hour to drive through it. We used to think it was put there to impede all the hot cars in Boone County, but actually it had more to do with controlling Beaver Creek, which often became an ocean after rains. The second and more famous thing about Saint Edward is Cletus, Kenny, and Rex Fischer grew up and went to High School there. They all played six-man football for Saint Ed, and became stars for the Cornhuskers. If you're not a native Nebraskan or Cornhusker fan, this means little to you, but in Boone County it's real important.

This main street had an attractive Methodist Church right next to the big dip on Main Street. You couldn't help but notice and admire this pretty, brick structure as you slowed down to drive through the dip. A block north and west stood an equally impressive brick Presbyterian Church. The Methodists had their parsonage, the Presbyterians their manse. Seeing these two structures in tiny Saint Edward was always a symbol of stability and a reminder of a proud pioneer heritage.

About a month ago, my work took me up to Saint Edward. It was the first time I had been there for a while. The Beaver Creek bridge still greets you when you come in from the west. The downtown looked familiar, but the big dip is gone. Another noteworthy change was the Methodist and Presbyterian buildings are no longer there. In their place, where the Methodist church used to be, sits a brand new building with the name "United Methodist-Presbyterian Church of Saint Edward."

It's a curious thing that Methodists and Presbyterians are able to unite. John

Wesley had a close friend and fellow pastor, George Whitefield, who was considered the most eloquent preacher among the early Methodists. In the 1740's Whitefield and Wesley had a falling out. Historians called it the Calvinist/Arminian controversy. For us it has to do with a difference of opinion concerning the nature of God. Calvinists, later known as Reformed which includes Presbyterians, Congregationalists, and Baptists considered human beings to be totally depraved. That is, it is God alone who can rescue, save, restore, and free us. Humans, they believed, are totally incapable of grasping the reality of God, except as God gives the gift of understanding. John Newton, who wrote the hymn "Amazing Grace," and Charles Wesley, along with Whitefield became Calvinistic Methodists.

Strict Arminians, on the other hand, held a more hopeful view for humans and most early Methodists remained Arminians. They believed that people are not totally depraved. As a matter of fact, John Wesley taught that human beings have been endowed by their creator with the potential to become perfect, to be like Christ, to be imitators of God. Wesley taught that God gave each person a spark of divinity and there was no limit to human potential.

I wonder if the Methodists and Presbyterians of Saint Edward discussed these ancient controversies before they took down their old buildings and joined together. I doubt it. Most churches are concerned with far more mundane matters. The point is both Calvinists and Arminians are correct: Christians need to be humble and realize we are dependent upon God, and we also should know we are important and can do great things.

Jesus said: "The greatest among you will be your servant." The good news is it matters not if you think you are totally depraved or going on to perfection. What matters is that you belong to God, and when you respond to God in service to others, you have been exalted.

Postscript

This sermon produced some unintended consequences. An angry Episcopalian was in the audience and took offense at the words, "And call no one your father on earth, for you have one Father - the one in heaven." She wrote a scathing letter to the **Columbus Telegram**, announcing to the world that St. Luke's UMC in David City was encouraging a holy war against Roman Catholics and Anglicans because these groups insist on referring to their pastors as "Father."

I received a call from the pastor asking me what I might have said to provoke this gathering storm in peaceful Butler County. What a wonderful luxury it is to be a guest preacher, I thought. I sent her a copy of my words and contacted a Masonic brother in the David City church, requesting his interpretation of events. Not to worry, he said, the injured complainant was a documented goofball, and the Columbus newspaper often published senseless remarks.

I wonder if anyone was offended hearing the masculine bias in our Bible? Besides, if one believes the Bible equals the language of God, the verse I read from Matthew's Gospel belonged to Jesus not me.

Post Postscript

The church in St. Edward voted to become United Methodist only, so it truly doesn't matter anymore.

+++

I had no regrets about my job change but I did keep looking for something more satisfying. Our year of 1999 was summarized for the annual Christmas letter and included the following:

As Regional Representative for CMIC my territory stretched west to Cherry County and south to Interstate 80 - about 40,000 square miles. However, lots of the work was done by phone. It had been interesting and challenging. Perhaps best of all, it gave me the a chance to observe and pontificate upon the state of contemporary Christianity in a variety of settings.

Our house got a face-lift. The fake stucco, compressed siding, and wood fascia was in need of repair. So we replaced it with steel and vinyl covering everything but the roof and brick. We also had an underground sprinkler system installed.

Chris kept things steady around our house. She had a couple of "minor" surgeries early in the year - to deal with ganglions and endoscopic things. She continued to work as a roving substitute in the kitchens of the Lincoln Public schools and served as an officer in a local TOPS club. Of course, the largest and best block of time was reserved for watching Emma, which she did four days a week for three to four hours.

Emma was changing every day (she was 2 in January 2000). Highlights for 1999 included her first steps, a growing vocabulary (which includes grandma and grandpa - well, both words sound like "bo-pa"), and most important, lots of smiles and hugs every time we saw her.

Seth, Sarah, and Emma lived in Clatonia. Sarah was with Friendship Home in Lincoln and Seth was in his final year at Saint Paul seminary. Their lives were full of exciting changes. Seth was looking forward to his May 2000 graduation and Sarah was expecting our *second* grandchild.

Ana continued at Ameritrade. She moved from Lincoln to Omaha in April. This move followed a very courageous decision *not* to relocate in Arizona. She was happy and busy and we got to see her frequently.

On January 1, 2000 we ushered in the millennium with very little fanfare. Bob and Betty Ellis came to see us on the last day of 1999 and we went downtown and hooted our horn at the right second. All the alarmists, conspiracy theorists, and other assorted crazy people were wrong; the world did not come to an end. We all went to Clatonia on New Year's Day and spent some time with Seth, Sarah, and Emma.

Since I had a real job now, it was back to work on January 2. I was determined to add a few customers during the year and win a trip to Hawaii.

In the spring of 2000, I stopped at St. John's African Methodist Episcopal Church in north Omaha. Their building is on the National Register of Historic Places, and is of the "Prairie Style" made famous by Frank Lloyd Wright. Beginning with a basement in 1921, it was not completed until 1956. This church was in the direct path of a devastating tornado that twisted through Omaha in 1975. During that storm the concrete roof was lifted a few inches and set down again, a testimony of a sure foundation. St. John's became a customer I enjoyed and often visited over the years.

Seth received his degree from Saint Paul School of Theology in May 2000. Two weeks later, he was at AC and awaiting the imminent arrival of his second child. He was ordained a Deacon at the close of conference, and still no baby. Family and friends were at our home after the ordination when Sarah and Seth left for the hospital. Cora Erin was born breech later that evening.

Seth's first full-time appointment was in Aurora, about 80 miles west of Lincoln. They were scheduled to move when Cora was just two weeks old. We spent part of four days helping them pack and unpack. It was a big event for Emma, who was then 2½.

When we got to Clatonia the day of the move, she was standing on the front porch looking at the huge truck in front of her house. She said, "That's a moving truck....but it's not moving."

We helped them get settled in Aurora, and were there the next week and took Emma to Grand Island to do some shopping. On the way home we stopped at KFC and picked up supper. It had been another long day for Seth, and he was sitting casually when his plate full of chicken, coleslaw, mashed potatoes and gravy slid off the table. Part of it ended on his lap. He said, "Crap!"

Emma's eyes got very big and she exclaimed, "Daddy said crap." Then she told each one of us starting with Mommy, "Daddy said crap." I'm pretty sure she had no idea what crap might be.

In August I was sent for another week of training in Merrill, Wisconsin. While there I received a call from a large church in Norfolk, saying they had accepted my proposal. Except for that good news, the week was a colossal waste of time.

On our 25th Anniversary, I promised Chris a trip to Niagara Falls. That was in 1995. We finally made it there in September of 2000!! It was a wonderful trip with great weather. We took a first class tour of the Falls (including the boat ride that gets you all wet). We also drove to Thousand Islands to see the beautiful Boldt Castle. We went through Canada, and stopped in Indiana Amish country on the way home.

In the fall of 2000 I was invited to quote the Omaha Chinese Christian Church. This congregation included many young professionals, who had come to this country to attend college. Most of the folks on the church council also fit that description. I made my presentation in English (obviously), and their questions were all in English. At one point the council chair made what seemed to be a summary, but it was in Mandarin, as was a brief discussion. Then silence; and a young man said to me, "you have our business."

Anastasia continued to live and work in the Omaha area. She was now a "New Accounts Senior Representative," which was a supervisory position at Ameritrade, Inc. She made it to Lincoln frequently and out to Aurora whenever possible.

My first full year in the insurance business was a successful one. I increased my book (total premiums in my territory) by 14%, and added a couple of large churches, a Lutheran high school, and my former church in Ceresco. I also continued to add United Methodist churches to the group worker's compensation program which produced little income but gave me all-important "unit credits." The end result was a nice bonus and a trip to Hawaii.

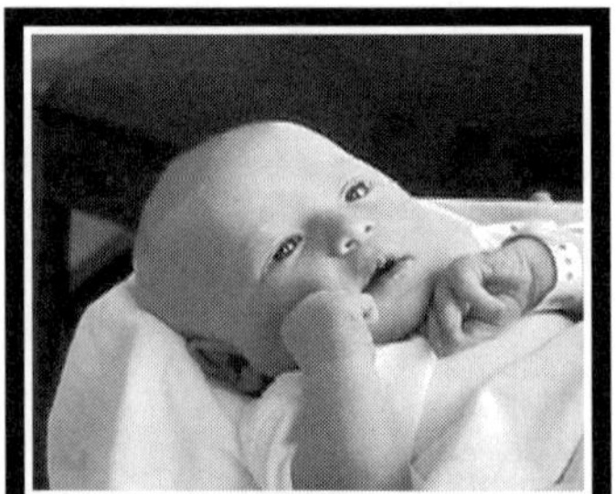

Cora at one day

Chapter 20
Adventures Of A Happy Wanderer

CMIC decided to offer insurance services to senior/assisted living facilities. Regional Representatives were summoned to the home office for training, and I flew to Merrill, Wisconsin in early February 2001. My colleague, Dave Allen, had driven to Des Moines, and caught a ride with one of the Iowa salespersons. On Friday we were ready to head home, and were told the airport in Mosinee was closed because of heavy snow.

The Iowa guys and Dave decided to drive home, and I went with them. Dave and I climbed into a Ford Taurus that was being driven by a former stock car racer turned insurance salesman. Another car was occupied by four Iowans, and we agreed to communicate via cell phone regarding road conditions. Our driver was a bit of a show-off to say the least. No snowdrift was too big, and he conquered them all as we headed west toward Minneapolis. In those days, Dave refused to wear a seat belt, and I became concerned when I saw him buckle up. At supper time, we zipped through the Twin Cities and our chauffeur decided we should stop to eat.

An hour later, we were back in the car and it was dark all around us. It was 250 miles to Des Moines, we had a full tank of gas, but we weren't on a mission from God. We discovered the other group hadn't wasted their time at a restaurant, and were about a hour ahead of us. Our driver did his best to catch up via slick roads and blowing snow.

It was close to midnight when we arrived in Des Moines, where Dave had left his car. Our division manager implored us to stay at his house, but it was only a three hour drive down Interstate 80 to Lincoln. Dave was driving a year-old Pontiac Grand Am with no dashboard lights, but we would not be approaching the speed limit on this night. The snow had let up in Des Moines, and away we went.

At Stuart, 40 miles west of Des Moines, it was snowing in clumps and the visibility was terrible. We decided to look for a motel. The first one was full; the second one had a 18-wheeler blocking access to its parking lot. Back on the Interstate I saw something I didn't know existed: thunder snow. We drove on and secured the last available room at Adair, 18 miles west of Stuart. The next day we were rewarded with a blue sky and bright sun and made our way back to Lincoln.

In my initial training time mention was made of achieving goals and going on a trip as a reward, but not in such a way that it really turned me on. However, the possibility of going to Hawaii was appealing, so I worked a little harder, and in February 2001 we were bound for Honolulu.

We got up early, drove to Omaha, then flew to St. Louis and waited for the Hawaiian connection. When we got to the Waikiki Hilton, we were so tired we napped for a while before the evening events. At 7 pm we walked across a wide expanse of green, listening to Hawaiian music. The weather was perfect and I was thinking, "this is paradise."

For four days we toured the main island including Pearl Harbor, the U.S.S. Missouri, Chinatown, the Polynesian Cultural Center, National Cemetery, and many other places. Our trip home was interesting to say the least. We were scheduled to leave at 6:40 pm, but did not do so until midnight. We arrived in St. Louis at mid morning, but Lincoln flights were full, and we ended up with first class tickets to Omaha where Ana picked us up. Our luggage was nowhere to be found, so Ana took us to the Lincoln airport where our car was parked. Magically, the luggage was also in Lincoln.

Unfortunately during the week my stepfather, Donovan R. Walters, D.D.S., died in Lincoln. He had been battling heart issues for several years. Don was our family's dentist in Albion. He was the only dentist I went to until I was 26. One time he filled a cavity for me, and said there was another starting on the upper front. I said to go ahead and fix it. He just started drilling without any Novocain, and after less than a minute said, "it's gone." I never had a problem with it again.

Don and his first wife were divorced in the late sixties when the kids left home and he built a small house. At the same time, my mother was looking for a place to live, and she bought Don's four-bedroom place at 6th and Fairview in the south end of Albion in 1969. They were an item by the time Chris and I were married in 1970.

In 1973 Don sold his dental practice, and moved to Watertown, South Dakota where he taught dental assisting at the Community College. Mom and Don were married on Christmas Day, 1973, at the Albion UMC, with yours truly officiating. They bought a nice place across from a park in Watertown.

They moved to a new house west of Beatrice in 1975 when Don became a staff dentist at the Beatrice Developmental Center. He retired ten years later, and Mom and he had several good years before health issues crept up on them. My children and nieces and nephews called him Grandpa Don, and we were very grateful for the companionship he gave our mother.

Grandpa and his girls in 2000

As of January 13, 2001, I was entitled to be called "The Reverend Worshipful Brother Sir Knight Charles Wesley Leypoldt," but Grandpa Chuck suits me just fine.

Grandma and her girls in 2001

In the spring of 2001, a pastor in Grand Island called me seeking insurance coverage for a presbytery of which he was the moderator. I met him at his church office, also the presbytery office, got the information necessary and visited a while. When I left, I walked through the church sanctuary and had a "déjà vu" moment.

I went back to the office, and asked the pastor about the church's history. He said it had been built by the Seventh-Day Adventists. Aha! My father had a cousin in Grand Island, who died in 1960 and we attended the funeral in this sanctuary. It's fascinating how things float around in your head for years, and land unexpectedly.

On September 16, 2001 I preached at Good Shepherd Presbyterian Church in Lincoln, which was the Sunday after the World Trade Center attack. A portion of my sermon follows…

My spouse claims that when I tell family stories, I tend to embellish the details; and when that happens, my memory becomes selective and I always emerge a hero. I have decided this morning to "bare my soul" and admit to you that I do have a couple of serious hang-ups and I have put my family through suffering because of them.

The first is that I think of myself as a happy wanderer. Perhaps you know the song: *"I am a happy wanderer along the mountain track; and as I go I love to sing, my knapsack on my back."*[44]

I wasn't inspired to go back-packing or anything like that, but I do enjoy traveling the back roads and taking my own sweet time about it. The next big problem I will confess to this morning can be summed up by what I've seen printed on tee-shirts: "real men don't ask directions." Yes I love to wander, but I also wonder when I wander, because often I get lost, and when the family is along, they become real grouchy real soon. *"Oh, may I go a wandering until the day I die."*

I have been lost in several of America's largest cities. Every summer we add a new one. Last year it was South Bend, Indiana and Rochester, N. Y. A few years ago it was Madison, Wisconsin. I think it all started in 1969 when I went to seminary in Kansas

City. During those three years I got lost in some of the finest and worst neighborhoods. Throughout the years, I've been lost in Wichita, Oklahoma City, Philadelphia, Baltimore, Washington, D.C., Portland, Memphis, Nashville, El Paso, Dallas, Fort Worth and both Minneapolis and Saint Paul. I have never been to Columbus, Georgia, but I have been lost in Columbus, Ohio, Columbus, Mississippi, and Columbus, Nebraska. And yes, even the city of Angels, Los Angeles, California.

The most lost I ever got was a day that I was on foot, and my family was thousands of miles away. I was in the old city of Jerusalem on a Sunday. I had gone to church, and then did some shopping. It's hard to describe the sights, sounds, and smells of this ancient city. It's somewhat like a shopping mall - except that the passageways are very narrow and the shops are quite small. The merchants meet you in the door or in the walkways. Prices are determined by bartering.

I was with four colleagues. We had a couple of hours before we needed to be back at the hotel for the tour bus departure. I was distracted by a very persuasive Armenian shopkeeper, and fifteen minutes later I was alone. I looked in vain for my companions in the nearby markets. I decided to head back to the hotel by myself. After walking for blocks the better part of an hour, I simply could not find my way out of the old city. For a while I was the only non-Arab within sight. I was worried. I was embarrassed. I was scared.

I was about ready to do the unthinkable - ask for directions - when I spied some familiar faces. They were other American clergymen equally lost in this holy city. Fortunately, we soon met up with one of the clergy women on our tour. She asked for directions, and we found our way out of the old city and back to the hotel.

In Luke's Gospel, the 15th chapter, we find three examples of how God manages the problem of our tendency to get lost. The point of today's lesson is that God knows there are folks who get lost. God knows even the most faithful become complacent and disinterested in the ways of Christ, but that never stops God from searching to find us.

Jesus encouraged us to hear and understand that God is looking for us. The parables also proclaim joyous conclusions. The shepherd, the housewife, the prodigal's father, all gather friends and neighbors for a party when the lost is found. Jesus said there is no greater joy than a lost child returning to God.

All of us have been affected by the tragic and horrible events of this past week. The stories in Luke strengthen us today. They remind us God is always searching for ways to make us whole. God is with us whether we know it, recognize it, or understand it. Jesus said he came to "seek and save." Against the backdrop of rescue workers looking for survivors, or a grieving nation looking for answers, our faith reminds us of a God who never gives up, who never quits, who is never silent.

The woman in Jesus' parable searches diligently and finds her lost coin. She is so happy that she plans a big celebration for her friends and neighbors. She wants to share her good fortune with her friends. God is looking for us to be the people who tell the story of Jesus and his love. Even within the tragedies of violence and the possibility of war, there are opportunities for witnessing and service. The generous response of so many this past week teach us that. More than ever, we as Christians, cannot wander aimlessly. We cannot not be silent or complacent. We must reach out, with joy, to others in all circumstances.

Weighing heavily on my heart that morning was the death of my close friend and colleague, Bob Ellis. He was 15 years older than me, and one semester ahead of me in seminary. He had been a meat-cutter in his home town of Montezuma, Iowa for 13 years. He had four kids with Betty, our equally close friend, when he decided to study for the ministry. The Iowa Conference gave him a full-time church, and he became a full-time student at William Penn College in 1964. In 1970 he moved his family to Platte City, north of Kansas City, and served the church there.

There is no question that Bob became the big brother I never had. He was like so many pastors I admired in my youth: the unconventional, unabashedly liberal ones, who were grounded in changing society and making a difference in people's lives. His spouse Betty went to work at the seminary when they moved to Platte City, and she was and is a valued member of our extended family.

Our close seminary friends had come from different places, and went back after graduation to Kansas, Missouri, Iowa, and South Dakota. Over time we've stayed in touch as babies, moves, career changes, joys, disappointments, and health issues have impacted our lives. In the days before internet and unlimited long distance were available, we called each other after 11 pm, and sometimes fell asleep on the phone.

The year after we left seminary, Bob and Betty bought a lot at Clear Lake, Iowa near the church camp facilities. Seth was a year old the first time we went there. A cabin shell was in place, but there was no running water. Year by year we went, and improvements were added. As our children grew, and other changes happened, the Ellis cabin was a constant. During the winter we found warmer places (like hotels), but we got together and our children had the benefit of honorary aunts, uncles, and cousins.

Bob was appointed to the church in Garner, Iowa in 1989, which was only 15 minutes from the cabin. In 1997 he retired from the ministry, and they bought a home in Garner. On November 29, 2000 he had a liver transplant at the University Hospital in Omaha, and Ana and I went to see him the next day. He was uncomfortable, but very optimistic. We were chased out of the room by a professor/surgeon and a group of resident physicians. As I left, I told them Bob was very concerned he might have received the liver of a Republican. The teacher was not amused, but the prettiest resident gave me a big laugh.

Bob was out of the hospital room and in an apartment in the adjacent Lied Transplant Center by New Year's Eve. The Grenzes and us got apartments there, too, and we had a great celebration. All of us were hopeful Bob would make a full recovery soon. Bob and Betty made frequent trips to Omaha, and we saw them when possible. Unfortunately, he was very ill at the end of August and had to be hospitalized in Omaha once more. 9/11/2001 was a horrible day for our country, and it was also the day I said good-bye to Bob Ellis. He slipped into a coma and died on Saturday, September 15.

+++

In the fall of 2001 I got a call from the Trustee president at my home church, Albion UMC, telling me they were interested in an insurance quote. I tried to sell them a policy the previous year, but I wasn't competitive on price. They were insured by Guide One via a broker who contacted local independent agents, and offered them a shared commission on sales.

The local agent in Albion was Ralph Schmadeke, one of my childhood friends, who was a member of the church. Ralph was more interested in saving the church money than in retaining business, so he was happy to give me another chance. He set up a meeting at his office for me to present a proposal. The incumbent broker was also there, and we made our pitches in the presence of one another. My bid was accepted as it was lower with improved coverage. It was the first and only time I made a sale under these circumstances.

I had another great experience at the United Methodist Church in Aurora, where my son, Seth, was one of the pastors. Steve Leach was an insurance agent in Aurora and an active member of the church. I had become acquainted with Steve before Seth moved to town, and learned that the Aurora church was insured by him on a brokerage basis with the UMC Insurance Program. I told Steve about the worker's compensation program that was available, but didn't push for the multi-peril coverage.

In October of 2001 Aurora's trustee president called me and asked me to quote the church's insurance program. He said Steve Leach was on the Finance Committee and told folks their premium would be increasing and said, "you should call Seth's dad and see what he can do for us." With that very gracious invitation I prepared my proposal, discussed it with Steve and the Trustees, and made a nice sale. The next year Steve referred another church in the area to me and I was able to help them as well.

Our Christmas Epistle follows:

In the beginning of 2001, God created a new year and presented it to Chuck and Chris. God said, "You will have dominion of this year and I will help you make it a good one." And verily, Comet Lodge #229, AF & AM installed a new Worshipful Master, and Chuck took his place in the East. All gave homage that was due. But behold the January winds began to blow, and the white fuzzy things fell on the lawns and driveways of suburban Lincoln. But God gave unto the Leypoldts digital cable with more than 100 channels, and a new furnace, and memories of sugarplums danced in their heads. Nebraska survival instincts abounded, and peace and harmony prevailed in the house.

And God said to Anastasia, "New employment and a new home shall be yours during 2001." And God led her to the Omaha World-Herald and gave her good and wholesome instruction for her labors. Then God appointed two men and a truck to take her belongings to a new domicile on South 37th Street in Omaha.

Then God said to Chuck and Chris, "You shall vacate this land in February and navigate to the land of Eden that some call Waikiki." And Chuck took up his wife and several suitcases and went on the large silver bird and spent one week in paradise. And when the lucky couple returned they brought grass skirts and the granddaughters wore them and Don Ho played upon the harp and lire and all was well.

Yet sadness fell upon the Hawaiian adventure when Grandpa Don Walters died. His funeral was held in the Albion UMC, with grandson Seth assisting in the service.

And God told Seth and Sarah, "In the sixth month you shall take hammers and nails and all sorts of building supplies and rent a van and recruit young people from the regions of Aurora and Bradshaw and traverse south to the land of Mexico. There you will find a family needing a new home and you will help build it." But Seth and Sarah asked, "We have two children and a golden canine. How can we leave them." To which the Lord God replied, "I have appointed grandparents to care for these little ones." And it was done. Emma and Cora and Hannah the golden canine spent six days in Lincoln. Behold, Grandma and Grandpa knew why 50-year-olds were not supposed to have children. And they were very tired. And the summer winds blew and the heat index was elevated on the plains of Nebraska. But God gave unto the Leypoldts central air conditioning and underground sprinklers and five more cable channels and all remained pretty good.

In the month of September, sadness again descended upon the land. Despite receiving a new liver, a dear friend from seminary days, Bob Ellis, died in Omaha. Chris, Chuck, and Ana said good-bye to him with many others in Garner, Iowa.

And behold God gave unto Chuck a vision of bright lights and twangy music and time share discussions. And God said, "You shall take your wife and journey forth to the land of Branson, there to eat barbecued meats, and to walk your feet off." And Chuck did as he was told. And in Branson they listened onto the prophet Yakov Smirnoff and were refreshed by the Platters. And again it was very good.

And the days grew shorter, and the nights cooler, but mild weather remained in the land of Nebraska. And in the land of Lincoln, the bright lights shone and the Leypoldt yard was cheerfully decorated. And God said to Chuck, "Well done, you good and faithful servant. Church Mutual now protects 45 more congregations because of your efforts. You shall find a passport and take your wife and journey onto Cancun next February." And Chuck replied, "But there are nude beaches there and I have a meek and bleached whale look about me." But God said, "Do not be afraid. I will be with you."

Then God reminded Chuck and Chris to say: "Happy Christmas to all and to all a Good Night."

+++

2001 was a very bad year for the insurance industry, as it was hit by a perfect storm of disasters. The stock market was in sharp decline, and many companies had invested unwisely. Hurricane and other storm activity was much worse than average. In addition, the attack on the World Trade Center resulted in monumental losses for insurance companies. CMIC was well-positioned to deal with each of these challenges. Our reserves were conservatively invested and actually showed a gain in value, storm losses were kept in bay, and we lost nothing on 9/11. My book of business soared past $1.1 million with over $120,000 in new business.

Our year 2002 began at the Ellis Cabin near Clear Lake, Iowa. Because of Bob's illness, they had been using it less and were intending to sell the place. Betty invited us and the Grenzes to come up one last time. Chris Grenz joined his parents Ken and Jeanette, and Ana, Seth, Sarah, Emma, and Cora were able to be with us as well. It was very cold, but we had no road problems getting there and back.

In February we made our way to Cancun, Mexico as a benefit of reaching my sales goal. It was a really interesting place and kind of strange to experience heat and humidity in the wintertime.

Chris had trigger finger surgery on May 29. This was the result of pointing said finger at her spouse in an accusatory manner over the years. It was fixed, but doctors advised her to refrain from the aforementioned syndrome.

Seth was ordained an Elder in June and reappointed for a third year to Aurora and Bradshaw. Ken Grenz and I stood behind him at the event which took place at Saint Paul Church in downtown Lincoln. At the following reception I visited with Mel Ireland, who was ordained with my father at the same church in 1945.

Later in June, the Leypoldt clan gathered at Fort Robinson to celebrate my mother's 85th birthday. It was a grand observance as we filled one of the large brick houses which once served as an officer's residence. At that time, her progeny numbered 31 including children, grandchildren, great-grandchildren, and spouses. They were all there for most of a week.

In September Chris and I traveled to the Mackinac Straits area of Northern Michigan. There we found a unique bridge, an unconventional island which prohibits motorized vehicles, and several lighthouses.

In 2002 the insurance industry was still reeling because of the "perfect storm" in 2001. Church Mutual increased its rates significantly, but Dave and I were able to retain business because our increases were lower than others. My book grew by $385,000. New business included two large camps and several large churches.

I'll never forget the experience I had at a small UMC in northeast Nebraska. The treasurer had invited me to her home to make a proposal. She fed me and the trustees present, with wonderful homemade bread and vegetable soup. After my presentation, she said she would call me back after their renewal policy arrived. In a week or so I received a voice mail, telling me their current premium was increasing 400%! Needless to say, I wrote that one.

Something similar happened when I was invited to quote the coverage of the church in Lincoln that I now attend. They were among the few in Nebraska who were part of the UMC insurance plan, whose two previous carriers had gone bankrupt. My bid was much lower than the current premium. They called back and told me to write it up as expiration date was approaching, and they had received nothing from the incumbent.

Even though things were going well for me at CMIC, I still kept my eyes open for another job. I looked at employment listings in the daily paper and checked the Nebraska Bankers Association website periodically. On a July evening in 2002, I saw a listing for a position at the Albion National Bank. I quickly dusted off my resume, and sent it the next day to Wayne Boilesen, the bank president.

He called me within a few days, and on July 9 I sat down with him at the bank. Wayne had been a teacher and business owner in Albion before joining the bank in 1983; he had just recently become president, and was looking to fill his former position of Senior Vice President. We had a cordial and frank discussion, and I felt confident about a job offer.

We left his office, and Wayne drove me around town to look at housing possibilities, and to sell me on the idea of living in Albion. Back in the office I was given salary, benefits, and bonus expectations. My current income included salary, commissions, and bonuses, so it was a little difficult to compare the two jobs. I was nostalgically inclined to move to Albion, but Chris certainly did not share my sentimentality.

After scribbling a few Albion numbers, and comparing them to current expectations for the year at Church Mutual, I realized what I should do. I called my wife and said, "We are not moving to Albion, and I'll give you 25,000 reasons why." When Church Mutual's bonus was received in February of 2003, I did better than expected. I was $31,000 ahead compared to the bank job.

Chapter 21
The Leader Of The Pack

I was optimistic and excited about getting into the assisted/senior living market. However the CMIC underwriters made it very difficult. I spent many hours measuring and photographing buildings, surveying the management about all kinds of issues, conversing with and relaying information to the home office Thereupon I submitted a signed application and waited for an underwriter's approval. In contrast, most church new business could be quoted after a brief on-site visit and an hour in the office. With few exceptions, church underwriters were not consulted until business was sold.

On March 14, 2003, I was briefly hospitalized - my first such experience in 39 years. I was cured of the ailment, and just as the Philistines learned in 1 Samuel 5, some things should be sent away and never mentioned again. The recovery from my surgery was brief but excruciatingly painful, and I learned how it might feel to have a rasp inserted in a certain body cavity and thrust up and down a few times.

The ailment from which I suffered was something I dealt with for at least 40 years. My New Testament teacher in seminary, Lindsey Pherigo, speculated this might have been the thorn in the flesh that Saint Paul mentioned in 2 Corinthians 12:7. It's presumed that Dr. David Livingstone succumbed to its horrors in 1873 in Africa. My father, George Brett, Jimmy Carter, Karl Marx, and Marilyn Monroe are among the millions who have suffered from this malady. Ironically it was my barber, rather than a doctor, who shared a remedy (Metamucil) with me, but far too late to avoid my lamentable fate at the hands of a surgeon. I also discovered that Vicks VapoRub is a really good ointment for all kinds of ailments.

Two weeks after my aforementioned hospital experience, I sat on a pillow and drove out to North Loup, about 150 miles west of Lincoln, to visit a community-owned "low-income" apartment complex. It was a well-managed, attractive facility in this little town with a population of 300. Each unit was supplied with emergency buttons in bathroom and kitchen, which sounded an alarm on the outside wall. These were approved and inspected periodically by maintenance people and the state fire marshal. My underwriter was concerned that these were not connected to and monitored by first responders. "Who would hear the alarm?" she asked. "Everyone in town," I answered. She also was troubled when she learned there was no rescue squad in town. I explained that help would come from Scotia, which was four miles away and could be there in less than ten minutes. Finally, I asked her if she had ever been in a small town, and you can guess her answer.

Another time I was asked to quote a large, new, and very nice assisted living facility in a small city near Lincoln. This time the application process was going smoothly, and I was thinking positively. One issue ruined it. CMIC underwriters required there be a minimum ratio of one staff person for a given number of residents. In this case it needed to be two, and they had only one person on duty during the overnight hours. They were in compliance with all government regulators, their loss history was excellent, but a nonsensical, arbitrary guideline was wreaking havoc. The owner told me he had the overnight person doing laundry and odd jobs, because there was nothing else to do. He also said full-time employees cost his business about $40,000 per year. I didn't waste any more time on this prospect.

In June of 2003 the city of Aurora was visited by a hail storm. The stones were documented to be the largest ever recorded in the USA up to that time. Seth and Sarah picked up several from their yard, photographed and measured them. The largest was 3.5 inches. I had five Aurora churches insured at the time. Only the Covenant Church parsonage suffered damage, and that was discovered when the hail stopped and rain water began rushing into the living room.

When I was a banker I was able to go to 3 or 4 Nebraska football games each year, but hadn't done so for quite a while. In September 2003 a friend had some tickets available, and I called Seth asking if he wanted to go see the game against Troy State. He said yes, but later called to say he had been given a pair of tickets from someone in Aurora. No problem; I would go with one of my brothers. Seth said, "Emma wants to go," so we had a plan. Emma was five at the time, and her grandmother said she'd be bored to death, but Seth brought her to Lincoln and we went to Memorial Stadium. When we got to the East Stadium, we needed to go through separate entrances. Seth asked Emma if she wanted to sit with him or Grandpa, and she chose me, so off we went. She really liked all the pre-game music and excitement, and then the game started. With 10:38 left in the first quarter she asked, "can we go back to grandma's house now?" I said "not yet," and she was bored but very well behaved. At half time we went over to see her dad, and then went out so she could play in front of the stadium. I had my radio and followed the game, and the Huskers were picking up an easy win. We went back inside for the fourth quarter. She had a fun time, but to this day has never asked to go to another game.

In 2003 CMIC went digital. Previously we were using Polaroid instant pictures. They supplied us with awful Canon "powershots." We had battery chargers which we traveled with, and used every day that we were on the road. That year I booked $1,970,961 in insurance premiums, an increase of $1.1 million since 1999. New business that year included three assisted living facilities, three large churches in Fremont, a Buddhist Temple in Omaha, and a small college in Norfolk. I now had the privilege of looking after the insurance program of all four ELCA churches in Fremont and all four LCMS churches in Columbus. In many small towns in northern Nebraska, I insured all the Protestant churches in town. For the first time in my life, my income was in six figures.

One reason I was successful in selling church policies, was that I targeted prospects that had buildings for which we were most competitive on rates. We offered huge credits to churches less than 24 years old, masonry buildings with heavy laminated beams, and steel non-combustible buildings with proper gauge steel decks and supports. If a house of worship met the above criteria, and was less than 15,000 square feet I drove away with dollar signs in my eyes.

Traditional churches generally had one of three kinds of roofs: A.) concrete (rare) B.) wood trusses with plywood deck (common) and AB.) joisted masonry with heavy beams supporting a tongue-in-groove deck. Even some older buildings without beams qualified as AB if their trusses were supporting a clay tile or slate roof. I was after the AB's. Sometimes these classifications were tricky. Roof decks might be hidden behind false ceilings or a building might be brick veneer, but "stick built."

CMIC contracted with Insurance Services Office (ISO) to establish ratings for all buildings in excess of 15,000 square feet and those with sprinkler systems. However, they made numerous mistakes. I had a large church in Grand Island which was 100%

steel and concrete. ISO called it frame because they had nailable fiberboard on the steel deck, so they could install asphalt shingles. I called the architect and got copies of all kinds of tests to prove it was still non-combustible. CMIC, of course, paid a fee for ISO's erroneous initial opinion.

Another time, I quoted a church that ISO rated masonry with a B roof. A year later ISO sent a report to the underwriter, and the church was now rated A (non-combustible with cement roof and floors) and they received a much lower rate. This was wrong also, but I didn't follow-up with anyone. A few years later the building had no substantive change but they became AB non-combustible, which was still wrong! I've got more, but you get the idea. Several times I had customers who added sprinkler systems to their buildings. More than once, the new ISO rates were higher than our standard rates. Try explaining that one.

We were given a laser measuring tool to get more accurate readings of ceiling heights and all distances. At a training session a few weeks after we got our lasers, I told my colleagues the best thing about the laser is "if you're not sure whether you're looking at an AB roof, point it at the ceiling and if the light comes on, its AB." Underwriters needed some documentation, and I crawled into more than one attic with my camera to provide it.

This is how I summarized the year 2003 in our annual Christmas Epistle: 2003 was a good year for us…lots of family time…a couple of great trips…we were happy and (relatively speaking) healthy. As anticipated a year ago, we went to the Bahamas in February. We left Omaha in the early am (it was snowing and zero temp), laid over in Atlanta for a while, and reached our destination about 4 pm. At this time the stewardess announced, "Welcome to Havana, Cuba," which sort of curbed our enthusiasm. But she was only kidding, and we spent five days enjoying the 70 to 80 degree weather.

Our August trip found us in Missouri, Illinois, Kentucky, Tennessee, Georgia and Alabama. We followed highways 127 and 59 and stopped frequently to experience the world's longest yard sale. On the way home, we visited the Country Music Hall of Fame and Museum in Nashville.

Chris stayed busy in 2003 with occasional jobs at Lincoln school kitchens, attending auctions and garage sales, serving as treasurer for TOPS, quilting and other crafts, and best job: babysitting. Chuck was in his fifth year with Church Mutual…60 new customers translating into big bucks!! And best job: grandpa!!

Ana was still in her apartment in Omaha. She gave the retail world a try, but went back to AmeriStar…doing very well. She acquired a new Jeep Liberty. Seth, Sarah, Emma, and Cora were in Aurora. Sarah became Director of Social Work at The Hearthstone in York, and Seth continued with the Aurora and Bradshaw churches.

Emma turned five in January, and now had a semester of kindergarten on her resume. She was also a Daisy Girl Scout and attended dance/gymnastics school. Her favorite color was pink. Cora was three and started pre-school, Sunday School, and dance/gymnastics classes.

In February of 2004 we found ourselves in Tucson, Arizona for CMIC's annual Presidents Circle party. Once again we were in a very nice resort, and a visited some historical sites including the Bisbee Copper mine and the old town of Tombstone. On awards night I was recognized as the Division Sales Leader, which meant I was the top 2003 producer in Nebraska, Iowa, Colorado, Wyoming and Utah.

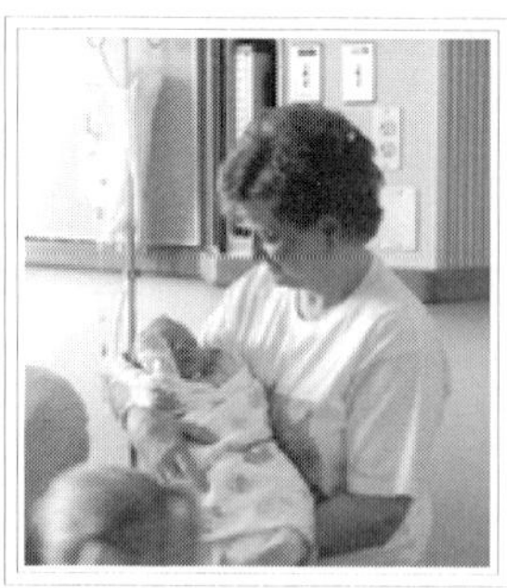

Pictures from 2004

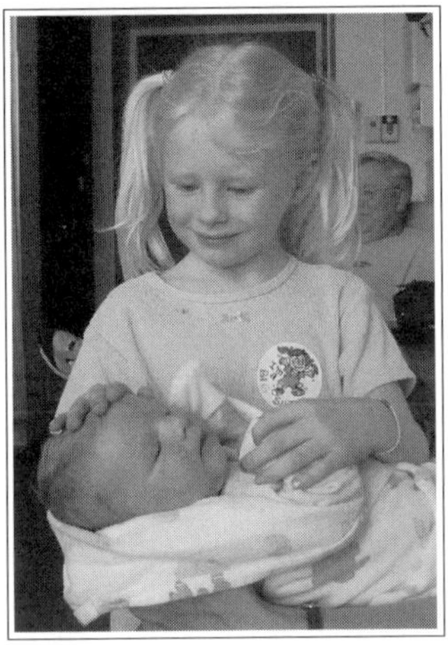

More pictures from 2004

In 2004 I had another great year in insurance sales. It started out slowly, but I got a big boost when a large Grand Island church with a parochial school came my way. In April I was able to convince the United Methodists at Ithaca, one of my former churches, to buy a policy and managed to pick up a portion of Epworth Village's insurance program. In October I wrote a big camp and a sizeable LCMS congregation with a school. That one month's production was over $75,000. The year ended with my book growing to over $2.5 million and attrition (customers lost) was only 1.28%.

Best of all I qualified for a Caribbean cruise and was Division Sales Leader for second year in a row. Our year was summarized by our very precocious granddaughter in December:

Hi! My name is Olivia Jo Leypoldt. I arrived into this world on June 21, 2004. I live in Aurora, Nebraska with my Mommy Sarah, Daddy Seth, and Sisters Emma and Cora. I also have four grandparents, five great grandparents and lots of uncles, aunts, and cousins.

My Grandpa Chuck said his youngest grandchild gets to write the Christmas letter for him and Grandma Chris. I asked my sisters about this, and they said to watch out for him because he's an EGGS-ZAD-JER-ATER!!! And then I thought, "How can I write a letter? I only talk baby babble, can't sit up very well, and don't really know much about these two old people." But Grandpa's got this really neat computer where you just sit down, and stare real hard at the screen, and all your ideas jump out. So here goes.

My Grandpa runs around Nebraska selling insurance to churches. Sounds pretty dull to me. But Grandpa must do pretty well. Grandma Chris still works at the school kitchens around Lincoln. This year she found time to finish a house quilt, and also makes wonderful pretzels and does cross stitch. Her house is full of Barbie dolls, Fisher Price toys, puzzles, and other stuff. There's a sign on her door that says, "Little people always welcome. Service includes: meals, lessons, entertainment and lots of hugs." My sisters have a lot of fun there, and I'm starting to as well.

My Daddy is a pastor in Aurora, and my Mommy is social work director at the Hearthstone in York. My biggest sister Emma is in the first grade, and my bigger sister Cora goes to pre-school. My Aunt Ana Leypoldt lives in Omaha, and works at AmeriStar.

Well, that's all. Grandma and Grandpa hope you have a great 2005, and want you to work and pray real hard, so next Christmas we can celebrate Peace On Earth once again!

It's been a good year
To you it must be clear
Our grandchildren are so dear
We close with this good cheer
Merry Christmas to all far and near!

+++

CMIC had grown rapidly from 2002 to 2004, and the ratio of premiums written and funds to secure losses was a little out of whack. Therefore, our sales goals in 2005 were reduced, and we had to limit our quote activity. My life was made much simpler when Long Term Care sales were moved into a separate division.

In many ways my job was pretty easy. Dave and I were the only insurance agents in Nebraska who worked for a company who specialized in the religious community. We had a very good reputation regarding claims, and provided all kinds of safety materials free of charge to churches, whether they were customers or not. Many independent agents had no source for church coverage, so they referred people to us. I didn't mind a quote limit, because I already had over 40% of potential customers in my territory on the books.

Not all churches were prospective clients. The Archbishop of Omaha was Board Chair of Catholic Mutual, so the three dioceses in Nebraska had no choice on insurance. I knew my territory pretty well by this time, and didn't bother those who were locked in with a local agent. I thought the Episcopal churches were out of reach as well, but was mistaken.

The Episcopal Church owns an insurance company: The Church Insurance Company. I had removed all their congregations from my prospect list. One day a warden from an Episcopal Church in Lincoln came to our office, asking about insurance coverage. He showed me their renewal policy, which was very expensive. I quoted and sold this policy in 2005. I added all the Episcopal churches back into my data base, quoted nearly all of them including the Cathedral, and sold several more policies. Never say never.

One memorable sale happened at Utica, 40 miles west of Lincoln. On January 12, I made a sales presentation at a church which also operated a large school. Before the meeting, the school principal said he had received the current policy in the mail that day. When I passed out my proposal, I saw the principal pointing to the two documents and smiling; I knew I made a sale. But I really enjoyed driving home, and listening to the Nebraska women's basketball team defeating Number #1 Baylor in triple overtime.

In March of 2005 Seth decided being an associate pastor for five years was long enough, and he asked for a change. His DS told him he was under consideration for three places and, without any guarantees, he asked him for preferences (I know DS's aren't supposed to do this, but they all do). Seth asked my advice (I know UMC pastors aren't supposed to do this, but some of them do). One of his possibilities was a church I insured. I knew the property and several people there. It was a few miles west of Grand Island, still close enough for grand parenting the girls.

The other two places were way out west. On March 22 Seth called to tell us they would be moving to Chadron, 450 miles from Lincoln. Aurora was just an eighty minute drive, and we had spent many, many hours with our granddaughters the past five years. It was hard for us, but certainly a good thing for Seth and Sarah. It worked out well for them, and I developed a strategy for Church Mutual to help us keep in touch with our grandchildren.

When driving across Nebraska on I-80, I discovered the York radio station (KAWL) kept people informed about bad weather by taking calls from local residents. One summer afternoon I was driving home, and saw a bank of dark clouds north of the Interstate. Tuning to KAWL, I listened to various reports from callers. One fellow called in from the unincorporated village of Thayer. He said there were softball-size hail stones hitting the town and you could actually hear loud thumps as he talked. I insured a church in that village which had about 20 houses. I called the pastor the next day to ask if the church was damaged. He said, "no, but I heard there was damage on the south side."

Another time I was driving on I-80 near York, and KAWL was reporting 60 mph winds in the city of York. A little later it started raining cats and dogs, and I stopped under an overpass for a few minutes. The wind was shaking my Ford Fusion like crazy! In five minutes, the rain stopped. In ten minutes, the sun came out, and I went on my way with no problems.

One of my fun experiences was meeting a gentleman in Broken Bow by the name of Gene Goben. Gene was the evangelist at the non-instrumental Church of Christ in Broken Bow, which I insured. He was also the mayor of Broken Bow, and worked for an auction business. He had a garage filled with antiques and other collectibles including a 1954 Studebaker. He told me one of his kids had connections with an advertising agency that was looking for old cars to include in a promotion for Coca Cola. He said his Studebaker was in the ad, but he hadn't seen it yet. A couple of months later I saw several Coke items at a mall in Omaha, including a tray which had that Studebaker I'd seen in Gene's garage. I bought two of them, and presented one to Gene on my next trip to Broken Bow.

I had a mind-blowing experience at the little town of Hadar in the summer of 2005. I insured a Lutheran (WELS) church and school in this village north of Norfolk. They had a new pastor and had enlarged their parsonage, and I needed to update their policy. I stopped at the house and a pretty, young woman with a pierced nose diamond opened the door. I silently wondered, spouse, daughter, babysitter? I took a chance, "are you Mrs. So-and-so?" Yes, she was! Another stereotype was shattered.

When we were young, Chris was often mistaken as the pastor's daughter. As my hair turns whiter, it's happening again. I don't have to look for a trophy wife, I already have one.

In 2005 CMIC altered its sales divisions. I was now in the Heartland Division which included Nebraska, Iowa, Kansas, and the western half of Missouri. Even with the quote and sales limitations I grew my book to over $2.8 million and kept my attrition below 3%. We were qualified for a trip to Acapulco, and I won my third Division Sales Leader award.

+++

In 2005 our Christmas Epistle was sponsored by the letter **D.**

Decade

We've been here at 2830 North 74th for ten years now.

Dotage

In the past decade we've seen a lot of changes in our house and family. But the very best thing has been our ascent into the status of doting grandparents. This position became more challenging when Seth accepted the Chadron UMC appointment on July 1st. However, we've been able to visit there five times since July. As a matter of fact, we celebrated 3.5 decades of wedded bliss on July 11 while in a cabin at Chadron State Park.

Sarah has taken to being a stay-at-home Mom for the present. Emma is in 2nd grade, Cora in Kindergarten, and Olivia is a cute and cuddly 18-month old.

Ana continues with her job at AmeriStar and lives in Omaha.

Chris has made 3 quilts this year and continues occasional work at school kitchens, is president of TOPS, still makes the best pretzels in town, and recently joined the Bell Choir at our church.

Digital

One thing that's really changed in the past decade is the growth of things digital. We're now on our fourth digital camera. We enjoy digital cable television, especially the digital video recorder, and watching DVDs. *I've even learned to endure the annual digital exam necessary for men my age.*

Dramamine

We didn't need this little pill in February but we thought we might: we took a

Caribbean Cruise. We flew to Fort Lauderdale for ship departure and stopped at Key West, Cozumel, and Belize before circling back. It was a fun time!

Decrepit?

Not yet; but last summer we attended the Albion alumni banquet. It was 40 years ago that Chuck received his high school diploma. The after banquet party was at the bowling alley, which was the high school hangout back in the sixties.

Division Sales Leader

Once again my employer recognized me as the Division Sales Leader. It's a curious thing for someone who is more than a little skeptical about capitalism and consumerism to accomplish this; but anything to hasten retirement is a good thing. Sometimes the end justifies the means.

Dodgers

I've been a Dodger fan for five decades. Last June they were in Kansas City for a three-game series with the Royals. Chris, Ana, and brother Gary went with me to celebrate this unique event and the glorious 1955 World Series champions took on the hapless Royals. The resulting sweep by the home team gave way to contemplative thoughts regarding childhood predilection and fantasy. Of course we live in "next year country."

Dream

We're hoping for a peaceful world in 2006 and wish the very best for all of you!

+++

I've written elsewhere about how important Christmas was to our mother. In 2005 she was too weak to host a party or to travel anywhere. She still remembered us all with gifts and money. The six Nebraska kids got together in Lincoln and went down to Beatrice on December 26. We took pictures, and made the best of it, feeling certain this would be her last Christmas.

The next year, in late February, she was hospitalized in Beatrice and a week later transferred to Bryan Hospital in Lincoln. Because of my father's cancer, Mom nagged us to get annual exams but she failed to do so herself. She readily admitted she had "white coat syndrome," meaning doctors and hospitals made her nervous and she had to be really sick to call her physician.

After ten days at Bryan it was determined she had cancer, and we all agreed there was no good reason to submit her to treatments. We moved her to the hospice wing at a facility in Lincoln. She did not like it at all, and we took her home after six days.

The next week I called my brother Gary to talk about a basketball game, left a message, but didn't hear back from him. I tried a couple more times with no response. I talked to Jim and Cathy and they hadn't heard from him either. The next morning I was headed for Beatrice to see Mom, and called Gary again to ask if he wanted to go along. This time my message was, "If you don't call me back I'm going to call the police." Chris heard me and reminded me we had a key to his house.

Gary lived six miles from us in south Lincoln which was on the way to Beatrice, so I took his newly remembered house key and hit the road. When I arrived and saw several newspapers on the stoop, I got a very somber feeling. I went inside, called his name, and found him in bed. He said he had scooped walks, developed a bad cold, and went to bed. He heard my phone messages, but could not get up to answer them. I could see that an ear drum had burst.

I called 911 and a fire truck and rescue squad were soon at the door. Why there was a fire truck I don't know. Gary was in very bad shape and they took him to Bryan Hospital and he spent 48 hours in intensive care. His type 1 diabetes warped into type 2. The doctor said he was lucky I came when I did. I'm glad to say he went home after less than a week in the hospital.

When I called Steve (who lived with Mom in Beatrice) about Gary, he said she was ready to come to Lincoln to take care of him. But we all knew that wasn't possible and Gary called her to say he was OK. Janice came from Oregon on April 3 to be with Mom and Steve. Cathy was there often as well and the rest of us went down as work schedules permitted. We were all there on Sunday, April 9. Mom was in bed, in and out of consciousness, and complaining of pain.

Our friends, Gil and Connie Karges, stopped by as well. We took turns holding Mom's hand and talking to her when it appeared she was awake. As I was sitting there, she woke up, opened her bright blue eyes, and spoke to me. I could not understand her until she said, "I'm done. Go get someone else." She repeated in similar fashion to all seven of us. I'm pretty sure she was giving us some final instructions.

I knew from many experiences that people nearing death could linger, in and out of consciousness, for hours, even days. Gil mentioned this as well. We left for Lincoln at 7 pm, and Steve called about 10 to tell us Mom had died.

Here are a few things I'll remember about my mother. She loved babies. This is obvious because she delivered seven of them. But she loved other people's babies, too. My Dad felt the same way. I don't think she cared too much for adolescents or teenagers. Once past that stage, she spoiled and babied us.

One of Mom's great disappointments was that she did not go to college. As mentioned earlier, her college plans were foiled by a bank failure in 1935. She was a proficient typist, and became an office manager for Remington Rand in Omaha. In 1943 she married my dad and went to Madison, New Jersey where Dad was in seminary. Because of her office skills, she made a little money as a typist for professors and students. This served as compensation for her lack of a college degree. Through association with these scholars, and by helping them transfer their ideas to the written page, she cultivated her own intellectual pursuits.

As a teenager and young adult she was very active in her local church. This was in the 1920's and 1930's when Methodist theology was undergoing tremendous change. Due to the eminent scholars at Drew (Edwin Lewis, Lynn Howard Hough, Carl Michalson), it was a great place to live and study. When James Thomas was elected a Bishop in 1964, Mom remembered helping him prepare his 1944 Master's Thesis.

I didn't realize it when I was growing up, but she was very progressive theologically; much more liberal than my dad. She believed in human rights and racial equality, felt war was a terrible solution to world problems, and knew God's love was as free and boundless as a mother's undivided love for her children.

She loved music and loved to sing, but she could not carry a tune. None of us kids wanted to sit by her in church, but she sang lustily nonetheless. She was a wonderful pianist. One of her proud self-taught experiences was mastering the pipe organ at the Crawford church.

My mother had a favorite chair in her family room. It was next to the patio door and the right distance from her television set. She was a voracious reader and real multi-tasker. She could seemingly be deep into her book, follow a TV show and all the surrounding conversations, and talk on the phone as well. It was amazing!

On the lamp table beside her chair were a TV booster speaker, a pen or two, a small pile of books, some pictures, and scraps of note paper. We found this poem during our vigil on the day she died:

I'd like your memories of me to he happy ones.
I'd like to leave a memory of smiles to fuel an afterglow.
I'd like to leave an echo whispering softly down the ways
Of happy times and bright and sunny days.
I'd like your tears of grief to dry before this day is o'er
And fond happy memories will fuel your afterglow.

It was written in her own hand, but not completely original. I think she found something she liked and rearranged the thoughts to match her own feelings of life and death and legacy. And we were so glad that she did! ***She proudly meets Olivia Jo in July 2004:***

+++

Because long term care was now in a separate division, my book of business slipped below $2.8 million in 2006. However, I was compensated for the loss and happy to get away from that line of coverage. I wrote a policy for the largest Protestant church in my home town and a beautiful historic building in Lyons, Nebraska. I was able to keep my attrition at a respectable 3.5%. I must have been anticipating this book as my 2006 Christmas letter took this form: **2006 Christmas Blog.**

January 1....Council Bluffs Hampton Inn with Ken, Jeanette, Betty…near AmeriStar Casino where Ana worked. Jan 26….Chuck got a crown (from his Dentist) ….Jan. 27-29...in Chadron for Emma's 9th birthday party…Cora stayed with us at motel…said Grandpa's snoring was annoying.

February 3....bought "new" clothes at Salvation Army store.. Feb. 7…got lost looking for *Cheeseburger, Cheeseburger* in Omaha…eventually met up with Ana… Chuck picked wrong day to leave cell phone at home…Feb. 8...Chuck almost killed by manure spreader south of Pender. Feb 18...Chris went to Bryan Hospital luncheon where her sister Shirley had decorated a table with some of her Dad's miniature tractors…Feb

20..left home at 5 a.m. to catch 8 a.m. flight to Acapulco…laid over in Houston at noon….arrived at the Acapulco Princess Hotel around 4 pm….we're on the 16th floor, overlooking the ocean! Feb. 21...toured the countryside…Feb 22...toured the city sites Feb 23...went shopping downtown…fun fiesta party in the outdoors that evening..Feb. 24..packed for home and flew out around noon, stopped in Houston again….long delay….back in Omaha about 9:45 pm…..daily temperature difference about 70 degrees (because of wind chill)! Feb. 26..Chuck's Mom in Beatrice hospital…he and Gary went down. **March** 2..Chuck's Mom at Bryan hospital in Lincoln…Mar 8...took Ana to Granite City for belated birthday supper...March 11...Moved Mom to Tabitha Hospital in Lincoln…March 17..Mom went home to Beatrice…under hospice care…March 23...On way to Beatrice, Chuck stopped to see his brother Gary and he was very sick….had to call 911 and Gary spent a few days in the hospital.

April 6...Chris' dad stayed overnight in hospital…April 8 and 9: spent most of time at Mom's house in Beatrice…she died about 10 pm on the 9th…April 16 (Easter Sunday)..after church headed to Albion. April 17... Mom's funeral at Albion UMC. All seven children were there along with most of the spouses, grandchildren, and great-grandchildren. Our Aunt Bobbie from Beatrice Mosaic Home was there, too. Seth helped conduct the service. Mom's resting next to Dad in the Rose Hill Cemetery overlooking Albion. April 21...went to Chadron…gas is $2.98 per gallon…April 22: Chadron is celebrating Earth Day on courthouse lawn…temp reached 90 degrees. April 23..Olivia shushed Grandpa at church. April 24: headed home…temperature hovering at 32, five inches of wet snow on car.

May….yard work and garage sales….May 21...took a fun tour of Wyuka Cemetery May 29 (Memorial Day): had lunch in Douglas and visited a few more cemeteries. Ana has enrolled in Master's program at Bellevue University and was working at Dillard's in Omaha Crossroads Mall.

June 2....headed west on insurance business and on to Chadron next day. June 4: Cora and Emma lit candles in church so we had to sit in front row with them….Cora's 6th birthday party in afternoon…back home June 5. June 14..Seth called…Olivia broke her arm…we went to Kearney for AC and back there again on the 16th and 17th … Kearney got about ten inches of rain during the week. June 23..Chris got her left trigger finger fixed. Now she's had two carpal tunnel surgeries and two finger surgeries…we call her the bionic grandma.

July 3..Sarah and the girls came to visit…next day went to Waverly where most of the Landons were celebrating the 4th. July 7: girls left for Chadron…July 11: our 36th Anniversary…went to Prairie Home Companion movie and supper. July 14 & 15...Chris had garage sale in Waverly…July 16...Chuck's 59th birthday. His wife gave him a cane. July 28...the hills south of Chadron are on fire…Seth and Sarah had to evacuate their home for a short time. July 30...we head to Chadron for our scheduled vacation. State Park is closed so we stay at Seth's for two nights.

August 1...Fire is under control…we moved into our cabin at Chadron State Park…Emma and Cora stayed overnight with us…Cora advised it would be best if Grandpa did not fall asleep until after she does because she's a sound sleeper and his snoring won't bother her then….Rapid City one day…Fort Robinson another. Aug. 4…. headed home…stopped at Lake Minatare (site of one of two Nebraska lighthouses)… climbed all the way to the top and took pictures to prove it. Aug. 23...went to photography exhibit downtown and discovered the power of using a selenium tint. Aug.

25 & 26...Seth and Sarah and girls came for overnight visit. Aug. 27...went to Grinnell to meet our friends Jeanette, Ken, and Betty…next day we ate lunch at the wonderful Maid Rite in Marshalltown and headed up to Clear Lake. After supper we took a cruise aboard the "Lady of the Lake"…Aug. 29..toured the "Wright"-style neighborhood in Mason City and Music Man square, then back to Grinnell…Aug. 30..ate lunch in Montezuma and drove home…great mini vacation!

September 3...went to Nebraska State Fair (first time in many years). Sep. 10...Big celebration for Harold Landon's 80th birthday. Lots of friends and family met at Valentino's for supper and party. Chris made a quilt which everyone signed. Sep. 15...headed west on business and ended up in Chadron. *Sarah is a graduate assistant and working toward Master's at Chadron State College.* Headed back home on the 17th. Sep. 22...Chuck had work to do in central Nebraska so Chris went along and we took in the "Junk Jaunt" which included Grand Island, Cairo, Ravenna, Mason City, Litchfield, Broken Bow and other places…gas is back down to $2.09 (election day is coming).

October 6..visited our new grand-niece at the hospital…Oct. 7..Bionic Chris went to a friend's retirement party...Oct. 18..celebrated Chris' birthday (late because Chuck was sick on the 14th) with movie and a meal. Oct. 30 ...headed to Chadron to help girls celebrate Halloween. Emma was a witch, Cora was Lady Gweneviere, and Livi was a Nebraska cheerleader…cool night for trick or treat, single digits in Chadron.

November 1..headed back home. TV and radio making big bucks on political ads…glad it's almost over. Nov. 7...Democrats winning…some people do care about corruption and competence…gas prices headed back up within a week. Nov. 19...attended 125th anniversary of Davenport church…we lived there 35 years ago.

December finds us getting ready for Christmas…another trip to Chadron this weekend…all will be at our house later.

In January 2007 Church Mutual rolled out a new cost estimating system and I took another wintertime trip to northern Wisconsin. This time Dave and I flew up and back without weather problems. The major change was a new way for us to estimate the value of art glass. Little did I realize it at the time, but this new approach would lead me to a new passion.

In February of 2007 Chris and I were bound for Costa Rica to enjoy some time in the sun. The airport reminded me of a county fair grounds with its open pole sheds. After a bus ride on a dirt road, we were at a swanky resort with iguanas and lemurs wandering loose. We later toured a jungle area which featured crocodiles, Capuchin monkeys, and hundreds of exotic birds. We heard the music of the marimba. Very early on Friday we loaded up and were back at the airport. It took several hours of shuffling through lines, checking in, and waiting before we boarded the plane.

Before takeoff we were informed there was a toilet malfunction and an oil leak. Because there was but one mechanic at the airport we sat for 90 minutes before departing for Houston. It was raining in Houston and our Omaha flight was delayed. Finally, in the air our pilot shifted into high gear and we landed at Omaha close to scheduled time. It was raining in Omaha and the temperature was just above freezing. Fortunately our company car, a 2005 Ford Taurus, was indoors in the parking garage.

We drove cautiously as we took exit 446 toward Lincoln at 6 pm. I was going 50 mph and noticed some slush on the road, so slowed to 40, and we hit a patch of ice and started sliding sideways across the four-lane westbound highway. I tried to tell Chris to brace herself for an airbag explosion when we spun around and hit a large concrete barrier on the driver's side. Fortunately, because of the weather, the traffic was very light and we avoided any other collision. The engine was dead, but I turned the key and the car started. We continued to Lincoln and the rain turned to snow with very poor visibility.

We got home three hours later and pulled in to our garage. The car was smashed on the left front fender, bumper, and headlight assembly (but the lamp still worked). We had no trouble getting in to the trunk and took all our things inside and tried to wind down before going to bed. Saturday was spent unpacking, scooping driveway and walks, and sorting through the souvenirs. Late in the day I called to report our accident.

CMIC leased cars through ARI, a fleet management company. CMIC gave us a few options and we decided which car we wanted to drive for two years or 60,000 miles, whichever came first. I averaged a new auto every 18 months. Ironically I had a new 2007 Ford 500 waiting for me when I left for Costa Rica, but didn't have time to pick it up before our trip. Sure glad I didn't.

ARI said not to worry about repairs and I left the battered Taurus at a local dealer and drove away in my new Ford, by far the nicest company car I'd driven. At the office, I told Dave about my wreck, and he said he did a similar thing a little further west, went into a median and was able to get back on the pavement. Fully five months later I received a later from Rick Schaber, CMIC's Risk Control Manager. Here's what it said: "On February 24, 2007, you were involved in an accident while driving your company leased vehicle. The CMIC Accident Review Committee has thoroughly reviewed all the facts at our disposal concerning this accident. It is the committee's unanimous decision that this accident was preventable. A preventable accident is one in which the driver failed to do everything reasonable possible to avoid it. In other words, you were not driving defensively at the time of your accident. All operators of CMIC vehicles are expected to employ defensive driving skills at all times. Hopefully, through this unfortunate occurrence, you have become more aware of the importance of driving defensively and will adjust your driving habits accordingly. It is the recommendation of the Accident Review Committee that you receive this written reprimand. No further action will be taken at this time."

I emailed requesting a copy of the report and all other information utilized by the Accident Review Committee in their investigation. I thought it strange their "thorough review" did not include interviewing Chris or myself about what happened, or possibly talking to Dave about the weather that night. Schaber sent me a one-page loss report describing the accident as "iv lost control on ice covered rds, bumped median, no other veh's involved." Very thorough indeed.

Later that year I was talking to one of supposed members of the committee, and he told me the same letter was sent to another CMIC representative, also five months after an accident. Only in this case, the employee was killed and his family got a dose of not so thoroughly reviewed corporate compassion. Speaking of the Ford 500 - I really loved that car! Ford has renamed the model a "Taurus," and if I ever buy another sedan I'll be shopping for one of them.

In March of 2007, Chris' dad was diagnosed with Alzheimer's Disease and moved into the Ashland Care Center. Chris' stepmother Eunice went to see him at least once a day, and Chris was there at least twice a week. He was also hospitalized twice, the second time with a broken hip. He enjoyed visits and was able to attend family Thanksgiving and Christmas events.

On a spring day in 2007, I was asked to quote a small church in northwest Lincoln. My practice was to measure the building, count the pews, take notes on various building items, and then take copious pictures of the inside and outside of the building. On this occasion, my Canon camera quit. However, I always kept spare batteries charged up and I slipped in new ones. But the camera still didn't work. I was certainly glad this didn't happen when I was 200 miles from home!

I called the "help center" and they agreed to send a new camera ASAP. I went home and picked up my "real" camera (a Sony) and finished up at the Lincoln church. The next day I was scheduled to do some work at O'Neill and Albion, so I took my Sony with me. Help center sent me a second-hand Canon A70 that I continued to use, but in May of 2007 I bought my first Sony digital single lens reflex (the A-100), and took that along on most of my trips.

In June of 2007 I was driving through Anselmo, which I believe to be the geographic center of Nebraska. Travelers can't miss Saint Anselm's Catholic Church west of highway 2 in this tiny village. I decided to stop. My Sony and I spent some time recording this Nebraska treasure, the first of many visits to Catholic churches.

On July 16, 2007, I passed through the portal of oldness. We celebrated the big 6-0 in Iowa with our friends Betty, Ken, and Jeanette, including another cruise on the Lady of the Lake in Clear Lake, Iowa. If you're ever in Ames make sure you check out Hickory Park restaurant.

My ego got a big boost in 2007 when the TV show **Chuck**[45] came on the air and continued for five seasons. He even had a pretty, blue-eyed, blonde wife like I do. A movie, **Good Luck Chuck**[46], came out in 2007 as well. Names may or may not help us in our search for identity. Years ago the University of Alabama basketball coach was fired because he struck his secretary in this face. His name: Wimp Sanderson. The athletic director's name was Hootie Ingram.

I sent a proposal to a church in Hartington and they invited me to a meeting in November of 2007. Because I had an appointment in nearby Crofton the next day, I decided to stay overnight at Hartington's only motel. I called and the motel owner said, "I'll be out of town, but I'll leave the key at the office." So I checked myself in, ate at the Subway, and went to my sales meeting. Early the next morning I headed north on Highway 57, a route I'd never before taken.

Driving north on this nippy fall day, I sighted a tall steeple in the distance. As I grew closer I was more and more curious. At the end of 57 to my right was Bow Valley and the magnificent church of Saints Peter and Paul, with a 200 foot tower and on a hillside to boot. I had no time to stop that morning, but was back a year later to photograph this wonderful place and another one six miles away in Saint Helena.

My sales results were so-so in 2007. I had just enough sales to off-set the sheep who went astray. I discovered something interesting about a competitor during the year. Brotherhood Mutual had not been very active in Nebraska, but they were contacting our folks and their rates were very competitive. We were usually close enough to save business when we had the chance to compare coverages. The **Wall Street Journal** reported that Brotherhood refused to insure a church because of their denomination's (UCC) inclusive posture regarding gay clergy and same-sex marriages.[47] I sent that data to our home office and they made use of it in material provided about our competitors. Sometime later Brotherhood became more aggressive, and I often shared this information with customers and prospects. It certainly helped me with United Methodists.

In my thirteen years with CMIC I had 3 managers who worked from either Des Moines or Kansas City. I got along with all three, and because I was meeting or close enough on the numbers they didn't bother me much. They each did annual evaluations but only one, Joel Barcus, asked me to submit ideas which might benefit Church Mutual. I dutifully made a few suggestions including:

- offer coverage to day care centers, whether religious or not
- develop a broker relationship with local independent agents
- sell to all camps and private schools, whether religious or not
- expand to groups such as lodges, legion halls, senior centers
- consider writing insurance for public schools
- enlarge my territory to include the Nebraska panhandle

I always thought it was strange that my territory ended where it did. It supposedly followed the lines of the time zones, but I had Hooker and Cherry counties which are in mountain time, so they weren't following their own rules. The remainder of western Nebraska was handled by a representative in Denver and later on, Cheyenne, but they didn't have time to cover that large area. When Seth and his family moved to Chadron I stepped up my lobbying efforts.

At the end of 2007, Joel Barcus informed Dave and I that we would be selling in all of Nebraska. He asked us to divide up the counties. I added Sioux, Dawes, Sheridan, Box Butte, and Scotts Bluff counties and Dave had the rest. All my other ideas were devoured by gravitational singularity at the home office.

In December of 2007 Chris and I went to Chadron to see our grand children's Christmas programs. It was overcast when we started and was raining pretty good when we turned off the Interstate at Ogallala. A little later the rain turned to snow, and it was getting dark as well. The terrain in northwest Nebraska includes wide open spaces and some steep hills so we were more than a little tense. However, it wasn't terribly slick and the Ford 500 was doing well.

About 15 miles south of Chadron, we caught up with a snowplow just as we were descending a steep hill near the Job Corps facility. We followed the blade at about 30 mph all the way to town.

In 2007 my new accounts were offset by those who left and the book stayed even. I did just enough to qualify for another company trip, but this one would be quite different: we were heading north.

Chapter 22
Change We Can Believe In

Church Mutual changed my compensation plan in 2008. For the previous nine years I was paid a salary, 10% commission on all new business, and a $50 bonus for every three-year church package policy that renewed. The new arrangement would continue salaries and 10% commissions, but replaced the renewal bonus with a percentage of the book each month. This would give me a higher guaranteed income.

On February 7, 2008 Ana and I decided to go hear Senator Barack Obama speak in Omaha. I was running late, and my garage door opener malfunctioned. I then pulled the door shut, and in my haste got three fingers smashed. As I sat in the Omaha Civic Auditorium waiting for the rally to start, my right trigger finger turned an ugly shade of purple and throbbed painfully. I mused, if I could just get close enough to touch the hem of Obama's suit jacket, maybe I would be healed. No such miracle occurred that day; but a bigger one sure took place on November 4! The best quote I heard during the presidential campaign was: "What did you like best about the last time a Democrat was in the White House, the peace or the prosperity."

Later in February, CMIC sent Chris and me to Banff in the Canadian province of Alberta. From 2001 to 2007, because of my hard work and superior skills in salesmanship, we spent one week each winter in a warm place. President Whitburn announced this destination while we were basking in the warm sun at a Costa Rican resort. We had no clue where this might be, but soon learned we would be sent in a northerly direction to a frigid place. Even though I missed the beaches and bikinis, it turned out to be a great experience. We stayed in a swanky hotel which resembled a Scottish castle. We saw ice sculptures, frozen waterfalls, hot springs, and attended a unique indoor/outdoor barbecue. I even took a trip on a ski lift (the Banff Gondola).

In March 2008, Erin Andersen of the **Lincoln Journal-Star** asked the public to send her some funny things that kids say. Chris records all the sayings of our grandchildren in her diary, and we contributed several items to Erin. They follow.

One time the older girls were telling us that their little sister pulled the hair out of one of their toy horses, and now the horse looks like a donkey. This made their grandma laugh, so Cora told her, "you need to write that in your diary."

Our 2½ year old granddaughter, Cora, was at our house for lunch. I asked her if she wanted a wiener and she replied, "no. I want a hot dog." Some 30 years previously I asked her father the same question, and he gave me a similar response which became a sermon illustration.

Cora's older sister was celebrating her 5th birthday. When we called to wish her happy birthday, Cora got on the phone as well. Grandma asked her "what did Emma get for her birthday?" to which the 2½ year-old replied earnestly, "presents."

5-year-old Emma was at our house during a big snowstorm. Because we needed to attend a wedding, I went outside to clear the driveway and then took a shower. While I was still in my underwear I told Emma I was ready to go to the wedding. She said seriously, "people will laugh at you."

Emma and Cora spent the day with their grandmother. At suppertime she brought home some Chinese food. Cora had just awakened from a nap, so she sat on grandma's lap while they ate. When grandma starting talking Cora said, "Grandma, don't talk while you eat."

When Cora was 3 her mother put her blonde hair in braids quite often. One day they were visiting friends who had a six-year-old son. When he saw Cora's hair, he said, "I like your bracelets." But she didn't like what he said very much.

When Cora was three she loved cottage cheese, but she called it "cotton cheese."

Emma asked her grandma, "what's your name?" Grandma replied, "Chris." Then she asked, "how do you spell it?" Grandma answered, "C-H-R-I-S." Emma then said, "no, it's I-T."

Cora told us she knew a baby boy named Chuckie. I said that was my name when I was a baby boy as well. To which she replied, "then you changed your name to grandpa."

When Emma was five, she told us she was going trick or treating as a princess. And the next year, when she was older, she would be a queen.

My favorite cartoon character is Wile E. Coyote, and we have all kinds of mementos to prove it. When Cora was 3½, she called him "Kylie Wyote."

Cora stayed with us for a week when she was four, and we took her to the county fair. She went on a ride which swung her around about 15 feet off the ground, which was a little too much for me to watch. However, she appeared to be having a good time, and was talking to another little girl while on the ride. When it was over I asked her if she was scared, and she said, "no, but I thought I was going to throw up." Then I asked her what she was talking to the other girl about, and she said, "I asked her if she felt like throwing up." Later she wanted to ride the ponies. The attendant asked which one she wanted to ride and she said, "the blonde one."

Cora was almost five and her baby sister, Olivia, was nine months when they came to visit. When they were ready to leave, Grandpa said to Cora, "I think Olivia should stay here with us." Cora said, "Oh no, she would starve death."

Then I said, "we would feed her." Cora rebutted, "you don't have any milk."

I then assured her that we had some milk, and Cora concluded the argument by asserting, "but you don't have a breast."

Emma was asked how old her baby sister was, and she said "zero and one-half."

Grandma Chris went to Aurora to look after her granddaughters. There seemed to be a lot of train activity that day, and she remarked to 5-year-old Cora "there goes another train." Cora replied, "no, there is only one train, and it goes back and forth all day."

Chris bought a Princess and the Pauper coloring book for 5 year-old Cora. As they were coloring together, Cora told her that she already had a book just like this one. Then she whispered in Grandma's ear, "you gave it to me for my birthday." Her grandmother replied that she was old, and sometimes forgets things. Cora then said, "yes and Grandpa's even older."

One day Cora was sitting on my lap. Looking up at my chubby face, she asked, "what's that line?" and pointed at the crease which divides my chin from some flabby skin around my throat. I told her that the line separated my two chins. Cora ran upstairs, and exclaimed to her mother "did you know Grandpa has two chins?"

Olivia was not quite three when I asked her, "let's look at this book, shall we?" To which she replied, "I'm not Shallwe, I'm Olivia!"

On her seventh birthday, Cora was listening to a hymn on the car radio. Her dad told her it was the same hymn that was sung in a church service the family attended the day she was born. She told him "I thought it sounded familiar."

Ten year old Emma had a friend who attended the Catholic Church. She told us when a Catholic baby is baptized they get a fairy godmother.

I was showing this publication to Olivia, now ten, and told her in case my book is made into a movie she needs to decide who will portray her. She said, "your life is not intense enough to be a movie."

Two pictures of Olivia from 2006:

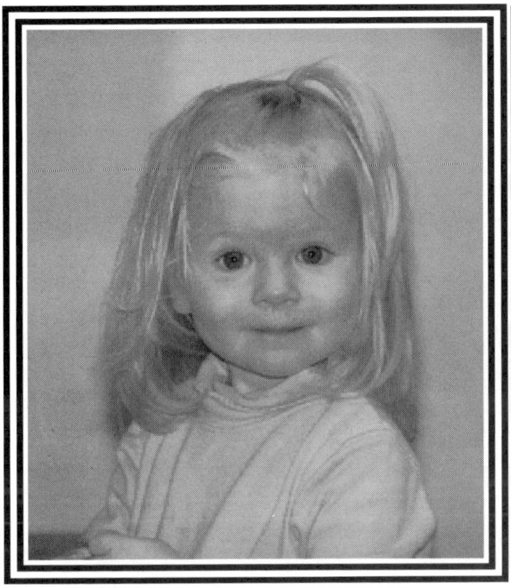

In 2008 I took full advantage of the new opportunities in the Nebraska panhandle. One April morning it had snowed and blown so much that the Chadron schools were closed. I had appointments in Alliance, Morrill, and Scottsbluff that day, and started down Highway 370, which was open but snow packed. After 30 miles, I decided to call the pastor in Morrill to make certain I could get there on time. He said the sun was shining, and they had no snow.

I pulled in to Alliance, as I needed some photos at the Presbyterian Church. The snow was so heavy that portions of the church were not visible. A few miles south of Alliance the snow stopped, and the highways were clear. Temperatures in the fifties greeted me at Morrill, and when I got back to Chadron nearly all the snow was melted.

In May of 2008, I was contacted by a Realtor who was selling a church building in Lincoln to a Russian congregation. The building was appropriately located in what is sometimes called the North Russian Bottoms. The church was built by Lutherans, and most recently occupied by an independent Orthodox sect, who had left all their furnishings and vestments behind. When I got my proposal ready, I called the pastor to set up a meeting at my office.

He spoke little English, but brought his daughter who had graduated from a Lincoln high school. We discussed coverages, and I asked the pastor to what denomination he belonged. He said, "M. B." I thought a few seconds and queried,

"Mennonite Brethren?" I asked if the Mennonite Brethren were active in Russia. The daughter said, "No. But they loaned us the money for the church, so we joined them." It appeared like sound theology to me, and I made the sale.

I used to brag about the fact I insured every Protestant church between Lincoln and Wahoo. This included the towns of Raymond, Malcolm, Davey, Ceresco, Swedeburg and Ithaca. I didn't feel so smug on the night of June 4, 2008, when I sat on my patio listening to storm reports concerning the area.

Ceresco was hit the worst with high winds, heavy rain and a tornado. The next morning I called CMIC's claims department to alert them to expect several calls from Nebraska. I also contacted and left messages for several friends in Ceresco, but because electricity was off they couldn't call back for three days. On Sunday there was still no power in town but all three churches were worshiping. Their times were staggered, so I attended each service. The UMC, which I served 30 years previously, took a direct hit and needed numerous repairs, but was structurally sound.

They have what I earlier described as an AB roof, and I honestly believe a frame building or lower quality masonry structure would have collapsed. In July 2005, the UMC at Valentine was hit by either a tornado or 90 mph winds. A small window at the north end of the sanctuary blew out, and these winds caused tornadic activity in the room with chandeliers and books flying around. A HVAC unit flew off the fellowship hall, and through the sanctuary roof to stop the mini tornado. The wind then escaped via the southeast corner of the sanctuary by cracking a support beam, and pealing the bricks from a block wall. Once again, this church was saved by an AB roof.

Later in June of 2008 I scheduled a renewal survey at Zion Baptist Church in Omaha. This historic African-American group has served Omaha in a single location since 1887. Their present building was erected after the 1913 tornado, and survived the 1975 tornado. I was photographing art glass windows with my DSLR camera, and found a surprise up in the balcony. Baptists do not believe in sprinkling babies or anyone else at baptismal ceremonies, but one of their balcony windows had a baptismal font on it. Reg Jackson was Zion's head trustee, and I said to him, "you must have had a Lutheran architect design this church." "How so?" he asked, and I told him about the window. "Well, we'll see about that!" he exclaimed good naturedly.

In 2007 Seth Leypoldt was chosen to represent Nebraska United Methodists at the Jurisdictional Conference in Texas, which would be held the following year. The only real function of the conference was to elect Bishops, and Seth had a great time interviewing candidates and getting to meet people from several conferences of our church.

In July of 2008 I drove to Alliance on business, and then stayed the night at Chadron. Seth and Sarah were headed to Texas for Jurisdictional Conference that week and the girls including Sophie, a chocolate lab puppy, would be staying with us. I had a couple of stops to make on the way home, and 8-year-old Cora accompanied me. We saw some beautiful thunderheads building as we drove through the Sandhills, and I stopped frequently to take pictures.

At 6 pm we met the rest of the family for supper, and Emma joined Cora and me for the ride to Lincoln. At Aurora the rains came in torrents, and the girls loved the thunder and lightning strikes the rest of the way. The next day I took Seth and Sarah to Kansas City to catch a plane to Texas, and we entertained our granddaughters for a week.

At this time, they were ten, eight, and four years old.

Gateway Mall was having their annual Lemon Days event, and one morning we loaded the van and headed that way. It took a while to find a parking space, and once inside, we discovered a few thousand others were shopping along with us. We meandered through the racks of bargain clothing and piles of ½ price shoes, and perused the shelves of discounted books until it was time to head toward the food court. But first, we took a potty break.

The food court has many choices, and it seemed the five of us went in different directions as we surveyed all the food and drink choices. Grandma supervised Emma and Cora while Olivia, the four-year-old, was with me. She and I chose Subway because they had chocolate milk. And a pretty long line as well.

As we shuffled along and talked about what might go well with chocolate milk, we found ourselves close to the front and Livi announced it was time for another trip to the toilet. Off we went...and fortunately the Mall has a family lounge, so I didn't have to worry about going to the Men's room or standing outside the Women's room. It was busy, and we had to endure a line once more. The trip was successful, and we headed back to Subway.

By this time Grandma, Emma, and Cora had their food, and were conveniently settled with their trays and packages and were enjoying lunch. After 15 or 20 minutes Livi, and I joined them with our six inch subs and chocolate milk. Pretty soon, Emma and Cora were finished. Because there was much more to see, away they went with Grandma following. Grandpa remained to supervise Livi's bites of sandwich and sips of milk.

But first things first. Emma and Cora needed to visit the necessary room and Chris said, "can you clean up this table?" and "I'm leaving my purse on this chair, so don't leave without it." "No problem," I replied as I leisurely chewed away on ham and cheese, and slurped my flavored cow juice.

For a few minutes, I looked around the busy food court, eyeing several other grandparents, and casting longer looks at a few young mothers. All the while, I reminded my granddaughter to eat her lunch and drink her milk. Suddenly my precocious little sweetheart announced, "I have to go potty again," and she vanished.

Holy Buckets! The trays? They can wait. The purse? I had no other choice but to pick it up, and head south toward the necessary rooms. I moved as quickly as possible. A 61-year-old man wearing a Wile E. Coyote t-shirt, khaki colored shorts, black crocs, and carrying a purse, was hurrying toward the restrooms at Lincoln's Gateway Mall. An overweight security guard glanced my way, as did two teenagers with coal black and pink-streaked hair. No time to waste. My little girl was on the loose.

As I entered the restroom hallway, panic set in. I hadn't seen Olivia since she left our table. Surely she went this way, but what if she went to the ladies restroom to find Chris and the other girls. What to do? Maybe I should holler out her name? Or stop at the door of the girl's toilets and ask someone to seek out Chris? No, it's been a while, they're probably no longer there. What shall I do, what shall I do?

Well, the thing was, Livi had already been to the family lounge twice in the past hour, so I thought, I'll check there first. I entered the room. Several young mothers and about a dozen little kids were present and milling around. They all looked at this old guy with the purse. Some stared. Others glanced at me, and quickly looked away. My grandpa eyes darted around the area but saw no Olivia.

At the right moment, an attractive young woman with a little one in a stroller asked me, "are you looking for a little blonde?" "Yes," I said, reassured. She directed me to a closed door where the familiar child-sized lavatory was. I opened the unlocked door, and found my 4-year-old granddaughter comfortably doing her thing. And telling me, "please leave and shut the door. I need my privacy."

Oh, yes, I also got a speeding ticket on the way to the Mall that morning.

Olivia and Sofie on July 16, 2008

+++

On September 29 I received a call from Virginia White in Grand Island informing me her brother, Duane Donaldson, had died. Duane was my classmate at Albion, and the first kid I met when we moved there. His family was very active in our church.

Virginia told me their pastor was on vacation, and wondered if I could conduct Duane's funeral. It had been almost 15 years since I functioned as a pastor, and I didn't think I would be emotionally prepared to help bury one of my childhood friends, so I declined. Driving to Grand Island, I deeply mourned the loss and knew I made the right decision.

We went to church camp, youth fellowship, and Sunday school together. He was an athlete and I wasn't, but he still included me. At the end of the football season, his folks invited the whole team to their house for a steak supper. Duane made sure I was there as well. Perhaps his greatest accomplishment was being named Outstanding

Student his senior year, even though he wasn't in the top ten academically.

His older sister, Carolyn and her husband Scott Maricle, managed Camp Fontanelle in 1965 when I was working there, and he came to visit often. He went to Kearney State and then joined the Marines and ended up in Vietnam. Then he went back to school, graduated, and started teaching in Grand Island.

He switched to banking about the same time I did, and I ran into him a couple of times because of that. Mostly we saw each other at events in Albion. In 2005 he was planning to attend our 40 year reunion, but had an accident fixing fence and was in the hospital. They discovered cancer at that time. I saw him and called him a few times, but he lost the battle. I wish I could have paid him tribute, but his life was a far better sermon than anything I might have said.

Another Albion friend who I met very early was Jim McCoy. Like Duane, he went to a country school, and I met him in Sunday School. Jim's folks, Wes and Patty, had married young and they were like a couple of kids. They started inviting me out to their place, and I spent several nights there. I was 13 the first time I tasted a T-bone steak, and it was at the McCoys.

The Albion area was a popular destination for pheasant hunters, and their season started in November. I was at the McCoy farm on a November weekend in 1961. One morning, I went with Jim to usher the dairy cows across the road to the barn. A car full of hunters drove by slowly and stopped. One of them rolled down his window and asked, "can you tell us how to get to Albion?"

Jim told them it was 2 south, 1 east and another 3 miles south. Another one said, "my god, that's where we spent the night." Alcohol, guns, and city slickers don't mix well.

Wes' folks owned a meat market and he learned to be a butcher, but Patty's dad needed help and they moved to the farm. Wes was like the flip side of my father. He drank, smoked, cussed, and told dirty stories. When I went to college, they bought the locker in Osceola which was right on Highway 92. I stopped there many, many times on my way home from Wesleyan.

As time went on, they got acquainted with Chris and Seth as well. We were living in Ceresco when I got the call that Wes had died of a massive heart attack. It was May 30, 1975, and he was only 50. Jim said, "you're doing the funeral," and I didn't hesitate to agree. I was almost 28 and an ordained elder; I could do anything back then.

It was to be a morning service in Levander's funeral home in Albion. We drove up without having seen anyone ahead of time. I spoke to Jim and Patty and the other relatives I knew as a kid. Albion's pastor and dear friend, Les Anderson, gave me some words of encouragement. I walked to the casket, saw my friend motionless, and it sunk in that I need a little comfort myself. But I did okay.

We continued to see Patty every once in a while, and after a couple of years, I discovered Duane Schmoker had become more than a friend. On December 5, 1978 they drove to Hebron where I led their marriage ceremony. We stopped to see them from time to time. Duane died in 1994 and in March of 2002, Jim called to tell me his mother was in a Lincoln hospital and was very ill. I went to see her, and later Jim walked me outside to say his mother wanted me to conduct her funeral. I wasn't 28 anymore, and had been away from a pastorate for 8 years; not sure about this.

Patty went back to the Osceola hospital, and died on March 18, 2002. Jim called and asked me to be a casket bearer and speak at the funeral. I called my pastor friend in

Osceola and told him I would say a few words at the cemetery.

I made the following remarks at her committal service. "Every one of us lives in a home filled with rooms: bedrooms, living rooms, parlors, and kitchens. We've come to appreciate special rooms and places as memories are formed. When I think about Patty, I'll remember special times in different houses. First, there was the farm house northwest of Albion. Then, during my college days, I was welcome into the little house north of the highway in Osceola. But more often, I found Wes and Patty in their second home at the locker plant. Then for the past few years, I saw Patty in her last home in Osceola. My favorite room in the farm house was the kitchen. Not only because she fed me well, but because in Patty's houses, the kitchen was the place for conversation and fellowship and good times.

"A week ago I saw Patty in a hospital room. Later she was in another hospital room. In a very real sense, it was a delivery room. It was a place of pain, and preparation, but also joy, because it was the room from which Patty was released from the burdens and frustrations of life. Just as the hospital's baby delivery room is a place that we leave after its function ceases, Patty's last room served as a place of preparation for her to enter the home that we call eternity. Jesus once spoke about eternity in this way, 'In God's house there are many rooms. I would not tell you this if it were not so. I am going now to prepare a place for you.'

"The rooms that we use and the rooms that God has prepared for us have one great thing in common: they are places that have been filled by love. In the 13th chapter of the First Letter to the Corinthians, Saint Paul writes to tell us that love is the most important gift that God gives us, and in the same way, love is the most important element in human relationships. Listen again to what the apostle is saying: You may know a dozen languages, be the best preacher in the country, have the highest I.Q. in the state, possess great faith, give away everything, sacrifice your life for others, but if you are unable to love, these things do you no good whatsoever.

"Then Paul describes what love is. 'Love is patient and kind; love never gives up; love is eternal. It is not: jealous or conceited or proud or ill-mannered or selfish or irritable.' In the letters of John we learn even more about the importance of love. These letters teach us that God's love came into the world in a mysterious and wonderful way in the flesh and blood of Jesus Christ, and that because of this divine love, we human beings are instructed to share God by loving one another.

"One of the reasons we are here today is to thank God that we have come to know God's love. And that love is very much like a woman who fills the rooms of her home with love, and the virtues that accompany love - faith and hope. Now Patty's body will remain in this place. We should not think we are leaving her here. Because she has loved and received love, she will continue to fill the rooms of our hearts."

+++

Because of the new contacts in the Nebraska panhandle, 2008 was a very busy year for my insurance work. I picked up new accounts in Alliance, Scottsbluff, and Hemingford, and spent time getting acquainted with existing customers and prospects. One could say I had a branch office at the West Hills Inn in Chadron. Chris went with me for most of the trips, and we spent many, many hours with our granddaughters.

On November 4, 2008 I watched with joy and fascination as Barack Obama was declared winner of our country's presidential election. I was extra proud he won an electoral vote from Nebraska's second congressional district. When the race for the White House began in 2006, I thought John Edwards was the best person for the job. I liked his United Methodist connection and desire to end poverty. But when Mr. Obama won the Iowa caucus, and I heard him speak, I felt he was a winner and sent his campaign a check the next day. When I listened to him in Omaha on February 26, it truly felt like a revival service, and I realized something magical was unfolding in America.

I have always been captivated by the world of politics. The first election I can remember was the one in 1952. The presidential race was between Dwight Eisenhower and Adlai Stevenson. I was at the polling place and when my dad disappeared behind the curtain to cast his vote, I tried to go along but was prevented. I remember being asked who I would vote for, if I could. "Ike" I replied. Nebraska gave Eisenhower 70% support that year.

In 1956, I watched with interest the two party conventions on television. I remember Terry Carpenter of Scottsbluff, Nebraska, refusing to vote for Richard Nixon to be Ike's running mate. I didn't know whether to be proud of, or embarrassed for, Nebraska. In 1960, we entered a new era of politics and witnessed the televised debates between Nixon and Kennedy. For the first time, every citizen was able to make a decision without the filters of the media. (Remember, these were pre-cable days, so there was nothing else to watch when the debates came on). I was 13, and an eighth grader with presidential aspirations.

In 1964, I was a huge Goldwater fan. I even joined Young Americans for Freedom and people called me Au H_20 Jr. Early in 1968 I worked for the election of Senator "Clean Gene" McCarthy, and when he dropped out I was for Bob McCloskey, a Republican member of Congress, who urged us to get out of Vietnam. An assasin eliminated Bobby Kennedy, clearly the best hope for our nation.

On July 16, 1968 I turned 21. Vice President Hubert Humphrey and former Vice President Richard Nixon were the choices for my first presidential vote. Because of the Vietnam war and the Democrats' treatment of protesters in Chicago, I voted for Nixon. I often joke that my unforgivable sin of voting for Nixon forced me to seek atonement by attending seminary and becoming a pastor.

Along the way, I discovered the prairie populists of days gone by, such as, William Jennings Bryan, Bob LaFollette, and George W. Norris. It was then natural for me to give my loyalty to the most gifted man to ever run for president of the United States - Dr. George McGovern of South Dakota. He was the son of a Wesleyan Methodist pastor, a former Methodist seminary student himself, and a professor at Dakota Wesleyan University. No one, before or since, has been more qualified to occupy the oval office. I had an audience with Mr. McGovern in Lincoln on July 1, 2007, and this experience cleansed the guilt of my Nixon vote.

Some think it strange to admire both the right-wing apostle Barry Goldwater and the so-called liberal George McGovern. In Barry Goldwater's later years he showed his independence. "Mr. Conservative" supported a woman's right to choose, gays and lesbians in the military without restrictions, and endorsed a Democrat for Congress in Arizona.

What drew me to them is that they were both non-conformists. In Christianity we have depended a lot on non-conformists. Jesus: "My kingdom is not of this world." Peter: "I now know God shows no partiality." Stephen and others faced death rather than conformity. More recently: Martin Luther in the 1517 Reformation, John Wesley in the

1700's, and Popes John XXIII and Francis. In history people like Columbus, Galileo, and da Vinci refused to conform to outmoded scientific theories of their day.

Senator McGovern and me in 2007

It is often not ideas or philosophies that attract us; it is admiration for a person's integrity. Goldwater, McGovern, Obama - each of these stood for independence and courage to stick to minority opinions, and put truth ahead of desire for political office.

In 1976 I voted for Jimmy Carter somewhat reluctantly. This peanut farmer from Georgia warned us we needed to end our dependence on foreign oil. In 1980 I voted for John Anderson to help push him past a threshold of receiving matching campaign funds. Carter had painted himself into too many corners and was simply unelectable. I admire him as a great humanitarian and was able to meet him and Rosalyn in 1998.

The Reagan years were a disaster in nearly every aspect, and I proudly cast a vote for another Methodist preacher's kid, Fritz Mondale, in 1984. George H. W. Bush was saddled by one poor decision after another, and my generation was thrilled to see Bill and Hillary Clinton move into the White House. It was a time of peace and shared prosperity, but it gave rise to a new generation of right wing demagogues who thrive on greed and division.

Their first victory went to a decent but incompetent man, controlled by advisors who led us into two wars, unrestricted criminal activity in the financial industry, a corrupt tax policy where the poorest folks pay twice the percentage of the wealthiest, and a disappearing middle class. Hope and change were needed and Barack Obama gave us both. There is more about presidential politics in Chapter 23.

It's much easier to elucidate and complain about politicians than it is to be one. My own emergence into politics was slow but deliberate. I was elected secretary of my freshmen class at Albion High School. The next year at 15, I became sophomore vice-president. In September of 1963 I was elevated to the A.H.S. equivalent of the Oriental Chair as I was chosen president of the Junior Class of Albion High School. This was no small accomplishment. The two previous class presidents - Duane Donaldson and Gary Siebler - were both football players. I had to overcome the "non-jock" stigma and won anyway. My presidential ambitions were reaching fruition.

Gradually, I became aware my newly-acquired power had its pitfalls. My vice president was a girl who turned out to be more responsible than ambitious, and she constantly reminded me that my job had duties along with its obvious glory. You see, the Junior Class paid for the Junior-Senior prom and banquet. This meant fundraiser after fundraiser, week after week, from September to April.

I should have gone out for sports. It was a lot easier than being Junior Class president. Junior Class presidents popped popcorn - night after lonely night - first the oil, then the kernels, then you waited, then you bagged. The lines at the window grew longer and more restless. I can still hear my vice president shouting, "more popcorn!" Remember 1963 was also the year the other president, John Kennedy, was murdered. This whole thing pretty much ended my presidential ambitions. Since then I've had only occasional bouts with ambition. In 1980, for instance, I won election to the Board of Education, Otoe County District #44. Basically, I have come to believe that ambitious people are not very wise people.

Historians will surely place Barack Obama in the top tier of Presidents. He was given the Nobel Peace Prize within his first year in office. His policies saved us from a depression, guaranteed health care for all citizens, decreased unemployment by 40%, restored market confidence with DJIA gaining over 100% since he was inaugurated, guided us toward renewable energy, bolstered efforts against terrorism, eliminated barriers for gays in the military, created pathways for marriage equality, paved the way for elimination of the federal budget deficit, and established immigration reforms.

He did most of this without the cooperation of Congress, whose favorability rating is consisently around 10%.

+++

In 2008 I got a call from the President of the Central Plains Classis of the Reformed Church in America. He needed liability coverage for the organization, and property coverage for a couple of buildings they owned in Papillion: the former Papio Theater and ex-Masonic Lodge. That's how I became the insurance agent for the place where I watched **The Blob** in 1957.

After nine years of trying, in 2008 I picked up perhaps my most coveted insurance customer. Loretto is a village six miles north of Albion. Their UMC is a Gothic building with beautiful art glass, and unique pews made from native cottonwood. My dad was their pastor for nine years, as they are part of the Albion charge. I preached my first "in church" sermon in Loretto back in 1966. I used to brag I insured every United Methodist Church (in my territory) on Highway 14 except Loretto.

On a wintery day in November, I got a call from Chuck Crosby, the Loretto church treasurer. I had sent them another proposal, and put the file away. But this time the stars were aligned, and they voted to come my way. Ironically the call came while I was driving south of Norfolk, only 40 miles from Loretto. I quickly made my way to the Crosby home, and got the necessary signatures. I then had a wonderful visit with Chuck and Twylla, and headed back to Lincoln in a very contented mood.

Due to my success in western Nebraska my book of insurance business grew to $2.8 million in 2008. Attrition crept up to 3.71% which was the highest since my first year with Church Mutual. The numbers were good enough to win us a trip to the Dominican Republic, which turned out to be our last one with CMIC.

In February 2009 we had an event-filled week at the Punta Cana resort in the

D.R. One night we ate at a resort restaurant and visited with two women at the next table. One was the wife and daughter of Dr. Frank Schubert whose books about Fort Robinson I've read. Another time we drank rum from a coconut shell, and stopped at a cigar factory where I bought a box of cigars. Why I did this I don't know; I still have the full box. One night we watched the fascinating Cirque de Soleil.

Upon departure we flew to Atlanta and boarded our 9 pm Omaha flight at 11 pm. It sat on the tarmac for another hour as the plane was overweight, and the captain pleaded for three people to give up their seats. We lifted off and had a bumpy 2 hour ride to Omaha. We were lucky to retrieve luggage, as several passengers found none. We got to our car at 1:30 am and drove though a snowstorm, arriving home at 3 am.

Working for CMIC gave me a glimpse into corporate America. The company was started in 1897 to provide fire insurance protection in a small area of northern Wisconsin. They grew steadily, but did not become a national provider until 1952. In 2003, when Hawaii was added, they were selling policies in all 50 states. In 2005 they doubled the size of their home office, and in 2006 they became a billion dollar company. There were three company presidents in my 13 years with CMIC, and Chris and I were on a first-name basis with each one and their spouse. One of them, Charmaine Whitburn, remembered the names of our granddaughters and asked about them each time we saw her.

Dieter Nickel was company president from 1971 to 2001. I got acquainted with him at my first training session in 1999. Dieter gave all employees a generous gift package of meats and cheeses each Christmas. In 2000 we received the gift the same week Nebraska was playing Wisconsin in the NCAA volleyball championship, and I sent Dieter an email saying: "Thanks for your generous gift. All the best to you and yours at this season, but this does not apply to the Badger volleyball team." Within five minutes I got a phone call from Dieter asking me what I meant about the Badgers, as he didn't follow volleyball. When I explained he challenged me to a wager, and I bet him $5 Nebraska would win. A few days later he mailed me a five dollar bill.

Gerald Whitburn became CEO of CMIC in 2001. I also met him back at my first training session. He called me in 2003 to discuss the structure and decision making process of The UMC. CMIC's officers were meeting with the General Church finance people about setting up a denominational insurance program. That didn't happen, but I dealt with some Nebraska UMC issues quite often.

CMIC had insured the Conference since 1993, and as Conference Treasurer I renewed the 3-year policy in 1996. I helped expand the coverage in 1997 when CMIC established a voluntary group workers' compensation program. I renewed their package as an agent in 1999, and in 2000 I set up a group program which gave every church a credit. It also helped Dave Allen and I to sell more policies. The Nebraska UMC Conference was far and away my biggest customer.

In 2004 the United Methodist Property and Casualty Trust (UMPACT) was established. Church officials were certain they could broker protection, and give churches a bargain. It was especially popular in coastal states where rates were highest. After Katrina hit in 2005, UMPACT was in trouble and started pushing the Bishops to get into the program. Nebraska's Bishop was a fan of this idea and pressed our Trustees to go for it.

In the spring of 2008 I was told the Nebraska Conference trustees would consider a proposal from UMPACT. Their policy renewed 9/30/2008, and I alerted my underwriter and Division Manager, who contacted the others in the chain of command. My underwriter, Elaine Nass, was carrying the ball at the home office and she gave me periodic updates. She was lobbying for improved coverages and pricing tools to help me keep the business. In June the Conference Treasurer told me the UMPACT folks would make a presentation on August 4, and I should be prepared to do the same.

The summer wheels turn slowly in northern Wisconsin. Our proposal needed to be ready at least a month before the August meeting, so I could review and revise and be ready for the Trustees. The deadline passed, but Elaine called to say she was meeting with #2 and #3 people at CMIC to finish it up on July 6. The next day, she told me those two didn't show and everything was on hold. I then decided on a new strategy.

I emailed all I knew to be involved in developing the proposal, detailing my work, my suggestions, my conversations with church and company people, and my frustration. I copied in Mr. Gerald Whitburn, CEO of CMIC, and hit "enter." The next morning I had a call telling me to be in the office at 3 pm, as Whitburn would be calling. For about ten minutes he interviewed me to clarify several issues. Little did I know that several red-faced underlings were sitting in the room.

Elaine called to say wheels were moving, and I got the proposal in plenty of time to prepare for August 4. The meeting was held and we saved the account. My division manager, Bruce West, told me to never contact Mr. Whitburn directly again. It seems Whitburn called in #2 and chewed on him, #2 assailed #3, and so on down to Bruce, who very politely gave me the message. Apparently corporate America and the schoolyard bully system have a lot in common.

The next and last time I heard from Mr. Whitburn was on a July afternoon in 2009. His secretary tracked me down on my cell phone while I was walking through the Brass Armadillo antique mall on a work day. At any rate, he was calling to tell me I had been promoted to Senior Regional Representative. This status came with a deferred compensation plan, which more than doubled my CMIC pension.

+++

I've reported earlier about the Oakland West Side church. When I attended the church's auction in 1997, the church windows were the last items sold. Several windows had been purchased and removed by church families, but quite a few remained. One or two were sold, and then the auctioneer opened bids for all the rest. When bidding ended, the winner announced the windows would be taken to a museum in nearby West Point.

As I was now into photographing windows all over the state, I made it a mission to find the West Side windows. Someone referred me to La Mae Johnson, a former member of the West Side church, and I gave her a call and went to see her in April of 2009. She had been widowed for several years, but still lived in her farm home between Oakland and West Point. We had a wonderful visit, and she shared many letters and pictures of our family that Mom had sent her over the years. My dad married she and Linder in 1945. I discovered the West Side windows were in a building at the Cuming County fairgrounds in West Point.

A few weeks later I went through West Point and found the structure. It was a former German Lutheran church, which was moved to this location several years previously. A new roof was being installed, and the building was unlocked. The original frosted glass had been replaced by West Side's art glass, which was just the right width.

An elegant altar with the outstretched arms of Jesus greets visitors, and restored windows still bearing Swedish names of donors give light and beauty to this little chapel. I put together a photo album with new pictures of the windows, and our family photos from Oakland days, and presented it to La Mae at the West Side reunion in September 2009.

+++

In October my Wesleyan class of 1969 had a reunion. After thinking about all the changes in the city of Lincoln in the past 40 years, I wrote an essay entitled "The Saga of Rip Van Leypoldt," and published it on my website.

It began "I dreamt that I was still a college student at Nebraska Wesleyan. I woke up in a parking lot and immediately started thinking, 'whoa! I must have been at Der Loaf 'n Stein again last night!' Once I got to my feet and rubbed the sleep from my eyes, I looked up the alley and saw the Delta Zeta house and down the street southwest and there was Zeta Psi. I couldn't remember they painted it, though. To the north I spied Alpha Gamma Delta, but thought there should be a big old house next door to it.

"Then I looked straight ahead and a concrete slab for parking was all there was. No Alpha Kappa Lambda. What the….? Damn pledges really pulled a good one this time! But wait. This is THE place. Street sign definitely says 50th and Huntington. I must be having a Clara Urania Mills moment.

"I stumbled up the sidewalk to the door of the first non-apartment building on the block. This friendly gentlemen opened the door. He looked kind of familiar but I wasn't sure I'd met him previously." The rest of the story is posted on **pylodet.com**.

+++

My Christmas Epistle listed a few more things about the year 2009.

I started driving a Ford Fusion in April; its no Taurus but I adjusted. What's really cool is the Sirius radio: oldies music, comedy, liberal talk, even a Disney channel for our girls. Sarah received her Master of Arts in Education degree at Chadron in May. Later that day Cora and I scaled a "mountain" south of Chadron, which event became You Tube video. On May 15 I launched a website: **pylodet.com**. I started sending our Christmas Epistle via the internet to those on Facebook and others who have e-mail addresses known to me. The web version had more pictures and a couple of videos.

July 13, 2009 our Anastasia and Jeff Grinvalds were married in New Orleans. Our families and friends came together at a reception for them in Omaha on August 15.

In September new triple pane windows were installed at our house; thanks to progressive policies in Washington, we received a tax credit the following year. We went shopping for new curtains. Chris told a sales clerk that our bedroom drapes matched the wallpaper and I hadn't noticed it previously (in 14 years). The windows were guaranteed to reduce our energy costs 30% the first year. November 2009 gas bill was 40% lower than last year's. Chris had a milestone birthday in October and we also attended my Wesleyan class of '69 reunion on October 31.

Chris stayed busy with quilting, TOPS, garage saling, substitute kitchen work, and weekly visits with her Dad. I reported having 15,957 photos in my "church art" files, 3,682 cemetery headstone pix, and another 4,998 miscellaneous (mostly grandkid) photos taken so far in 2009. My computer had 2.14 terabytes of storage with 1.67 still available so my Sony cameras will be busy for some time. I did attempt to spend a little time with my day job as well. I was counting down the days to retirement.

+++

My insurance results in 2009 were less than inspiring. I wrote two more large churches in Scottsbluff and one in Alliance; also, a large church in Columbus, two large churches in Grand Island and a big child care facility in Omaha. My attrition was a very respectable 2.8%. The bean counters started using loss ratios against us and that disqualified me from the annual trip.

Our North 74th Street Home in 2009

Early in 2010 I stopped at a church north of Henderson. They asked me to quote their insurance the year before but I was unable to close the deal. In these situations, I usually followed up so prospects would know I was still looking for business. The church was unlocked but no one was around.

I noticed the church pews had been moved to the narthex and fellowship hall and the sanctuary was in process of major repairs. I saw a letter posted on a bulletin board, which detailed an insurance company's offer to pay a claim following the collapse of the sanctuary roof. I called my underwriter to tell her that my failure to sell this account, resulted in saving Church Mutual $80,000. Speaking of claims, some notable ones are burned into my memory. I had only one customer who suffered a total loss, and it was due to arson. It was a small church, and the total claim was less than $300,000. A culprit was never found, but a church member was pretty sure it was the former pastor who had been dismissed because of marital infidelity.

Another church was sponsoring a Halloween party, and a teenage girl was hurt while using an inflatable slide. She spent a couple of days in the hospital, but fully recovered. The hospital expense was $19,000, the family had no insurance, and the church had a $5,000 limit for medical expense. Because the party was well supervised there was no negligence, so no reason to pay more than $5,000. The church held a series of fundraisers to help the girl's family.

An Omaha church submitted a claim for ceiling damage caused by a roof leak. CMIC sent an adjuster to look at the roof, and he brought along a roofer who had made an unsuccessful bid to install the roof a few years previously. The pastor was upset with the adjuster for doing this, and I agreed completely. I called the claims supervisor, and said I felt the adjuster's contract with CMIC should not be renewed. The claims supervisor told my underwriter that I hurt his feelings.

Another Omaha church with a parochial school had a teacher who became exasperated with an unruly child. At day's end she tied the child to a chair, using material that would not hurt him in any way. After a few minutes, she realized her mistake and told the principal what happened. Corporal punishment liability was not yet covered on all our policies. When the principal called me, I checked and happily reported we would take care of any damages.

Another Omaha church, a Baptist congregation with a predominately black constituency, was using an accountant who embezzled $25,000. Not all churches had bonding, and we were adding it on renewals. Unfortunately this church was not covered. They had been customers of CMIC for over 30 years. The vice president of claims called me about the situation. I said, "let's pretend they are Wisconsin Synod Lutherans and pay the claim." He did so!

Yet another Omaha congregation had two unusual claims. In 2000 they built a large addition on to their church, and decided to upgrade their pipe organ. The console was taken to a shop, but the pipes were stored in the parsonage basement. This house was unique in that it had a basement under the garage area, and that's where the organ pipes ended up. You might guess what happened during the winter. Melting snow and ice from vehicles dripped down on the organ pipes. Fortunately, there was no damage.

The second potential claim occurred in 2007. The church in question was formerly a rural congregation and as Omaha grew, the farmland became very valuable. Several parishioners shared their good fortune with the church. Their congregational president concocted a plan, whereby he would invest $250,000 of the church's money to buy land, and sell it for a profit. Instead, he used it for personal gain and got caught. A judge ordered him to repay the stolen amount plus interest and legal fees. And he spent some time in jail. CMIC lost nothing and the church learned a valuable lesson.

+++

On July 11, 2010 Chris and I observed our 40th wedding anniversary in Indiana. We rented a nice room in a bed and breakfast in the heart of Amish country. We were able to combine my interest in Amish culture, Chris' love of quilting, and our joint hobby of shopping for bargains and collectibles. We went to the Shipshewana flea market. We also took an Amish "extrusion" which included a buggy ride, visit to a dairy farm, and supper in an Amish home.

On July 29, 2010 my father-in-law, Harold Wayne Landon, died at the age of 83. He deserved far more than to have his final years stolen and ravaged by an affliction known as Alzheimer's. He lived his life working the family farm and raising his family. He rose above the losses of his wife Arlene and daughter Kay to cancer. When hospitalized, I heard him tell a nurse about those two deaths, and say how grateful he was that Eunice came into his life.

Harold met Eunice Johnson on a blind date in 1972. It was a scheme of three couples: one knew Harold, one knew Eunice, and one who knew both couples independently. Contacts were made and Harold called Eunice. The rest, as they say, is history. Eunice was born and raised in Wakefield, attended Luther College in Wahoo, and taught in my dad's home town of Hershey. She went back to college and got a B.A. at Bethany in Lindsborg, Kansas, taught in Goodland, Kansas and then in Lincoln. In the meantime she earned her Master's at UNL. Eventually she served as a consultant to the administration, specializing in physical education programs.

What a challenge it must have been to marry someone with four grown children and two little grandsons in 1973. Harold and Eunice remodeled a house on one of the Landon farms, and she left education for agriculture. She has been the glue holding us together since. When Kay became ill in the early 1980's, she was there for her. She is Grandma Eunice to ten grown kids, and oodles more great-grandchildren. She made life bearable for Harold as his health declined, and helped us all do our best to care for him.

When I was orphaned in 2006, I realized how lucky I was to still have Eunice for a mother. A couple of years later, Chris gave her the highest of compliments when she introduced her as "my mom" to one of our friends.

Chris' father was buried next to his children's mother at the Cedar Hill Cemetery, just a few miles from where he lived and farmed his whole life. Eunice has chosen to be there, also, well into the future. His grandson Seth Leypoldt presided at the committal on August 2, 2010. These words from Genesis help me remember my father-in-law and other stewards of the land: "As long as the earth remains, there will be planting and harvest, cold and heat; winter and summer, day and night (8:22, CEV)."

+++

In 2010 Church Mutual hired more Risk Control people, and established new underwriting guides that made the job difficult for anyone who was not two years from retirement. In 2010 I picked up just enough new business to keep the wolves from my door. My attrition shot past 8% as our competition moved in aggressively; but storm activity in Nebraska was hurting us. The average church building is covered with asphalt shingles, and runaway oil prices drove their price literally through the roof.

On March 5, 2011 I meandered out to western Nebraska to visit a couple of my insurance customers. It turned out to be a real nice trip with temperatures in the 50's and 60's. After completing the "work" portion of the journey I headed back east on the super slab known as Interstate 80. I stopped for lunch in Ogallala. Nearby was one of my favorite spots for bargain hunting: Pamida (now Shopko).

But first I must share a confession. I used to be a smoker. According to my self-guided psychotherapy, tobacco was not the real problem. In truth, I had an oral fixation. You see I sucked the index finger on my left hand until I was nine. That finger is smaller than the right pointer to this day. My parents tried all kinds of child psychology tricks to cure me. But one day, I decided to quit on my own. That's when I took up smoking. When I was ten, I found an almost full pack of cigarettes in the street. I hid them next door in the church my dad was serving, and snuck one or two a day until they were all gone. Maybe that's why I'm the shortest boy in the family. As time went by, I kept an eye out for an idle pack of smokes, and helped myself a few times. Mostly I just finished off a discarded butt (sordid, but I told you this was a confession). In Junior High and High School it was easier to find ciggy piggies.

A lot of my friends were smokers, and they could snatch a few cancer sticks from their folks or buy some out of town, and I could get in on the action. After I received my coveted driver's license, I had no problem satisfying my hankering. One could go to St. Ed or Petersburg and buy almost anything. A pack of cigarettes only cost about a quarter in those days. My little weed neurosis grew steadily during my college years. Not only was it legal to smoke in the fraternity house, it only cost about 2 or 3 cents per coffin nail. Some of my buddies even substituted smokes for breakfast. About this time I became more sophisticated, and started smoking menthols and was buying them by the carton (because it was cheaper, not because I was smoking more).

When I went to the seminary in 1969, I was concerned that the ancient Methodist ban on tobacco might be a problem. So I kept my Salems hidden for a while...about an hour actually. The first guy I met in the dorm was a professional inhaler! My oral fixation was deemed acceptable; it's even possible we smokers were in the majority. I was introduced to Kools during a break in Church History class. I gradually transitioned into pipe smoking. I had a pretty nice collection of pipes and several little racks to display them, and humidors to keep the tobacco fresh. I found tobacco that smelled and tasted perfect for my growing obsession. I quit preaching and starting banking, and became a public smoker. I also ruined shirts, ties, car upholstery, a few carpets and endured lectures from dental health professionals.

In 1986, I was a 39-year-old banker in Douglas, Nebraska. During the year I developed a persistent, hacking cough and chronic pain in my chest. It didn't really slow me down or bother me that much, but Chris noticed it and after her remedies failed, she talked me into a trip to the doctor in Nebraska City. My physician was a college friend and non-smoker. He checked me out, and said the best thing would be to visit the x-ray room at Saint Mary's Hospital. Whoa! Wasn't expecting that. No problems showed on the x-ray. However, I started a systemic liquidation of my pipe collection. I tried cigars for a while. Even the ones with pipe tobacco flavor didn't appeal to me.

My compulsion mutated toward bubblegum. I searched the candy sections and specialty stores for sticky confections with minty, long-lasting flavor, preferably sugarless, and able to make huge bubbles. For several years I was stuck on Bubble Yum; even won a contest for biggest bubble at a church picnic once. A couple of years ago, Bubble Yum quit making the peppermint stuff and I was really bummed. I went looking for a substitute and quit chewing for a while. Then I discovered Big League Chew. It's the best! Just the original, none of those sissy flavors for me.

Emma loved to pop my bubbles.

This brings me back to the Pamida in Ogallala. It was a good source for Big League Chew, and I was running a little low. Couldn't find it in the usual place so I went back to the candy department. None there either. *What the heck!* So I did something I rarely ever do - asked for help. "I think there's some in the close-out section," said the friendly clerk. Sure enough. Not only several packages but it was reduced down to 50 cents from the regular $1.25.

So now I'm feeling pretty good and enjoying the weather even more, and hop back into the Fusion for additional time on I-80. I popped in a big wad of chew, and headed east. After 90 minutes or so, both my bladder and my gas gauge were telling me to pull over at Lexington. For twelve years I'd driven a company-leased car and filled up with a gas card. I hate to admit this, but I didn't pay much attention to gas prices. I found my way to a Conoco place called Fat Dogs in Lexington.

It wasn't real busy, and I pulled right into a middle spot. I always use Super Unleaded with ethanol. I activated the pump and saw that corn gas was up to $3.729. Yikes! I washed off the headlights, walked back to the stinky pump handle, and saw a sign I hadn't noticed previously. It said Super Unleaded $3.379. Interesting. I'll have to ask about this.

I went inside and used the filthy men's room, then sauntered up to the idle guy behind the counter. This is exactly what I said, "doesn't really matter to me, I drive a company car, but just wondering why the sign says 3.379 and the receipt says 3.729." He tells me something like the cheaper price is only found at pumps 1 & 2. "Well that explains it," I replied and walked out. Sure enough, there was some fine print at the gas pump explaining the situation. Of course I didn't see it until I was told about it.

Oh well. I saved more money on the gum than the company lost on the gas purchase. Who cares if they lost $3.50 because I wasn't paying attention. One big corporation screwed another big corporation: that's the way capitalism works. Doesn't matter to me.

But it does matter. Deception is wrong. Big signs that mislead and fine print that offers disclaimers are dishonest. Perhaps it was legal; but still crooked. I'm sure I won't buy gas at Fat Dogs in Lex again.

On a lighter note, here's two things I mull over but don't know where to put them. My favorite soft drink is Diet Code Red, but I still haven't forgiven Coca Cola for taking away Black Cherry Vanilla Diet Coke. And, whenever I visit the grocery store, I mourn the mysterious loss of Kitty Clover all over again.

+++

I saw a print at Our Savior's Lutheran Church in Plainview, Nebraska that I really liked. It depicted a little girl holding a toy lamb, and looking at an art glass image of the Good Shepherd. It was entitled "Feed My Sheep," and was the work of Kathryn Andrews Fincher. I began to think about this image more often, and wondered if I could insert my granddaughters into a similar picture. I imagined the Good Shepherd window from my home church in Albion and Emma, Cora, and Olivia looking up at it.

In March 2011 I went to see my friend Randel Anderson in Norfolk, and discussed the possibility of him doing this painting for us. I brought pictures of the girls and the Albion window. We ended up using one from September 2006 when Emma was 8, Cora 6 and Olivia 2. It looks wonderful above our fireplace in the living room.

The United Methodists in Albion have a unique window and I believe it is inspired by these words from John 10: "The one who enters by the gate is the shepherd of the sheep. The gatekeeper opens the gate for him and the sheep hear his voice. He calls his own sheep by name and leads them out…Jesus said to them '…I am the gate for the sheep...I am the Good Shepherd.'" I've seen one like it at First Baptist in Omaha and First Presbyterian in Wichita, Kansas. The window is based on the work of Sybil C. Parker, a British citizen, born in 1860. She called her Good Shepherd rendition, "The Door of the Fold." It can also be seen at The Campus Church at Stanford University and in First Presbyterian, Jefferson, IN, State Street UMC, Bristol, VA, First Christian, Hammond, IN, and Dexter Avenue UMC, Montgomery, AL. These places are on my bucket list to visit. You can see the painting and more information about Sybil Parker's works at **pylodet.com.**

In May 2011 I renewed a policy in Platte Center and upon leaving, I heard the radio reporting a tornado on the ground heading for Osceola. Ordinarily I would go home via Osceola on Highway 92, so I switched my route to the 4-lane Highway 30 east of Columbus. The skies looked nasty as I hurried through the Platte County seat.

A few miles east, the heavens opened as wind, rain, and hail pelted my Ford Fusion. I decided to pull over in Schuyler and wait this one out, but it quit before I got there. I thought about Osceola where I had two nice churches with parsonages insured, but there was no new news. The sun came out and I buzzed home.

The next morning, I read in the paper that the Osceola twister had lifted just as it approached the city limits. In 2007 I had survived a crash in the company car, and was told, more or less, that I was responsible for bad weather. Evidently my power over the elements had now saved the company $4 million in losses at Osceola. I reported same to home office.

When I was hired by CMIC in 1999, my manager said the practice of renting office space would soon be discontinued, and we would work from our homes. It finally happened on June 1, 2011. I rearranged my furnace room to accommodate a large desk, bookcase, and storage and filing cabinets. I also moved some files and other materials, and was all set. I concentrated on renewing policies and sending out a few proposals to keep the manager happy.

Operating from my furnace room/office was kind of like taking care of Seth in the Davenport parsonage: I found a lot of distractions to keep my mind off work. I was multi-slacking my way through life. Even my road trips involved some new adventures.

On an August day in 2011, I went searching for the Beaver View Brewing Company in Albion, Nebraska. I looked for it once before and couldn't find it, so this time I asked around, and was told the libation was on tap at a local bar. Keep in mind: this is my home town where my father gave temperance sermons at least once a year. The bar was also the place people in Albion went for coffee in the afternoon.

I stopped at the saloon about 3 pm. When I opened the door I was no longer 64, but felt like a kid who was using a fake id to buy beer. I asked about Beaver Brew, and they had two choices. The waitress started filling a jug of the award-winning Little Blind Blonde ale. I looked around and saw a couple who were faithful members of the UMC in Albion, and walked over to say hello. "So what brings you to Albion, Chuck?" I was asked. I told them I heard about the brewery, and thought I should give it a try. He looked shocked; she asked, "didn't you sign one of your father's abstinence cards?" The whole table waited for answer. "What can I say," I mumbled.

+++

CMIC was in trouble in 2011. Increased storm activity throughout the nation took away our profitability. Underwriters began to non-renew policies and deny permission to quote numerous prospects, based on loss histories or other criteria. The annual incentive trip was canceled.

In the previous year company assets increased to $1.2 billion. However, more than 1,700 tornado touchdowns and $156 million in damage to customer properties along with a decrease in premium volume, required some changes in operating costs. We had a big powwow in a Chicago suburb in September of 2011, and predictive modeling became part of the company jargon.

Generally speaking, predictive modeling uses the past to anticipate the future. All kinds of statistics and analytical methods are utilized to identify patterns and predict losses. In property insurance, rates have always been subject to claims history, age and condition of buildings, and safety concerns. CMIC would soon join many other companies already using multivariate techniques to provide even granularity and better analysis of individual risks. Sales representatives would input information, underwriters would review these inputs and mine more data, and a customized premium would be generated for each customer and prospect. If I had any doubts about retirement, they all faded away.

The best thing about the Chicago meeting was that I drove the company car over there, and Chris went with me. We made some leisurely stops on the way home. At the end of 2011 my book of business fell below $2.8 million, and attrition was one tick under 10%. Here's how my Christmas epistle reported the year:

Twenty-six Random Thoughts and Fun Facts About 2011

A. Our Whirlpool washer and dryer needed replacement, and Sears advertised a great deal on Maytags. After patiently listening to an impassioned plea to add a Service Agreement, which we declined, we agreed to buy. After the delivery and hook-up, we discovered the hot line was connected to cold water, and surprisingly we fixed that by ourselves. Our new washer sounds like a jet plane warming up: there's no **agitator!**

B. On July 14 I woke up with a sharp pain in my shoulder area...thought I'd "slept wrong." Couldn't sit comfortably in the car, but spent 2 days driving all around the Panhandle. Went to a Chiropractor in Chadron and then to my G.P. in Lincoln, and he said I had a **bulging disc.**

C. **Cora** is eleven and in the sixth grade at Gering. She plays saxophone and volleyball and is a computer whiz kid.

D. Said goodbye to my **DSLR** A-350 and bought a Sony a65, which uses different technology.

E. **Emma** is thirteen and attending Gering Junior High. She plays clarinet (first chair) and is the proud owner of an iPhone.

F. In 2003 my company provided me with a new **Ford** Taurus, and another one in 2005, and a **Five** Hundred in 2007, down to a **Fusion** in 2009. This year I had two choices: **Fusion** and Chrysler 200. I chose poorly. My disc starting bulging about the time I started driving rhe Chrysler.

G. Speaking of **Gering**...Sarah went to work at the Panhandle Mental Health Center in July, and she and Seth bought a house in Gering. Their girls decided to switch schools. Though he spends a couple of days each week in Gering, Seth is still with the Chadron church until June. His future plans are in process.

H. As reported last year, Church Mutual's **home** office is now in my basement. Therefore, I have two man caves in which to hide.

I. Climate change and runaway oil prices are wreaking havoc on the property **insurance** industry. Brace yourselves.

J. **Jeff and Ana** remain in their home in North Omaha. Jeff is teaching at Westside High School. Ana is with Telecare, which assists severely mentally ill folks. Kyle is 18 and will graduate from High School next spring. Maija is 13 and an eighth grader.

K. Chris continues on call in various **kitchens** of the Lincoln Public Schools. She also volunteers at Fabulous Finds, our church thrift shop, and makes the best pretzels in Lincoln.

L. **Let it be.**

M. In 1981 I was a banker paying 17.22% for six month certificates of deposit and was charging 19% for farm loans. Today our **mortgage** rate is 3.75% and Ally Bank sells what they call a High Yield Certificate of Deposit that pays .74%. You do the math: me thinks the banks are gaining on us.

N. There is **No** Place Like **Nebraska**!

O. **Olivia** is seven and a second grader at Keil School in Gering. She rides her bike and makes pictures with a Sony of her own.

P. If you want to learn all about **pylodet** (and so much more), visit pylodet.com.

Q. In July we were in Chadron looking after Olivia. Chris decided to do some baking, and asked this **question:** "Where does your mom keep the sugar?" Livi replied helpfully: "In the kitchen"

R. I can see clearly now. The sixty-fifth anniversary of my birth will be July 16, 2012, and my intention is to **retire** shortly thereafter. Can't wait.

S. We took on a really big art project this year. I dreamt up a portrait featuring our girls and one of my favorite **stained** glass windows.

T. From the "why did it take you so long?" department: we now have a Smart **TV** in the family room. This means plasma, high definition, and Internet access on one beautiful 42 inch screen.

U. **Uncensored:** I'm thinking about writing a tell-all book after I retire so you better be nice to me. *Writer's note: long range goals do help.*

V. Not much time for a big **vacation** this year. We spent four days at Fort Robinson in August with Ana, Emma, Cora, Olivia, Seth and Sarah. The highlight of our trip was attending the Post Playhouse production of **The Spelling Bee,** or more accurately, the walk from our cabin to the theater. As we casually strolled on that beautiful summer evening, a curious bull snake appeared along our path. We were so busy chatting and enjoying the night, that we didn't notice him right away. I actually stepped over him, and looked down in the same instance. Then, in a moment of recognition, I exclaimed, "snake!" Chris immediately shrieked, and moved quickly into the street. About twenty fellow playgoers were in front of and behind us, and reacted in a variety of ways. Sarah took a picture with her camera phone. Too bad I didn't have a video camera running.

W. In June our whole family made a nostalgic visit to **Wurst Tag** in Eustis. It was so great to see our friends, and eat lunch at Lucky Chuck's. The grandkids stayed with us while their parents attended Seth's High School reunion.

X. I have expanded my collection of church photos by a few thousand this year. Most of them have been captured on my regular business trips, but one special visit was to the Basilica of Saint Francis **Xavier** in Dyersville, Iowa. This also helped me identify another image of St. Francis in a Nebraska church.

Y. It's been a good year for **youth-hood**. A grand-nephew and three grand nieces have been welcomed to our world.

Z. We have reached the **zenith** of our annual message. As always our wish for you is a very merry Christmas and a happy and prosperous new year.

Chapter 23
Turning Sixty Five

It should be abundantly clear to all concerned, that my job was seriously interfering with my hobbies. Shortly after January 1, 2012, I gave notice to my manager that I planned to retire on August 17, 2012, which was 32 days past my 65th birthday. On April 14 I received an email from Joel Barcus, a Regional Manager (a step above Division Manager) of CMIC. He praised me for my performance in the first quarter, and told me to take Chris out to dinner and charge it to the company. By the time I quit in August, I was ahead of my sales goal for the year, but couldn't have cared less.

When Ana was in college, she was taking an Economics class, and the teacher asked the group if they knew anything about their parents plan for the future. Ana said, "All I know is my dad wants to retire as soon as possible." She knew me so well!

In May the UM Conference Treasurer called to tell me the church at Pilger was closing, and I needed to add the property to the AC policy. It was ironic I was reckoning this church as a customer, three months previous to my retirement. There are two towns in Stanton County: Stanton and Pilger, and a total of nine churches including one Catholic. In 1999, only two were customers of Church Mutual.

There was an agency in the Pilger bank, who wrote the Pilger churches. The LCMS church came my way, and the bank's manager was treasurer of the ELCA congregation, and invited me to quote their church. While at the church, the pastor told me he also served St. Luke's Lutheran in Stanton, and I quoted it as well. Both congregations bought policies, as did two others in Stanton.

Don and Virginia Barnes Johnson were Albion natives who lived in Pilger. They were the first couple married by my father at Albion in 1959, and they were active in the Pilger UMC. Don owned the Pilger bank which branched out, and became Midwest Bank. When I was conference treasurer, I asked him to serve on the Conference Board of Pension and Health Benefits, and he did so for several years. Thus, I figured he would be open to me quoting my last non-customer Protestant church in Stanton County.

I tried 2 or 3 times but they just weren't interested in a replacement cost policy, as they felt they had a limited future. On June 16, 2014 the former Pilger UMC and St. John's LCMS and parsonage, were all destroyed by a massive tornado.

+++

In July our families planned an adventure for the five Leypoldt brothers. We were sent off without knowing where we were going until receiving instructions as we went. It was called the Quest of the Brothers 5. I filed the following report.

Friday, July 13 - Got the family truckster ready and loaded up my stuff. Chris and I motored to Jim and Missy's about 9:30 am. Doug and Nancy were already there, and informed us that Steve was indeed going with us. We drove to the alley and began loading. Gary arrived.

Cathy stopped by to see us off. Where is Steve? Doug said, "he's sitting in the shade in the back yard." We started tossing in the bags and coolers. Oh, darn! I forgot a cap. Chris goes home to fetch one.

Just about loaded. Where are Steve's things? Better go find him. Turns out he's a cardboard replica known as "Flat Steve." Chris brings five caps for me to use. I chose the one with Douglas Grain, Inc. logo. Cathy, Missy, Beth, Ben, Chester, Charli, Cairo and Aderha are in the farewell throng along with Chris and Nancy. We're ready to depart, and received numerous gifts and salutations. Our first destination was Clay Center. Better hurry; we're already behind schedule, it's after 10 am.

Headed west on I-80...**BIG DELAY DUE TO CONSTRUCTION.** We detoured south at Milford on Highway 15, then took 6 all the way to 14 intersection. Arrived just a little late at Kay and Buck's house in Clay Center. What a wonderful hostess is Kay Doupnik! Subway sandwiches and dessert. Pretty soon we're off for a challenge at the Clay Center golf course. The manager set up several putting exercises. I actually got a couple of holes-in-one, but Jim was the overall winner. Drinks are served in the clubhouse, and the driver sticks with Diet Coke while a couple guys drank an Ultra ice tea. All the while, we were interviewed by the editor of the **Clay County News**.

Took a few pictures in Clay Center, and were directed toward Albion. On the way, I photographed the Hamilton County courthouse and Seth's former home in Aurora. Stopped in Central City for gas, and opened Aderha's demand to wear rain hats while pumping gas, which we did. Our next summons required each of us to be photographed with a person we knew in Albion. Upon our arrival in our hometown (about 4 pm), we went to Ralph Schmadeke's insurance office and found three persons (including Ralph) to pose with Gary, Flat Steve, and myself. Next, across the street to the **Albion News** where the editor took a group shot to be published in his next edition. We then proceeded to the **Boot Rack** to find the Reynoldsons who graduated with Doug. They were gone for a few minutes, but Chelse offered to pose with Steve, which was well-received by all of us. Darlene Reynoldson came in, and was pictured with Doug. Thereupon, we headed to the funeral home and found Ron Levander who stood with Jim.

We checked into the Dunes Motel. It was time for supper, and we went to the Albion Country Club. Our waitress was an attractive young lady, who told us she would soon be a senior at Boone Central H.S. Her grandpa was a kid who grew up in Loretto, and was several years younger than me. An Albion teacher, Randall Henning, was also there and sat down to visit with us. He had Doug, Cathy, Steve, and Jim in his classes. A girl from the class of '66, LeAnne Buhlmann, was in the dining room, but we didn't recognize each other. Another high school friend, Greg Packard, the facility manager, mentioned to LeAnne that I had been there. Shame on me.

Saturday, July 14 - Up early. We went to Casey's for coffee, and ate one of Jim's nutrition bars. We drove past the Albion UMC and noticed the sign said "welcome." Was that for us? We drove to the cemetery, and marveled at how many more were there with Mom and Dad. We left flowers supplied by our trip planners. Soon, we're on Highway 91 heading west. Gary reflected on his friendship with Stephanie Stejksal, and we remembered driving/riding on the roller coaster hills west of Albion.

Upon entering Spalding, I wanted to check on the Catholic Church, as they had a recent fire and were remodeling. The church was locked, but Flat Steve needed to stretch his legs. We placed him in front of the school sign (across from church). The immediate ultimatum before us was three-fold: 1.) picture of Burwell UMC, 2.) picture of Steve at welcome sign, 3.) find Missy's friend Mary at a Calamus campground. We needed to *git 'r done* before noon. In Burwell, the first two pictures were easy, but goal #3 involved a geocache at a little church near the lake. We found the chapel, and the cache, but further instructions were confusing. In a rare moment of spontaneity, I bought a park permit at the store near the church.

We rambled across the dam road, looking for camp site #10. We found the place but not Mary. We scattered to see what we might see. A park ranger stopped by, to ask exactly what we were doing. The campsite occupants left their air conditioned camper to visit as well. The ranger checked my brand new park permit, and didn't know what else to do. Just then Missy's friend Mary appeared, and the joke was on us (and the ranger).

We were directed by Cairo to skip a rock 20 times on the lake. Gary, Jim, and Doug found at least twenty rocks and skipped them several times. Doug found a $20 bill at the lake's edge. Turns out it belonged to Jim, as he dropped it when pulling rocks out of his pocket (at least that's what he told us).

It was noon and Mary recommended a restaurant south of Burwell. I've heard good things about this place, too, and off we went. We skirted the edge of Burwell, and went south on Highway 11 to the little town of Elyria where I mistakenly thought the place was located. We found a friendly soul who advised us to take the "oil road across the highway, and we couldn't miss it." This was also the road to Fort Hartsuff.

The place called **Country Neighbor** turned out to be quite special for all of us. We missed the noon crowd, and parked ourselves in a booth. Three of us ordered the crispy chicken salad, and Gary had a piece of pie. We were so hungry we forgot Flat Steve, and when he came in, our fellow patrons really perked up! A youthful grandmother along with granddaughter were the first to be photographed with Steve. Turned out she was the owner of the place. Two young ladies found three different ways to approach Steve, even trying to spoon feed him! Then we crashed the meeting of the local Red Hat Society, or as Gary called them: the "red-hot" ladies. We and they took lots of pictures, and they were happy to learn two of the brothers were bachelors. We turned down a very generous offer to purchase Flat Steve. The group's president was social editor of both the **Ord Quiz** and the **Burwell Tribune**, so a little publicity could come our way.

We piled into the van and headed up the road to Fort Hartsuff, a restored military fort which had a limited existence in the 1870's. It was 102 degrees, but we were inspired to rove around the parade grounds, and tour the buildings. There was a field of tall corn next to the fort, and Flat Steve disappeared into it. He emerged and asked, "is this heaven?" to which we replied, "no, this is Nebraska."

After bailing Steve out for another trespass, we motored up to Highway 91, and then west toward Alliance. Approaching the Loup County seat, Taylor, we noticed several scluptures depicting villagers. We stopped and photographed many of them.

Further on highway 91 we came upon another Nebraska county seat, Brewster, where the Blaine County courthouse is located. This may be the only county seat without a post office. It appears Uncle Buck's is still in operation, as is the United Church of Christ. We noticed the flags were at half-staff. Upon further review, we discovered it was in honor of former Governor Norbert Tiemann, the last Republican governor in Nebraska who was not a total doofus.

We stopped at Halsey's National Forest, and climbed the tower, taking pictures to prove it. On to Hyannis, another Sandhills county seat, where we filled up with gas. We pulled into the Alliance Inn and Suites about 6 pm (gained an hour thanks to Mountain Time). Our next task was to visit Carhenge at sunset, so off we went. This is an interesting place I've visited several times. It was a nice evening, and we walk around and I take a lot of great pictures.

We met a very nice New York family, and one of them took a group picture for us. We headed back into Alliance for a late supper, ending up at Ken & Dale's. Nice place; nicer waitress. Doug starts telling her our story, including the brother who is out moping in the car. Doug goes out and gets Flat Steve, and the whole restaurant is pretty excited. We get a photo of Steve and ***all*** the waitresses! When we leave, another gal and her grandma ask us our story, and they pose too! Steve's ego, and perhaps his id, is now out of control.

We shifted into conflict resolution. Our guide was providing two rooms for us each night. This meant Steve had to stay overnight in the van. He was perfectly happy to do so at Albion, however now that he was a proven babe magnet, he wanted to move inside. At an executive session, we voted 3-1 to make him stay in the van. Gary was the hold-out, and as a compromise he suggested Steve could occupy the recliner in our room.

After walking all over Hartsuff, climbing the Halsey tower, and hiking the trails at Carhenge, we were pretty tired. So we settled down for long summer naps while visions of buxom waitresses, our wives (and old girlfriends in Gary's case) danced in our heads, and we drifted off to sleep. Flat Steve was right there beside me in his recliner chair. I awoke once during the night, only to see his unchanging expression and beady red eyes glaring at me.

Day Three: Sunday, July 15 - this place has a continental breakfast but is crawling with pubescent boys and their parents preparing for a baseball tournament. We ate what we could find, packed up, and headed toward the Pine Ridge. Our first assignment was to find Cochran Park, south of Crawford, and recreate the 1955 Easter Egg hunt that's in our family video. In less than an hour, we arrived at Cochran Park. Sadly, most of the park is now private property. However, there is considerable right-of-way along the blacktop, and we get our job done.

We were instructed to go into Crawford, and take Flat Steve to the place where the flesh-and-blood Steven Wayne was born on June 13, 1955. Although it's no longer a hospital, it's easy to find and we get our documentary photographs done. Drove around town a little. The parsonage has been replaced, and the old house moved to a new location, which we drove past. The big house on 3rd and Paddock is still there, although painted blue. The old grade school is long gone, but our little church looks the same. Went by the old Plymouth garage which is now an antique store. The owner let us inside, and we made a few purchases.

It's 10:30 am and we received orders to be at Gering between 1 and 2 pm. Lots of time, so we stop at Fort Robinson. Flat Steve entices a couple of biker chicks to pose for us, as do three little kids from Hay Springs. We drove through Smiley Canyon and Harrison, and decided to visit Agate Fossil Beds. None of us had been there previously, but Professor Gary prepared us for some natural history on display. What a wonderful place and, even better, a pretty young ranger was on duty. Flat Steve was brought in, and she offered to let him wear her hat!

On to Gering where my precious grandchildren (and their pets and parents), were awaiting us. First we stop at Jimmy John's, and munch happily away. The whole family presented us with three new projects: 1.) find and photograph the UMC in Scottsbluff; 2.) visit the site of the Junior College our dad had attended; 3.) scale the Scottsbluff National Monument, observing from there, the Hull Church. We easily accomplished these things, however the Hull Church was a tiny speck when viewed from the monument. We went back to Seth's house, and were told to relax and not leave until 5 pm. By the way, Steve was introduced to two more female rangers at the Scottsbluff National Monument.

As the clock struck five, we were sent to an address in Sidney, which is about 90 miles from Gering. Along the way, we stopped at Chimney Rock for a group picture. What's up with this Sidney destination, we wondered? I had a pretty good idea. Our dad had a cousin who lived in, and raised his family, in Sidney. His name was Niles Leypoldt. Because of Facebook connections, I had discovered Nyla Leypoldt Hobson, whose son married the daughter of my friend Lori Storbeck of Crawford. I met Nyla at our church in 2011, and she knows Beth Leypoldt, a fellow employee of Cabela's. I didn't know where Nyla lived, but was not surprised she hosted an excellent party for us.

What did astound me was the moment Seth and his family arrived. His girls can really keep a secret! We got to know Nyla, her husband Randy, two of Nyla's brothers, her three granddaughters, and her mom, who was married to Dad's cousin Niles.

At 10 pm we went to the AmericInn in Sidney. On the way, I committed a crime which I feel I must confess but my brothers made me do it. We were traveling south on 11th Avenue and stopped for a red light, intending to go left on Old Post Road. Maybe five cars came by, but no one was behind us. We must have been stuck there for ten minutes. A vote was taken, and all but Flat Steve advised me to ignore the malfunctioning light. And off we went down Cabela Road toward the motel.

Day 4: Monday, July 16 - I awoke a year older. AmericInn has a great breakfast, and lots of places to sit and enjoy it. At 9 am we were on Interstate 80 heading east, with Doug driving. First stop: Hershey, where our father was born in 1915. The Hershey UMC is on the main road into town, and we stopped there first. It was locked, but we walked around the building, and I pointed out the location of the "Leypoldt window."

We drove up and down a few streets. Two trains went by in the short time we were there. Then we headed toward the Interstate, and a pickup was parked at the church. A loyal church member was preparing to remove a bird nest from the cross and flame. We scurried out of the Sienna, grabbed his ladder, and Doug scampered up to remove the unsightly aviary. This kind gentlemen unlocked the church and Gary, Doug, and Jim saw the Leypoldt window for the first time. Flat Steve headed for the pulpit, where he was photographed. It was a great experience, and we all wished Dad and Steve could have been there with us.

We visited the North Platte cemetery, and paid homage to several Leypoldt ancestors, then meandered into the **Come and Get It Barbecue** for lunch. After another photo with Steve and a waitress, we went in search of Three Brothers Wine, and checked out the Golden Spike Tower. We dropped by the impressive war memorial at the I-80 interchange, where Doug planted a kiss on the Canteen Lady. Next we traveled to the Fort McPherson National Cemetery, where aunt and uncle Alyce and Frank Eckhoff are buried.

We were instructed to get the wine, and be at Dino's in Lincoln by 6 pm. Jim had called the Farnam winery when we were at the BBQ place, and was assured they would be open until 6 pm. It would mess with our schedule, but decided to buzz down to Farnam. Roger Welsch has called Highway 47 north of Farnam among the most scenic in the state, and we followed that trail off the Gothenburg exit.

No one was at the winery and we called the owner once more. "Sorry," he says. "You might find our product at Lucky Chuck's in Eustis." We sped east on 23. Nostalgia overcame me as I cruised into Eustis. **Oh no!! Lucky Chuck's is closed on Mondays.** Three Brothers could not supply these Five Brothers on *unlucky* Chuck's 65th birthday. Gary took the wheel, and soon we were back on I-80. We stopped for gas one more time, and arrived at Dino's in Lincoln a little after seven. All our Lincoln family was there, plus Nancy, Ana and Jeff. Missy showed a video of the places and people we encountered in the previous 80 hours. **It was an amazing and fun-filled experience.**

P.S. I was serenaded with "Happy Birthday" that evening and I'm pretty sure I saw Flat Steve's lips moving during the song.

+++

As I rambled around the state on my final weeks with CMIC, my mind wandered to many events. I thought about our family trips. I recalled seeing the four faces on Mount Rushmore when I was 4. A few years later, we spent a week in the Rocky Mountains, made snowballs in July, and fed pieces of bread to tiny, tame chipmunks. I remember eating a lot of minced ham sandwiches on our family vacations. Seth renamed them "circle meat" when he was learning to talk.

My children took some memorable trips as well. They always enjoyed the luxury of an air-conditioned Pontiac Catalina or Ford Crown Victoria. When we went camping, it was to places like Holiday Inn, Ramada, or Best Western. "Roughing it" was a motel with only one television set, and four persons picking four different programs. A real challenge was finding the right radio station. I know of none that alternate between classical, oldies, rock, and country.

As reported earlier, I was and am a wanderer. I love the back roads and little towns that time has forgotten. Unfortunately, I was the only one in our family who felt that way. Sometimes they'd quietly endure my little detours, and sometimes they would patiently follow me into the dusty antique stores and roadside museums. But mostly I deferred to the 3-to-one majority, and passed by the sights which intrigued me.

Long after she grew up, we found a long forgotten verse, penned by a little girl not enjoying her family's vacation trip. She said:

My dad is boring, boring!
He's going to places his children does not want to go to!
He is no fun.
Nothing, no fun, when he goes to museums.
It is so boring, boring, boring.
My dad is always boring.
He never wants to do things his children want to do.
All he does is things he wants to do!!!!!!!
And that's boring, boring, boring!!!!!!!!!!

CMIC paid me to emulate the great Charles Kuralt. I loved his "On the Road" features on the CBS Evening News, and he loved Nebraska also. He wrote, "And still I wander, seeking compensation in unforeseen encounters and unexpected sights, in sunsets, storms and passing fancies....The little roads without numbers are the ones I have liked the best, the bumpy ones that lead over the hills toward vicinities unknown."[48]

Were it not for the company car and free gas, I might have never been to Pilzno, Mills, Burton, Lillian, Mirage Flats, Nysted, Orum, O'Connor, Bazile Mills, Rose, Saint Helena, Worms, Venus, Pleasant Point, or Swaburg, and all kinds of other local wonders I've found in beautiful Nebraskaland.

I also thought about my experiences in north Omaha. One time a church on North 15th Street asked me for a quote. I drove past without seeing a place to park, so I decided to go around the block. But there were two guys working on a car in the middle of the street, so I flipped a Louie and pulled up on the church lawn.

Greater St. Paul COGIC in north Omaha has a great ministry. They have two worship centers and outstanding pre-school and tutoring programs. They owned several houses around the main church, which were used for various purposes. One day I was working on a policy renewal, and driving slowly down the street, taking pictures. A scantily clad woman, high on something, took exception to my activity and ran after me, calling me various things. The last thing I heard was, "get the hell out of here." And I quickly obliged.

During my time with CMIC, I became involved with several building programs. I had one church in Omaha that started a new sanctuary in 1985, but postponed their project, leaving a shell while they worshiped in the fellowship hall. They finished the whole building about 20 years later, and it is a beautiful facility today.

I saw a modest little church in Bassett transformed by flipping the altar area with the narthex. Their pastor is a United Methodist turned Episcopalian, who has been my friend since 1987. Dozens of churches built completely new facilities, and it was fun to share in the excitement that accompanies those ventures.

Two situations were fraught with frustration. I visited a church in west Omaha which had just completed a large addition. When the pastor was giving me a tour, I noticed there were two fire alarm panels side-by-side. I asked why, and he said "this is the one the fire marshal told us we needed when we started construction, and this is the one he told us we needed before occupancy. We left them both here so we could answer questions like yours."

A country church had built a fellowship hall/classroom addition next to, but not connected, to the church. Before the building was complete, a fire marshal told them they needed to fasten all the tables in the hall to the floor, so they could not be removed. His ruling was based on occupancy; 200 was the maximum number sitting at tables, while 400 could sit on folding chairs without tables. If 400 people were the occupancy, they would need to sprinkle the building, and because of rural water, they would have to add an auxiliary pump. The building was all on one level, with more than adequate exits.

+++

On my last day of work, August 17, 2012, I drove my company car to Omaha and left it at the home of Lance Baker, who was hired to replace me. Bruce West, my boss for the previous 5½ years, drove me back to Lincoln, and Dave Allen joined us for lunch. It was a nice quiet end to an interesting and mostly positive experience.

CMIC publishes a monthly magazine, and I enjoyed reading the interviews and accolades written about new retirees. When traveling alone on rural highways, I rehearsed what I might say when the editor called me. What did you like most about working for CMIC? Eight trips to places I never imagined I would visit. Also, a chance to photograph beautiful church buildings. Also, the opportunity to meet new people and work with others I'd known for a long time. Also, as written above, the freedom to roam the back roads and city neighborhoods in the state I love.

This quote from Bob Uecker, baseball player and actor, sums up my career in insurance: "To last as long as I did with the skills I had, with the numbers I produced, was a triumph of the human spirit."[49] Strangely, no one from CMIC wanted to hear my story of 13 years, 5 months, and 17 days. No matter. They'll be sending me or Chris a check for many years to come.

+++

In 2012 we were treated to an entertaining presidential campaign. The incumbent, Mr. Obama, easily defeated a challenge from a billionaire. The one percent launched a vicious and dishonest barrage of media announcements, but supporters of Obama's progressive agenda held firm.

In the fall of 2012 I wrote a little essay about politics entitled **Mitt and the Metropolitan.**

I am among the minority of American citizens who are registered and will be voting in this year's presidential election. I take this responsibility very seriously, and have voted in every presidential election since I turned 21 in 1968. Even before that I was keenly interested in national politics, and read a series of presidential biographies which I found in the Crawford Library around 1955 (obviously tailored to the skills of an 8-year-old).

As recorded earlier, Republicanism guided me from Kindergarten through my sophomore year in college. In 1952 (the first election I can remember) Nebraska supported Dwight Eisenhower. He was one of us: a small town boy from neighboring Kansas. Our Governors, Senators, and Representatives were all Republicans.

In 1960 the winds of political change were shifting. Our beloved Ike was forced into retirement, but his protégé Richard Nixon received the mantle. His opponent was young and likable and had a beautiful wife. On a November morning in 1960 we awoke to a disturbing reality: a Catholic had prevailed over Mr. Nixon. Nebraska held firm, giving Nixon his highest percentage of support. We braced for the probability of a new Vatican in America.

The Sixties were filled with challenges. The war in Vietnam was escalating, John Kennedy was murdered, and Lyndon Johnson moved into the White House. Civil rights, women's rights, and the war on poverty were hot topics. I loved Barry Goldwater. I went to college. Some of my friends went to Vietnam; several were killed. Martin Luther King, Jr. and Malcolm X were assassinated, President Johnson dropped out, Richard Nixon was back. I was no longer so certain about Republicanism.

The party of Lincoln, George W. Norris, and Margaret Chase Smith no longer cares about ethnic minorities, the disadvantaged, women's health or equality. The "G" in GOP certainly is not grand for the middle and lower economic groups.

I was always a little curious about Democrats, but there didn't seem to be any around me. My father was a Republican, though not very dogmatic about it. He was born in 1915 and given the name of the sitting Democratic president. My mother was also a Republican, but she was raised by an unabashed Progressive and voted for Franklin Roosevelt in 1940. My uncle Bill Hennings did help me expand my horizons though. He lived in Washington state so we didn't see him very often. He was a conscientious objector, an agnostic, and married to a relative of Adlai Stevenson. He was also a Yankee fan; but I really admired him anyway.

Surprisingly, I found some more answers at my local **Jiffy Lube.** While waiting for new oil and a tire rotation, I picked up the July 2012 issue of **Car and Driver** magazine. I discovered Mitt Romney and I share an admiration for Nash Metropolitans. He bought a used convertible when he was 15. My dad let me drive his 1956 coupe when I got my driver's license. You can read the magazine article on pylodet.com.

There are some differences. I wasn't allowed to drive a Rambler on the golf course before I was 16, and my dad didn't have a chauffeur to give me driving lessons. I still don't know what credit-default-swaps are, and had to work as a camp dishwasher to earn money for college. I don't think I've ever been in a house big enough to drive a car into, even a Nash Metropolitan. I guess that's why the Romney family needed more than one maid. Probably the biggest difference between me and Mitt is that I always had to wash the car myself. Evidently Mitt and I both have a sense of humor.[50]

P.S. I voted for Barack.

That's my story and I'm sticking to it.

Olivia and Emma in April 2005

Cora in 2005 and 2006

Chapter 24
If Jesus Is The Answer, What Is The Question?

The first sermons I remember were those preached in Crawford. My dad had a practice of removing his wristwatch and laying it on the pulpit. Then he preached without notes, standing beside the pulpit. I asked why he did this. He said he was criticized for appearing dependent on his outlines, and this satisfied his instructor. Microphones forced him back in the pulpit in succeeding years.

You've read about the Methodist parsonages that were home to me. They were older houses, but they were no worse than most others in town, and they were always filled with adventure and love. My mother tried to keep one room in these homes nice and clean at all times. These spaces were called the "front room," a kind of throwback to parlor days.

These rooms were kept "up to snuff" because you never knew who might stop by, including a couple wanting to be married. There was a mystery surrounding those parlors, too. They contained our best furniture, and drapes, instead of curtains. On the floor were rugs, rather than linoleum or hardwood. And they always smelled a little musty from being closed up.

I preached my first sermon in one of those front rooms. I was probably four or five, and bored to death on a summer day. I convinced my younger brothers to help me "play church" and we sneaked into the front room, sang "Jesus Loves Me," and I held forth the Word of God.

My little brothers, aged 2 and 3, were not impressed and didn't show up for my next sermon. But that didn't stop me. The Columbus DS gave me a license to preach in 1966, and I've stepped into pulpits at least 2,000 times since then.

At the end of my first year in college, I began thinking seriously about the ministry. I talked it over with my dad, and he suggested I preach a few sermons during the summer. I gave my first one at the Loretto and Albion churches on May 22, 1966 and titled it, "Our Unpaid Debt." I also preached at Stromsburg, Cedar Rapids, and Belgrade that summer.

In 1967 I went home to my summer job, and was a guest preacher at Palmer, Archer, Ewing, Bloomfield, Polk, Swede Plain, Greeley, Wolbach, Carroll, Winside, Seward, Loretto, and Albion. In September I started my work at Alvo, giving an occasional sermon, attending meetings and working with the youth. The main thing leading me to the ministry was hero worship of my dad, and admiration of several other pastors I knew. Glenn Bush was a great friend and mentor as well. When my junior year ended, I was pretty sure I would attend seminary after I finished college.

The next summer (1968) I preached at Methodist churches in Albion, Loretto, Osceola, Seward, Aurora, David City, Bellwood, St. Paul, and Fairdale. In the fall I spoke at a district youth rally in Columbus. I continued with the Alvo church, and enlisted my future wife to teach Sunday School through May 1969. After graduation from college, I went back to Albion to paint houses. I also preached every Sunday during the summer of 1969 at the little church in Marquette, about 50 miles south of Albion.

From June 14, 1970 through June 14, 1981 I exhorted the faithful virtually every Sunday morning. I generally used a couple pages of notes, and was partially extemporaneous. One Sunday in the fall of 1970, I ran short of preparation time and effectively lifted a sermon from one of Bishop Gerald Kennedy's books, and read it to my congregations at Cheney and Palmyra. I received positive and helpful advice from Miss Frances Monahan, a retired teacher at Palmyra. She said, "your sermons are so much better when you don't read them." And I never did it again, except for funerals.

The Bible is the place we go to find both answers and questions. Our ancestors in the faith gave us this collection of letters, stories, sermons, legends, songs, and prophecies to help us in our life journey. The Bible tells us about a people in search of meaning, who often looked for it in wrong places. In time, a savior appeared to clarify who is searching for whom. After the death of the savior, God continued searching for us with a message of resurrection and forgiveness. This message is communicated through preaching.

When I photograph sanctuaries I like to stand in the pulpits, and imagine what the pastors experience when they look at their flock. The older Lutheran churches have pulpits which require a stairway with several steps for entrance. Among most impressive are in rural churches at Wausa, Hampton, Arlington, Bancroft, and Columbus; also in the villages of Kronborg, Nysted, and Bazile Mills. In those settings, I experienced the sacramental nature of the Gospel being proclaimed and received.

The art of preaching is called homiletics. Homileticians fret about types of sermons, the use of poetry, visual aids and humor, avoiding plagiarism, and the proper length of a sermon. A lot of folks are interested in that last one. My present theory is a sermon should be long enough to give people their money's worth, but the investment starts losing value after fifteen minutes.

The Hebrews had a different philosophy. Nehemiah, in his 8th chapter, tells about Ezra who read the scriptures to the people for six hours. Here is the amazing thing: it also says, "the ears of all the people were attentive (NRSV)." There's more: they stayed around for a couple of more hours while Ezra and Nehemiah interpreted the scriptures to them. All this happened outside, without benefit of padded pews or climate-controlled thermostats.

One Sunday my friend Ken Grenz made a surprise visit at the Douglas church and afterward said, "that story of mine has really gotten around since seminary." All preachers borrow stories when constructing sermons. It's been challenging to find documentation for this book. I have posted a lot of material on my website and when searching the web for end note references, I often find myself as the source.

I tried to use hyperbole in my sermons as well. According to Matthew, Mark, Luke and John, Jesus did the same. Hyperbole means using overstatements, not to be taken literally, but to gain attention. I was never afraid to say something outrageous, and let people choose what to do with it. Hopefully homiletic hyperbole always directs us to the truth. Long before talk show chatter masqueraded as news, I believed it was OK to say, "I report, you decide."

During my last year in seminary I was required to take a class in preaching, which should be obvious. Our teacher was Dr. Larry Wagley, who was a real professional in the art of communication. My seminary gave three grades for all our course work: credit, non-credit, and honors. I received honors in only one class: preaching. I saw Dr. Wagley in 1985, and he asked about my current pastoral appointment. A little sheepishly I replied, "I'm on Honorable Location and managing a bank."

In June of 1987 I was back in the pulpit on a regular basis, and using a sketchy outline. However, after I acquired my first computer in 1988 my style changed to manuscript preaching. I discovered it takes four minutes to read one page of text; therefore I worked hard to limit myself to 4-page sermons. I didn't "read" my sermons, but the script was in front of me at the pulpit, to keep me on schedule.

I'm now an occasional guest preacher, but I'm content to be a listener. I agree with George Burns who said: "The secret to a good sermon is to have a good beginning and a good ending, then having the two as close together as possible."[51] Improvements in sound systems have allowed speakers to wander instead of staying in the pulpit, but this can be a distraction. I suggest staying behind the pulpit and/or altar table at least part of the time to remind folks the message, not the messenger, is the reason they are in church. In addition preachers need to be good story tellers, with many tales from their own personal experiences. And, of course, it's always appropriate for both listeners and preachers to get lost in wonder, love, and praise during the sermon.

Some of my favorite borrowed tales appear next. Jerry Clower tells about a deacon's meeting at the North Fork Church. Uncle Versie Ledbetter was up in years and he didn't go to many Deacon's meetings anymore, because he thought the youngsters - those about 50 or 60 - could take care of the church business. But he got word they were fixin' to spend some money so he got Newgene, his grandson, to take him over to the church house for the meeting. They got into a big discussion about buying a chandelier. Someone said, "I move we buy a chandelier for the church." Another deacon said, "I second the motion." The moderator said, "is there any discussion?" Uncle Versie said, "Sir, I'd like to speak. I want all of you to know that if we go buy a chandelier, there ain't nobody in our church got enough education that when we order it from Sears and Roebuck, they could spell it. Then, if we ordered the chandelier, there's nobody in our church that knows how to play it. And what I'm concerned about, is we don't need to spend this money on no chandelier as bad as we need lights in the church." [52]

O Henry's story entitled **The Gift of the Magi** needs to be heard often. It's about a young couple who are short of money, but desperately want to buy each other Christmas gifts. Unbeknownst to Jim, Della sells her most valuable possession, her beautiful hair, in order to buy a platinum fob chain for Jim's watch; while unbeknownst to Della, Jim sells his own most valuable possession, his watch, to buy jeweled combs for Della's hair. The essential premise of this story has been copied, reworked, parodied, and otherwise retold countless times since it was written.

Another of my favorite yarns is one I never had the courage to include in a sermon. A Catholic priest was assigned to a church in the inner city. His church had a soup kitchen, food pantry, and thrift shop with many committed volunteers. The priest made it a point to be on the street day after day, getting acquainted with the homeless, doing all he could to make life better for people. There were always a few who rebuffed him, but he never got discouraged.

One day he was a block away from the church, and he saw someone he recognized going into the building. It was somebody he had diligently tried to get close to, but he always told the pastor to get lost. Perhaps something had changed, and this person was ready to receive help from the church.

The priest high-tailed it down the street, and went into the sanctuary. As he opened the door, he saw the man go into the confessional, so he went there quickly. He sat down, pulled back the curtain, and asked, "Is there something I can do for you, my friend?"

The guy answered back, "Yeah, there isn't any toilet paper in here. You got some over there?"

I never told this one in a sermon either, but wish I had. It's for those who believe a place of eternal punishment exists. A man who had spent his life chasing women, going to parties, and drinking every kind of alcoholic beverage, died and was sent directly to Hell.

He was met by a devilish looking guide and ushered to a doorway. His escort led him inside, and the view before him was completely unexpected. He saw a room filled with tables. As he walked around he saw beautiful, alluring young women sitting at every table with inviting glances. He also saw large decanters with labels of various liqueurs from all over the world.

"My gosh," exclaimed the newly deceased, "if I had known Hell would be like this, I would have come sooner." To which his companion replied, "take your time, you will be here for all eternity. You will soon discover all the flasks have holes in their bottoms, but the women do not."

Here's one about a woman who taught a third-grade Sunday School class in a United Methodist church. In her class were twin girls. They seemed very happy, and never missed church or Sunday School. They came from a poor family, and their dresses were always worn and out of style, but it didn't seem to bother them. One day their teacher talked to some friends at church, took up a collection, and bought these girls some beautiful new dresses.

The next Sunday, the twin girls were missing. The teacher called their home immediately after church, fearing they might be sick. "Oh no, they are not sick," explained their mother. "They just looked so nice in their new dresses, that I sent them to the Presbyterian Church."[53]

A small girl was sent by her mother to the grocery store. She was gone an awfully long time, and her mother was starting to worry. Finally, she walked in the door, and mommy immediately asked "where have you been?" The little girl said, "well, I met Mary, and she was crying because she had broken her dolly." Mommy asked, "did you help her fix the doll?" "Oh, no," the little one replied. "I helped her cry."

John Craig told me about a parishioner named Freddie. She was a widow who lived on a limited income, and was also burdened by medical bills. Thanksgiving was approaching, and Freddie shared her joy about hosting her four children and several grandchildren for the first time in many years. John and his wife Edith wondered how she could afford the feast most of us have on Thanksgiving Day. So they cooked up a plan.

On Sunday morning, he announced from his pulpit there was a needy family in the community. He encouraged his congregation to donate some food to help them. He told them to bring a few things to the parsonage, and he would deliver them. Shortly after finishing Sunday dinner, the doorbell rang at the parsonage. It was Freddie. She was the first one donating something to help the anonymous family in need.

Bruce Larson told the story of a Catholic priest living in the Philippines, a much loved man of God, who carried a burden of long past sin buried deep in his heart. He had committed that sin once, many years before, during his time in the seminary. No one else knew of this sin. He had repented of it, and suffered years of remorse because of it, but still had no peace, no inner joy, no sense of God's forgiveness.

There was a woman in this priest's parish who deeply loved God, and who claimed to have visions in which she spoke with Christ, and he with her. The priest was skeptical of her claims. He decided to test her visions and said to her, "you say you actually speak directly to Christ in your visions. Let me ask you a favor. The next time you have one of these visions, I want you to ask him what sin your priest committed while he was in seminary."

The woman agreed and went home. When she returned to the church a few days later the priest said, "well, did Christ visit you in your dreams?"

She replied, "Yes, he did."

"And did you ask him what sin I committed in seminary?"

"Yes, I asked him."

"Well, what did he say?"

"He said, 'I don't remember.'"[54]

My commentary: to imitate Christ, we all need to learn how to forgive and forget at the same time.

Here's a story I love. When the Nazi army invaded Denmark, every Jew was ordered to wear an armband with the Star of David clearly visible for identification. The King then stood on the balcony of his palace, wearing an armband with the Star of David. A German officer said, "Your majesty, I did not know you were a Jew."

"I am not. These Jews are my people, and I am their King," he replied. Within a week, every Dane in the capitol city was wearing the Star of David on one arm.[55] When following Jesus, there is nothing more important than loving your neighbor.

Another of my favorite jokes comes from the great comic Buddy Hackett. He said he got a leather wallet for a gift that was very special. It came from the foreskin of an elephant's penis, and when he rubbed it, it turned into a suitcase. So far I've refrained from using this in a sermon.

Perhaps you have heard the story about the woman who was bitten by a dog that was suspected of having rabies. She was rushed to the hospital for treatment, and left in a room to wait for an autopsy report on the dog. The intern on duty decided he should explain the seriousness of her situation, and he told the patient her injury could be fatal. The woman asked him a lot of questions, and by the end of the interview, the intern felt he had said too much too soon. She was visibly shaken.

He left the room, and when he came back, he found her sitting on the side of the treatment table with a pen and note pad. He saw her pause occasionally and stare into space, and then resume writing. The doctor thought she was writing her will or recording funeral instructions. He asked if she were writing a will. "Oh no," she said, "just in case I've been infected, I'm making a list of people I want to bite before I die."

Here is a true story told me by Tex Sample, who knew the family well. Nancy Cruzan was 26 years old when severely injured in a car accident. She was comatose for seven years before her life support system was removed. Her parents were members of a small-town UMC in Missouri. They came to believe Nancy had a right to die, and finally won this approval from the United States Supreme Court.

The Right to Life movement protested the decision as an act of murder. They set up a vigil outside the hospital in Mount Vernon, Missouri. Some shouted words of protest at Nancy's parents. "Why are you killing your daughter?" they asked. On Friday, December 21, 1990, Nancy Cruzan's father left her bedside and went outside to talk to the protesters. It was not a confrontation. He brought along a coffee pot, cups, and a long extension cord. He knew what they needed on this shortest, and perhaps coldest, day of the year.

Nancy died five days later. Bob Cruzan, more than anyone else, was acutely aware of what his daughter Nancy needed most - not a tube feeding, but a caring family who would be with her in the valley of the shadow of death, and who loved her enough to let her suffering end. It may not be true in every case, but surely this was one time when father knew best.

Three small children in a family begged their parents for a pet hamster. They promised they would take care of it, and finally they got one. They named it "Danny."

Two months later the mother of the children found herself doing all the cleaning and feeding. One day she also found a possible new home for the hamster.

She sat her children down, and told them about Danny's prospective new home. She was quite surprised to see how well they were taking the news.

One child remarked, "He's been around for a long time - we'll miss him." The mother said, "Yes, but you need to know that he's really too much work for one person."

The second child said, "Maybe if he wouldn't eat so much and wouldn't be so messy, we could still keep him." But the mother was firm. "It's time to take Danny to his new home now," she insisted. "Go and get his cage."

Then, all at once the three children stood up, and began to cry and scream. They exclaimed: "Danny? We were confused. We thought you were talking about Daddy."

My favorite story of all time has to do with the method used by Native Americans to name their children. I heard it when I lived in Eustis, and told it to a Lutheran friend when we were alone in the coffee shop. He laughed so hard, I was afraid he would have a heart attack. I went down the street to see someone else, and walked past thc shop 15 minutes later, and he was still in the same chair, red-faced, and guffawing. Sorry I can't share it; it's a bit racist and profane, and I have granddaughters who like to read.

Following is part of a sermon I preached on February 27, 1994. As far as I know, this was the only delivery I made which prompted listeners to contact the District Superintendent. See if you can understand why this happened.

Today's Gospel lesson (Mark 8:27-38) is a familiar one. Mark tells us that Jesus is concluding his Galilean ministry of preaching, healing, and exorcisms. Jesus took his disciples to an area north of Galilee known as Caesarea Philippi. I'm tempted to give you a geography lesson this morning. Just ten days ago I was at the site of Banyas, the ancient capitol of Caesarea Philippi.

However we have other matters to consider on this second Sunday of Lent. We hear Jesus saying some things that are hard to hear. He talks about going down to the Holy City, Jerusalem. He speaks of his future suffering, rejection, trial, and death. Peter didn't like the sound of that trip to Jerusalem. "You are too pessimistic, Lord. We'll take care of you. We'll even destroy these enemies with God's help!"

With anger in his voice, Jesus rebuked Peter in front of all the disciples. "Get behind me, Satan!" he said, "for you are setting your mind not on divine things but on human things."

Then a crowd gathers, and Jesus preaches a little sermon on the meaning of his Messiahship and our Discipleship. "If any want to become my followers, let them deny themselves and take up their cross and follow me. For those who want to save their life will lose it, and those who lose their life for my sake, and for the sake of the gospel, will save it. For what will it profit them to gain the whole world and forfeit their life? Indeed, what can they give in return for their life? Those who are ashamed of me...of them the [Messiah] will also be ashamed when coming in the glory of God..."

There you have it! The Disciples were no longer following a meek and mild Jesus along the shores of Lake Galilee. They now must go with a tough and determined Jesus to the dangerous area of Jerusalem.

Now a question: what things are happening in today's church which might evoke a rebuke from Jesus? What are we doing that would cause the Messiah to be ashamed of us? I can think of a few.

First the question of authority. Jesus was mad at Peter because he refused to listen. Remember, the voice of God saying, "This is the Messiah, the Chosen One, listen to him!" We have some authority problems in our day, too.

Here is a story about Senator Bill Bradley of New Jersey. The senator was attending a dinner in Washington. When the waiter came by with the butter, the Senator said, "I'd like two pats of butter, if I may, please." To this the waiter replied, "Sorry, sir, it's one to a customer." "Well," said the Senator, "I guess you don't know who I am. I'm a senior member of the United States Senate. Before that, I was an All-Star basketball player with the New York Knicks. And before that, I was a Rhodes Scholar at Oxford."

The waiter was not impressed. "I guess you don't know who I am," he retorted. "No, I don't," said Bradley. "Who are you?" The waiter drew himself up to his full 5 feet 5 inches, and said proudly, "I'm the guy with the butter."[56]

Every once in a while, people get confused about who is really in charge. In many restaurants, it's the waiters. Ultimately, in all things, it is Jesus Christ. In some things, it is those called and ordained by the Church of Jesus Christ.

Many who call themselves United Methodist do not understand our system of shared authority, even though every Full Member pledges their loyalty to this system. When I was ordained, I promised to abide by the authority of the Bishop. The Bishop, in turn, gave me authority to preach, administer the sacraments, and by appointment, to manage the work of this local church. Like it or not, this is the way we do things. In this place, I'm the guy with the butter!

God is not pleased with disloyalty, and what is sometimes called "micro-management." Perhaps this is what Jesus saw in Peter when he scolded him, "you are setting your mind not on divine things but on human things."

Hmmm…maybe that was it.

If Jesus is the answer, what is the question? It might be "What would Jesus do?" The Decalogue is still the basic outline of ethics for all civilized societies. Jesus summarized these Commandments by focusing on obedience to God and love of neighbor. Many years ago, Charles Sheldon wrote a little book titled **In His Steps**. His thesis was if you have an ethical question, you should ask "What would Jesus do?" Further light could be gained by consulting Jesus' teachings in the Gospels.[57]

The problem for us is Jesus said nothing about abortion, premarital sex, drug dependency, fracking, climate change, marriage equality, terrorism, the common core, and many more topics that create discord. The religious right can give answers, but only by claiming they know more about Jesus than do Matthew, Mark, Luke, and John.

What would Jesus do? He quotes the Torah, "You shall love the Lord your God with all your heart, and with all your soul, and with all your mind. This is the greatest and first commandment. And a second is like it: You shall love your neighbor as yourself. On these two commandments hang all the law and the prophets (Matthew 22:37-40)."

What would Jesus do? He would have us revisit the Golden Rule, making its words of wisdom guide our thoughts and actions. Both Matthew and Luke record: "Do unto others as you would have others do unto you." I believe Jesus would have us begin all our decisions with this rule. When our conduct is tempered with love, God is there. Eight different times the Bible says "you shall love your neighbors as yourself." There is simply no better way to follow Jesus.

Never forget: the people who follow Jesus are a victorious community. "IN HOC SIGNO VINCES"[58] is our motto. It may be difficult to understand the historical Jesus, but our hero is one whose sacrificial love led to death on a cross, yet still lives in this message: "In Christ God was reconciling the world to God's self, not counting our trespasses against us, and entrusting us with the message of reconciliation (2 Corinthians 5:19)." This, or a variation, should be part of every Christian sermon. I also think it's OK for pastors to say "do as I say, not as I do" once in a while.

At Ceresco we had a lot of children in the church, and once a month they sang, which really gave our attendance a boost. I started doing a children's sermon on those Sundays. For the remainder of my parish ministry, I had a children's sermon every Sunday. I found some resources that helped tie the children's sermon to the lectionary, and I tried to develop an object lesson for the kids. Two things I learned were to be prepared, and don't ask too many questions. A pastor in Douglas used to start by asking the kids questions, and we parents cringed at some of the answers. One time she was trying to make a point about boredom, and asked the group, "have you ever been bored?" To which my son replied, "I'm bored right now."

In Geneva I had lay persons who did about half of the children's sermons. Quite often we had 30 to 40 children under 12 in worship. One time I used a CROP Blanket as an object lesson, and I draped it around several of the kids as I told them how the blankets were made and several of the ways they were used by people. Then I passed out $5 dollar bills to every child, and asked what they would like to do with their gift. Without any prompting, they all said they wanted to buy a blanket for someone. We raised well over a thousand dollars for CROP that Sunday.

My grandfather took a clock out of an old Buick, and put it in a wood frame. It's very unique, and I used it to show children how things can appear to belong in the trash, but still be useful. One of my brothers stabbed me with a pencil many years ago, and there is still a mark on my right arm. I used this to illustrate how wounds heal, and scars remain so we can teach others about courage.

I had a little girl in Farnam jump on my lap almost every Sunday during my first couple of years there. I reminded her of that when I saw her at Chadron State College many years later. My most precious memories came from my years in Douglas, when my daughter was 3 and 4 years old. She always gave me a kiss on the cheek when I finished my children's sermon.

If Jesus is the answer, what is the question? In his little book **Man's Search For Meaning**, Viktor Frankl said people should not ask what the meaning of life is because we are responsible for providing the answer. Meaning is there all the time, and waits to discover you.[59] A friend once told me her son had been through years of struggle, but things were better because he found the Lord. I understood what she meant, and was happy that she was happy, but I kept thinking "I didn't know God was lost." Read the 15th chapter of Luke's Gospel; we do not find Jesus, Jesus finds us. Christian faith did not begin the day you first accepted it. The only way to answer to God's question is to hand over yourself.[60]

If Jesus is the answer, what is the question? Jesus wants to hear from us. He is looking to us for answers, and he is the questioner. One fine day at Caesarea Philippi, Jesus asked two questions of his disciples. First, "Who do people say that I am?" Second, "Who do you say that I am?" Jesus wanted answers, but Peter and the Disciples appeared to have flunked their test. There's more. On the first Easter, Jesus questions Mary Magdalene twice: "Why are you weeping?" and "Who are you looking for?" Mary passed her exam. Ben Garrison said, "We do not find Jesus. Jesus finds us."[61]

+++

Along with preaching, pastors are also responsible for administering the Holy Sacraments of Baptism and Communion. I was reading Jeff Foxworthy's **The Final Helping of You Might Be A Redneck If….**[62] and was reminded of an experience from my days as a small town pastor. A young mother and her children moved to town and were very faithful in church attendance. She had a two-month old baby who was not yet baptized, and requested I stop at her home to discuss a time for scheduling the rite, which I did. I had not met her husband, but she assured me he would attend the baptism.

On the designated Sunday I arrived at the church, prepared the font, and went about greeting folks. When the baby and family arrived, I went outside to visit with them and meet the father. He was a big guy with a full beard, and finishing a breakfast beer in the car. He stayed long enough to see his daughter baptized and disappeared.

The oldest child in the family was a boy who was one of the most attentive listeners in the congregation. He always sat at pew's end in a middle row. One time I told a story to explain the Epiphany, and ended it with, "who do you think opened the window?" and this boy answered right out loud, "God!" It felt as though he and I were having a one-on-one conversation.

I believe every baby deserves to be baptized. I don't care what a dad had for breakfast, or if a mother wants to show off an expensive christening gown. Baptism is a sign that grace is real, and this tiny infant is loved and accepted by God almighty, and we cannot withhold the gift. You can read about how Jesus felt in Mark 10:13-16.

I also believe everyone is welcome at the simple banquet called the Eucharist or Holy Communion. Early in my ministry, I restricted this meal to those who were baptized, but I escaped this arrogance long ago. I understand and respect the several forms and schedules churches employ, but it must be open and available to all or it is not authentic. Saint Paul makes this very clear: "since all have sinned and fall short of the glory of God, they are now justified by God's grace as a gift, through the redemption that is in Christ Jesus (Romans 3:23-24)."

+++

Once upon a time people named Leypoldt, Landon, Hennings, Reed, McGill, Talcott, Renwanz, Sanquist, Read, Thompson, Jordan, Alexander, Coleman, Loder, McVoy, Masten, Beiler, Hildreth, Schultz, Chalker, Holke, Dettman, Coun, Blish, Conrad, Lowe, McConnell, Mathis, Robertson, Birdsall, Canby, Witt, Ropeken,

Michaelis, Schlunz, Knutel, Prigge, Peterson, Johnson, Carlsdotter, Houck, Frey, Osswald, Gaylord, Kunz, Mueller, Shenefelt, Burns, and Harrison left their European homes behind and came to a new land called America.

They settled in Pennsylvania, Indiana, Iowa, Kansas, and Minnesota, the District of Columbia, and Nebraska. They were Methodists, Lutherans, Catholics, Presbyterians and Freethinkers. They had no right to be here, but if they were healthy enough, and had pale faces, were told "come on in!"

Many of them came by way of a giant statue called Lady Liberty and they may have read these words:

"Keep, ancient lands, your storied pomp!" cries she
With silent lips. "Give me your tired, your poor,
Your huddled masses yearning to breathe free,
The wretched refuse of your teeming shore.
Send these, the homeless, tempest-tost to me,
I lift my lamp beside the golden door!"

The blood of those people in the first paragraph runs through my veins, and my wife's veins, and those of our children and three granddaughters. We didn't have to say or prove anything to receive the blessings of liberty; it was our birthright.

I take seriously the words in a book written by people who took them even more seriously, and certainly shape Christian behavior. They are found in the Gospel of Matthew, Chapter 25, and I dare every member of Congress who claims church membership to read them: "When [Jesus] comes in glory with all the angels, then Jesus will sit on the throne. All humans will be before the throne, and will be separated as a shepherd divides the sheep from the goats, on the right and on the left. Then our Ruler will say to those on the right, 'Come, you that are blessed by God, inherit the world prepared for you from the foundation of the world; for I was hungry and you gave me food, I was thirsty and you gave me something to drink, I was a stranger and you welcomed me, I was naked and you gave me clothing, I was sick and you took care of me, I was in prison and you visited me.' Then the righteous will ask, 'when was it that we saw you hungry and gave you food, or thirsty and gave you drink? And when did we see you as a stranger and welcomed you, or naked and gave you clothing? And when did we see you sick or in prison and visited you?' And the Ruler will answer them, **'Truly I tell you, whenever you served one of the neediest members of my family, you served me.'** Then our Ruler will say to those on the left, 'You are condemned, go into the eternal fire; for I was hungry and you gave me no food, I was thirsty and you gave me no drink, I was a stranger and you did not welcome me, naked and you gave me no clothing, sick and in prison and you did not visit me.' They asked, 'when did we see you hungry or thirsty or a stranger or naked or sick or in prison, and did not take care of you?' The Ruler will answer them, 'Truly I tell you, just as you did **not** do it to someone in need, you did not do it to me.' And these will go away into eternal punishment, but the righteous into eternal life (my paraphrase)."

+++

A few words about my love/hate/dislike relationship with The UMC now follow. I love my church's social outreach ministries which help people all over the world. I love their history of establishing hospitals and colleges that continue to thrive. I love the ways they provide open doors and open hearts in thousands of cities and small towns.

I hate the misguided attitude my church has toward lesbian, gay, bi-sexual, and transgender persons. I dislike the itinerant appointment system. The appointment system is both a blessing and a curse. It is a blessing because it assures congregations they will have a pastor, and a pastor is guaranteed a job with great benefits. It is a curse because lay folks, and sometimes clergy, are often treated like pawns in the process.

In The UMC change is difficult. ACs are supposed to find ways so that clergy and lay persons each have 50% of the voting members. The congregation I attend has 900 lay members who are represented by one lay member at the AC. It has six clergy members (including me), who represent themselves.

We support work beyond the local church by paying apportionments. Each Conference decides how to raise the money, and most try to make the formula as fair as possible. In my first year as Conference Treasurer, the budget was the next to last agenda item at the AC. It was one of those "we've always done it that way" things. After the session closed, a lay member who happened to be married to one of my college friends, told me point-blank that our system is a joke. In any given year about 75% of churches send lay members to conference, and because they have other responsibilities, many leave before the conference ends. Active clergy are required to attend, and stay the entire session unless excused. The ratio of clergy to lay can easily be 2 to 1.

The disgruntled lay member mentioned the overwhelming majority of clergy voting on the budget, and said in a colorful way, "most of them couldn't balance a (expletive)[63] checkbook!" That's probably unfair, but the point is our decision-making process is flawed. We now have a new Conference which encompasses two states, so even fewer lay members will have time to attend annual meetings. Two things are needed: clergy should not vote on financial matters, and decisions should be made at smaller regional meetings.

I once floated the idea that Districts, rather than individual churches, be given an apportionment. The DS would convene a meeting, and each church would send a delegate to present their unique needs and resources. They would then work out a fair share, and own the process.

Another proposal I made when Conference Treasurer was to reduce the number of District Superintendents from 8 to 4, and change their duties to exclude almost everything but personnel matters. It marked the beginning of the end for me as Conference Treasurer. In 2007 the Nebraska AC reduced districts to six and made other changes similar to my suggestions. My pastor at the time, Ed Bonneau, was one of the proponents of the change. I said something to him about what was happening many years after I proposed it and he said, "The trouble with you, Chuck, is that you've always been about ten years ahead of everyone else."

Our Nebraska AC's declining numbers have forced us into a merger with the two moribund conferences in Kansas, and I am now a member of the Great Plains Conference of The UMC. The philosophy that bigger is better will not save our denomination, neither will connectionalism, bishops without term limits, and the archaic appointment system.

Another issue is The UMC is growing in the south, shrinking on the coasts, barely holding on in the populist midwest, and exploding in emerging nations. The net result is a drift away from the social gospel.

The UMC system of electing and assigning Bishops is ridiculous. The Peter Principle, people being promoted until they reach their level of incompetence, is rampant in our denomination. Bishops should be chosen by ACs. The appointment system should be scrapped, and replaced with a system of negotiation between church, pastors, and bishops. Serious discussions about uniting the UMC with ELCA and Presbyterians, needs to happen now, with UCC, Disciples of Christ, and Metropolitan Community Churches in the mix as well. I would also like to see the BoD changed to allow individual congregations to affiliate with other denominations.

Having said these things, it is appropriate to remember the example of Gamaliel. In Acts 5 he said of the early church, "...if this plan...is of human origin, it will fail, but if it is of God, you will not be able to overthrow them."

Thank you for indulging me; I feel better now.

Emma and Olivia in 2005

Chapter 25
On Being An Older Brother

I gave this sermon in Eustis and Farnam on March 29, 1992. I am proud to say some people told me they disagreed, but no one said I shouldn't have delivered it.

I was the victim of child abuse. I must be quick to point out that I wasn't harmed by my parents in any physical or emotional way. The abuse I suffered came as the result of my birth order. I grew up in a family of five boys and two girls, and I was the oldest boy. My sister Janice was first-born. Child psychologists often say first-borns get a lot of attention, a lot of glory, and a lot of pressure.

They are only partly right. Janice was "Miss Perfect." She got almost all A's all the way through college, and she never got into trouble. In May of 1966, I finished my first year at Wesleyan with a 2.5 G.P.A., happy to have passed Biology. That same year, Janice graduated "With High Distinction," and joined the Peace Corps.

When we were growing up, it was like there were three adults in our family: Mom, Dad, and Janice. When chore time came, Janice either supervised or disappeared. When baby brother had a dirty diaper, guess whose name was called? (it wasn't Janice) In a very real sense, I was the oldest sibling. However, Janice got the attention and the glory, and Charles got the pressure. At least that's the way I felt.

I must confess I resorted to hyperbole[64] in this sermon, and my big sister has always been better to me than I deserved.

One of my friends and former employers was Alan Dunlap. He was the oldest of four boys who grew up in a banker's family in Douglas, Nebraska. He told me about a July day when he and his brothers went "skinny dipping" in the Little Nemaha creek, which runs along the south edge of Douglas. It happened that while Alan and his brothers were enjoying the mud slides and cool water in the buff, Art Zech and his brothers snuck up and stole their clothes. When noon approached, they heard their mother call them for dinner, and discovered the dastardly deed committed by the Zech boys. Again their mother called. All they could do was hurry home, and hope no witnesses appeared on the streets of tiny Douglas.

Along the way, ten-year-old Alan began to carry his five-year-old twin brothers. As they left the shrubs and crossed the tracks, only the grain elevator stood between them and home. In complete horror, Alan saw the line of trucks and wagons. It was July - wheat harvest time! Again, mother called. There was nothing left to do. Alan strained past the line of waiting farmers, now carrying all three of his younger brothers, covered only by the dried mud of the Little Nemaha. Everyone can empathize, but only an older brother can fully understand the pathos of that moment.

Today we will focus our attention on an unnamed man Jesus spoke about in one of his parables. This man had a younger brother who left home with an inheritance he did not deserve, and was clearly a wasteful deadbeat. Their father welcomed back the younger son with a party, but the older brother is pictured as angry, resentful and self-righteous. As we consider this older brother's feelings, perhaps we will see ourselves and our discipleship in a new way.

In his fifteenth chapter, Luke gives us four parables. Three of them concern something which was lost and then found: the lost sheep, the lost coin, and the lost (or commonly called) prodigal son. The fourth parable concerns the attitude of the elder brother.

The scriptures are a little rough on elder brothers. In one of the creation stories, Adam and Eve have two sons. The oldest one, Cain, murders his younger brother, Abel. One of the biblical heroes, Joseph, had ten older brothers who sold him into slavery. The great King David's oldest son, Amnon, raped his younger half-sister Tamar. When David died, his next eldest son, Adonijah, was passed over as new king in favor of the younger Solomon. Finally, Jesus presents us with the image of an older brother who is a sanctimonious party pooper.

Tradition has viewed the father of the two sons as representing God. I no longer accept this. In the first place, the father is lacking wisdom. It was unthinkable to give the younger son his illegitimate inheritance. Old Dad would be an awfully soft touch to do so. Secondly, God would not let us off the hook so quickly. When the prodigal returned, he did make a confession of sin. However, it was not followed by the necessary "I will not do it again." God loves us, but God also wants us to avoid patterns of self-destruction. A third way the father is not like God, is his treatment of the older son when it came to the party invitations. The older one didn't get one. He came in from work, and heard the music and partying. God allows us to refuse invitations, but God would never ignore any of us like this.

I agree with those who say these parables teach us about "agape" love: the love given to us without our deserving it, and which expects nothing in return. Luke portrays Jesus as one who connected with people who assumed they were beyond the reach of God's love. Jesus showed them God's love is infinite and unconditional; it includes everybody. Luke says Jesus went to both the righteous and sinners. He went to the younger brothers, and he went to the older brothers. The major point is that Jesus expects his followers to practice unconditional love in all their relationships. Regardless of all other interpretations, the older brother simply could not grasp the meaning of this limitless love. Today's church still struggles with agape love.

When I began my pastorate in Hebron, I learned that one of our most active families had stopped attending church, and was planning to join another denomination. In visiting with them, I found they were leaving because they had heard some Methodist preacher somewhere had commented that he believed self-avowed homosexuals could be ordained clergy. I wouldn't let what somebody thought that somebody else said determine where I was going to attend church.

Many Christians, including United Methodists, are in real trouble on this issue. Valid scientific research shows that sexual orientation is genetic. Thus, when we condemn a homosexual, we also reject the God who created him or her. There are three brief references to homosexuality in the New Testament. If you study these passages carefully, you will learn they are there to illustrate the harmfulness of dysfunctional relationships, not sexual orientation.

Those who have an irrational fear of homosexuals are called homophobes. The older brother in Jesus' parable would probably be one. He was unable to love or be loved. He was unable to accept differences. When the partying started he stayed outside on the porch.

The scriptural stories of Jesus' death, and its meaning are always before us. Paul wrote: "Christ did die for all of us. He died so we would no longer live for ourselves, but for the one who died and was raised to life for us. (2 Corinthians 5:15)" We Christians must be careful. Jesus promised he would draw all persons to himself. Shall we join the celebration, including the rainbow of cultural diversity, or we will stay outside sharing the misery of the older brother?

The good news is that God loves us unconditionally. God loves older brothers with stiff necks, and younger ones who are dirty rotten scoundrels. God also calls us to express divine love by reaching out to others who feel lost and rejected by society.

Window on page 247 is from Zion ELCA in Albion
The buffalo was caught in repose at Fort Robinson in 2006

Two pictures from September 2006

Chapter 26
Credo

In my last year of seminary, I prepared a paper called Credo (which means "I believe") for a third and final time. This document was written on December 10, 1971, and presented to Professors Tex Sample and Carl Bangs, both ordained pastors in The UMC with advanced degrees including Ph.D.s. I started my composition with a bit of religious autobiography, and hoped to articulate a theological position. I used orthodox terms to support a social gospel.

I then met with Bangs, Sample, and another teacher to discuss my mini dissertation. I don't remember much about this meeting except I "passed," and had to take a couple of remedial classes in theology and church history. I received my Master's degree on May 15, 1972, and was ordained an elder in The UMC a year later.

On December 21, 2008 I joined Facebook, and was asked for my religious views. In addition to United Methodist, I wrote eclectic, evangelical, existentialist, which are thus explained: ***Eclectics*** use elements from many traditions, philosophies, systems and processes. ***Evangelicals*** believe God's love is generous and unlimited, and this message needs to be shared. ***Existentialists*** are concerned with today, individual choices, and the journey.

During the ill-considered Iraqi war, Secretary Rumsfeld said, "There are known knowns. These are things we know that we know. There are known unknowns. That is to say, there are things we know we don't know. But there are also unknown unknowns. These are things we don't know we don't know." It made me wonder if Mr. Rumsfeld was an existentialist, too. The thing is, existentialism helps me stick with things I know are real.

Were I to write a Credo today, some 43 years after my last one, what would I say? The statement would be much briefer, more honest, and my denomination might encourage me to look for another professional path to explore. I quit the parish ministry in 1981, The UMC took me back in 1987, and I retired early in 1999. All the while, I pondered as I wandered.

First of all, I agree with Søren Kierkegaard who wrote, "life is not a problem to be solved, but a reality to be experienced." I tend to do my deep thinking sociologically. This means I try to analyze what motivates my thoughts and behavior. Just think of the many layers of influence which pile on to cover up the real person inside you. At my friend Curtis Trenhaile's funeral in 2001, I heard Bette Midler singing **In My Life.**[65] It captures well the places and people that impact our life experiences.

On February 1, 1948 my parents chose the path of Methodist Christian for me. I affirmed that choice later, and reaffirmed it several times, but I knew what I was doing and I knew why I was doing it. When my dad got sick and was going through treatments to destroy cancer, I prayed many times he would get well. I even made a few bargains with God, offering something in return if God would cure my father. I gave this up when I realized there was no hope, but I didn't blame God for what happened to my dad. This tragic experience started me thinking theologically. Life ends. I, too, will die some day. Finitude is for real.

A song I've heard at funerals starts: "I don't know about tomorrow, I just live from day-to-day. I don't borrow from its sunshine, for its skies may turn to gray. I don't worry about my future…"[66] The first time I heard it the existentialist in me was feeling good, but then it launched into some poor theology, and the sociologist in me ushered me to another place.

When I strip away agony and ecstasy, fear and hope, despair and joy, failure and success, falsehood and truth, questions and answers, sickness and health, I get to the basic me. And it starts with finitude: the realization that I shall die. It could happen tonight; or I might live to celebrate my 100th birthday. But I will die, and be gone forever. There was never one dramatic moment when this reality came to me; but the gradual impact of my inevitable demise was real.

Most folks don't manage the death issue well. An elderly parishioner was in the Hebron hospital. Her younger brother had died unexpectedly, and her daughter wanted me present when the mother was told. This well-meaning daughter used every cliché for death she could think of without simply saying, "Uncle Joe died last night." We took a lunch break, and I came back before the daughter and asked her mom, "did you understand what she was trying to say?" She said no, and I told her "your brother Joe died in his sleep yesterday." She replied, "I wondered what she was talking about!" The daughter was greatly relieved when I told her what happened, and thanked me.

I went with my dad to a graveside committal when I was four years old. We traveled down a dusty road near Ravenna, to a cemetery where a handful of mourners and a funeral director were waiting for us. The mortician pried open the casket, and a little old lady dressed in black was viewed for the last time by those present. It was not a scary time. A few years later, I saw my beloved grandfather in repose at an Omaha funeral home. I was sad but he looked serene lying there, and I wasn't terrified in the least. Ten years later, I helped my mother choose a casket for my dear father at the Levander Funeral Home. I went to Penney's and bought a new shirt and tie, took them and his best suit to the funeral home. Mel Levander called us later in the day, and we went down to view the remains of a 54-year-old man who had nurtured and inspired me for 21 years. It was a tearful experience, but I remember thinking he looked so peaceful, and had been freed from the awful malignancy which devoured his body.

Somewhere in these experiences, I developed a process to deal with the reality of my finitude. Initially I took the easy way. If you were a Christian, your soul magically flew away to another dimension called heaven. If you weren't a believer, you had no soul, and you just disappeared. My reaction to finitude was to pretend it wasn't real by buying into the dualistic "mind over matter" theory of the Greek philosophers.

Gnosticism is the Christian version of dualism, and wasn't very popular at my seminary. I unenthusiastically warmed to the notion that God was prepared to create a new spiritual body for us when we die. We may have to wait a few thousand years, but on the day of resurrection we'd fly away to a celestial banquet in our new garments. I got this from 1 Corinthians 15 which talks about perishability, imperishability, mortality, and immortality, which perhaps is a more illusive kind of dualism.

I also learned that hell, which I never believed in anyway, was either the city dump (Gehenna) in Jerusalem or permanent separation from God. I was a proponent of universal salvation at this time as well. In other words, I was still looking for something to help me reject finitude.

As I transitioned into a pastoral role, I was pretty much a confirmed existentialist and death was not much of an issue for me personally, but, I had to conduct funerals once in a while. My approach was to stick to our Book of Worship. My sermons focused on the living and the values of precious memories, always reminding folks that "nothing could separate us from the love of God in Christ Jesus our Lord (Romans 8:39)." The 23rd Psalm and Isaiah 43, verses 1 & 2, were read at graveside.

My favorite humorist, Garrison Keillor, described questions about the afterlife in this way: "My people aren't paradise people. We've lived in Minnesota all our lives and it took a lot out of us. My people aren't sure if we'll even like paradise: not sure that perfection is all it's cracked up to be. My people will arrive in heaven and stand just inside the gate, shuffling around. 'It's a lot bigger than I thought it was going to be,' we'll think. We'll say, 'No, thank you, we can't stay for eternity, we'll just sit and have a few minutes of bliss with you and then we have to get back.'"[67] That's pretty good theology. Jesus taught it was better to wait in quiet humility than to assume a place of honor (Luke 14:7-11).

Karl Marx was right when he said religion is opium for many people. Some folks find comfort when given a list of absolutes to follow, hoping these will induce God to make room for them in heaven. The problem with this approach is: virtually no one can pass the test. Matthew, Mark, and Luke tell us it is easier for a camel to pass through a needle's eye, than for someone with money to get into heaven. Surely you remember how disappointed the rich ruler was (Luke 18). That's the bad news.

Dr. King wrote "Death is not the ultimate evil; the ultimate evil is to be outside God's love."[68] The good news is you need wait no longer to bask in the eternal sunshine of God's love. I believe salvation, eternal life, and heaven are present, not future, events. Consider what Jesus said to Zacchaeus: "**Today** salvation has come to this house…" Paul to the Corinthians: "As we work together, we urge you also not to accept the grace of God in vain. God says, 'At an acceptable time I have listened to you, and on a day of salvation I have helped you.' See, **now** is the acceptable time; see, **now** is the day of **salvation** (2 Corinthians 6:1-2)!" John's Gospel is filled with existential declarations including: "Very truly, I tell you, anyone who hears my word and believes the one who sent me has **eternal life**, and does not come under judgment, but has passed from death to life (John 5:24)" and "Very truly, I tell you, whoever believes has **eternal life**" (John 6:47). I also like the way Brenda Carlisle expressed this sentiment in her song **Heaven Is A Place on Earth.**[69]

Norman Duane Green lost his life in Vietnam on February 18, 1968 at the age of 19. He was a Number One Son and had two younger brothers. Norm was a year behind me in school. We went to Sunday School and youth fellowship together. His folks and his grandma were active Methodists. His funeral was one of the last my dad conducted. One of Norm's brothers had a terrible time dealing with the loss, and when my father died exactly one year after Norm, he told his mother "Norm's OK now. Reverend Leypoldt is with him."

I am very sentimental, and there are things I read in obituaries and hear at funerals that appeal to me. One of these is the notion that we will be greeted by loved ones if there is an afterlife. I shed tears when I hear Brad Paisley sing **When I Get Where I'm Going.**[70] However, I can't find anything in scripture to support this kind of possibility. There's another song that may say more about our desire to be reunited with the dead in a conscious and recognizable fashion. It was sung by the incomparable Dusty Springfield and titled **Wishin' and Hopin'.**[71] She's telling young lovers there is more to relationships than day dreaming and scheming; you've got to get real!

I feel the Gospel is diminished when longing for a pie in the sky crowds out the call to serve others. With all the confusing and conflicting theories, I've concluded it's best to heed the wisdom relayed to Isaiah: "For my thoughts are not your thoughts, nor are your ways my ways, says God. For as the heavens are higher than the earth, so are my ways higher than your ways, and my thoughts higher than your thoughts (55:8-9 NRSV)." The question of eternal security is God's business, not mine.

Therefore, finitude is real. Heaven is a place on earth. How about a supreme being? I cannot remember a time when I did not believe in God. In Philosophy 101, I heard the prime mover argument and needed nothing more. Reflecting upon Christology was more difficult, but once I focused on the Word made flesh, I understood. In Romans 8, Paul describes the process by which God remains active in our lives via the Holy Spirit, and Trinitarian I am.

F. Forrester Church, a Unitarian pastor, defined me when he wrote: "When I was growing up, I believed in God without questioning what I really meant by this. God was God and that was that…when things were going well, when I did not need God, God was there. I believed in God without worrying too much about why…the power which I cannot explain or know or name I call God. God is not God's name. God is my name for the mystery that looms within and arches beyond the limits of my being. Life force, spirit of life, ground of being, these too are names for the unnameable which I am now content to call my God."[72]

Except for the idea of God, I've never been good at accepting things "on blind faith." If I came across a concept which didn't make sense to me, I subjected it to analysis. I blame this on sociology, and my bias is there is a reason why people believe and practice their faith.

Many religious folks believe in the beliefs of their particular group, but can give you very few reasons why they are who they think they are. But I needed a little more. Paul Tillich was a theologian who helped me analyze my search for meaning. He described salvation in this way: "In times of despair, when separation is keenly felt, answers cannot be found, voices are heard but not understood, all joy and courage are destroyed. Sometimes in that moment a wave of light breaks into our darkness, and it is as though a voice were saying: 'You are accepted. You are accepted by that which is greater than you.'"[73] A simple affirmation from a great mind.

John's Gospel records several moments where "I am" is used by Jesus descriptively. This helps us see Jesus as the Word in the human form. Luke contributes this "...Jesus came to Nazareth...went to the synagogue on the Sabbath...stood up to read [from Isaiah]...and found...where it was written: 'The Spirit of God is upon me, and has anointed me to bring good news to those who are poor...to proclaim release to the captives and recovery of sight to the blind, to let those who are oppressed go free, [and] to proclaim the year of God's favor.' Jesus rolled up the scroll, gave it back to the attendant, and sat down. The eyes of all in the synagogue were fixed on Jesus. Then Jesus began to say to them, '**Today** this scripture has been fulfilled in your hearing (Luke 4:16-21).'" Some have proposed the historical Jesus, his death, and resurrection was all a hoax. If that could somehow be proven, it would not change my theological method. The key to understanding Jesus is not flesh and blood, it is the message.

The redeeming work of God through the heroic sacrifice of a perfect human transcends history. The death of the unblemished one does not destroy this message. The resurrection appearances of Jesus, including the one at Pentecost, affirm that the Living Word is eternal. John magnifies the concept of **Jesus equals Message** by writing, "In the beginning was the Word, and the Word was with God, and the Word was God (John 1:1)." "And the Word became flesh and lived among us, and we have seen the Word's glory, the glory as of a parent's only child, full of grace and truth (John 1:14)." Paul put it this way: "In Christ the people of this world were reconciled to God, not counting their trespasses against them, and entrusting the **message** of reconciliation to us (2 Corinthians 5:19)." This verse tells us how vitally important it is to hear **and** share the Word with others.

There was a time when I needed to move past mind games, and pay attention to these words of Jesus: "If any want to become my followers, let them deny themselves and take up their cross daily and follow me. For those who want to save their life will lose it, and those who lose their life for my sake will save it (Luke 19:23-24)." It is one thing to learn intellectually that salvation, eternal life, and heaven are within your grasp, and quite another to realize that this truth has also been written on your heart: "...this is the covenant that I will make with Israel, said God: I will put my law within them, and I will write it on their hearts; and I will be their God, and they shall be my people (Jeremiah 31:33 NRSV)."

In the first chapter of Acts we learn about the Ascension: Jesus told the Disciples "...you will receive power when the Holy Spirit has come upon you; and you will be my witnesses in Jerusalem, in all Judea and Samaria, and to the ends of the earth." Jesus was carried away, and the disciples stood gazing upward when told by God to get back to work (Acts 1:9-11). Jesus prepared the first disciples to ground themselves in service. We may need to look to the mountains for inspiration, but the essence of the Gospel is within us, and multiplies as we identify with the needs of others.

An ancient catechism advises "The chief end of man is to glorify God and enjoy him forever." I prefer the closing comments of the Risen Christ, who in John 21 tells Peter, "Feed my lambs, tend my sheep, feed my sheep." God is glorified in our deeds of love and kindness. I sincerely believe actions speak much louder than words, and what you do is far more crucial than what you say or believe.

Among the most significant verses in the Bible is 1 John 4:20 "Those who say, 'I love God, and hate their brothers or sisters, are liars; for those who do not love a brother or sister whom they have seen, cannot love God whom they have not seen.'" It occurred to me quite early that people are more concerned with "sins," that is, bad behavior, than they are with Sin, which is defined as estrangement from God. For example, the commandment "Thou shalt not take the name of the Lord thy God in vain" was presumed to frown upon using swear words. But I learned it was far more damnable to say "I speak for God" or "God hates fags."

"The self is the one and only thing we own," wrote Dr. E. Stanley Jones. Socialization enables us to choose directions for our individual self. Ultimately, there are only two choices: self-realization or self-surrender. It's a process. It's not easy. Whether religious or not, everyone needs to find a way that will provide meaning. Self-realization means the answers are in you: "know thyself," "accept thyself," and "express thyself." Each of these proposes a direction that is self-destructive because a power beyond the self, and the companionship of other humans is not part of the formula. Some folks never consciously participate; for them not to decide is to decide.

Religion should assist those who seek answers, but it ain't necessarily so. A few years after Jesus' death, the early church failed to accept non-Jews into the movement because they were burdened by the Law. The Roman church created sacramentalism, papal infallibility, limbo, purgatory and sold indulgences. The Reformers objected to Rome but insisted on a new orthodoxy enforced by executions of freethinkers. Sectarian groups appeared, and tossed out many traditions. Some invented legalistic views that led to immersion, fundamentalism, and revivalism which endeavored to scare people into the church. Principalities and powers managed to exploit the confusion and the admonition to "love your neighbor as yourself" was sidelined in favor of patriotism and other forms of civil religion. Unfortunately, weapons of mass deception have now silenced the Gospel in many churches. "We deceive, you believe," is the motto of civil religion, and in America today many churches are merely branches of the Republican Party. It's not surprising some folks are cynical about Christianity.

I was fortunate to be raised in a home where rules were enforced, and forgiveness was practiced. I also was nurtured by church camps, youth rallies, a Methodist college and seminary, and numerous lay and clergy friends. Therefore, when I needed to express my beliefs, I did so within a Christian context. I've been blessed to participate in several faith communities where people supported one another, welcomed others, and gave generously to ministries beyond their walls. Our model of perfection is found in Acts 2:44-45: "All who believe were together and had all things in common; they would sell their possessions and goods and distribute the proceeds to all, as any had need."

I was once asked, "Do you expect to be made perfect in love in this life?" To which I answered, "yes." To get on this track, I surrendered to the realization that meaning, that is, heaven on earth came my way when I accepted the offer of One who taught me to be a follower. I am indebted to Dr. E. Stanley Jones for his book **Victory Through Surrender** which helped me understand the above ideas.[74] To summarize, my Credo is 1.) I know and accept that I will die someday. 2.) I needed to surrender my self in order to accept the invitation to be a follower. There is one more thing I believe: 3.) Imagination is more important than knowledge.

John Lennon released his song **Imagine**[75] in 1971, but I don't think I heard it until 1994. The occasion was the Eustis-Farnam High School commencement. I was amazed to hear these words coming from the gymnasium p.a. system as the kids departed the platform. I was even more surprised I'd never heard the song before. No doubt the students loved the tune and didn't pay much attention to the political philosophy, but I'd like to believe a former pastor with existential and socialist ideas influenced someone along the way. When I graduated high school in 1965, one of the popular songs was **What The World Needs Now is Love**.[76] Hal David wrote it, Jackie DeShannon sang it, and many in my generation believed it. My idealism has been tempered by sociological realism, but I dream of a time when every child in the world will experience the rights of life, liberty, and the pursuit of happiness.

When I was a teenager I met a girl who liked me back, and thought I was in love. I must have been really serious, because I asked my mom for advice. She told me, "I don't think you're in love with her, you're just in love with love." And she was right because I've only loved one girl, and she didn't come around until I was 21.

I've concluded this about religion: we have faith in faith, we believe in beliefs.

You might say we're wishin' and hopin' and thinkin' and prayin', but we're missing the message that God in Christ has chosen to be with us, and when we accept God's acceptance of us, we are on the path of meaning and discovery. This separates Christianity from religion. Let me hasten to add that I agree wholeheartedly with Paul's advice "...work out your own salvation in fear and trembling (Philippians 2:12)." It's important for all folks to listen and develop their own "theological method."

The following Bible verses teach us about prayer.

"Be still and know that I am God (Psalms 46:10a)."

"Likewise the Spirit helps us in our weakness, for we don't know how to pray as we ought, but that very Spirit intercedes with sighs too deep for words (Romans 8:26)."

"I believe; help my unbelief! (Mark 9:24)"

"Pray always and don't lose heart (Luke 18:1, the parable of the Unjust Judge)."

"When you are praying, do not heap up empty phrases as the Gentiles do, for they think they will be heard because of their many words. Do not be like them, for God knows what you need before you ask (Matthew 6:7-8)."

"You have heard that it was said, 'You shall love your neighbor and hate your enemy.' But I say to you, Love your enemies and pray for those who persecute you, so that you may be children of God; for God makes the sun rise on the evil and on the good, and sends rain on the righteous and on the unrighteous (Matthew 5:43-45)."

Prayer is communication with the mystery called God. Kierkegaard said, "Prayer does not change God, but it changes the one who prays." I don't think we should pray for rain, healing, victories over opponents or enemies, winning lottery tickets, or anything else that would be selfish. God knows all about us, and we should be centered on others, not ourselves.

Even though your forgiveness is a done deal, it's a good idea to confess sins to get them out of your system. There are many sung prayers in our hymnals that strengthen our sense of community. *Let There Be Peace On Earth* (UMH #431) and *Pass It On* (UMH #572) are just two of hundreds. Prayerful communication opens us to answers about life and strength for the journey.

Let me now confess to you that I did something in two Nebraska parsonages and at Fisk Hall in Kansas City, that may have been amerciable. I also did something that was very stupid at the Casey's store in Albion back in 2004, and have yet to share with my spouse. If you can guess what either of these actions were, and swear to me that you will never reveal, and always conceal them, I will refund the price of this book.

In addition, though the sociologist in me remains strong, I still treasure imagination. Perhaps there is an eternal dimension beyond this life. If so, every single creature will be included, and the vilest, most horrible monsters will have been transformed, because grace is more powerful than evil. I love the last scene in the 1984 movie **Places In The Heart**. It portrays folks receiving communion in the church. Everyone is there - living and dead, murderers and victims, betrayers and the betrayed.[77] That's the kind of afterlife which I can begin accepting.

I've long defined a liberal as a radical with children. I've now returned to the far left on most subjects. Please remember: what you do is way more important than what you say or believe. Much of the New Testament was written when Christians were persecuted, and folks needed to hear there would be a better future. The phrase "Thy will be done, on earth as it is in heaven" directs us to a perfect and just society, where all people live in harmony with God and others, thus producing a heaven on earth.

Dr. King wrote he found a plaque that many families had in their homes during the struggle for civil rights:

Fear knocked on the door.
Faith answered.
There was no one there.[78]

I am captivated by this verse: "There is no fear in love, but perfect love casts out fear; for fear has to do with punishment; and whoever fears has not reached perfection in love (1 John 4:18)." There are senseless phobias we all deal with but when fear produces nationalism, racism, sexism, homophobia and irrational resistance to change, our human community is in peril. Dr. Walter Brueggemann preached on this verse, saying: "We are, all of us, a mixture of love and fear. We go back and forth between them. When we are addressed in love, we are able to be open, receiving, peaceable, ready to be concerned for others. When we are overpowered by fear, we are likely to be hidden and closed, either cowering or aggressive, agitated and anxious, mostly preoccupied with ourselves. We go back and forth, trying to sort it out, yearning for love, reacting to the power of fear."[79]

I believe it's no accident the Bible uses words of hope to address times of radical change. This message is "do not be afraid."

At the genesis of monotheism, God came to Abram, saying, "Do not be afraid, Abram, I am your shield; your reward will be very great (Genesis 15:1 NRSV)."

In the fullness of time, a precursor of the Living Word was sought, and God sent this message to his parents: "Do not be afraid, Zechariah, for your prayer has been heard. Your wife Elizabeth will bear you a child, and you will name him John (Luke 1:13)."

At the annunciation another message was delivered: "Do not be afraid, Mary, for you have found favor with God (Luke 1:30)."

At another annunciation to working people: "Do not be afraid; for see, I am bringing you good news of great joy for all the people...(Luke 2:10)."

When Jesus grew to adulthood and started his ministry, he chose helpers. To the fisherman, Peter, he said "Do not be afraid; from now on you will be catching people (Luke 5:10)."

Jesus knew his words were challenging, and he comforted the flock as he traveled to Jerusalem. "But even the hairs of your head are all counted. Do not be afraid; you are of more value than many sparrows (Luke 12:7)" and "Do not be afraid, little flock, for it is God's good pleasure to give you the dominion (Luke 12:32)."

After preaching and teaching, Jesus sent his disciples on a boat ride and later appeared, frightening them and said: "Take heart, it is I; do not be afraid (Mark 6:50, Matthew 14:27, John 6:20 differs a little)."

On another occasion Jesus took three disciples to a mountain, and they witnessed a transfiguration of his appearance, and assurances from a voice in the cloud, but were scared and fell down, and Jesus said, "Get up and do not be afraid (Matthew 17:7)."

On the night before his crucifixion, Jesus told the disciples: "Peace I leave with you; my peace I give to you. I do not give to you as the world gives. Do not let your hearts be troubled, and do not let them be afraid (John 14:27)."

We also have the inspired words of Charles Wesley who reminds us we have been changed from "glory into glory" and our lives of service lead us to be "lost in wonder, love, and praise," which in turn prepare us for every experience.

Each of us will face the transition called death. We should not be afraid. Nothing worse than uninterrupted, profound slumber awaits us; anything more or less, I am content to leave to the imagination of the boundless mystery we call God.

Get ready! Glamour shots are on the next page.

Above: Ana and her little cousin in 2007
Below: Olivia in 2010

Chapter 27
A Daisy A Day

Chris' grandmother Grace McGill was a gatherer of antiques and collectibles long before it was fashionable among the masses. She had ten grandchildren, and gave her treasures to them at birthdays and Christmases. In 1985 she decided to buy each one a case to display the items. We went with her to furniture stores, but Chris couldn't find anything she wanted. Grandma then offered us her beautiful curved glass cabinet, which has been an important part of our living rooms since.

Grandma was born on February 22 (Washington's birthday), and she collected all sorts of hatchets. Our daughter arrived on February 21, and we decided to call her Anastasia Grace to honor her great-grandmother. Grandma gave her hatchet collection to us for safekeeping, and we've passed them on to Ana.

Chris and I went to auctions for a time, but now we concentrate on estate sales. One of my treasures is a roll top desk. It was priced at only $250, which got my immediate attention. Upon closer examination I found it was composed of several parts, original and new, and I was able to buy it for $125.

I collect Nebraskana and Masonic items, also clocks, calendars, religious icons, anything made in Israel, toy vehicles, music CDs and books. I have Roy Rogers and Garrison Keillor CDs with their autographs. We have a table from the Gordon MacRae estate, a Husker shot glass from Coach Jim Ross, and a bust of Teddy Roosevelt once owned by Clayton Yeutter.

My grandfather Hennings and my dad both took many pictures. I bought my first camera in 1957, and Dad taught me how to develop pictures. However, I soon relied on my friends at the drug store for negatives and prints.

When I was 14, Dad bought an Argus 35 mm that I still have. I took that camera with me on the Youth Mission Tour in 1964, and learned to use it well. When my kids came along we had a couple of crude Instamatics, but mostly took super 8 movies. I bought a Minolta 35mm and used it on and off from 1975 to 1997. In 1994 I took hundreds of slides in the Holy Land with the Minolta. I've now converted all the 35 mm slides to digital images and stored them on my computer.

In November 1997 I purchased my first digital camera (a Sony Mavica), and my interest in photography was rekindled. That camera saved images to a small floppy disk, and made pictures which were 640x480 only. It had a fixed lens and no eye viewer. Within two months, I ascended to the status of grandfather.

On April 13, 2001 I upgraded to a Mavica FD75 with 10x zoom lens, eye viewer, and it allowed me to make very short videos. I also acquired a device which enabled me to take 1280x960 photos on this Mavica. By 2004, digital camera technology improved dramatically, and I purchased a Sony F-828.

The F-828 had a Carl Zeiss lens, two memory stick slots, longer movie capability, and took 8 mega pixel photos. I purchased my first Digital Single Lens Reflex (DSLR) camera in May of 2007 but was still using my F828 because the DSLRs had no movie function. This Sony A-100 quit on me in October 2008, so was glad I had the F828 in reserve. In November 2008, I bought a Sony A-350 which took 14 mega pixel images. I left the cheap company camera in the office, and was using my own equipment exclusively at that time.

In November 2011 I read Sony was offering a new camera. It was a Single Lens Translucent (SLT) with several enhancements compared to the A-350, namely 24 mega pixel stills, high definition videos, fixed mirror, and an improved alpha lens. The price tag, however, was $2,500. I stopped at a camera store in Omaha to purchase a small accessory and asked about the new camera. The clerk showed it to me and I gushed over it, but said I couldn't justify the cost. "How about this one?" he asked and handed me a lighter camera (model a65), which went for $1,000. That I could afford, but could I rationalize the transaction?

Shortly after Thanksgiving I was telling my son-in-law, Jeff Grinvalds, about the new camera. He said if I was planning to give him anything for Christmas (he knew I was), a used Sony A-350 would be much better than his old Canon. That, of course, was music to my ears. I bought the a65, and gave both the F828 and A-350 to Jeff.

My photographic skills improved with each camera, and I anticipate making pictures until these tools slip from my nerveless grasp. My favorite subjects are grandchildren (mine and those of Chris' and my siblings), landscapes, flowers, and church art. Links to the best of the best are at **pylodet.com**.

A little boy went to church with his mother on a sunny morning. He was fascinated by the many colorful figures he saw in the art glass windows, and he asked his mother who these people were. She whispered this was such and such a saint, and that was another. Some time afterward, in Sunday school, the teacher asked if anybody knew what a saint was. The excited boy, raising his hand, said "I do! A saint is someone who the light shines through!"

I learned this lesson much later in life. I now have over 20,000 photos of church art (windows, altars, pulpits, banners and statuary), and interiors and exteriors of houses of worship. I would love to publish a book with these color images. The most spectacular photos came from churches in Crawford, Swede Home, Nebraska City, Lyons, Bow Valley, Bloomfield, Broken Bow, Bazile Mills, Pender, South Sioux City, O'Neill, Randolph, Albion and Lincoln. They're posted in several places on the web and featured on **pylodet.com**.

For many years I thought it would be fun to travel Nebraska and stop at each of our 93 county courthouses. In June 2013 I put together a plan to do so, and invited my four brothers to accompany me. Three of them agreed to participate. Our truly laudable pursuit would be done in three day trips to towns in the eastern third of our state, with the remainder requiring two overnight stays out west. Later on, we added a fourth short day trip to finish our quest.

We started on Monday, July 22 in Lincoln, made a loop through southeast Nebraska, ending in Beatrice to help our Aunt Bobbie celebrate her 77th birthday (our fifth brother, Steve, joined in this event). On the following Monday, July 29, we traveled the eastern seaboard of Nebraska and received generous rainfall as we went through Tecumseh, Pawnee City, Falls City, and Auburn, thence along the Missouri River, veering west to Ponca, and ending our day in Fremont. On July 31 we made an initial visit to Wahoo, journeyed through east central counties all the way to Butte, and back home through the Sandhills and Osceola.

The following week we were down to three brothers as Doug was recuperating from surgery. On Monday, August 5, we survivors departed Lincoln, and made an initial stop at Kearney. Next came Minden and all of southwest Nebraska, including Ogallala, where we spent the night. The next day we motored to Oshkosh, ate lunch with my granddaughters in Gering, and meandered through the Panhandle until we stopped at Thedford. On Wednesday the 7th of August, we arose early, drove to Valentine and Springview, then made an orderly descent toward North Platte, arriving in Lincoln about 10 pm. In North Platte we also happened upon the Leypoldt & Pennington building.

The abbreviated and final day was August 11 when we repaired to Grand Island, Loup City, St. Paul, and our hallowed hometown: Albion. Our sister Cathy joined us on this final day as did Doug and his wife Nancy. We spent 85 hours on the road and metered 4,000 miles on my Honda Fit. We visited every county seat in Nebraska and were inside about half the courthouses. I took 427 pictures including every courthouse and many other buildings, which are now posted on **Google Earth**. We consulted my copy of Oliver B. Pollak's book **Nebraska Courthouses**[80] at every stop as well as researching on-line via smart phones.

On the first day of September in 2013, Chris was working at our church's thrift shop. She called to tell me she had a flat tire and I headed her way. Her car is a 2005 Toyota Sienna we've had since it was new, and in 2013 it had less than 40,000 miles. As I drove there I was thinking I'd never changed a tire on this car, nor did I know where the spare or jack might be. When I arrived a young fellow had stopped, and already taken care of us. It was great to experience the generosity of an angel unaware.

My 2013 Christmas epistle was titled "A Tale of Two Houses" and included the following: Eighteen years ago at this time we were in a parsonage and cheerfully living among the United Methodists in Geneva, Nebraska. The bright lights of the metro won us over, and we moved to the capitol city. We bought a 4-bedroom multilevel home in northeast Lincoln, and moved in on a cold day in January of 1996. We were in our forties in the nineties, and five flights of stairs and a basement laundry room didn't bother us one bit. Over time we replaced the roof, added lawn sprinklers, affixed vinyl siding, procured new HVAC and windows, and installed tankless hot water.

After my retirement in 2012, we developed a casual interest in finding a different place to call home. Estate Sales and Open Houses gave us many opportunities to snoop around other people's houses at leisure. A seller's market boosted value at our old place, and we got serious about a change.

On November 17, 2012 we went to a sale in the Cripple Creek area of south Lincoln. This house had a lot of things we liked and was in excellent condition. So we inquired, but listing price appeared to be above our budget. Christmas week we found another one a little cheaper and very nice, but it had a BIG lawn. I checked, and the Cripple Creek place was still on the market; we looked at it twice more (falling mortgage rates also allowed for budget reconsideration).

Because Chris was still on the fence, I suggested we make a "low ball" offer, which I did on January 8. Lo and behold we had a motivated seller, and we started to pack our things. We closed the deal on February 19, and began moving a few belongings right away. At the end of that week, I ventured alone to my new house along with a load of stuff and my 6 foot aluminum stepladder. After unloading, I decided to check out the attic area above the garage.

The garage ceiling is 10 feet above the floor, so to get my head up through the opening I had to stand on the top step of the ladder. I looked around for a minute or two, and the rickety thing holding me up went down. I was hanging by my fingertips, and my feet were maybe 5 feet from the concrete below me. In my mind, of course, I was on a tightrope 30 feet off the ground with no safety net. After brief reflection, I let go, was not hurt, and gained a sermon illustration. At my next physical, however, I somehow lost an inch of height. Our two properties were about eight miles apart, and day after day we made 1, 2, or 3 trips using both cars with brother Gary giving us invaluable assistance, including a pickup truck.

Our home in Lincoln

On March 18, a local firm sent two men and a truck to load and deliver our remaining furnishings. But, alas, we still had two houses, and the one on North 74th Street needed some sprucing up. We hired a contractor to take care of most of it, brother-in-law Les helped as did Gary, and we trudged back and forth throughout April. Finally, on May 12 we listed the old house with our friend Jack McVay. It was sold for full price four days later! However, we did not close until July, and we still made occasional trips up north. We had two garage sales in March at the old place, and three more after we moved. It took us a while to get settled, but it was well worth the effort.

In his latest book Bishop John Shelby Spong wrote, "I can see more than I can say. I can experience more than I can describe. That is as far as words can carry me."[81] Well said, and I'm almost finished.

I've decided if there was only one book in the Bible it should be John's Gospel. It begins at the beginning, and ends with this common sense: "…there are also many other things that Jesus did; if every one of them were written down, I suppose that the world itself could not contain the books that would be written."

Earlier, John told us how Jesus' friends were handling his death and disappearance: "Late Sunday afternoon the disciples were hiding behind locked doors because they were afraid. Jesus appeared saying 'peace be with you' and showed them the wounds in his hands and side. The disciples rejoiced and Jesus said again 'peace be with you. As God sent me, now I am sending you.' He breathed on them and said, 'receive the Spirit. When you forgive sins of anyone, they are forgiven. If you fail to forgive, people will be excluded.' All were there except Thomas, and they told him what they had seen, but he was skeptical and needed to see for himself. A week later at the same place and time, all the disciples were together, and the doors were shut. Jesus again appeared and said to Thomas, 'put your finger in my wounds. Quit doubting and believe!' Then Thomas said, 'My Lord and my God!' Jesus said to all of them, 'Have you believed because you have seen me? Blessed are the ones who do not see me, yet believe I am who I am'" (John 20:19-29 my paraphrase).

These early disciples seemed to have forgotten everything Jesus taught them. They were lost and alone, especially Thomas. Mary got the message and told them about it, but here they were, behind locked doors. It's like when you know better, but your gut keeps telling you something's missing.

Late afternoons are difficult for many. I was fifteen in 1963 when I started my job at Camp Fontanelle. On a May Sunday Mom and Dad took me to the place I was going to spend the entire summer. I moved into the dishwasher's cabin - a 10 x 12 shack with studs covered by canvas. I thought I was ready, but a very lonely feeling overtook me when my parents drove away late in the afternoon.

A few years later, I moved into my freshman dorm room at Nebraska Wesleyan on an August morning. Dad and I then spent a few hours at the State Fair. Late in the afternoon, he took me back to campus, dropped me off, and I felt a real emptiness. A similar feeling came many years later when I left my son at that very same dormitory, and three years after that, my daughter in a building nearby.

In April of 2014, our Anastasia found an appealing new job in Oregon. She applied on-line, was interviewed via Skype, and a few days later accepted a position as a case worker with the Coos County Department of Health & Human Services. She borrowed our van and rented a trailer; we drove her Subaru and it took three days to get there. It was morning when we left Ana and headed back to Nebraska, but it most certainly felt like late afternoon.

Chris and I have lived in nine communities and 13 houses, four of which we've owned. At the time we came to Lincoln in 1996, we had relocated on average every three years. I know many of my reasons for moving had to do with elusive dreams, and not always well constructed objectives.

In the seventies a singer/songwriter named Jud Strunk appeared on television. His most popular tune was titled, "Daisy a Day." It's a love song about a down to earth, small town couple. In their courtship time he started picking a daisy from the green fields, and giving it to his lady fair. In the days of raising children, he would hand her a golden-yellow and white flower each night. After her death, in the twilight of his years, he could be seen walking slowly to the hillside cemetery, still presenting his loved one with a daisy each day.[82]

I can't claim to be this devoted or romantic. Nor can I adequately express the love and admiration I feel for my spouse Christine Lu Landon Leypoldt. She keeps me grounded in all my wanderings, and is always on my mind. When the loneliness of a late afternoon creeps toward me, she's always there for me. She is my greatest hero and best friend forever. And full of surprises, too.

Returning from Oregon in our Toyota Sienna, I learned that my wife of 44 years drove barefoot on long trips. Once more, I was simply lost in wonder, love, and praise.

Our 40th Anniversary
July 11, 2010

Chris entertains Anastasia at Ponca State Park in 1976

Our children on vacation in 1984

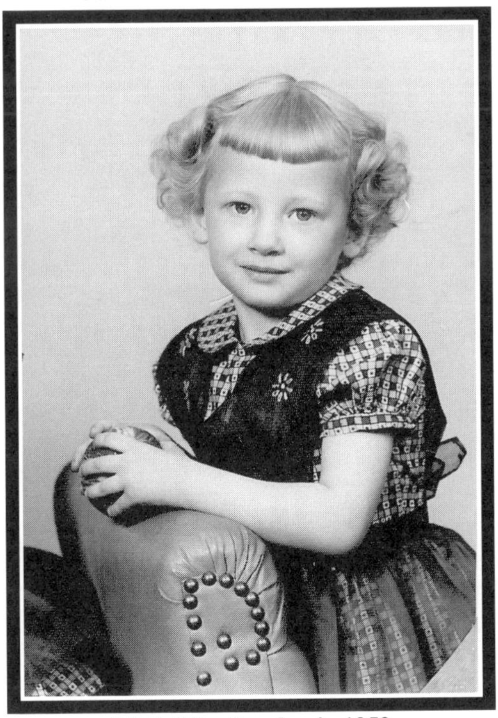

Little Miss Landon in 1953

My mother and her children in 1988

My mother and her children in 2002

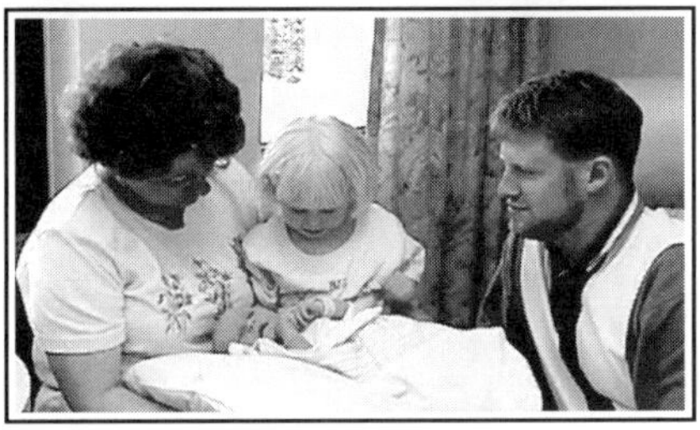

Pictures from 2000 and 2001

Ellis Cabin, Clear Lake, Iowa in 2002

Leypoldt & Pennington Building in North Platte

Masonic window at Grace Episcopal Church in Columbus

A sample of the many art glass windows I've photographed. Images are from Broken Bow, Nebraska City and Fontanelle. To see them in living color go to pylodet.com.

West Side Church in 1997

Emma & Cora in '05 & '07

Chris' dad with his twin great grandsons in 2003

The Leypoldt children in 1951

Glossary Of Acronyms

AC - Annual Conference
AF & AM - Ancient, Free & Accepted Masons
BoD - Book of Discipline
CCFA - Conference Council on Finance & Administration
CEV - Contemporary English Version of the Bible
CMIC - Church Mutual Insurance Company
COGIC - Church of God in Christ
CROP - Christian Rural Overseas Program
CYME - Conference Youth Ministries Event
DS - United Methodist District Superintendent
DSLR - Digital Single Lens Reflex
ELCA - Evangelical Lutheran Church in America
EUB - Evangelical United Brethren
FDIC - Federal Deposit Insurance Corporation
ISO - Insurance Services Office
GOP - Grim Obstructionist People
KCI - Kansas City International Airport
LCA - Lutheran Church in America (before ELCA)
LCMS - Lutheran Church, Missouri Synod
NRSV - New Revised Standard Version of the Bible
NWU - Nebraska Wesleyan University
SCC - Southeast Community College
SPRC - Staff Parish Relations Committee
TOPS - Take Off Pounds Sensibly
UCC - United Church of Christ
UMC - United Methodist Church
UMH - United Methodist Hymnal
UMYF - United Methodist Youth Fellowship
UNL - University of Nebraska-Lincoln
USDA - United States Department of Agriculture
WELS - Wisconsin Evangelical Lutheran Synod
YAC - Youth Annual Conference

Unless otherwise noted, all scripture references are from
The New Testament and Psalms: An Inclusion Version (New York: Oxford University Press, 1995)

End Notes and Bibliography follow

1 Joseph Campbell, *The Power of Myth with Bill Moyers (*New York: Doubleday, 1988) p. 229
2 Dale Evans wrote Happy Trails in 1952. She and Roy Rogers sang and released it the same year
3 Dan Schiltz & Randy Travis wrote Heroes and Friends. Travis released the single in 1991
4 Swedish translation of "Lost In Wonder, Love, and Praise" from Charles Wesley's Hymn *Love Divine, All Loves Excelling*
5 Carl Dietemeyer, "Westside (sic) Methodist Reaches 70th Birthday," *The Nebraska Farmer, 10/18/47*
6 Tex Sample, *Ministry in an Oral Culture* (Louisville, KY: Westminster/John Knox Press, 1994) page 1
7 Dr. Everett Jackman, *The Nebraska Methodist Story (*NE Methodist Historical Society, 1954), p. 247
8 Bruce Fierstein, *Real Men Don't Eat Quiche* (Pocket Books, 1982)
9 The Movie *Odd Jobs* was released by Tri-Star in 1986
10 Albert Schweitzer, *The Quest of the Historical Jesus* (New York: Macmillan Co., 1964), p. 403
11 *Rain Main* was released by United Artists 12/16/88
12 Allen Shamblin wrote *He Walked On Water.* Randy Travis released it for Warner Brothers 4/26/90
13 www.eisenhower/archives January 17, 1961
14 David Corn, *motherjones.com ,*August 28, 2013
15 Hartzell Spence, *One Foot in Heaven* (New York: Grosset & Dunlap, 1940), page 4
16 Vater Unser is German for Our Father
17 *Dear Hearts and Gentle People* by Sammy Fain and Bob Hilliard, 1949
18 Julie Gold wrote *From A Distance* Bette Midler released it 1990, Atlantic
19 *Teen Wolf* released by Atlantic in 1985
20 "*One Hundred Years of The United Methodist Church, Albion, Nebraska"* 5/28/72
21 Harold Bosley, *Doing What Is Christian* (Nashville: The Graded Press, 1960)
22 *Animal House* distributed by Universal Pictures in 1978
23 *2001: A Space Odyssey* distributed by MGM on May 15, 1968
24 John A. T. Robinson, *Honest To God* (Norwich: SCM Press, 1963)
25 Randy Sparks wrote *Today* and released it in 1964
26 Donald K. McKim, ed., *How Karl Barth Changed My Mind* (Grand Rapids: Eerdmans, 1986)
27 *American Graffiti was distributed* by Universal Pictures in 1973
28 Will Willimon: Pulpit Resource, Volume 26, #2, Year C, 1998
29 Shakespeare, *Romeo and Juliet*, 2.2
30 Arthur Schopenhauer 1788-1860, often quoted, no original source given
31 Willimon, op. cit.
32 See Chapter 24 for a definition of hyperbole
33 *Amerika*, ABC mini-series in February 1987
34 From the French poet Alphonse de Lamartine (1790-1869)
35 *As The World Turns* was on CBS-TV from 1956-2010
36 *The Naked Gun* was released by Paramount in 1988
37 E. Stanley Jones, *Is the Kingdom of God Realism?* (New York: Abingdon, 1940)
38 Paula Schwed, *I've Got Tears In My Ears…* (Kansas City: Andrews McMeel, 1996)
39 Tim Vivian, The Other Side Magazine Volume 28, Number 1, January/February 1992
40 *One Fine Day* written by G. Coffin & Carole King in 1963. Recorded by many, but Chiffons were first.
41 Joe Siegler *Ranger Player From The Past* ranger fans.com 9/13/2000
42 James T. Garrett, *God's Gift* (C.S.S. Publishing Co., 1991)
43 Kathleen Norris, *Dakota: A Spiritual Geography* (New York: Ticknor & Fields, 1993), p.18
44 adapted from a 19th century German folk song *Mein Vater var ein Wandersmann*
45 The TV program *Chuck* was on NBC from 2007 to 2012
46 *Good Luck Chuck* was distributed by Lionsgate in 2007
47 J. B. Guess, *For anti-gay reasons, insurance company refuses coverage quote to UCC church*, www.ucc.org, 9/14/2007
48 Kuralt, Charles *A Life On The Road* (New York: G. P. Putnam's Sons, 1990) page 11
49 baseball-almanac.com/quotes
50 Mitt Romney as told to Bruce McCall, Car and Driver, July 2012
51 Found in numerous places; original source unknown
52 Jerry Clower, *Stories From Home* (University of Mississippi Press, 1992) p. 74
53 Illustrations Unlimited James S. Hewett, ed. (Tyndale House July 15, 1988) page 216
54 James L. Moore, *Jesus' Parables of Life* (Dimensions For Living, 2005), p. 31
55 May be fictional, but Danish Christians did protect Jews during WW II

56 Bradley story has often been used, original source unknown
57 Charles Sheldon, *In His Steps* (Chicago Advance, 1896)
58 "In Hoc Signo Vinces" is Latin for "by this sign (the cross) we are victors"
59 Viktor Frankl, *Man's Search For Meaning,* (New York: Washington Square Press, 1959), p. 172
60 R. B. Garrison, *Seven Questions Jesus Asked* (Nashville: Abingdon, 1975), p. 91
61 R. B. Garrison, op. cit., p. 65
62 Jeff Foxworthy, *The Final Helping* (Atlanta: Longstreet, 1999)
63 I think I heard her correctly, but I was a little shocked. The adjective began with F.
64 See Chapter 24 for a definition of hyperbole
65 Lennon & McCarthy wrote *In My Life* & EMI released it 12/3/1965
66 Hymnary.org says the author is Ira F. Stanhill, limited information found
67 Garrison Keillor, *Leaving Home* (New York: Viking, 1987), pp, 217-18
68 Martin Luther King Jr., *Strength to Love* (New York: Pocket Books, 1963), p. 143
69 Rick Nowels & Ellen Shipley wrote *Heaven Is A Place On Earth* and Brenda Carlisle released it in 1987 for MCA
70 Paisley released *When I Get Where I'm Going* in October 2005 on the Arista label. It was written by Teren & Rutherford.
71 *Wishin' and Hopin'* was released by Dusty Springfield in 1964 for Philips Records. Score by Bacharach and David.
72 F. Forrester Church, *Everyday Miracles* (New York: Harper & Row, 1988) pages 159-61
73 Paul Tillich, *The Shaking of the Foundations* (New York: Scribner's 1948), p. 162
74 E. Stanley Jones, *Victory Through Surrender* (Nashville: Abingdon Press, 1966) pp. 26-47
75 John Lennon wrote *Imagine* in 1971 and released it on the Apple label
76 Bacharach & David wrote *What The World Needs Now Is Love* in 1965-de Shannon released it on the Imperial label.
77 TriStar Pictures released *Places In The Heart* in 1984.
78 M. L. King, Jr. *Strength To Love*, p. 144
79 Walter Brueggemann May 10, 2009 Washington National Cathedral "Perfect Love Vetoes Fear"
80 Oliver Pollack, *Nebraska Courthouses* (Chicago: Arcadia Publishing, 2002)
81 J. S. Spong, *Eternal Life: A New Vision*, (New York: Harper One, 2009), p. 211
82 Justin Strunk, Jr. wrote and recorded *Daisy A Day* in 1973

Happy Trails To You!

With François Rabelais, I am now off "in search of the Great Perhaps"